Healthcare Ethics, Law and Professionalism

Healthcare Ethics, Law and Professionalism: Essays on the Works of Alastair V. Campbell features 15 original essays on bioethics, and healthcare ethics specifically. The volume is in honour of Professor Alastair V. Campbell, who was the founding editor of the internationally renowned *Journal of Medical Ethics* and the founding director of three internationally leading centres in bioethics, in Otago, New Zealand, Bristol, UK, and Singapore.

Campbell was trained in theology and philosophy and throughout his career worked with colleagues from various disciplines, including law and various branches of healthcare. The diversity of topics and depth of contributors' insights reflect the breadth and impact of Campbell's philosophical work and policy contributions to healthcare ethics. Throughout his long academic career, Campbell's emphasis on healthcare ethics being practice-oriented, yet driven by critical reflection, has shaped the field in vital ways.

The chapters are authored by leading scholars in healthcare ethics and law. Directly engaging with Campbell's work and influence, the essays discuss essential questions in healthcare ethics relating to its methodology and teaching, its intersection with law and policy, medical professionalism, religion, and its translation in different cultural settings. Chapters also grapple with specific enduring topics, such as the doctor-patient relationship, justice in health and biomedical research, and treatment of the human body and the dead.

Voo Teck Chuan, Assistant Professor, Centre for Biomedical Ethics, Yong Loo Lin School of Medicine, National University of Singapore, Singapore.

Richard Huxtable, Professor of Medical Ethics and Law, and Director, Centre for Ethics in Medicine, University of Bristol, UK.

Nicola Peart, Professor, Faculty of Law, University of Otago, New Zealand.

Biomedical Law and Ethics Library

Scientific and clinical advances, social and political developments, and the impact of healthcare on our lives raise profound ethical and legal questions. Medical law and ethics have become central to our understanding of these problems, and are important tools for the analysis and resolution of problems – real or imagined.

In this series, scholars at the forefront of biomedical law and ethics contribute to the debates in this area, with accessible, thought-provoking, and sometimes controversial ideas. Each book in the series develops an independent hypothesis and argues cogently for a particular position. One of the major contributions of this series is the extent to which both law and ethics are utilised in the content of the books, and the shape of the series itself.

The books in this series are analytical, with a key target audience of lawyers, doctors, nurses, and the intelligent lay public.

Series Editor: Sheila A.M. McLean
Professor Sheila A.M. McLean is Professor Emerita of Law and Ethics in Medicine, School of Law, University of Glasgow, UK.

Available titles:

Health Research Governance in Africa
Law, Ethics, and Regulation
Cheluchi Onyemelukwe-Onuobia

Revisiting Landmark Cases in Medical Law
Shaun D. Pattinson

Healthcare Ethics, Law and Professionalism
Essays on the Works of Alastair V. Campbell
Edited by Voo Teck Chuan, Richard Huxtable and Nicola Peart

Religion, Medicine and the Law
Clayton Ó Néill

For more information about this series, please visit:
www.routledge.com/Biomedical-Law-and-Ethics-Library/book-series/CAV5

Healthcare Ethics, Law and Professionalism

Essays on the Works of Alastair V. Campbell

Edited by Voo Teck Chuan,
Richard Huxtable and Nicola Peart

Routledge
Taylor & Francis Group

LONDON AND NEW YORK

First published 2019
by Routledge
2 Park Square, Milton Park, Abingdon, Oxon OX14 4RN

and by Routledge
52 Vanderbilt Avenue, New York, NY 10017, USA

First issued in paperback 2020

Routledge is an imprint of the Taylor & Francis Group, an informa business

British Library Cataloguing-in-Publication Data
A catalogue record for this book is available from the British Library

Library of Congress Cataloging-in-Publication Data
A catalog record has been requested for this book

ISBN 13: 978-0-367-58410-8 (pbk)
ISBN 13: 978-1-138-06079-1 (hbk)

Typeset in Gaillard
by Out of House Publishing

MIX
Paper from
responsible sources
FSC
www.fsc.org FSC™ C013985

Printed in the United Kingdom
by Henry Ling Limited

Alastair V. Campbell, photograph taken by Michael Campbell (2017)

Contents

List of contributors

Anita Ho, Associate Professor, Centre for Biomedical Ethics, University of British Columbia, Vancouver, Canada.

D. Gareth Jones, Emeritus Professor, Department of Anatomy, Bioethics Centre, University of Otago, New Zealand.

Gordon M. Stirrat, Emeritus Professor of Obstetrics and Gynaecology, University of Bristol, UK.

Grant Gillett, Professor of Biomedical Ethics, Bioethics Centre, University of Otago, New Zealand.

Jacqueline Chin, Associate Professor, Centre for Biomedical Ethics, Yong Loo Lin School of Medicine, National University of Singapore, Singapore.

Jing-Bao Nie, Professor, Bioethics Centre, University of Otago, New Zealand.

John McMillan, Professor, Bioethics Centre, University of Otago, New Zealand.

Julie Woodley, Senior Lecturer in Radiography, University of the West of England, Bristol, UK.

Lynley Anderson, Associate Professor, Bioethics Centre, University of Otago, New Zealand.

Margaret Brazier, Professor, School of Law, University of Manchester, UK.

Michael Campbell, Researcher, Centre for Ethics as Study in Human Value, Department of Philosophy, University of Pardubice, Czech Republic.

Neil Pickering, Associate Professor, Bioethics Centre, University of Otago, New Zealand.

Nicola Peart, Professor, Faculty of Law, University of Otago, New Zealand.

Peter Skegg, Emeritus Professor, Faculty of Law, University of Otago, New Zealand.

Raanan Gillon, Emeritus Professor of Medical Ethics, Faculty of Medicine, School of Public Health, Imperial College London, UK.

Richard Ashcroft, Professor of Bioethics, School of Law, Queen Mary University of London, UK.

Richard Huxtable, Professor of Medical Ethics and Law, Centre for Ethics in Medicine, University of Bristol, UK.

Robin Gill, Emeritus Professor of Applied Theology, Department of Religious Studies, University of Kent, UK.

Roger Higgs, Professor Emeritus of General Practice, Kings College London, UK.

Ruth Macklin, Distinguished University Professor Emerita, Department of Epidemiology & Population Health, Albert Einstein College of Medicine, USA.

Sheila McLean, Professor Emerita of Law and Ethics in Medicine, School of Law, University of Glasgow, UK.

Thomas H. Murray, Senior Research Scholar and President Emeritus, The Hastings Center, USA.

Voo Teck Chuan, Assistant Professor, Centre for Biomedical Ethics, Yong Loo Lin School of Medicine, National University of Singapore, Singapore.

Dedication and acknowledgements

This book is dedicated to Alastair V. Campbell as an acknowledgement of his friendship and his leadership in making ethics in healthcare a relevant, inclusive and relatable field.

We are very grateful for the ideas and assistance given to us in putting together this collection of essays. Inspiration for the book came from Jacqueline Chin, who suggested an editorial collaboration between faculty members from each of the three universities where Alastair helped to establish bioethics centres.

We would like to thank each of the chapter authors for devoting their time and effort towards this book, and for their enthusiasm for the project, which reflects the collegial spirit that Alastair inspires. Our thanks also go to Tom Murray for his personal reflections on Alastair as a scholar, teacher, colleague and friend, and to John Coggon for suggesting that we invite Alastair to add his own reflections.

We would also like to take this opportunity to express our gratitude to Alastair's wife, Sally, for supplying Alastair's biographical information for Tom's piece and for being a co-conspirator in keeping the project a secret until it was sprung on Alastair as a surprise during a dinner held in his honour at the 2017 International Conference on Clinical Ethics Consultation. We have witnessed the support she has provided to Alastair throughout his career and to the centres he has led. We have all enjoyed her generosity and kindness, her hospitality and good humour, and the friendship she has extended to us.

This book would not have been possible without help from Will Zhang, research assistant at the Centre for Biomedical Ethics, National University of Singapore, and Kyla Mullen, research assistant at the Faculty of Law, University of Otago. They provided supreme and consistent support in getting the chapters into publishable form. Lastly, we would like to thank the editorial team at Routledge, in particular Alexandra Buckley for her patience and guidance. To quote Huxtable's proudest acronym creation, this volume on **H**ealthcare Ethics, **L**aw and **P**rofessionalism greatly benefited from all their help.

Voo Teck Chuan, Richard Huxtable and Nicola Peart

Part I

Introductions

Alastair Vincent Campbell
Scholar, teacher, advocate, leader, friend and colleague

Thomas H. Murray

The first time I met Professor John Eu-Li Wong, he informed me that he had obtained funding to create a Chair in Biomedical Ethics. My task, he explained, was to find the person who would be the initial holder of that chair and the director of a new centre at the Yong Loo Lin School of Medicine at the National University of Singapore. I was taken aback, to say the least. But John was so earnest and persuasive that I agreed immediately to do what I could to help him find the ideal candidate for this important post. John had a clear vision of the qualifications he sought, among them that the individual should be both an international leader in the field and a physician.

I added another criterion: The person should be a builder – that is, someone who understood what was required to create a thriving programme, able to recruit very promising junior colleagues and to nurture their development.

I cannot recall all the names we discussed but it soon became clear to me that restricting the search exclusively to physicians narrowed the pool excessively and, in my view, needlessly. Many fine programmes had been created under the leadership of physicians. But so had many other excellent ones by non-physicians, including programmes at leading medical schools. Would he consider candidates who were outstanding in all respects but not physicians? John agreed.

I had no one particular in mind when I made this suggestion. But, as happens on occasion, I woke in the middle of the night with an epiphany. I knew exactly the right candidate: An internationally renowned scholar who had built not one but two outstanding programmes, with all the intellectual, social and political skills needed to create an excellent programme at the National University of Singapore. There were additional factors in his favor: He was about to step down from the leadership of his current centre at the University of Bristol; and, I happened to know, he and his partner were adventurous, not at all intimidated by the prospect of learning to navigate a new culture and new institutions.

I immediately contacted John and suggested I introduce him and Alastair V. Campbell to each other via email. He agreed and you know more or less what followed. My recollection is that things moved swiftly from there (at least by the usual standards at the National University of Singapore). Alastair became the first Chen Su Lan Centennial Professor and the Centre for Biomedical Ethics was born.

Alastair's colleagues at Bristol had celebrated the completion of his tenure as programme head with a day-long symposium – a series of challenging scholarly papers, one relentlessly following another. They slotted my presentation as the very last on that long day. To me this meant two things. First, the audience was likely to be weary. No matter how stimulating the papers, a full day of paper after academic paper would wear out most human beings. Second, however scrupulously the session chairs tried to keep on schedule, by the time my presentation began we would be running out of time and people would be eager to call it a day. I wanted to do something that would be warm, humorous, on target, and quick. Fortunately, Alastair's wife, Sally, and my wife, Cynthia, agreed to be co-conspirators, which required them to find somewhere in Bristol just the right item of clothing. To be precise, a hat. Not just any hat, a wizard's hat. The premise of my presentation that afternoon was that no normal human being could have accomplished what Alastair had done and, therefore, we needed to look for an alternative explanation. Which I was delighted to provide: Alastair, I explained, was in fact the great wizard and head of Hogwarts School, Albus Dumbledore, in disguise. As proof, I showed photos of Dumbledore and Alastair side by side. In any event, once we placed the wizard's hat on his head, the identification was indisputable.

That hat followed Alastair to Singapore, Even if you have not seen it in his office, indisputable proof exists that his wizarding power was undiminished: The Centre for Biomedical Ethics's astonishingly rapid growth from a gleam in John Wong's eye to a potent international force in Bioethics, a major mover in the School of Medicine, and a valuable source of ethics support for the government of Singapore. Of course, the Centre's success cannot be attributed to any one person. It required many people's vision, support, collaboration and dedication. But it is also true that the success of any institution or programme depends heavily on the skill, integrity, wisdom and work ethic of the individual who leads it. In Alastair, the National University of Singapore chose well. Of course, if the best predictor of future success is a track record of past successes, it was not much of a gamble. If there is another prominent Bioethicist who has founded three successful centres, I am not aware of who that might be. Alastair could be described, I suppose, as a serial founder.

One way to understand how Alastair has been able to accomplish so much is to consider key roles he has filled in his distinguished career: as thinker; as teacher; as engaged in critical policy debates; as leader; and as friend and colleague. The account that follows is indebted to Alastair's former colleagues Nicola Peart and Richard Ashcroft, his current colleague Voo Teck Chuan, his partner in life Sally Campbell, and my recollections of our time together.

Thinker

When I first began writing as a scholar I was thrilled to be published. Later I wanted whatever I had published to be read. Finally, I realised that what was ultimately important was to participate in significant public conversations – that is, to publish, to be read and (at least mostly) understood, and to have a constructive impact on how we think about and act towards matters of great importance. By any and all of these criteria, Alastair has had an altogether worthwhile career as thinker and scholar. According to Google Scholar, his work has been cited well over 2,000 times by other scholars. It ranges broadly from pastoral and professional care to a host of important issues in medical ethics and medical education. His recent book, *The Body in Bioethics*, is a revealing extended meditation on the human body's significance in life and, hence, in Bioethics. Through his reflections on the meaning of donated versus purchased organs for transplantation, cosmetic surgeries, the 'Body World' displays of plasticised human corpses and controversies over the repatriation of ancient human remains, Alastair shows the moral myopia that can follow from a naive embrace of Cartesian dualism, from which comes the belief that our minds and bodies are fully separate and distinct entities. *The Body in Bioethics* is an extended argument for the view that:

> we remain what we inevitably are – vulnerable living tissue, located in time and space. Our bodies and the bodies of our fellow humans are always with us, an inescapable concomitant of being living, conscious beings. If we ignore this aspect of human life, we will end up with an abstract, theoretical and ultimately irrelevant bioethics.[1]

I should add that this moral myopia also leaves us vulnerable to transhumanist fantasies of disembodied consciousness uploaded onto immortal computers, and makes it difficult to understand what is at stake when, for example, we pump athletes full of anabolic steroids and other performance-enhancing drugs.[2] Appreciating what it means to be an embodied, conscious, reflective creature goes a long way toward enriching our understanding of many controversies in Bioethics.

Teacher

Alastair's decades of wrestling with complex moral and practical problems in medical ethics served the National University of Singapore well when he arrived and began sharing what he had learned. His philosophically trained colleagues, in some cases, took a while to appreciate fully his practical wisdom, as Voo Teck Chuan describes:

> In the early days of CBmE [the Centre for Biomedical Ethics], Alastair was giving talks to the healthcare community on medical ethics so as to publicise CBmE and the nature of ethics teaching. Jacqueline Chin (then

---

1 A.V. Campbell, *The Body in Bioethics* (Taylor & Francis 2009) 119.
2 T.H. Murray, *Good Sport: Why Our Games Matter and How Doping Undermines Them* (Oxford University Press 2018).

Research Fellow) and I (then Research Assistant) were roped in to help with the research based on an earlier talk he gave in the UK. Alastair said it would be a case of *cauld kail het up*, a Scottish phrase which he explained as 'reheating and serving leftover cabbage', so we should just update his slides with the latest relevant literature rather than look for fresh arguments. At that point in time, I read the phrase as essentially pejorative. As a philosophically trained, junior researcher, I thought all academic work should focus on 'originality', whatever this means. It is only in 2017 – the 10th year anniversary of CBmE – that I realised there is certain wisdom, in that context, to using 'leftover cabbage'. I found out recently that figuratively, 'cauld kail het up' may be interpreted as reviving an old tale. It was serving up accumulated years of insight and reflection on the subject matter and considering their relevance against the backdrop of advancements in medical ethics and medical ethics education. The talk was transcribed and published with the title 'How can we know that ethics education produces ethical doctors?'[3], co-authored by the three of us, a well-respected bioethicist and two philosophers transitioning to the field. The article highlights the limits of ethics education – for all the effort tutors put in, we cannot know for sure that a student will turn out to be an ethical doctor. But it also urges the need for academic rigour in teaching and assessment, with the concept of a 'reflective practitioner' as an ideal we guide students toward. Despite changes in topics and teaching methods, this remains the key approach of our undergraduate longitudinal Health Ethics, Law and Professionalism (*HeLP*) curriculum.

Under Alastair's leadership, admirably comprehensive educational programmes for people training in medicine, other health professions, as well as advanced degrees in Bioethics were organised at Otago University in New Zealand, the University of Bristol in the UK and the National University of Singapore.

Engaged public actor

In their insightful essay in this volume, 'Healthcare Ethics in New Zealand', Lynley Anderson and Nicola Peart describe in detail the crucial role Alastair played in helping the citizens of New Zealand come to terms with the revelations of unethical research performed on women with carcinoma *in situ*. The investigation that followed, known as the 'Cartwright Inquiry' after the distinguished judge who chaired it, rattled the faith of New Zealanders in their physicians and scientists and unsettled those professions.

Alastair's contributions to the Inquiry helped to set medicine and science on a sounder ethical basis and instituted a new norm for who should have a

---

3 A.V. Campbell, J. Chin and T.C. Voo, 'How Can We Know That Ethics Education Produces Ethical Doctors?' (2007) 29 *Medical Teacher* 431.

voice in approving research. Among the reforms he championed, the committees reviewing research protocols with human subjects were reconstituted. They were now required to have equal numbers of lay and professional members, and the chair was to be chosen from among the lay members. (My two visits to New Zealand were both to teach in summer workshops aimed specifically at those lay committee participants. I found the people I met to be thoughtful and serious about their responsibilities.)

Peart describes the broad and lasting impact of Alastair's leadership:

> Alastair developed the Bioethics Centre into a centre of national significance. Its advice was sought from around the country and its influence nationally was significant. It was a time of great change and Alastair played a key role in that change. His success was largely due to his ability to bridge diverging views, to find compromise and to help health professionals deal with ethical issues in a constructive and unpatronizing manner.

Alastair found many more ways to contribute to public deliberation and public policy in New Zealand, as he did in his subsequent roles. In the UK, he served as Chair of the Ethics and Governance Council of UK Biobank, and as Vice-Chair of the Retained Organs Commission. In Singapore, he served as an adviser to the Ministry of Health. Taking seriously his work as thinker and as teacher, Alastair recognises an obligation to participate in the world outside the academy. When one's scholarship makes it clear that the human subjects of research must be fully respected and their informed consent provided, public advocacy for that respect follows closely. If one's scholarship leads to strong conclusions about the nature of a just healthcare system, then one should grasp opportunities to press for justice in one's own system. If your investigations reveal that markets in human organs for transplantation exploit the poor and that better alternatives exist, then, as Alastair has done, argue on behalf of those alternatives.

Policy is driven by many forces and competing interests. You will not win every argument, and what you win today may be undone tomorrow. But those are not reasons to give up the fight. Alastair continues to advocate for what he believes is right and good. One way to keep up the good fight is to seed institutions that can nurture others able and willing to join in the effort, and that he has done with great success.

Leader

For all that he has accomplished as thinker, teacher and engaged public actor, there is a powerful argument to be made that Alastair's successes as leader and founder of multiple institutions may be the most remarkable of all. He was the founding editor of one of the most prominent journals in the field, the *Journal of Medical Ethics*. He played a key role in organising the International Association of Bioethics. And, of course, he was essential to the growth and success of three different centres of excellence in Bioethics – Otago, Bristol and Singapore. Richard Ashcroft, Alastair's former colleague at Bristol, describes what a good leader does:

> I first met Alastair when I applied for the role of Lecturer in Ethics in Medicine, to join him in the newly founded Centre for Ethics in Medicine. Alastair and Sally welcomed me into their home before I took up the job, so I could get to know Bristol and the University before I got started. That set the tone for our whole working relationship. Alastair and Sally took a warm interest in me, as with all the staff and students who joined the Centre under Alastair's Directorship. He helped me find a home in Bristol, he got me started, he introduced me to all sorts of interesting people, he gave me chances.
>
> Alastair believed in hard work, but also in work-life balance and in good fellowship. It was important to be able to have fun and relax, as well as to put in long hours when necessary. He was understanding when personal difficulties or illness made working difficult or impossible, and he is a wonderful listener. But equally he would brook no nonsense in terms of unprofessional behaviour, rudeness or sloppy work. He set the tone. I have now been working in higher education for more than 20 years, but I have never had a boss who was a true leader like Alastair. You want to please and impress him. You do not want to let him down.
>
> He brings out the best in people, and he gives people lots of opportunities which might otherwise not come their way. I got invaluable experience representing the Centre in committee work, in course development, in making speeches on professional occasions, in leading research projects and in publication which it would be unusual for academics as junior as myself to be allowed or encouraged to do thanks to Alastair. In part this was because there was an explosion of work to do which he could not possibly do all by himself, but in part it was because he believes in people and in developing their talents and competences. I am not a natural risk taker, but with Alastair in my corner I felt able to take big steps and even if they failed I knew he [would] support me. All of this without in anyway being a softy himself. When Alastair gave you a rocket, you did not forget in a hurry. It is not true that 'we never had a cross word', and there is one period in particular when things were quite strained between us, but in hindsight I think that was largely because he thought I was doing something which would lead to personal disaster (and it turned out that he was half right). I did hurt him, and I did let him down, but, and this is the important thing here, we made it up and talked it through and he did not hold a grudge. And I think that tells you a lot about Alastair the man.

It is not, I believe, a coincidence that Ashcroft's recollections focus on the character and personality of Alastair, for those are vital to understanding Alastair as a friend and a colleague.

Friend and colleague

Although I had met Alastair on my two visits to New Zealand, I did not know him all that well until his sabbatical year at John Carroll University, located in a suburb of Cleveland, Ohio. Alastair, Sally and their sons rented a house not far from where my family lived at that time, which afforded opportunities to work together and to socialise. I came to appreciate and to prize his many virtues, among them great warmth, loyalty, perceptiveness, abundant common sense, generosity of spirit, a profound commitment to justice and a marvelous sense of humor. He was unfailingly supportive of all that was good and honorable, and, as Richard Ashcroft noted, quick to detect pretentiousness, falsity and defective character.

It should be no surprise that the same virtues that make Alastair such a fine friend and colleague also underlie his many accomplishments. His fertile intellect, perceptiveness and work ethic make it possible to be a prolific and influential thinker and writer. His commitment to knowledge and abundant capacity for nurturing make him an exceptional teacher. His love of justice and his compassion, especially for the poor and the powerless, provide the motivation and the courage to participate in the sphere of public debate and public policy. Together, these traits make him an extraordinary leader and a builder of enduring institutions.

Final thoughts

Alastair's remarkable career was aided by a happy combination of personality, passion and preparation. His studies in both philosophy and theology contributed greatly to his intellectual abilities. His training, along with his scholarship in pastoral care, may have also sharpened the skills that enabled him to be so extraordinarily successful in the multiple roles he filled. I suspect that his theology credential may have helped attract support from organisations that aided in the founding of the centres at Otago and Bristol. Sally notes that seed money for the Bristol Centre came from religious organisations. Anderson and Peart report that the Otago Centre was established by cooperation between the university and the Presbyterian Synod of Otago and Southland. Alastair's earlier sabbatical in New Zealand had been funded by a variety of organisations including Presbyterian, Anglican and Roman Catholic agencies. I imagine these early supporters should feel very satisfied by the return on their investments.

Richard Ashcroft has some final words about the sort of person Alastair V. Campbell is:

> Alastair remains my academic mentor, and I often have turned to him for advice, about work and personal matters, and he always gives good advice, even if I'm not too good at taking it. And as I find myself becoming more senior in the profession I often find myself asking what Alastair would do

in a given situation. I judge myself by that standard; I judge others by that standard. Not many people measure up.

I agree with Ashcroft. Alastair is an uncommon leader and mentor. He is also a fine person, an exceptional colleague and a treasured friend.

An accidental ethicist

Reflections on my career in medical ethics[1]

Alastair V. Campbell

Plans

One of my favourite jokes is this one-liner: 'What makes God laugh? – having plans!' Well, from my teenage years, I certainly had plans, and maybe the outcome in my life history is causing some heavenly mirth? It is hard to know where to begin, but probably some early encounters with medicine had something to do with it. My mother had breast cancer and died relatively young (I was 19 at the time), and I still recall her struggle with illness over many years, but most especially the way her body was ravaged by the early attempts at cancer treatment. Her chest was deeply scarred and burned from radiotherapy, which did extend her life for some years, but at a huge cost to her general health and especially her self-esteem. Then, at the age of 12, I was to become part of a surgical experiment (although I did not realise that was what it was at the time). I had suffered for some years from chronic flat feet (making it difficult to carry on with my love of rugby), and an orthopaedic surgeon in Glasgow decided to try some major surgery on both my feet in an attempt to lift up my fallen arches. After 6 months in plaster up to both knees, I was able to experience the result – better than before, certainly, but with such a strangely shaped left foot that there should be no problem with identification in a morgue should that be required! However, the most powerful memory from that time was not of my own relatively minor problems but of the many fellow patients in the orthopaedic ward. These were all boys of around my age or younger, who had contracted polio. The ward looked like a mediaeval torture chamber, with what were known as 'stretcher beds', designed to help straighten contorted limbs, and 'iron lungs', vast steel caverns, which were early forms of ventilator to ensure that the patient could still breathe. I knew, even then, that many of them might never be able to walk again, and that some would be confined to wheelchairs for the rest of their lives. In that context, being prevented from playing rugby for a year seemed

1 The central section of this chapter was previously published in Alastair V. Campbell, 'Medical Ethics, Then and Now: A 40-Year Perspective' in Richard Huxtable and Ruud ter Meulen (eds), *The Voices and Rooms of European Bioethics* (Abingdon, Routledge 2015) 11–16. Permission to re-use it is gratefully acknowledged.

pretty trivial, and the enforced inaction turned me into more of a bookworm than I had been before.

So, it might seem that these early experiences set my mind on a medical career of some kind, maybe even a career in medical ethics (although in those days this was not a subject people talked about at all, at least not in the way we do now). Not so! My plans a couple of years later went on a totally different track. Medicine was never an option, since I was deeply bored by science (as it was taught in those days), and felt utterly at home in the humanities, most especially English, French and Ancient Greek. I also enjoyed public speaking and picked up a couple of prizes at school (plus a new status as the conjurer at the annual school concert, with a real rabbit produced out of a top hat!). Then came a visit to Glasgow to attend a massive crusade led by the American evangelist, Billy Graham. Full of adolescent fervour, I gave my heart to Christ and that is when the teenage plan was made – I would be a Christian minister, helping people and preaching the Gospel. That was to be my calling. When, starry-eyed, I told my father the good news (he was a Presbyterian minister, who had been Professor of English at Madras Christian College in India), he offered words of caution. 'Take your time, son', he counselled. It was wise counsel, but it took me years to discover where my real vocation lay. At the time the path seemed clear and it gradually took a more definite shape – an arts degree, then a divinity degree, then off to tend the faithful, at first as a missionary in India, as my parents and my grandparents had been. (My grandmother was one of the first female medical graduates and, with my grandfather also a doctor, founded a hospital in India that exists to this day.) Plans! At this stage I am tempted to quote Robert Burns – 'The best laid schemes o' mice an' men gang aft agley.'

Looking back, I think the change in my awareness of what I could best do in my life began with my 4 years studying philosophy at Edinburgh University. This taught me how to think critically and how to write – in a style I consciously copied from Bertrand Russell – with precision and brevity. After that, some of the dogmatism evident in the Divinity Faculty at that time was hard to swallow, but I found my intellectual salvation in teachers like Professor John McIntyre, who held the ancient Chair of Divinity and had no truck with sloppy thinking or uncritical faith claims. It was McIntyre who steered me in a quite new direction after I graduated in systematic theology. To my surprise, an application for a Harkness Fellowship of the Commonwealth Fund of New York was successful, and this meant 2 years of fully paid study in the States at any university of my choosing. I sought McIntyre's advice, thinking of studying at Harvard or Yale on a topic exploring language about God. 'What a waste of time!' said my mentor, 'You could do that anywhere. Why not study something only the Americans are doing? – It's called pastoral psychology, I think.' So, by that time married and with one child, I ended up taking my first wife, Paula, and our first daughter, Fiona, all the way to California, for me to study at San Francisco Theological Seminary and at the University of California at Berkeley. These were amazing years, with in-depth study of psychology and psychotherapy and many months of practical experience in a highly experimental and innovative day treatment centre for seriously ill psychiatric patients. At the end of my practical training, I ended up as a counselor to patients with severe delusions of a religious kind – something that was regarded with horror by the psychiatric establishment when I returned to Edinburgh!

It seems then that a path was opening up back to medical ethics, in some sense, but in fact it was to be another 10 years before this would happen fully. Because of the ill health of Paula's parents, plans to work in India were abandoned and instead I returned to Scotland to take up a job as Assistant Chaplain to Edinburgh University. Then a fresh impetus towards medical ethics came from an unexpected source. I was a few months into my new ministerial role when I was asked if I would also take on a part-time job at the Royal College of Nursing. It was to teach a course on ethics to senior nurses who were studying for a qualification to enable them to become nurse managers. (It was known flippantly as 'morals for matrons', although this was inaccurate because many members of the class were male nurses!) Whoever designed that course (I never found out who it was) was clearly sadistic. These unfortunate nurses were required to study the theories of Kant, Bentham, Mill *and* Spinoza! What is more, they had to pass a written exam at the end of the course. I do not know who were/was more terrified – they or I. But, for the record, I fainted shortly into my first lecture and this endeared me to the students for the whole year because I was now in *their* care.

After several years of struggling to get these moral theories across to the unfortunate nurses and relate them to real clinical situations, I realised that what was needed was a textbook that guided a clinically trained reader through the philosophical swamplands. Thus *Moral Dilemmas in Medicine* was born and, thanks to advice from the medical publisher of the book, it became a course book for both nurses and doctors (although it was from my nurse students that I got the real-life clinical dilemmas).[2] The book was published in 1972 and (despite my publisher's prediction that they would be doing this not for money but just for reputation) it went to three editions. Thus I finally became an accidental medical ethicist, and so, when in 1974 the Society for the Study of Medical Ethics decided to launch the *Journal of Medical Ethics (JME)* in collaboration with the *British Medical Journal*, they eventually turned to me to become editor, having looked in vain for a doctor who knew anything about the subject. Watching this 'baby' of mine grow into the high-impact international journal it has become today has been one of the great satisfactions of my life (and most of the credit for this has to go to Raanan Gillon, the second – and by far the longest-serving – editor of the journal and a doctor who *did* know about philosophical ethics). So now, as the founding editor of the *JME*, I had become an 'expert' in the field.

There was one final turning point. After the sudden death of the professor in the department in the Divinity Faculty to which I had been recruited after 5 years in the Chaplaincy, it was widely expected by my colleagues that I would be appointed to the Chair. However, I was unsuccessful and, at the time, I was bitterly disappointed, although I have since realised that it was by far the best

2 Alastair V. Campbell, *Moral Dilemmas in Medicine* (Edinburgh, Churchill-Livingstone 1972).

thing to happen to me, enabling a final move fully into medical ethics. From the 1980s onwards (with an increasing number of invitations to lecture abroad on medical ethics), it became more and more obvious that my two academic careers, in Christian ethics and practical theology (still at that time in my academic home, the Faculty of Divinity), and in medical ethics could not be sustained. I had to choose between them. Then came the offer of a Chair in Medical Ethics from Otago University, followed by one from Bristol University and finally one from the National University of Singapore. The decision was made, and from 1990 onwards I have been full-time in medical ethics and the founder director of three centres in the field. In these highly productive and exciting years, I have been hugely inspired and sustained by my marriage to my second wife, Sally, a true soulmate. The accidental medical ethicist finally found his true vocation.

Reflections

I fear these personal reminiscences might appear rather self-indulgent, but I hope they may help to set a context for the general points I wish to make in the rest of this chapter, based on over 40 years of my involvement in the field. These are as follows: first, the subject area is essentially interdisciplinary and, over the years I have been involved in it, this aspect has grown in both strength and depth; second, medical ethics and bioethics narrowly escaped from American capture, a threat coming from the sheer extent of the subject in the USA, and it has become truly global although risks of Western dominance remain; and, finally, there continues to be an uneasy tension between its origins in professional standards of practice (*of* doctors, *for* doctors and *by* doctors) and a genuine socio-political critique, both of the profession and of the wider issues of the ethics of healthcare. This tension remains, and probably can never be fully resolved.

1. Interdisciplinarity

The setting up of the *Journal of Medical Ethics* entailed a commitment to interdisciplinarity from the outset. With an editor trained in both philosophy and theology and two senior medical figures as consulting editors, the journal could not be seen as narrowly medical, yet still remained very closely in touch with, and focused on, medicine. The same was true of the inaugural editorial board, which had doctors, nurses, lawyers, philosophers, theologians and social scientists, all very senior in their disciplines, to steer the journal's development as a major scholarly resource for both practitioners and academics. Since those early days, the sheer range and volume of research and publication in medical ethics has been quite astounding. But, as important as quantity, is the quality of interaction between disciplines. No single perspective seems to have dominated for long, although the philosophers do seem to jostle for first place a great deal!

Of the many ways in which the disciplines have come together on a common cause, I would pick out two aspects. First, there is the rise of 'empirical ethics', with the social scientists playing a key role in devising appropriate empirical methods for enriching the factual side of medical ethics, but – more than this – challenging the 'is-ought' distinction, forcing a rethink of the philosophical fear of a naturalistic fallacy (defined by the *Encyclopaedia Britannica* as the fallacy of 'treating the term "good" (or any equivalent term) as if it were the name of a natural property').[3] This 'fallacy' was first identified by David Hume but became best known in philosophy after it was elaborated by G.E. Moore.[4] Related to this is an enrichment of qualitative research in the field, giving much greater prominence to the perspectives of patients in assessing the ethical issues.

Second, there is the contribution of legal scholars in making the discipline go beyond narrowly clinical questions (the 'sacred dyad' of the doctor-patient relationship) to the policy dimensions of ethical quandaries in medicine and the life sciences. Here the work of the UK Nuffield Council on Bioethics has been especially prominent, a notable recent example being its work on the use and retention of DNA samples by the police.[5] We should also note the huge range of research funded by the European Commission over the years, which has produced many insights into European and international policy matters. But these are just two examples, and one need only attend a conference of the European Association of Centres of Medical Ethics (EACME) or the World Congresses of the International Association of Bioethics (IAB) to see the exciting mix of scholars involved at the present time. Especially heartening is the large number of young scholars from many different disciplines who are keen to enter this field.

2. Globalisation

Some years back (in 2000), I wrote a highly critical review of Al Jonsen's book, *The Birth of Bioethics*,[6] which I published in the European journal, *Medicine, Healthcare and Philosophy*. I entitled it ' "My Country 'tis of Thee" – The Myopia of American Bioethics'.[7] Al Jonsen was a friend of mine (still is, I hope) but his book was a shocking revelation of the insularity of American bioethics. His account of the 'birth' made it look as though everything had started in the States and that the concerns about American health research and healthcare were all that mattered ethically. What is more, Chapter 12 of the book, entitled 'Bioethics – American and Elsewhere', was downright insulting in both its brevity and its inaccuracy about 'elsewhere'. When we think of the independent flourishing of the European scene, (originating around the same time as the Hastings Center

---

3 Editors of Encyclopaedia Britannica, 'Naturalistic Fallacy (Ethics)' (*Encyclopaedia Britannica* 26 July 2012). <www.britannica.com/topic/naturalistic-fallacy> accessed 20 March 2018.
4 George E. Moore, *Principia Ethica* (Cambridge University Press 1903).
5 Nuffield Council on Bioethics, *The Forensic Use of Bioinformation: Ethical Issues* (London, Nuffield Council on Bioethics 2007).
6 Albert R. Jonsen, *The Birth of Bioethics* (New York, Oxford University Press 1998).
7 Alastair V. Campbell, ' "My Country 'tis of Thee" – The Myopia of American Bioethics' (2000) 23 *Medicine, Healthcare and Philosophy* 195.

in the USA and with many centres in Europe), evident in the EACME cluster and in initiatives like the Erasmus Mundus Master degree, one wonders what our American friends see in their frequent overseas trips – just the tourist sights? Yet this history was written by a well-intentioned and open-minded scholar, who still could not see past the shores of his own nation.

This risk of American colonisation of the field has become much greater over the years through the amazing success of Beauchamp and Childress's *Principles of Biomedical Ethics*.[8] You find the 'Georgetown mantra' everywhere in the world, especially when doctors and other healthcare professionals have had crash courses in bioethics, often run by American academics. Of course, the authors themselves intended the book to be trans-cultural or perhaps 'supra-cultural', since they see the principles as capturing some fundamental human features of morality that transcend cultural difference. Moreover, in later editions of the book, the authors' approach has become increasingly nuanced with a recognition of the strength of other accounts of ethics, such as virtue ethics. But, on the ground, principlism assumes a distinctively American twist, whatever the authors intended. 'Autonomy' triumphs – this in the highly individualistic form so disapproved of by Onora O'Neill – and justice remains an afterthought.[9]

Fortunately, other forces in the field seem to have prevented this kind of 'MacBurger' approach to medical ethics. First was the vision of Peter Singer and Daniel Wikler, when they took the initiative in 1992 to inaugurate the IAB. The IAB constitution pays no heed to numbers of scholars in any given country. Instead, a strict allocation formula for electable places on the board prevents (at least to some extent) both national and gender dominance. We get a snapshot of this from the gender and nationality of the 13 presidents of the association elected since 1992: 9 male, 4 female; 3 from the USA, 3 from the UK, 1 from Australia, 1 from New Zealand, 1 from South Africa, 1 from Finland, 1 from Germany, 1 from Argentina and 1 from India. This is far from perfect equity in gender and nationality, but the WASP[10] dominance has at least been moderated a little. There remains a lot to improve, however, in terms of cultural diversity and gender equality.

Even more powerful forces ensuring internationalisation and inclusivity have come from the sheer diversity of theory in medical ethics and the wide geographical spread of scholars. Principlism cannot maintain any real dominance now that there are powerful advocates for culturally sensitive ethical approaches, a lively debate about 'East versus West' in ethics and the increased vitality of rival approaches, such as virtue ethics, care ethics and feminist approaches to bioethics. It is true that there are still few scholarly institutions in some regions (and Africa is especially challenged here), but still there is clear emergence of regional identities, especially in Asia – and here I must put in a plug for the journal founded

8 Tom L. Beauchamp and James F. Childress, *Principles of Biomedical Ethics* (7th edn, New York, Oxford University Press 2013).

9 Onora O'Neill, *Autonomy and Trust in Bioethics* (Cambridge University Press 2002).

10 White Anglo-Saxon Protestant.

by my centre in Singapore, the *Asian Bioethics Review*, a young journal still, but with a wonderful range of regional scholarship that has worldwide significance.

3. Socio-political critique

Let me begin this final section with a very rude comment made to me when I first met Ivan Illich (the author of *Medical Nemesis*).[11] He was speaking at a London Medical Group conference in London shortly after I had been appointed editor of *JME*. When he heard the title of the journal and my position as editor he remarked, ' "medical ethics"? – I would call it "medical masturbation"!' Of course this was quite consistent with Illich's negative view of modern medicine as a force driven by professional arrogance and allied to industrialist ambitions, largely destructive of health. Later, Ian Kennedy was to raise similar doubts in his Gifford Lectures, drawing on Illich's observation that the main gains in health in the twentieth century had come not from medical breakthroughs but from a rise in living standards.[12]

These negative accounts of medicine's achievements may appear extreme. They were to some extent the product of that heady time in the 1960s and 1970s when *everything* was under radical questioning. I still remember the student revolutionary movements, when Edinburgh, among many universities, was occupied by students demanding greater academic power. How changed things are now, when most students just hope to get some sort of job at the end of their studies, and the more radical of the academic disciplines (in humanities and social science) are clearly out of favour with governments looking merely for economic outcomes.

But we cannot dismiss these criticisms of medicine as merely the intellectual fashion of a bygone academic era. In so many ways, things are *worse* now than they were in the 1970s. The gap between rich and poor, healthy and diseased, has increased massively throughout the world in the post-1980s era of triumphant capitalism; and the pervasive economic influence of big pharma is to be seen everywhere, most notably in the 10/90 gap (a mere 10% of research funding goes to the health problems of 90% of the world's population).[13] Moreover, both research integrity and research ethics are under increasing threat as the rich world outsources the bulk of its clinical research to poor nations that can never afford the products of the research, and when the ever-mounting pressure to publish and to patent everything possible has led to both secrecy and outright fraud. Increasingly we hear from bioethicists in India and Africa of the bribery and corruption behind research and the inadequacy of ethical review. Another worrying sign of the times is the 'regulatory capture' by those with a commercial stake in research of the Food and Drug Administration and the other drug

---

11 Ivan Illich, *Medical Nemesis* (London, Calder Boyars 1974).
12 Ian Kennedy, *The Unmasking of Medicine* (London, Allen and Unwin 1981).
13 See Chapter 5 'Research' in Alastair V. Campbell, *Bioethics: The Basics* (2nd edn, Abingdon, Routledge 2017).

and device regulators. A strong indication of this is the constant controversy over revisions of the Declaration of Helsinki to make research more just and socially responsible.

Where has medical ethics been in all this? Well, of course there have been out-spoken critics of the current injustices, obvious examples being Thomas Pogge and Peter Singer, but for many in the field too much time has been taken up with questions of no relevance to the most urgent problems of our day. Indeed, the optimistic predictions of many libertarian and consequentialist writers about human progress and their (unfounded) predictions of so called 'human enhance-ment' (even moral enhancement!) seem to me to feed into the very socio-political influences that medical ethics should be combatting. The promotion of progress and liberty has been transmuted into the ever-increasing commodification of everything we prize as humans; and free market ideology seems to be everywhere, despite all the evidence that it causes immense injustice! I would like to suggest that for all of us, Michael Sandel's recent publication, *What Money Can't Buy: The Moral Limits of Markets*, becomes essential reading.[14]

So I think we have moved on from castigating the medical profession for being self-indulgent and self-aggrandising; indeed, we can see that profession itself as the victim of those very same forces that create and perpetuate injustice. But we have not escaped from the tension in medical ethics between getting the clinical encounter ethically right, and seeing that, more destructive than any failures of the profession, there is the sociopolitical context within which medicine seeks to promote and preserve human values. In a well-known phrase, we must surely watch out that we are not merely rearranging the deck chairs on board the *Titanic* even as the vessel sinks.

As I have progressed in my career through the last few decades and now that I have the honorific title of Emeritus Director, I have felt increasingly strongly that medical ethics is in increasing danger of becoming socio-politically irrele-vant and of being powerless in the face of major transnational forces that have no interest in humanitarian values but espouse either a crass form of materialism or (worse) a crude and divisive nationalism. One of my last lectures as Director of the NUS Centre of Biomedical Ethics was entitled 'Has medicine sold its soul?' It was very well attended and (sadly) many medical colleagues told me I was right, but that there was nothing we could do to prevent it. Maybe the preacher in me is finding a new voice in the end, but I am sure we *must* do something about it, or forego claiming to be teaching ethics at all. To be personal one last time, my father, first a college professor then a parish minister, was a socialist to the core. In the First World War, he was a conscientious objector and suffered vilification from some members of his own family for his stance. His socialism was deeply rooted in his Christian faith, and one of his more memorable remarks was 'In *theory* I can understand how someone might be both a Tory (Conservative) and a Christian, but for the life of me I cannot see *how*!' I no longer share the same

---

14 Michael Sandel, *What Money Can't Buy: The Moral Limits of Markets* (London, Allen Lane 2012).

strength of Christian belief that my father had, but his insistence on struggling for social justice is one of his great legacies I will always treasure. How to honour this legacy in the coming years of semi-retirement I am unsure. Certainly I have seen a return to virtue ethics as one way of creating the kind of self-reflective and committed practitioners that we desperately need in the doctors of the future. Beyond this, I think we simply must not give up. We need to question tirelessly the social and political authorities who try to silence genuine ethical debate and to turn medical ethics into mere social conformity.

Editors' introduction

Voo Teck Chuan, Richard Huxtable and Nicola Peart

Healthcare ethics is a field that explores, and where possible seeks to resolve, ethical issues arising in the delivery of healthcare services, and the related practices of research, biomedical innovation and public health. The issues are often complex and challenging, not least given the multitude of stakeholders and divergent interests, and the difficulties of judging which values are relevant or should predominate. Uncertainty of the consequences and moral (and other) costs of competing options, or of a new technology, and scope for differing interpretations of existing norms and standards complicate matters. Appropriate resolution usually depends on navigating the legal and regulatory frameworks that underpin practice, sourcing for good (if not best) practices and imbibing a healthy dose of pragmatism in how ethical standards and concepts can be applied 'on the ground', given personal, professional, institutional and epistemic limits.

At times, moral imagination, about how things could and should otherwise be, is not just ethically helpful but necessary. In advancing their arguments and claims, scholars, practitioners, policymakers and laypersons should be mindful of their practical, theological, political or philosophical presuppositions, which might otherwise obscure the reasonableness of, or commonalities with, other viewpoints. Healthcare ethics – like its more inclusive sibling bioethics – needs to hear and heed diverse perspectives. It is increasingly recognized that healthcare ethics needs an interdisciplinary approach: an 'all hands on deck' approach to gathering, exploring and appreciating information, experiences, perspectives and collective wisdom. This book of essays honours an early proponent of interdisciplinarity: Alastair V. Campbell. He argues that healthcare ethics, as a subfield of bioethics, should be advanced through a 'global perspective' so as 'to confront full on the forces which threaten human values, indeed which threaten the future of humanity itself'.[1]

In the opening essay of this book in which he reflects on his academic journey, Campbell calls himself an 'accidental ethicist'. 'Serendipitous ethicist' may be

---

1 Alastair V. Campbell, 'Bioethics Ten Years on – What Has Changed?' (2011) 25(8) *Bioethics* ii, iii.

equally apt. It was through, for example, taking on the task of teaching post-graduate nurses (at the University of Edinburgh), at a time when healthcare ethics education was an uncharted course, that Campbell 'discovered' the theoretical and practical gulf between philosophical moral reasoning and day-to-day clinical reasoning in problematizing and approaching dilemmas in the wards, and the utility of discussing cases (adapted from real experiences) as a bridge. Informed by this approach, his lectures were developed into *Moral Dilemmas in Medicine: A Coursebook in Ethics for Doctors and Nurses,*[2] which was recognized for its impact on the emergence of bioethics in British academia, including the value of the 'view from the sidelines' to mitigate the bias of healthcare providers.[3] Campbell thus charted a career path for himself and those not working directly at the bedside but in other practice settings to make meaningful contributions to ethics in healthcare.

From those early beginnings, Campbell forged a groundbreaking career in healthcare ethics, in which he has worked with numerous and diverse colleagues in various, also diverse, settings and countries. This book consists of 15 original essays by Campbell's peers, colleagues, friends and mentees (including Michael Campbell, his son). The essays engage with the significance of Campbell's scholarly work and his broader contributions to the shaping of healthcare ethics, its scholars and its activities. Campbell has addressed a diverse range of essential questions in the field. Aside from advancing methodological approaches to ethics analysis and teaching, his writings have examined the relationship of ethics to medical professionalism, law, religion and culture in healthcare. Campbell has also written extensively on specific, heavily debated issues such as the doctor-patient relationship, treatment of the human body and its parts, and justice in healthcare and research; these are topics that will endure and become more complex in an increasingly globalized and commoditized world.

We have arranged the essays according to Campbell's thinking about and influence on healthcare ethics theory and methods; the intersection of ethics with medical law and policy, theology and medical professionalism; bioethics in geographical and socio-cultural contexts; healthcare ethics education; and ethical issues in activities related to healthcare (like clinical research). In what follows, we provide, chronologically, a brief account of each essay, and some reflections they prompted from us about Campbell's distinctive arguments and ways of doing healthcare ethics.

Healthcare ethics in theory

To begin, John McMillan's essay 'Alastair V. Campbell and the "why" of medical ethics' distills two principles that Campbell promotes for approaching medical ethics: 'no special pleading' and 'engagement with experience'. 'No special

---

2 Alastair V. Campbell, *Moral Dilemmas in Medicine* (Edinburgh, Churchill-Livingstone 1972).
3 Duncan Wilson, *The Making of British Bioethics* (Manchester University Press 2014), 189.

pleading' makes the case for pluralism in medical ethics methods on the basis that no single moral theory or framework can address all moral issues encountered in healthcare in terms of description, justification and translation to action. 'Engagement with experience' argues for the value of understanding the issues *as faced and deliberated by* stakeholders, such as physicians and patients, which may be gained through close interactions with these stakeholders or from empirical inquiries. McMillan's essay is perceptive in showing that these two principles highlight the need to consider our primary reasons for establishing ethics as a subject and discourse in healthcare – to make healthcare ethics an inclusive field and ultimately to influence healthcare for the better, even as we present our preferred moral perspective on how some particular issue should be evaluated and resolved. In putting the 'why' of doing medical ethics in focus, McMillan presents a thought-provoking interpretation of the application of the two principles in considering the legitimacy of particular theories. 'No special pleading' rules out theories that *oppress* other perspectives, while 'engagement with experience' should include an important role for philosophical thought experiments and fantastic examples insofar as they 'lead us to understand, question, revise, or better some significant aspect of clinical reality'.

The Georgetown 'four principles' approach, commonly labelled 'principlism', has come to dominate bioethical analysis, at least with respect to clinical ethics. Whether this dominance is oppressive or imperialistic is arguable and might, for example, depend on how it is applied.[4] In *Principles of Biomedical Ethics*, Tom Beauchamp and James Childress affirm that beneficence, non-maleficence, respect for autonomy, and justice 'provide only a framework of norms with which we can start in biomedical ethics'.[5] How these norms are to be specified and balanced to address the nuances of particular ethical issues in healthcare may require guidance from higher order moral theories, such as virtue ethics. In wanting to propagate such an understanding, Campbell argued for the significance of virtue ethics[6] in healthcare ethics in debates with supporters of the four principles, in particular Raanan Gillon. In contest was the relationship between virtue ethics and the four principles. Campbell's position is that virtue ethics directs our attention to important aspects of the moral life, such as character and emotions, which enrich the application of the principles for a more adequate approach to ethics. This is a point that Gillon, as well as Beauchamp and Childress, are happy to accept. Continuing his debate with Campbell in 'Principlism, virtuism, and the spirit of oneness', Gillon further accepts, with support from evolutionary explanations, that it is plausible that human moral

---

4 Richard Huxtable, 'For and Against the Four Principles of Biomedical Ethics' (2013) 8(2–3) *Clinical Ethics* 39.

5 Tom L. Beauchamp and James F. Childress, *Principles of Biomedical Ethics* (6th edn, Oxford University Press 2009) 6.

6 In an email correspondence to one of the editors, Beauchamp wrote that 'I believe truthfully that Alastair is the [first and] only person to bring virtue theory to bear directly on bioethics prior to our 1979 publication of the Principles, in which we tried to do so'. Email from Tom Beauchamp to Voo Teck Chuan (28 March 2018).

psychology and intuitions are disposed towards virtue ethical reasoning. Nevertheless, he argues that it is conceptually necessary to rely on some moral standards, which the four principles can supply, in order to arrive at reasoned agreement, whether individually or collectively, on whether some character trait or action is a virtue or a vice. Citing Campbell, Gillon concludes with a call for a spirit of 'oneness' for connecting the four principles and virtue ethics in both theory and practice. The humour that Campbell possesses (an attribute also highlighted in Tom Murray's chapter and elsewhere in this volume) is a virtue in this cause.

Campbell is trained in theology and philosophy, and concepts and insights from the two disciplines often come together, whether consciously or not, in his theorization of healthcare ethics. In 'Professional relationships: covenant, virtue, and clinical life', Grant Gillett examines a model of medical care espoused by Campbell that, according to Gillett, integrates virtue ethics and covenantal models of the relationship between health professionals and patients. A covenantal model illuminates the commitments of health professionals to patient welfare that go beyond contractual market service. It may, however, suggest an alliance between parties of unequal status, and dispose health professionals to unjustified paternalistic behaviour based on assumptions of superiority. Nevertheless, as Gillett argues, a covenantal relationship between health professionals and patients should direct the former to adopt 'an ethic of the servant saviour' so that mutual trust and other relational values can develop for care to be effective. It is in such a conceptual space that Gillett interprets the relationship between virtue ethics and the four principles. As he submits:

> The virtues fostered by a covenant both supplement the four principles and highlight their deficiencies (or vices) by introducing further aspects of the clinical partnership, some of which allow the warmth and humanness of healthcare and the life of healthcare professionals to be acknowledged.

Healthcare ethics in disciplinary contexts

The discussion on the intersection between virtue ethics, philosophy and theology continues with Robin Gill's essay, 'Healthcare ethics and theology'. Gill distinguishes two forms of Christian theological approaches to healthcare ethics: fideist and realist. While both approaches may align with virtue ethics, a theological realist seeks to provide guidance on healthcare ethical issues in ways that do not create sharp differences between Christian thinking and secular humanistic reasoning. For example, while both a realist and fideist may highlight an ethics of compassion and care, a fideist, unlike a realist, may also bring up the virtue of (Christian) faith, or relate compassion and care to salvation. Placing Campbell within the realist camp, Gill argues that both approaches are important to address different audiences in healthcare ethics. A realist approach would be more suitable for a morally pluralistic audience: a fideist one more so for a Christian community. Gill advocates that fideists and realists should work together to counter fundamentalism and polarizing accounts of religion and secular philosophical ethics.

Roger Higgs's essay, 'In that (hard) case: could ordinary talk in clinical care have an extraordinary moral importance?' is a development of Campbell and Higgs's views on what it means to respect patients and their autonomy, which they earlier explored in their 1982 book *In That Case: Medical Ethics in Everyday Practice*.[7] Higgs argues here that 'ordinary talk' is a function of respect for patients in doctor–patient encounters. (Higgs does not define 'ordinary talk' but it appears to refer to modes of communication in everyday situations where politeness and queries about another person's life are used to forge relations.) With a focus on two types of 'hard cases' – those involving patients with medically unexplained symptoms and those in which physicians and patients become embattled – Higgs argues that ordinary talk could get patients to share their concerns and other personal information, which may be critical to resolving or preventing such cases. In reminding physicians of their 'obligations as *human beings*', ordinary talk, as Higgs writes, may have a transformative effect on healthcare, in opening up and shaping the appropriate choice(s) of treatment or care for patients. As a healthcare practitioner, Higgs provides us with an important perspective on healthcare ethics. While argumentation and provision of reasons to support or justify some medical decision are important features, healthcare ethics needs to attend to the 'how' of applying ethical principles in real-time, everyday practice.

Like Higgs, Margaret Brazier and Sheila McLean also each collaborated with Campbell, albeit in work that looked more to their shared area of expertise: law. In their essay, 'Human tissue: a story from a small state', they consider the question of how the law should regulate deceased organ donation in the UK. In 2015, Wales became the first country in the UK to introduce a 'soft' opt-out law that would respect family objections to donation for those who had not opted out. In 2017, the Scottish government announced its intention to bring forward similar legislative changes to increase organ transplantations. Brazier and McLean examine the resistance in England to follow suit. Drawing lessons from historical controversies in which human cadavers and their parts were illicitly taken for medical uses, they argue that policy making on use of the human body should reconcile the scientific, impersonal purposing of posthumous bodies and their continuing meaning for families. In this regard, they point to the importance of Campbell's defence of human bodily materials as gifts, which oppose their treatment as mere things or resources. Campbell's stance, as the authors observe, was probably shaped by his service on the UK Retained Organs Commission, in which he experienced the distress and violence felt by those families who discovered the non-consensual post-mortem retention of their relatives' organs in hospitals within the UK's National Health Service.

---

7 Alastair V. Campbell and Roger Higgs, *In That Case: Medical Ethics in Everyday Practice* (London: Darton, Longman & Todd 1982).

Healthcare ethics in cultural contexts

As Brazier and McLean note, the language of medical science was a contributory factor to the UK organ retention scandal. In some cases, families gave consent to donation of 'tissue' without realizing that 'tissue' in medical usage may refer to whole or multiple organs. Finding a common language between different stakeholders and communities is key to a common understanding and a foundation for co-operation. Michael Campbell and Jing-Bao Nie explore this theme in their essay 'Where our common language lies: virtues, embodiment and faith in global bioethics', in which they examine Campbell's aspiration for bioethics to take a global outlook. They raise the concern of whether the 'search for a common language for bioethical 'problem solving' can make us unable to fully appreciate the diversity of voices and approaches in bioethics', or 'fool us into thinking that the [moral] differences between people can always be bridged'. According to the authors, moral differences cannot be reduced to a matter of different weight being placed on a common range of principles or reasons (contrary to what principlism might suggest). With this insight, they argue that the way to finding a common language is to arrive at a suitable understanding of the experiences of those confronting the bioethical problem, and to recognize that the goal at hand is not to obliterate moral differences but to respond to them with creative solutions. Following (Alastair) Campbell, Michael Campbell and Nie conclude with the need for *faith* in ethics, which for them means believing in the 'possibility of mutual understanding, and in the possibility of meaningful change'.

We move from an account of global bioethics to a regional account in Richard Huxtable's essay 'On the open seas: pluralism and bioethics in Europe'. As Huxtable writes, the term 'European bioethics' might refer to distinctive ideas and thinking related to ethics that emerge from the particular geographical or cultural locale of Europe. Unlike bioethics in America, for example, European bioethics appears to give communitarian values or principles, such as solidarity, greater significance. Nevertheless, any apparent commonality should not obscure the fact that 'the ideas of Europe and European bioethics are fragmented, as there are different world views, different values, different times, and different influences to consider.' Rather than 'European bioethics', Huxtable thus prefers Campbell's idea of 'bioethics in Europe', which avoids the misleading depiction of a single ethical method or interpretation of ethical norms within this setting. Huxtable's use of the sea metaphor is apt here for it suggests the fluidity of ethical ideas across time and space in a globalized, increasingly open world. His broader claim is that ethical pluralism *is* a universal fact. Huxtable leaves us with the question of whether this empirical proposition (if true) means that bioethics *should* draw on plural moral values and approaches to address bioethical issues wherever they arise, which seems to suggest a global, unified outlook for bioethics, including healthcare ethics.

In 'Healthcare ethics in New Zealand', Lynley Anderson and Nicola Peart describe the monumental and lasting impact of the Cartwright Inquiry (1987–8) in institutionalizing a patient-centred approach in health delivery and research in New Zealand. The inquiry (led by Judge Silvia Cartwright) was initiated following revelations of an unethical study at New Zealand's largest women's hospital, which followed women with major cervical abnormalities without giving them standard treatment, and without their knowledge or consent, for two decades. At one level, the inquiry focused on the unethical behaviour of the obstetrician who conducted the study, but it also revealed a systemic lack of good oversight practices, the lack of distinction between healthcare and research, and a prevailing culture of paternalistic, doctor-centred decision making. As Anderson and Peart note, Campbell (by then already an internationally renowned ethicist) was called as an expert witness for the inquiry, and his evidence helped diagnose these deeper issues within the health system, and shaped the inquiry's final recommendations. Those recommendations, which were subsequently implemented, included the creation of a legislated code of patients' rights and the establishment of a nation-wide system of independent health research ethics committees with significant lay membership. Despite such promising developments, Anderson and Peart reveal that the number of ethics committees reviewing health (and disability) research and their scope of review has since been significantly reduced, in order to promote efficiency in review and attract industry-sponsored clinical trials in New Zealand. Anderson and Peart's essay thus grapples with a central theme of Campbell's work: the erosion of the protection of patients and research participants by commercial interests.

Healthcare ethics education

According to Anderson and Peart, the Cartwright Inquiry triggered the need for change in healthcare ethics education in New Zealand, and provided the impetus 'for the appointment of Campbell to a chair in bioethics and the establishment of the Otago Bioethics Research Centre' (now Bioethics Centre) in 1988, which became responsible for conducting and coordinating ethics education for medical students and staff at the University of Otago. The next three chapters, 'Healthcare ethics education at the University of Otago – and the Master of Bioethics and Health Law' (Neil Pickering, Lynley Anderson and Peter Skegg), 'Healthcare ethics education in the UK' (Gordon M. Stirrat and Julie Woodley) and 'Healthcare ethics education in Singapore' (Anita Ho, Jacqueline Chin and Voo Teck Chuan) provide enlightening accounts of the approach to, and challenges in, undergraduate healthcare ethics education in three geographical settings, led by centres (based at or affiliated to medical schools and teaching hospitals) in which Campbell played a founding role. Common themes, which reflect the pedagogical legacy of Campbell, are evident: ethics education must be multi-disciplinary and multi-professional, integrated with the medical curriculum throughout all years of study, apply a rigorous academic approach, and utilize sound teaching and assessment methods.

In addition to providing undergraduate ethics education, Pickering, Anderson and Skegg's essay describes the Otago Bioethics Centre's innovative development of highly regarded and popular postgraduate programmes, in particular the Master of Bioethics and Health Law. Covering the landscape of healthcare ethics teaching in the UK, Stirrat and Woodley's essay raises fundamental questions, such as whether medical professionalism and medical ethics should be taught separately, and the need to address the 'hidden curriculum' of role models in the clinical context. Ho, Chin and Voo describe the role of the National University of Singapore's Centre for Biomedical Ethics in building bioethics capacity in the city state of Singapore, which includes programmes for supporting the work of ethics committees and for 'training the trainers' – that is, teaching healthcare professionals to teach ethics to members of their own profession.

Health-related practices in ethical focus

The final section turns to specific areas of healthcare practice. In respective order, the three essays here address the use of dead human bodies for anatomical teaching and research, health research involving human subjects, and public health interventions.

In 'The dead human body: reflections of an anatomist', D. Gareth Jones brings to life the morally dubious past of anatomy in depending on unclaimed deceased bodies to sustain its scientific and teaching endeavours. He reflects that this practice was possible only by 'ignoring cultural inequities within societies'; the bodies were mostly those of people who, when alive, were impoverished or marginalized in society. In a climate that places a premium on respecting persons and their choice, bequest has become the norm (in at least certain countries) for supply of deceased bodies for anatomical practices, and this, as Jones writes, necessitates ethical thinking in cultivating anatomy as a 'humanistic discipline', in order to promote altruistic donation and address cultural or religious resistance. With reference to Campbell's views in his book *The Body in Bioethics*,[8] Jones argues that to humanize their profession, anatomists need to recognize 'that the embodiment of the person does not suddenly disappear at death, even though it will be let go in time'.

In 'Ethics in research: an appraisal of Campbell's remarks', Ruth Macklin responds to concerns about research ethics raised by Campbell in his book *Bioethics: The Basics*.[9] On Campbell's concern that voluntariness and consent would be undermined by in-kind food benefits to participate in research conducted during and in response to disasters, Macklin clarifies that it is more often the case that food is offered as humanitarian aid rather than as an incentive in this context, and that, even if it is an incentive for research, it is ethically more acceptable than monetary incentives. Macklin also points to the distinction between risk minimization and minimal risk as ethical requirements for research, and argues that the former is the accepted standard in international guidelines

8 Alastair V. Campbell, *The Body in Bioethics* (Routledge 2009).
9 Alastair V. Campbell, *Bioethics – The Basics* (Routledge 2013).

in research involving participants without capacity. Constraining the risk level to minimal risk would (unjustifiably) prevent many scientifically and socially valuable studies. In *Bioethics: The Basics*, Campbell argues that more needs to be done to rectify the unfair distribution of benefits arising from research conducted in resource-poor countries, because currently most of the benefits flow to the developed world. Drawing on this point, Macklin argues that entities from resource-rich settings have a post-trial obligation to make available successful products of research to the resource-poor community in which the research was carried out.

The final essay, 'The republic of health: motivating the republican turn in public health ethics' by Richard Ashcroft, pays tribute to Campbell's philosophical influence in making a case for civic republicanism as the appropriate political route to bridging healthcare ethics and public health ethics. In Ashcroft's view, contemporary healthcare ethics has drawn on liberal political philosophy's ideas of 'personal liberty and personal normative authority' to construct a patient-centred approach focused on individual autonomy. Ashcroft argues, however, that personal choice in the domain of healthcare or health-related decisions often lacks normative authority because of various cognitive errors and biases that affect decision making. What needs to be protected in such decisions, as Ashcroft submits, are individual values and not individual choice *tout court*. As we understand Ashcroft, civic republicanism is concerned with the normative structure of public reasons, which require (political) decisions to be reasonably justifiable or acceptable from each individual's viewpoint. In being directed to a similar understanding of normative authority, healthcare ethics and public health ethics can adopt common projects – aligned with civic republicanism – addressing human weaknesses in decision making and freedom from domination, and constructing a common good to which individuals can be committed. Ashcroft thus invites us to rethink the foundation of healthcare ethics and the implications of a liberal account of individual autonomy for individual and public health.

Conclusion

This collection of essays covers a wide-ranging set of issues relating to healthcare ethics, law, and professionalism, to all of which Campbell has made a significant and enduring contribution. From his early teachings in Edinburgh, he developed an internationally acclaimed career that took him all over the world. Of particular note are the three centres that he helped to found, first in New Zealand at the University of Otago, then in the UK at the University of Bristol, and finally in Singapore at the National University of Singapore. His achievements as a scholar, teacher, advocate, and leader are well described in the first chapter by Campbell's long-time friend and colleague, Thomas Murray, the retired director of the Hastings Center. His vision, dedication, work ethic, and collaborative approach, as well as his social skills and sense of humour, have given Campbell the wizarding power to achieve outstanding success in his work and to inspire many working in the field internationally.

As former colleagues of Campbell in each of the three universities where he founded bioethics centres, it has been a pleasure and a privilege to bring together the authors of the chapters in this book to showcase the immense contribution that Campbell has made and to acknowledge his tremendous legacy in the development of healthcare ethics in its broadest sense.

Voo Teck Chuan, National University of Singapore
Richard Huxtable, University of Bristol, United Kingdom
Nicola Peart, University of Otago, New Zealand
June 2018

Part II
Healthcare ethics in theory

1   Alastair V. Campbell and the 'why' of medical ethics

John McMillan

The *Journal of Medical Ethics* and two principles of good medical ethics

The *Journal of Medical Ethics* (*JME*) began in 1975 with Alastair V. Campbell as its founding editor. In an article published 40 years after the first issue of *JME*, Campbell ruminates upon the founding principles they used when starting what was at the time a bold initiative given the unknown prospects of the journal attracting a readership.[1] In doing so, he articulates the two principles he thinks characterise good medical ethics. The first is the idea that good medical ethics involves 'no special pleading', by which he means no theoretical or theological perspective should view itself as having a privileged position when it comes to making pronouncements about ethical matters. The second is that good medical ethics engages with the experiences of those delivering healthcare, those being treated, and those who frame healthcare policy.

While both of these principles will appear uncontroversial to many working within medical ethics, there are assumptions within them that others will not grant. In this chapter, I will explore the implications of both of these principles, defend them from a number of objections, and suggest some ways in which they can be extended.

'No special pleading'

The first editors of *JME* were concerned that medical ethics might be seen as captured by a specific ideology, be that theology or consequentialism. It seems reasonable to presume that this would have been partly motivated by Campbell's background in theology and philosophy, as well as an awareness that medical ethics (and bioethics more generally)[2] was developing as a secular area of inquiry.

1 Alastair V. Campbell, 'The Formative Years: Medical Ethics Comes of Age' (2015) 41 *Journal of Medical Ethics* 41, 5.
2 There is a distinction between 'medical ethics' and 'bioethics': the latter term has a broader scope and includes ethical issues from the life sciences in addition to medicine. Campbell is highly likely to agree that his views about 'good' medical ethics extend to bioethics so I will treat these terms as interchangeable for the purposes of this chapter.

Prior to the creation of 'bioethics', theologians were often called upon for pronouncements about moral matters. Arguably the most important early British statement about the ethics of donor-assisted insemination was the report of the Archbishop of Canterbury's working group on assisted insemination, usually referred to as 'the Cantuar Report'.[3] The Cantuar Report is worthy of study in its own right because sections of it contain insightful and vigorous ethical analysis.[4] However, it is also useful as an illustration of the way in which theology played an authoritative role in discussions about ethics and public morality. While the Cantuar Report uses a number of secular arguments, the definitive argument is theological:

> In the end, however, the judgment we reach on the subject of AID [artificial insemination by donor] will be shaped and determined by our view of the nature of marriage. If, with the Church, we hold it to be that exclusive contract and union 'for better or worse', the total commitment till death of each spouse to the other, then the part of the unknown donor must be seen as an unlawful intrusion, and the part of the wife – however innocent she may be of evil intent or motive – a breach of her marriage vows.[5]

There are, of course, exceptions, and examples of secular approaches to medical ethics from a similar time period, Glanville Williams in his classic *The Sanctity of Life and the Criminal Law* being one.[6] Nonetheless, even ethicists who argued in a secular fashion would be completely at ease with their views being framed as theological.[7]

Now when an ethicist argues from a theological perspective, it is usual for this to be declared and there are specialist journals catering for it, such as *The Linacre Quarterly* and *Christian Bioethics*. Some have argued that bioethics and Christian bioethics have become so distinct that the latter is at danger of being marginalised.[8]

No doubt Campbell could see that the future development of medical ethics would be primarily secular and multidisciplinary. It seems likely that we would have had in mind that this style was a feature of *The Hastings Center Report*, which had been established in 1971. There would also have been reactions to the

---

3 Church of England, Archbishop of Canterbury's Commission on Artificial Human Insemination, *Artificial Human Insemination: The Report of a Commission Appointed by His Grace the Archbishop of Canterbury* (SPCK 1948).
4 John McMillan, 'The Return of the Inseminator: Eutelegenesis in Past and Contemporary Reproductive Ethics' (2007) 38 *Studies in the History and Philosophy of the Biological and Biomedical Sciences* 393.
5 Commission on Artificial Human Insemination (n 2) 56.
6 Glanville L. Williams, *The Sanctity of Life and the Criminal Law* (Faber and Faber 1958).
7 Joseph F. Fletcher, *Morals and Medicine* (Princeton University Press 1954).
8 Christopher Tollefsen, 'Mind the Gap: Charting the Distance between Christian and Secular Bioethics' (2011) 17 *Christian Bioethics* 47.

utilitarianism of Peter Singer's *Affluence and Morality* and *All Animals are Equal* that were published in the early 1970s.[9]

It is clear from Campbell's later writings that there are other, and perhaps more important, arguments for 'no special pleading'. These arguments also help to explain the principle's scope as well as motivation. In his presidential address to the 1999 Tokyo International Association of Bioethics (IAB) conference, Campbell said:

> The fourth objective of the Association is 'To uphold the value of free, open and reasoned discussion of issues in Bioethics', and one of the ways this is to be implemented is by 'providing support for scholars whose freedom to discuss questions of Bioethics has been restricted or is under threat'. In some countries these restrictions and threats are all too obvious, emerging as they do from an insistence on religious, social or political conformity: but the threats are also there in ostensibly liberal countries, as the murderous activities of the extreme anti-abortionist lobby have demonstrated yet again in the USA. In this context, the position of the IAB is unequivocal: We oppose all such dogmatisms. We welcome the whole range of ethical arguments and viewpoints. As an organisation we take no position on any of the substantive issues of debate in Bioethics. We have a single moral position, that to be genuinely ethical, discussion of any issue must be 'free, open and reasoned'.[10]

Campbell is clearly not only concerned that a particular perspective might become too dominant in bioethics – this is also an argument for the importance of free speech and open debate as a counter to oppression. While 'no special pleading' in the context of the *JME* implies that all theoretical perspectives should be welcome, when applied to global bioethics or ethical issues where there are powerful vested interests, it implies that the freedom to pursue vigorous and critical conclusions is vital. So, a strong argument for 'no special pleading' is that privileging a particular perspective on ethics can silence perspectives that are vital when working toward sound ethical analyses. Moreover, it can be oppressive and function to legitimate oppression by vested interests.

It is worth noting that the objectives of the IAB were formulated and enacted by its founding members and Peter Singer played an especially important role in this. So, although some would argue that utilitarianism is too dominant in bioethics, it too is a voice in bioethics that some would try to silence. Although utilitarians tend to think that they have the correct theory of morality, that does not imply they are unreceptive to other ways of arguing about ethics.

---

9 Peter Singer, 'Famine, Affluence, and Morality' (1972) 1 *Philosophy and Public Affairs* 229; P Singer, 'All Animals are Equal' (1974) 5(1) *Philosophic Exchange* 103.

10 Alastair V. Campbell, 'Presidential Address: Global Bioethics – Dream or Nightmare?' (1999) 13 *Bioethics* 183, 185.

Free, open, and reasonable debate is valuable not only to avoid oppression. Campbell also thinks it is a way of reaching richer and more nuanced accounts of moral phenomena. When arguing with Raanan Gillon about the four principles approach to bioethics, Campbell claims that we need a multitude of theoretical perspectives:

> I am happy to concede the greater usefulness of the four principles in some of the scenarios suggested by Raanan. This approach can have more analytical force than virtue ethics in some of the standard cases which medical ethics considers. But the vice of principlism is its tendency to claims greater than it can justify. It points in the direction of solutions to some of our dilemmas – for example, by suggesting we calculate the benefit/burden ratio, but it is far from providing enough conceptual apparatus for making these difficult judgments. We need a diversity of approach in these complex human scenarios, and no theory should be seen as dominant.[11]

Campbell is a consistent and long-standing defender of a morally pluralistic approach to medical ethics, and this is a methodological reason why 'no special pleading' is important. Note also that the objection here is not that the four principles approach is redundant, or overly simplistic, but merely that its defenders have a tendency to view it as the magic key that unlocks bioethics. It seems that the aspiration to be the dominant approach to bioethics is what is most problematic for Campbell.

A related idea is that bioethics (and presumably medical ethics) should be interdisciplinary. This has always been a feature of *JME* and it is another way in which it has been committed to 'no special pleading'. The Hastings Center was established in 1969 and the *Hastings Center Report* followed not long after that in 1971. The Hastings Center is usually viewed as being the first bioethics centre and has influenced the shaping of this field significantly. It has always formed interdisciplinary teams for its research projects and has thereby promoted the presumption that bioethics should be conducted in an interdisciplinary fashion. The founding editors of *JME* would have been well aware of the Hastings Center's commitment to interdisciplinarity (Campbell is a recipient of the Hastings Center's highest accolade, the Henry Knowles Beecher award) and that is another argument for 'no special pleading'.

It is worth noting that while bioethics is nearly 50 years old, the scholarly discussion of medical ethics has occurred for much longer. The American Medical Association's first code of medical ethics was published in 1847[12] and like other early landmark statements, such as Percival's,[13] medical ethics was the domain of physicians.

11 Alastair V. Campbell, 'The Virtues and (Vices) of the Four Principles' (2003) 29 *Journal of Medical Ethics* 292, 296.
12 American Medical Association, *Code of Medical Ethics of the American Medical Association* (American Medical Association Press 1847).
13 Thomas Percival, *Extracts from the Medical Ethics of Dr Percival* (Clark and Raser 1823).

In summary, there are at least four distinguishable arguments that Campbell uses for 'no special pleading'. First, that it was important for the success of medical ethics that it not be perceived as 'captured' by theology or consequentialism. Second, because of the role that bioethics can and should have in speaking out against oppression and avoiding the oppressive effect that would result from a dominant theoretical perspective. Third, because moral problems are often nuanced and complex, so that using more than one theory is likely to give a better account of moral phenomena. Fourth, from its beginnings, interdisciplinarity was a feature of bioethics.

In the next section, I will consider the strength of 'no special pleading' and some objections to it, and offer my development of it.

The strength of 'no special pleading'

There are, or course, medical ethicists and bioethicists who nail their theoretical colours to the wall. Raanan Gillon is arguably the strongest advocate for the use of the four principles approach, stronger even than Beauchamp and Childress who formulated the four principles.[14] Does Gillon claim that the four principles are the best approach to medical ethics, and thereby should be in a 'dominant' position?

In one sense, he clearly does. The first edition of *The Principles of Health Care Ethics* included 90 chapters, all of which were about the four principles in an attempt to demonstrate how they could accommodate every issue in healthcare ethics.[15] However, in doing so, Gillon was trying to show how the principles could be interpreted in different ways and be consistent with most moral and theological traditions. The theoretical neutrality of the four principles is what leads Gillon to claim:

> [W]hatever our personal philosophy, politics, religion, moral theory, or life stance, we will find no difficulty in committing ourselves to four prima facie moral principles plus a reflective concern about their scope of application. Moreover, these four principles, plus attention to their scope of application, encompass most of the moral issues that arise in health care.[16]

That seems to imply that, if everyone adopted the four principles, that would not mean medical ethics had been captured by a particular perspective. Moreover, Gillon clearly thinks that they are not oppressive toward other views, can accommodate many views, and might even be consistent with the contribution of other disciplines. So, does it follow that the four principles approach does attempt to carve out a niche as the dominant approach yet does not imply 'special pleading'?

14 Raanan Gillon, 'Defending the Four Principles Approach as a Good Basis for Good Medical Practice and therefore for Good Medical Ethics' (2015) 41 *Journal of Medical Ethics* 111.
15 Raanan Gillon (ed.), *Principles of Health Care Ethics* (John Wiley and Sons 1994).
16 Raanan Gillon, 'Medical Ethics: Four Principles Plus Attention to Scope' (1994) 309 *British Medical Journal* 184.

The a-theoretical nature of the principles does seem to escape most of Campbell's worries, but perhaps not all of them. In his defence of virtue theory, Campbell is concerned that the four principles can create the impression that they are sufficient for medical ethics and important issues might be glossed over. The idea that four 'thin' principles can capture what is significant about diverse religious and moral theories does imply that they are made consistent at the expense of significance. So, while those advocates of the four principles approach claim that their account is consistent with other traditions, the watering down that inevitably follows does seem potentially oppressive, albeit in a more benign fashion.

There are ethicists such as Justin Oakley and Rosalind Hursthouse who write from within a virtue ethics tradition.[17] Both of them will often introduce the ethical analysis of an issue by stating they are about to 'give a virtue ethics' reading of that issue. Does this tendency of virtue theorists and other ethicists arguing from within a particular tradition amount to 'special pleading'? It would if they claimed their account was the only one that made sense and was capable of doing justice to the moral phenomena of a complex situation. However, virtue theorists, at least, tend to argue that they are providing an account of a moral issue that is richer and more nuanced than some other moral theories. In such cases, they are not attempting to capture or dominate ethical argument, but to enrich it. It might be that prefacing an ethical analysis with the rider that you are about to give an account based upon a particular moral theory unnecessarily limits the scope of your argument and is an open invitation for someone who is not sympathetic to virtue theory to cease reading, but it does not appear to be a case of 'special pleading'.

Trickier cases are when appeals are made to religious positions. Leon Kass is unusual in bioethics in that he overtly refers to God's wishes or conception of nature when arguing about the limits of biotechnology.[18] While bioethics is usually secular, Kass is unafraid to lead with his religious commitments. His argumentative strategy seems somewhat different in that while he might argue that he too is aiming at giving a fuller account of moral phenomena than is offered by secular moral theories, he appeals to considerations that not all would agree to and uses these considerations to reach conclusions about what such people should do. It seems implicit within Kass's account that those who do not agree that technologies such as in vitro fertilisation are an affront to God's conception of our reproductive nature are ignorant about the moral facts of the situation. When evaluated from the perspective of 'no special pleading', Kass's use of theory seems oppressive in that it claims priority over other theoretical perspectives and

---

17 Justin Oakley and Dean Cocking, *Virtue Ethics and Professional Roles* (Cambridge University Press 2001); R. Hursthouse, 'Virtue Ethics and the Treatment of Animals' in Tom L. Beauchamp and Raymond G. Frey (eds), *The Oxford Handbook of Animal Ethics* (Oxford University Press 2011).

18 Leon R. Kass, *Life, Liberty and the Defense of Dignity: The Challenge for Bioethics* (Encounter Books 2002).

gives an account of the moral phenomena that emphasise some moral features at the expense of others.

While there will appear to be nothing controversial about 'no special pleading' to those who read, write, and work within bioethics (and medical ethics), it is not a principle that would be granted by all who work on what we might call 'practical ethics'. While philosophers are unlikely to be happy with the idea that any specific moral theory is true and should therefore have a privileged position with respect to practical ethics,[19] they do tend to view practical ethics, and by implication bioethics, as being the proper domain of philosophy.

When characterising applied ethics, Archard and Rasmussen say:

> [T]he borderline between normative and applied ethics (1) is fuzzy; (2) may be drawn in different ways, depending on which normative theory is the right one; and (3) may not mark any deep divide, for instance in terms of the methods involved in these two branches of moral philosophy.[20]

In discussing the distinction between normative theory and applied ethics, they just assume that applied ethics is a branch of moral philosophy which, in turn, is a branch of philosophy. Philosophy is free to describe applied ethics as an area within the broader discipline. But when the range of issues described by anthologies such as Hugh LaFollette's *Handbook to Practical Ethics*[21] is very similar to what might be expected in similar companions to bioethics, that suggests that the primary difference between 'practical ethics' and 'bioethics' is that the former is a branch of philosophy and 'owned' by that discipline. Bioethics, on the other hand, is an area of inquiry where no discipline can plead that it is special and authoritative when it comes to these issues.

Disciplines such as philosophy are free to define themselves in whichever way they choose. However, the traditional view that philosophy has had of itself as 'the queen of the sciences'[22] is a view that implies a healthy sense of self-worth and dominance.[23]

There is some irony in the fact that the founding figures of bioethics such as Campbell and Callahan sought to create an area of inquiry where all cognate

---

19 Philosophers tend to use the terms 'applied ethics' and 'practical ethics' interchangeably. My preference is for the latter term because it captures the idea of an ethical analysis that is practically oriented, as opposed to one that merely involves the application of moral theory to real-life considerations.

20 David Archard and Kasper Lippert-Rasmussen, 'Applied Ethics' in Hugh LaFollette (ed.), *The International Encyclopedia of Ethics* (Blackwell Publishing Ltd 2013) 14.

21 Hugh LaFollette (ed.), *The Oxford Handbook of Practical Ethics* (Oxford University Press 2005).

22 David E. Cooper, 'Visions of Philosophy' (2009) 65 *Royal Institute of Philosophy Supplement* 1, 1.

23 It is worth noting that theology and mathematics have also considered themselves 'queens' of science. One presumes that there cannot be more than one monarch at any one time and that someone must be wrong.

disciplines could contribute, but it has been criticised as an enterprise that attempts to infiltrate or is subservient to vested interests. When reviewing two books critical of bioethics, Albert Jonsen remarked:

> Stevens tells a story of bioethics in which the bioethicists have become pusillanimous opportunists, subservient apologists for the powerful medical establishment. Smith's bioethicists, on the other hand, are insidious infiltrators of the ancient ethics of medicine, sapping its moral strength and injecting the poison of utilitarianism.[24]

Campbell is correct to identify and expand upon 'no special pleading' as a principle for bioethics. Given the drive of theology and philosophy, in particular, to carve out a privileged niche for themselves, maintaining a commitment to all being able to engage in free, open, and reasoned argument about ethical issues seems pertinent.

Campbell's second principle is related to the first in that its justification derives from the purpose of bioethics. Rather than being a purely academic enterprise, bioethics should be genuinely normative in that it engages with the issues that are relevant to those making and impacted on by difficult ethical choices.

Engagement with experience

Throughout his bioethical and theological works, Campbell has demonstrated a commitment to the good: his work is not narrowly academic in that he always has an eye to improving the world in some way.[25] When reflecting upon the founding aims of *JME* he remarked that:

> [G]ood medical ethics can be achieved only when the theorising stays closely in touch with the realities of healthcare. This entails talking to and working with doctors and other healthcare providers. It means engaging with the experiences of the recipients of healthcare and with the policy makers who set the framework for success and failure in healthcare delivery.[26]

When it began, the *JME* connected with clinicians by including the analysis of a clinical case in each issue. Those involved in medical education or clinical practice will know that clinical cases are a common currency in medical education and this made sense as a way of fostering interest in a scholarly approach to medical ethics.

---

24 Albert R. Jonsen, 'Beating up Bioethics' (2001) 31(5) *The Hastings Center Report* 40.
25 Alastair V. Campbell, *Moderated Love: A Theology of Professional Care* (SPCK 1984); Alastair V. Campbell, *Health as Liberation: Medicine, Theology and the Quest for Justice* (Pilgrim Press 1995); Alastair V. Campbell, *The Body in Bioethics* (Routledge 2009); Alastair V. Campbell, *Bioethics: The Basics* (Taylor and Francis 2013).
26 Alastair V. Campbell, 'The Formative Years: Medical Ethics Comes of Age' (2015) 41 *Journal of Medical Ethics* 5, 7.

While the *JME* no longer includes case commentaries, Campbell suggests that empirical approaches to ethics[27] are also a way in which bioethics can engage with the experiences of those involved in and affected by healthcare.

I will call this second principle 'engagement with experience'. It is worth noting that, while Campbell claims that this is important in order for good medical ethics and is therefore a necessary condition for good medical ethics, he clearly thinks that it is not a sufficient condition because merely being engaged with experience and a pluralist about theory is no guarantee that it is medical ethics, let alone good. Medical anthropology tends to be engaged with experience and open to different theoretical perspectives, yet might not work toward any ethical conclusions and thereby fail to be medical ethics at all.

Nonetheless, an implication of Campbell's principle is that medical ethics that fail to engage with the experiences of policy makers, healthcare professionals, and patients is weak or bad medical ethics. In his IAB presidential address in Tokyo Campbell posed a series of questions about the role and risk to global bioethics:

> Is 'global bioethics' in danger of becoming a kind of secular chaplain in this new imperial court, falsely assuring us that all is well because ethics is being given its due place in our appraisal of scientific advance? There is nothing like the seal of ethical approval to ensure an unimpeded advance of business – as one corporate leader expressed it, 'good ethics is good business'. Perhaps I exaggerate ...[28]

The worry is clear enough: this is an appeal for those involved in global bioethics to resist the temptation to merely discuss and legitimate scientific advance. The idea that bioethics more generally risks being reduced to giving the ethical *imprimatur* to new technologies is one that has exercised a number working in this field.

A strategy for countering this is 'engagement with experience'. If ethicists focus their analysis upon what a new technology is likely to mean for those accessing, providing, and framing policy about it, then perhaps bioethics will speak to what is significant and not merely legitimate. Take for example non-invasive prenatal testing (NIPT), which makes it possible to detect foetal DNA in maternal blood, thereby enabling the prenatal diagnosis of more conditions without invasive diagnostic procedures.[29] A superficial ethical analysis might point out that this is no different in principle from what we already provide and can do in the area of prenatal testing and that there are procreative liberty interests which mean NIPT should be permitted. However, an analysis of that kind on its own runs the risk of giving the stamp of ethical approval to

---

27 John McMillan and Tony Hope, 'The Possibility of Empirical Psychiatric Ethics' in G. Widdershoven *et al.* (eds), *Empirical Ethics and Psychiatry* (Oxford University Press 2008).
28 Campbell, 'Presidential Address' (n 10) 184.
29 Jeanne Snelling, Nikki Kerruish and Jessie Lenagh-Glue, 'Non-Invasive Prenatal Testing: The Problem with "Fast Cars"' (2016) 24 *Journal of Law and Medicine* 203.

a technology that has a number of subtle effects and is likely to change the nature of prenatal testing. These tests require only a blood sample. NIPT can be provided via mail from companies in any part of the world that may not help people interpret the complex information that such tests produce. Policy makers can be placed in an invidious situation in that they might not think that there is sufficient evidence of benefit but move to recommending access under a national health service in order to control the quality of NIPT. Off-shore companies are using social media to advertise their NIPT services directly to pregnant women, which might be seen as consistent with autonomy but could also be criticised as predatory.[30] Campbell seems right that genuine engagement with experience is a way in which bioethics can focus upon the issues that need attention and not become a superficial exercise.

'Engagement with experience' is a *prima facie* plausible view, and it is hard to imagine anyone working within bioethics arguing that it is not correct, nor conceding that their work failed to do this. However, it is potentially quite radical when you think of some famous examples of medical ethics that this condition is likely to pick out.

Judith Jarvis Thomson's article defending the permissibility of abortion is one of the most significant articles published in medical ethics. She argues via the construction of two thought experiments that are designed to isolate and test issues critical to the abortion debate.[31] In the famous violin player case, the reader is asked what their intuitions would be if they became connected to a violin player in such a way that staying connected for 9 months was essential for the violin player's survival. The argument goes that, although it would be morally admirable of the reader to stay connected to the violin player, they should not be compelled to do so. In effect, the thought experiment is a counter-example to the claim that abortion should be illegal because the foetus has the moral status of a person.

The problem is that one reaction to Thomson's thought experiments is to point out that this is a very unusual situation and it is hard to know what one would actually think if in such a predicament. It is a thought experiment that does not appear to 'engage with experience' because it is so far removed from actual pregnancies and terminations.

James Rachels' *Active and Passive Euthanasia* is one of the most highly cited articles in medical ethics and it is still provocative and challenging to those who believe there is a moral difference between allowing and actively causing death.[32] He too constructs a thought experiment designed to tease out a particular point about the active–passive debate. He asks his reader to consider two uncles, Smith and Jones, each of whom has equally wicked intent, the only difference between the two being that one actively drowns his nephew in the bath whereas the other

30 ibid.
31 Judith J. Thomson, 'A Defense of Abortion' (1971) 1 *Philosophy and Public Affairs* 47.
32 James Rachels, 'Active and Passive Euthanasia' (1975) 292 *The New England Journal of Medicine* 78.

fails to save his nephew when he easily could and passively watches him drown. Rachels claims that we should view Smith and Jones as being equally wicked and it is therefore not the case that there is always a moral difference between bringing death about actively as opposed to passively.

Physicians and medical students will often object that this scenario is so far away from the clinical realities surrounding the end of life that it cannot inform what should happen in a clinical context. Whatever is made of that point, it does seem that this is a thought experiment that does not engage with the experience of those treating patients toward the end of their lives.

Does Campbell's 'engagement with reality' mean that Jarvis Thomson and Rachels have failed to write good medical ethics? Taken literally, that seems correct. Philosophical thought experiments are usually designed to test the logical extent of concepts, so they are usually idealised and at least one step removed from reality.

My view is that this suggests a modification of 'engagement with reality'. Rather than the arguments and thought experiments having to be true to experience, what really matters is that good medical ethics aims are normatively motivated. By that I do not mean that medical ethics must aim at producing a normative conclusion (although I think that is true). Instead, medical ethics should aim at improving healthcare, or the world generally, in some way. The intention of good medical ethics is to lead us to understand, question, revise, or better some significant aspect of clinical reality.

Jarvis Thomson's article is good medical ethics because it aims at expanding our ways of thinking about the abortion debate and it invites us to frame the issue in terms of what someone should be permitted, rather than morally obliged, to do. It also requires people to question a central assumption that they had tended to make about the abortion debate: that the moral status of the foetus is the central issue. Likewise, Rachels pushes those who habitually defend the withdrawal and withholding of life-sustaining treatment on the basis that it is passive and not active to think critically about the assumptions they are making. So, I think that 'engagement with experience' should be interpreted broadly to include ethical analyses that are intentionally normative, in the sense of attempting to improve some aspect of the world.

Conclusion

I first started working in medical ethics at the Bioethics Centre in Dunedin where Alastair V. Campbell was Director. This was in the 1990s, a time when New Zealand was reacting to the findings of the Cartwright Inquiry.[33] I can recall him saying that it was important that we were always mindful that we were there primarily to work towards things becoming better for patients. I took that to mean

33 *The Report of the Committee of Inquiry into Allegations Concerning the Treatment of Cervical Cancer at National Women's Hospital and into Other Related Matters* (Government Printing Office 1988).

that, unless medical ethics aims at improving healthcare (or perhaps the world in the case of bioethics) in some way, it loses its point. That is a claim that I agree with: I think he is correct that those of us working in medical ethics and bioethics should not let it be reduced to a narrowly academic enterprise, nor think that their pet theory holds all the answers.

2 Principlism, virtuism, and the spirit of oneness

Raanan Gillon

Let me start with a slightly reluctant acknowledgment: throughout our careers Alastair V. Campbell and I have had – and continue to have – a marvellous but somewhat competitive friendship. And, alas, I have to admit that throughout our careers Campbell has always been at least a jump ahead of me. We first met when he was the founding editor of the *Journal of Medical Ethics* (*JME*). He published a piece of mine and before long he suggested I apply for the editorship, which he was vacating after 5 foundational years. I applied successfully and became the second *JME* editor (staying in post for 20 years until I thought I'd better retire before I was pushed). Soon after leaving the *JME* he was in New Zealand, once again founding away, this time a wonderful bioethics centre in Dunedin at the University of Otago, in which role he also became something of a New Zealand national bioethics guru. He and I were both elected to the board of directors – yes, the founding board of directors – of the International Association of Bioethics. And, of course, it wasn't long before Campbell was voted President (with, I should immediately add, my enthusiastic support). Then he was back in England founding yet another bioethics institution, the Centre for Ethics in Medicine in Bristol for which he obtained big bucks of external funding and under his outstanding leadership his centre immediately flourished and flourishes still. Then, having retired from his post at Bristol, Campbell went to Singapore to found yet another bioethics centre, the National University of Singapore's Centre for Biomedical Ethics, from which he has once again recently retired – though I wouldn't put it past him to found a new bioethics centre for the third age. In the competition between Campbell and myself for bioethics success, he is a clear winner, and I wholeheartedly congratulate him on his outstanding career.

Over the years I have naturally tried to learn the secret of Campbell's success. Clearly it's something to do with his virtue – or rather his manifold virtues. Intellectually he is very clever, rational, logical, and reasonable – but also wise. What however *is* wisdom? I wish I knew, but Campbell is an ostensive, if not definition, at least manifestation of what it is. Operationally he is effective, sometimes wily, unlikely to get himself into trouble – a safe pair of hands, as they say. Personally he is decent, straightforward, lively, interesting, again reasonable, and (for me particularly important) great fun. Given all these virtues, perhaps it is not surprising that over the years Campbell has become increasingly attracted to virtue ethics. I too have always believed in the importance of virtues as an essential aspect of ethics in real life – but I've always argued, and continue to argue, that there is no way of making any plausible theoretical – or indeed practical – sense of virtues without some moral standards – and those who know me will not be surprised to learn that the standards I advocate are the Beauchamp and Childress's four *prima facie* principles of beneficence, non-maleficence, respect for autonomy, and justice. So for many years the relationship between principles and virtues has been a recurring subject of discussion and debate between Campbell and me (in between the bioethics and other gossip, and our discussions about the existence and nature of God – discussions prompted by my atheistic but ever-interested probings). In the rest of this essay, I wish to look at the outlines of our and others' debates about virtues and principles and then – in a spirit of one-ness, about which more anon – I argue that the way forward is to acknowledge the importance of both these aspects of morality and try to move on, rather than waste many more words on debating the superiority or alleged priority of one or the other.

First, a reminder of the virtues of the virtues approach: Campbell has written eloquently on these.[1] They include the (to most of us obvious) fact that moral virtues are essential to the moral life of real people, in which they are grounded; that they are concerned with people's ways of life rather than just their particular actions; that they are concerned with attitudes and emotions as well as with rationality and actions; that they encompass a vast and complex range of morally desirable character traits. I won't go on – Campbell has and does it much better. I only wish to register my agreement with all these positive claims about the human virtues. My problems with virtue ethics theory only arise if and when the virtues are seen as competing with or even supplanting moral principles (or other moral standards or values) rather than interdependently coexisting with them.

Let me start with a story (something that we have been doing in medicine long before anyone invented narrative ethics). When I was a clinical medical student at Oxford in the early 1960s, medical ethics was supposed to be absorbed, not critically analysed. We students were expected to learn how to be good doctors by apprenticeship, picking up the ethical skills of all our virtuous teachers just as we picked up their technical medical skills. As I've explained elsewhere,[2] my problem then and now with this approach was and is how to decide which of my teachers were the virtuous ones, which (if any – perish the thought) the vicious

---

1 Alastair V. Campbell, 'Ideals, The Four Principles and Practical Ethics' in Raanan Gillon and Ann Lloyd (eds), *Principles of Health Care Ethics* (Chichester, Wiley 1996) 241; Alastair V. Campbell, 'Dignity of the Human Person in Relation To Biomedical Problems' in Peter Kemp (ed.), *Bioethics and Biolaw: Vol II* (Copenhagen, Rhodos International Science and Art Publishers, 2000) 103; Alastair V. Campbell, 'The Virtues (And Vices) of The Four Principles', (2003) 29 *Journal of Medical Ethics* 292; Alastair V. Campbell, 'A Virtue Ethics Approach' in Richard Ashcroft *et al.* (eds), *Case Analysis In Clinical Ethics* (Cambridge University Press 2005) 45; Alastair V. Campbell, *Bioethics – The Basics* (2nd edn, London, Routledge 2017) 18.
2 Raanan Gillon, 'What is Medical Ethics' Business?' in Martyn Evans (ed.), *Critical Reflections on Medical Ethics* (JAI Press 1998) 31.

ones (or should I use Philippa Foot's alternative term, the 'defective' ones?).[3] What were the criteria for deciding? This was a particularly difficult problem if these virtuous teachers were teaching or manifesting diametrically opposed ethical stances. Abortion was a simmering ethical issue at the time. It was illegal, and unethical according to the General Medical Council and medical ethics generally, unless the life of the pregnant woman was severely threatened (the, in my view, excellent Abortion Act was not to be passed by Parliament until 1967). However, thanks to the readiness of gynaecologist Alec Bourne to challenge the law in 1939, threats to the life of the pregnant woman now legally included threats to her psychological health, and so it had become legally acceptable for a gynaecologist to perform an abortion, given that he (usually 'he' in those days) was satisfied, and had psychiatric support for his opinion, that continuation of the pregnancy was a severe threat to the woman's psychological health. As a standard medico-legal textbook put it, 'The law and the medical profession then lived in harmony for many years; the Bourne decision was undoubtedly stretched to the limits of interpretation by many doctors but the authorities turned a sympathetic eye'.[4] Such was the background when I was learning my obstetrics and gynaecology and the wise and virtuous consultant on my 'firm' – as of course they all were – refused to carry out a therapeutic abortion on a 14-year-old schoolgirl. He did not do so on the morally coherent and morally respectable (though in my own view morally misguided) grounds that an abortion was – or at least was morally equivalent to – murder of an innocent person, for he was well known to carry out abortions when he considered them to be 'appropriate'. No, his reason was that 'the girl's a slut – an abortion would only encourage her to get pregnant again'. Argument on her behalf was to no avail (who did I think I was to question his decision, he curtly and rhetorically asked me) and no further explanation was felt to be required or given. Well this consultant was a man even then of considerable medical standing (and he went on to become one of the nation's medical great and good). I was a novice, there to learn by example. Yet I was intuitively disgusted and appalled by his example. (Indeed somewhere I think I still have a letter from the film director Ken Loach turning down a television play I sent him prompted by this episode; he was sorry but he had already begun work on a play with a similar theme; I think it was called *Up the Junction* though I wouldn't swear to it). But few, if any, of the medical staff of the time would have questioned the virtue of that consultant. His social standing and medical leadership role were somehow supposed to guarantee his virtue. And that is what worries me about the notion that virtues are in some sense freestanding, 'natural' characteristics, manifested and recognised without any need for accountability to criteria of moral justification other than social acknowledgment.

In some ways the very idea that an account of virtues is possible without resort to explicitly moral criteria – call them moral principles, standards, or

3 Philippa Foot, *Natural Goodness* (Oxford, Clarendon Press 2001).
4 John K. Mason *et al.* (eds), *Law and Medical Ethics* (6th edn, London, Butterworths 2002) 147.

values, it matters not in this context – seems to me to embody what Gilbert Ryle called 'a category mistake' (you know: she went home in a horse and carriage and a flood of tears). For virtues are explicitly defined as character traits. They are contrasted with vices, also defined as character traits. Elizabeth Anscombe back in 1958 claimed that it was 'not profitable' for philosophers to be doing moral philosophy 'until we have an adequate philosophy of psychology'.[5] Today impressive anthropological, psychological, neuropsychological, and neuroanatomical work is, as I'll outline later, beginning to provide a substrate for such 'an adequate philosophy of psychology', including the psychology of virtue and vice. But whatever the outcome of such studies it seems clear that in order for it to be conceptually possible to differentiate morally between the two types of character traits, virtues and vices, reference must be made to a moral criterion or criteria, whether these are moral principles, moral standards, or moral values. This fact does not entail any conflict between virtues and moral standards, whatever they are: it merely claims that if a character trait is to be classified as morally desirable and thus virtuous, or as morally undesirable and thus vicious (or 'defective', to use Murdoch's terminology), reference to moral standards of some sort is necessary. Nor will the technique of 'ostensive definition' do: that is, to point, as my Professor of Medicine at Oxford advised, at individuals or groups of people and say, 'Look, there's a virtuous person or group of people'. It won't do unless one is ready to accept the cognitive dissonance of ascribing virtue both to the consultant I have described, let's call him 'A', and those like him, and to those whose sympathetic characters, attitudes, and behaviour in similar circumstances are morally incompatible with those of A and his ilk (I think, for example, of the late Sir Dugald Baird, an early pioneer of a liberal and humane approach to abortion in his gynaecological practice in Aberdeen, a pattern that is now common in medical practice following the passing of the Abortion Act).

In our debates about virtues and principles, Campbell has riposted that of course there must be a moral criterion or criteria and that these criteria have, since Aristotelian accounts of virtue, rested in the eudaimonia or flourishing or agape of human nature.[6] I am inclined to agree with him that the source of morality lies in our human nature (although we will continue to disagree about the source of that human nature – for him it is God, for me it is the Godless origins of the universe and its subsequent evolution). But his riposte cedes the point I was making, which is that one can't make plausible sense of virtues (or vices) without recourse to some moral standard or standards. To explain that the moral standard against which to judge particular character traits is 'human flourishing' (or eudaimonia or agape) is analogous to the Kantian claim that morality is to be assessed against the standard of the good will acting in accordance with the categorical imperative; or the utilitarian claim that morality is to be assessed against the standard of welfare

5 Gertrude E.M. Anscombe, 'Modern Moral Philosophy' in Roger Crisp and Michael Slote (eds), *Virtue Ethics* (Oxford University Press 1997).
6 Campbell (n 1) (2003, 2017).

maximisation. In an Anscombian pursuit of philosophical moral psychology, all three accounts of morality can be reasonably asked for accounts of human characteristics that tend to conduce to their favoured ultimate moral objective and standard, and of human characteristics that undermine those standards. In the case of virtue theories (arateic theories), the former characteristics are virtues, the latter characteristics are vices.

Once it is agreed that categorisation of character dispositions as virtues (or as vices or morally neutral) necessarily requires some moral standard, we can engage in the further debate of what those moral standards should be and about the appropriate moral theory that explains and justifies those standards. As I've stated, the standards I've proposed for such assessment are the Beauchamp and Childress four *prima facie* principles: beneficence, non-maleficence, respect for autonomy, and justice. I don't purport to settle the issue of which overall moral theory best explains these principles – although it may be that Beauchamp and Childress themselves have gradually moved towards a position that claims that their own common morality theory does so. They may be right, or it may be that the four *prima facie* principles are best explained by some overriding Aristotelian or neo-Aristotelian theory of human virtue with eudaimonia or human flourishing or agape as its underlying explanatory moral value. Or it may be that the four principles are best explained by some version of utilitarianism with welfare maximisation as its underlying explanatory moral value; or by some version of Kantianism with the categorical imperative as its underlying moral value (and here let me acknowledge and recommend the fascinating synthesis of Aristotelian and Kantian virtue theory propounded by Nancy Sherman);[7] or by one of the religions; or by socialism, communitarianism, contractarianism, feminism, particularism; or – as I use it – that the four principles approach does not seek to adjudicate between these competing moral theories, merely to be consistent with all the purportedly universalisable aspects of all of them; and when they themselves are mutually inconsistent, to provide a mutually acceptable set of high-level *prima facie* moral commitments that all can subscribe to and use. The huge advantage of these four *prima facie* principles as I see them is their compatibility with the wide variety of 'overall' moral theories, religious and secular, that are themselves often mutually inconsistent – which includes of course their compatibility with 'virtuism'. The principles are, as Beauchamp and Childress assert, at the heart of the common morality: 'the set of universal norms shared by all persons committed to morality that all morally serious people share'.[8] I would go further and assert that these norms are reflections of their human nature. They are also compatible with the universalisable aspects of an even wider set of *particular* moral theories (theories 'which contain moral norms that are not shared by all cultures groups and individuals' – theories that again are often

---

7 Nancy Sherman, *Making a Necessity of Virtue: Aristotle and Kant on Virtue* (Cambridge University Press 1997).

8 Tom L. Beauchamp and James F. Childress, *Principles of Biomedical Ethics* (7th edn, Oxford and New York, Oxford University Press 2013) 3.

mutually inconsistent, but which can nonetheless agree to these four *prima facie* principles).[9] Such particular moralities include of course those of medicine and healthcare.

It has become evident to me over the years that no moral perspective plausibly rejects any one of the four *prima facie* principles, and Campbell accepts their value. But Campbell rejects the idea that the four principles are or could be *sufficient* 'to account for all our moral worries'. But of course I too do not believe or claim that they can be! (To be fair he doesn't say, 'I do claim this', only, when commenting on my paper,[10] that 'We are left with the feeling that, given scope, principlism can account for all our moral worries.')[11] As I recurrently acknowledge, the four principles approach does not resolve 'the moral worry' of irresoluble conflicts between the principles, nor does it resolve the moral worry about how to resolve disagreements about the scope of the principles. Furthermore the four principles approach is primarily concerned with accounting for our *prima facie* universal moral *obligations* – a minimal morality that all moral agents could accept. But as Beauchamp and Childress fully acknowledge, there is far more to a *full* moral life than acceptance of and behaviour in accordance with this minimal set of obligations.

This 'more' includes living virtuously, acquiring, and developing and exercising a huge range of character traits – 'habits of the heart' as Campbell is wont to call them – including trying to live well beyond the call of duty and aspiring to live in accordance with a wide range of ideals that are morally desirable. However it does seem likely that even non-obligatory or supererogatory moral objectives and ideals are explainable in terms of the moral values encompassed by the four principles, and thus why character traits conducing to these idealistic and supererogatory moral objectives should be considered as virtuous even when they are not even *prima facie* morally obligatory. Let us accept, for this discussion, Campbell's claim that eudaimonia or human flourishing is the end to which all the virtues are directed. The question then arises: are all the individual virtues simply to be assessed against this ultimate moral objective or are there some intermediate moral objectives, themselves contributing to human flourishing, but broader than the vast array of possible individual virtues? Similar questions arise with other monist moral theories such as utilitarianism and Kantianism. The four principles approach can provide such intermediate moral objectives that are compatible with each of these three morally monistic theoretical stances. In the context of virtue ethics, all the individual character traits or 'habits of the heart' that are candidates for being described as virtues or vices or morally neutral can be assessed in the light of these principles.

The example I offered originally claimed to show how character traits described as virtues in an earlier paper by Campbell – tolerance, sincerity, courage,

9 ibid 5.
10 Raanan Gillon, 'Ethics Needs Principles – Four can Encompass the Rest – and Respect For Autonomy should be "First Among Equals"' (2003) 29 *Journal of Medical Ethics* 307.
11 Campbell (n 1) (2003).

perseverance – might or might not be virtues; it depended on the context.[12] I gave the example of the notorious Nazi Eichmann who was said to be a sincere Nazi whose conscience troubled him when on one occasion he took pity on a Jew and failed to have her gassed. Campbell responded that sincerity (or any other character trait normally regarded as virtuous) that does not contribute to the moral end of all virtues – human flourishing, eudaimonia or agape – cannot be a virtue. But an Eichmann might argue – probably he would have argued – that exterminating Jews was a means towards achieving human flourishing or eudaimonia. If we accept commitment to the somewhat more specific (though still very general) four principles as concomitants of and conducers to human flourishing or eudaimonia or agape, we can refute such Nazi claims. Their extermination of people overrode and obliterated their autonomy; caused them massive harm; failed to benefit them; indeed, as subsequent history has shown, failed to benefit anyone including the 'Aryan nation' that it was intended to benefit; and was utterly unjust in terms of overriding the victims' rights including their right to life. Thus the sincerity and conscientiousness of sincere and conscientious Nazis in pursuing their murderous objectives were neither virtues nor virtuous.

So commitment to these subsidiary four *prima facie* principles by those committed to virtue ethics would seem to be likely to lead towards the achievement of their ultimate moral aim, notably eudaimonia or human flourishing or agape. Moreover assessment of any particular character trait or 'habit of the heart' on the basis of whether or not it conduces to or militates against the creation of benefits, the avoidance or minimisation of harms, respect for people's autonomy, and a striving for justice would seem at least to aid decision as to whether or not that character trait is likely to promote or undermine eudaimonia, human flourishing or agape, and thus whether and to what extent it should be regarded as virtuous, vicious or morally neutral. I suspect – and certainly hope – that Campbell would not disagree with these suggestions. In his 2003 paper he refers to Statman's analysis of types of virtue theory and asserts that his own approach to virtue theory is definitely in the 'compatibilist' category of arateic approaches, not seeking to reject the four principles approach but rather seeking to provide a broader account of morality than he believes that approach provides.[13] In his 2017 book Campbell somewhat cautiously indicates that this remains the case (as indeed he confirmed to me in a personal communication during my preparation of this chapter!). Thus, in an apparently sympathetic discussion of Beauchamp and Childress's *Principles of Biomedical Ethics*, Campbell cautiously acknowledges that 'properly understood' the four principles approach 'probably can' help us 'find a way through the dilemmas of bioethics'.

But if virtue ethics can benefit from reference to the four principles, can 'principlism' benefit from 'virtuism'? In particular, can virtue ethics resolve two

---

12 Campbell (n 1) (1996); Raanan Gillon, 'The Four Principles Revisited – A Reappraisal' in Raanan Gillon and Ann Lloyd (eds), *Principles of Health Care Ethics* (Chichester, Wiley 1996) 241.

13 Daniel Statman, *Virtue Ethics* (Georgetown University Press 1997).

moral problems that the four principles approach does not resolve, but that any fully adequate moral theory and any practical morality must resolve, one way or another? The first is what to do about unresolvable conflict between the principles – what to do about genuine moral dilemmas, where one line of valid moral reasoning leads to one conclusion and another line of valid moral reasoning leads to a conflicting and morally incompatible conclusion? The second concerns the scope of our moral obligations – to whom or to what do moral agents owe the *prima facie* moral obligations encompassed by the four principles? Certainly if virtue ethics can help us resolve either of these two problems, it will perform an invaluable service both for moral theory and for moral life.

In brief, I suspect that virtue ethics is no better – and that it would not claim to be better – at resolving moral scope problems than any other moral theory. For any moral obligation the question arises: to what is it properly owed? And the answers will have profound moral implications. I have argued elsewhere that the abortion argument, for example, is essentially a disagreement about the scope of our moral obligations rather than a disagreement about the substantive content.[14] Thus all moral theories agree that people should not kill other people – or at least not unless those other people are aggressors – but great disagreement arises about what falls within the scope of this obligation – particularly, in the context of abortion, about which living human beings are to be classed as people and why. It seems unlikely that virtue ethics is able to offer solutions to such theological and metaphysical disputes, although I am ready to be corrected. (And I have nailed my own colours to the mast earlier in this paper.)

So far as dilemmatic conflict between moral principles is concerned, perhaps virtue ethics can offer helpful ways of dealing with such conflicts? For any moral stance or theory that accepts the possibility of genuine moral dilemmas, there is the acute problem of how to respond to them in a morally acceptable way. A common approach – one that I personally am inclined to adopt – is that of casuistry: the application of general principles to particular cases in the light of paradigm or exemplary cases. (English case law is a form of casuistry.) But what should go on in such a process? Identification of the relevant principles is – presumably and usually – a straightforwardly cognitive process – and, if I am right, these *prima facie* principles are of a universalisable nature and so can be universally identified in the context of particular cases (acknowledging that variability of *interpretation* of the content of these principles may sometimes be an additional problem). But when it comes to what is often referred to as weighing them up or balancing them against each other when they conflict, the process is, I suspect, far less cognitive, far more open to such mental processes as intuition, emotion, imagination, empathy, aesthetic sensibility – and here perhaps virtue ethics can augment the cognitive processes of principlism.

For example, I have suggested previously that the very notion of 'weighing' may be mistaken as a metaphor for dealing with dilemmatic moral conflicts, because it

14 Raanan Gillon, 'Is There a "New Ethics of Abortion"?' (2001) 27 *Journal of Medical Ethics* 5.

implies that there is some sort of moral gravity 'out there' and that, provided we had a suitably sensitive weighing apparatus, we would simply need to place the opposing moral concerns in the apparatus and rely on this objective moral gravity to *show us* the right moral answer.[15] Perhaps harmonisation rather than balancing was a more appropriate metaphor for dilemma-solving aspects of the casuistic process; and perhaps there are certain character traits conducive to doing this well, rather as there are some people who are better than others at creating and discerning musical, other aesthetic, or even emotional harmony. Were this found to be the case, then it would surely be sensible to seek out people with such skills – skills that in many circumstances should presumably be properly classed as virtues – both in order to study and analyse the nature of such skills, and how to develop them; and in order to ensure that such moral harmony skills were at least represented in the moral decision-making process in cases of irresoluble moral conflict. Even if these admittedly unworked-out speculations could be supported, I would remain morally concerned not to leave such dilemma-resolving decisions entirely to those identified as having moral harmony skills, for the whole gamut of moral perspectives would be needed even if the objective were to try to bring them into moral harmony. But perhaps something like acknowledgment of moral harmony skills is (or should be) what goes on when ethics committee chair people are elected or appointed – that is, they are or should be chosen for such positions at least partly on the basis of their ability to perceive and create moral harmony out of moral disagreement (which of course is to say that they should be people like Campbell).

Whether or not such speculations are idle, of one thing I am convinced – and I'm pretty sure that Campbell agrees (see his *Bioethics – The Basics*, Chapter 2 on moral theories) that there need be and should be no mutual antagonism between principle-based ethics and virtue ethics.[16] Real and sustainable moral life needs both. Part of the way forward is surely to accept this (I hope uncontentious) assertion and to cooperate in finding ways of developing theoretical and practical ethics that incorporate both approaches.

In this regard, much work in recent years on anthropology, psychology, and the neuro-physiology and neuro-anatomy of moral reasoning and decision making, and especially on the relationship between reasoning and non-cognitive brain processes, has led to a tendency to support at least a toned-down version of David Hume's startling assertion that reasoning including moral reasoning 'is, and ought only to be the slave of the passions'[17] – or, in more prosaic and contemporary terms, that our moral decisions are at least for the most part the result of intuitive, emotional, and other non-conscious psychological processes rather than the result of conscious reasoning. Let me briefly outline three works that underline the powerful input that these non-cognitive aspects of our minds and brains have to our moral decisions.

15 Gillon (n 12) 327.

16 Campbell (n 1) (2017).

17 David Hume, *A Treatise on Human Nature* (edited by Lewis A. Selby-Bigge), Oxford University Press 1978) 415.

In *Thinking Fast and Slow*, Nobel Prize winner Daniel Kahneman (and his deceased collaborator Amos Tversky) showed, on the basis of extensive psychological empirical evidence, that many – indeed most – of the decisions we make, including our moral decisions, result from the workings of our unconscious and intuitive minds – what he calls 'System 1'.[18] Some of these decisions are endorsed by our conscious and deliberative selves – 'System 2' – but these endorsements usually occur after System 1, which works far faster than System 2, has already made a decision! And because System 2 is not only slow but also 'lazy', it is inclined to find easy justifications – rationalisations – for the more rapid decisions that System 1 has already made. System 1's rapid decision making is facilitated by a large number of intuitive and highly convincing shortcuts – heuristics – that on the whole are successful but in a proportion of cases result in what the rational System 2 classifies as bad decisions – when and if it is functioning rigorously and rationally to analyse them, rather than 'lazily' finding simple but cognitively mistaken rationalisations with which to endorse them.

Jonathan Haidt, a social psychologist who specialises in evolutionary explanation of moral psychology, also argues that moral intuitions come first and that reason is like 'a rider on an elephant's back' – but like Hume he argues that 'the rider's job is to serve the elephant' whose own main job is self-protection.[19] In addition to our powerful elephants, Haidt also hypothesises a relatively small population of metaphorical hive-maintaining bees altruistically ready to sacrifice themselves for their community. Haidt identifies six evolutionarily evolved domains of moral intuitions – domains within what he calls 'the righteous mind'. These include three domains from which emerge the moral concerns encompassed by the four principles (the domains of care/harm, fairness/cheating, and liberty/oppression) and he identifies – on the basis of transcultural psychological and anthropological research – three other domains of the 'righteous mind': loyalty/betrayal, authority/subversion, and sanctity/degradation. His main objective is to alert those whom Americans call liberals to the importance in human nature not only of the first three domains, which liberals tend to support, but also of the other three domains that conservatives (notably, in the USA, Republicans) tend to support. His message is that all six domains are part of human nature, that the reasoning side of human nature must acknowledge this fact and that conservatives and liberals must try to understand each other's perspectives and try to use their intuitive tendencies as well as their reasoning tendencies to come to a mutually agreeable and agreed accommodation.

In *The Chimp Paradox*, psychiatrist Steve Peters offers his psychological counselling clients – who include some very grateful, successful, and famous sports stars – a model of the mind based on a (very) 'admittedly simplified' tripartite account of brain anatomy and neurophysiology.[20] The model is of two conscious 'selves',

18 Daniel Kahneman, *Thinking Fast and Slow* (New York, Farrar, Straus & Giroux 2011).
19 Jonathan Haidt, *The Righteous Mind – Why Good People are Divided by Politics and Religion* (New York, Pantheon Books 2012).
20 Steve Peters, *The Chimp Paradox* (London, Vermillion Penguin 2015).

the 'human' and the 'chimp', coexisting in often uneasy relationship, both served by a powerful brain 'computer'. The evolutionarily younger rationally reasoning human self is in the frontal cortex of the brain, the evolutionarily more primitive and more powerful emotional chimp is in the limbic system of the midbrain. The computer, throughout the brain, stores memories, beliefs, values, and automatic behavioural patterns, both helpful and unhelpful, and can be 'programmed' by both the chimp and the human. The chimp – which Peters tells his clients 'can be your best friend and your worst enemy, even at the same time' – is concerned primarily with survival and reproduction. Its brain processes are faster than those of the human in the frontal cortex and it reacts rapidly, emotionally, and power-fully. According to Peters, direct confrontation between the human's rational will-power and the chimp's intuitional and emotional strength almost always results in victory for the chimp. Instead, the human must learn to manage and nurture his or her chimp by recognising its concerns, and praising and supporting what the human considers to be the good ones while programming the computer brain with reasoned strategies and behavioural patterns for anticipating and dealing with the chimp's bad tendencies. When the human fails to manage its chimp, the chimp runs the human's life – and then the human often fails to flourish.

Each of these descriptive models emphasises the importance and strength of intuitions, emotions, and what since Freud are called the unconscious aspects of mind. In terms of our moral reasoning generally, and specifically apropos the rela-tionship of principles and virtues, these models make it clear that the four principles are in no sense primary; we are born with brains genetically pre-programmed to respond to our environments automatically in a host of different ways, and these automatic responses are modified by environmental influences for the rest of our lives (as they have been even before we were born). Our reactions to our environ-ments remain for the most part unthinking, automatic, largely intuitive, and often emotional. Our reasoning selves are hugely influenced by our unreasoning uncon-scious automatic and intuitive selves – Peters' computer and chimp, Kahneman's System 1, Haidt's intuitive elephant and hive-maintaining bees. Even when our reasoning selves are called into action, largely in order to respond to problems, our reasons and reasoning are continually influenced by these intuitive, emotional, and automatic aspects of ourselves, which are especially powerful in the moral domains identified by Haidt. Nonetheless, when rational reasoning System 2 shakes off what Hahneman calls its 'laziness' and gets to rigorous work, it can sometimes thoroughly assess and sometimes actually correct the outcomes of System 1, even in the deeply embedded realms of morality.

The three works sketched above reflect relatively recent work in psychology and neuropsychology in which reasoning and rationality are hypothesised to be based on two distinct – though of course interlinked – psychological and neurological systems in the mind and brain – so-called dual-process theories.[21]

---

21 Jonathan Evans and Keith Frankish (eds), *In Two Minds – Dual Process And Beyond* (Oxford University Press 2009); Iain McGilchrist, *The Master and His Emissary* (New Haven, Yale University Press, 2009).

Thus Kahneman's System 1, Haidt's elephant and bees, and Peters' chimp are all manifestations of an evolutionarily older system of thought processes, largely unconscious, automatic, and very fast, which uses associative heuristics that have evolved to respond to specific adaptive problems during mammalian evolution. Conversely, System 2, the elephant rider and the human are manifestations of an evolutionarily more recent and specifically human thought system, conscious, controllable within consciousness, responsive to conscious reasoning, rule based, serial, and slow.

My suggestion is that in the arena of rigorous and rational moral reasoning the four principles can provide a mutually agreeable basis for individual and collective moral reflection about all the outputs of our unconscious minds. All the reasoning moral agents of Hahneman's System 2, Haidt's elephant riders, and Peters' 'humans' can use these *prima facie* principles as a basis for reflecting, individually and collectively, on the outputs of their corresponding non-rational mental systems – System 1, the elephants and the bees, and the chimps – and to feed the reasoned conclusions of those reflections back to those non-reasoning systems, sometimes (perhaps usually) to provide properly reasoned support where justified, but at other times to offer reasoned rejections and/or modifications of the intuitions and emotional responses by which, for the most part, we sensibly run our moral lives.

Within the six moral domains of Haidt's 'righteous mind', the four principles can be discerned as being not only evolutionarily plausible *descriptions* of how some of our moral decisions arise and are made but also as plausible candidates to be universalisable, mutually agreeable *prima facie* rational moral *normative principles* with which the reasoning elephant riders, or System 2, or the human may assess and respond to the intuitive responses of their emotional, intuitive, and deeply embedded non-cognitive counterparts, including the intuitions that concern the other moral domains that Haidt identifies, and about which, as he points out, there is unlikely to be cross-cultural agreement.

In the context of conflicts, both between these *prima facie* principles and between these principles and deeply felt moral intuitions, perhaps the more intuitive and emotion-sensitive approach of virtue ethics can help us.

For example, sanctity of life intuitions and the fundamental disagreements about them briefly discussed above are plausibly outputs from Haidt's 'sanctity/ degradation' domain. As both Haidt and Peters theorise, these intuitions are embedded in our evolved human natures. However, when we encounter deep disagreements – such as those about sanctity of life – concerning their relevance or importance in different situations and types of situation, while the four principles can provide our reasoning selves with an agreed set of rational principles with which to explain and assess such disagreements and with which to try to deal with residual incompatible intuitions, the more intuitive and emotion-sensitive approach of virtue ethics may help us make actual judgments about those residual incompatibilities. In such contexts, the Aristotelian 'triad' approach to characterising the virtues may be of particular value (e.g. too much 'courage' is foolhardy, too little is cowardly, but somewhere in between, *as appropriate to the context,* is virtuous). Virtue theory is constantly reliant on such intuitions about appropriateness and I have pointed to their dangers when detached from moral standards (the consultant who refused the 14-year-old an abortion was known to do abortions when he considered them to be 'appropriate'). But linked to explicit moral standards such as those expressed by the four *prima facie* principles, their value may be particularly important in seeking and finding 'harmony' in contexts of value conflict. Similarly, widely differing cultural attitudes and intuitions in relation to religion and the realm of the spiritual, to cleanliness and purity, to authority, to solidarity and group and individual loyalty, to betrayal, to homosexuality and other variants of sexuality, to racial and other deep-seated prejudices, are all plausibly explicable as culturally variable intuitive manifestations of the different moral domains embedded in our human nature and identified and described by Haidt.

The four principles are of course themselves also explicable as emerging from these evolutionarily older and deeply embedded moral domains. I've suggested they are also plausible candidates for widespread *reasoned agreement* across cultures. As such, they may provide us with agreed rational *prima facie* moral principles both to help reduce deeply felt moral disagreements emanating from those different domains of our moral minds and, informed by and in tandem with the intuitive and emotion-sensitive approach of virtuist approaches to ethics, may also help us deal with the moral disagreements that will undoubtedly remain.

Certain theoretical disagreements between virtuists and principlists may also (perhaps) be resolved by use of the four *prima facie* principles. Campbell describes the fundamental difference between action-orientated ethical theories and virtue-based ethics theories as encapsulated in the difference between asking 'What should I do?' and 'How should I be?'. I've pointed out that the very notions of virtues and vices pertain to descriptions – morally laden descriptions – of people's characters. Well, a commitment to these four *prima facie* principles can offer a way to link virtue ethics and the four principles approach simply by applying them to both of those questions, 'What should I do?' *and* 'How should I be?'. Just as people's actions can be morally assessed by reference to these principles, so too can people's characters and characteristics. For example, I'd *like* to be the sort of person who is helpful and useful, kind, loving, honest, tolerant, respectful of others, courageous, fair, consistent, determined, amusing, ready to compromise within the bounds of maintaining my integrity and incorruptibility. These are examples of virtues I'd like to manifest. Contrariwise, I'd like *not* to be the sort of person who does not wish to help others but instead enjoys harming them and being cruel. I'd like not to be disrespectful to, and unconcerned about, the views of others, not to be arrogant and overbearing, not to be unfair, self-centred, and corruptible. (And I'd definitely like *not* to be like A, the consultant I mentioned earlier!). But how am I to assess all these different characteristics as being either vicious and therefore vices or defects, or as being virtuous and therefore virtues? I'm entirely happy to agree with Campbell and other virtuists who use the overall criterion of their contribution to human flourishing. I am similarly ready to accept that utilitarians use the overall criterion of human (or, in some versions, general) welfare. Like most doctors and probably like many, perhaps even most, philosophers, I don't aspire to providing or having a satisfactory overall theory of ethics myself. But the four *prima facie* principles, while compatible with the overall moral objectives of human flourishing, welfare maximisation, and acting in accordance with one's conception of the requirements of morality, provide somewhat more specificity concerning human flourishing and human welfare and the requirements of morality – and very much more specificity when they are applied to particular cases and types of case in the processes described by Beauchamp and Childress as specification and balancing.[22]

Thus, from this four principles perspective, virtuous people are those who tend to contribute to human flourishing by aiming to benefit others; by trying to avoid harming others except insofar as such harm contributes (and with relevant agreement) to their overall benefit (the surgeon's knife, the oncologist's chemo-therapy provide obvious counter-examples for those who claim to reject *any* deliberate infliction of any harm – the 'above all do no harm brigade'); by tending to respect others' autonomy insofar as such respect is consistent with respect for the autonomy of all potentially affected by such respect; and by tending to be fair and/or just in their dealings with others. Similarly specific characteristics (courage, honesty, kindness, etc.) are classed as virtues insofar as they tend in par-ticular cases and types of case to be beneficial; not to harm – or, when harmful, to provide net benefit with minimal harm; to be respectful of autonomy; and to be just and fair. And of course the converse of all that in relation to vices.

Insofar as these characteristics are embedded in a person's personality (whether by nature or nurture, including by practice, by reason or emotion, by passion or dispassionate analysis, or by some combination of any or all of these), they are or become less and less the outcome of reasoning – though always open to reason – and more and more the outcome of the person's own variety and expression of embodied human nature, manifesting some combination of virtue and vice both in personality and in specific actions.

Thoughtful principlists will of course encourage the development and mainten-ance of such virtues – thoughtful virtuists will, I hope, encourage reflection about people's characters and ways of life by reference to these *prima facie* principles, which for them can serve at least as moral signposts to ways of achieving their overall objective of eudaimonia.

Finally, let me extol another of Campbell's insights: the importance of the principle (or virtue) of oneness, also known as the principle of bunnahabhain. Years ago, Campbell presented an account of this little known composite moral commitment to a conference on bioethics and biolaw in Copenhagen. Unfortunately this component of his lecture was never published and all we have recorded is a brief footnote in Tristram Engelhardt's published paper presented to the same conference.[23] Engelhardt reports the composite parts of the principle

---

22 Beauchamp and Childress (n 8) 17.
23 Hugo T. Engelhardt, 'Autonomy: the Cardinal Principle of Contemporary Bioethics' in Peter Kemp (ed.), *Bioethics and Biolaw: Vol II* (Copenhagen, Rhodos International Science and Art Publishers 2000) n 4.

of bunnahabain – also known, he says, as the principle of oneness – to be hale-ness, wholeness, hope, and heteronymy. I haven not consulted Engelhardt about this, and Campbell is strangely reticent when asked to enlarge. However my own take on this spirit of oneness – both a virtue and a principle, apparently origin-ating in a little-known work in Gaelic by an eighteenth-century Scottish phil-osopher, Lachlan McLeod – is that it can help to provide a basis for the needed rapprochement between virtue ethics and the four principles approach. Let me simply assert that anecdotal empirical evidence for its value recurrently emerged at spirited and harmonious meetings of the International Association of Bioethics Toasting Network of which Campbell and I have the honour to be founding members. However, scientifically more rigorous empirical underpinning of its value can be found in a subsequent paper written by Campbell and his colleague Teresa Swift.[24] Their study investigated the perceptions of people suffering from chronic diseases concerning the virtues they perceived to be needed to flourish despite ongoing pain and disability. Of particular importance were self-respect and respect from others; acceptance and courage; and communal involvement. But of special relevance to the spirit of oneness or bunnahabhain was their finding that a *sense of humour* was of crucial importance. Let me end this festschrift chapter by thanking Campbell for all his manifold virtues – including his very wicked sense of humour.

---

24 Alastair V. Campbell and Teresa Swift, 'What Does It Mean to Be a Virtuous Patient?' (2002) 5 *Scotland Journal Healthcare Chaplaincy* 29.

3 Professional relationships

Covenant, virtue, and clinical life

Grant Gillett

Introduction

Covenant, virtues, and human relationships are powerfully intertwined in an approach to bioethics that Alastair V. Campbell developed throughout his academic life. It found a ready audience among health professionals across widely diverse cultural and academic settings, and in many parts of the world. His approach, touching on so many features of ethics, had the ring of clinical authenticity so that caring professionals could think about the ethical aspects of their day-by-day practice. The effect was to enhance a clinician's ability to be part of genuinely caring and responsive healthcare teams, and to share with patients the skills needed to negotiate illness journeys together. The pastoral ideals and values emerging from this multifaceted bioethical analysis have ancient roots but an increasing relevance as the ongoing need for enduring and shared clinical relationships comes to the fore. To lay out an approach to healthcare ethics that does justice to these strands of thought is to understand caring as both professional and deeply humane. Those of us influenced by Campbell's intellectual rigour and dedication to the subject recognise his intellectual and moral influence on a conception of healthcare and its ethics that feels good to work with.

The covenant model

Campbell, reflecting his roots in pastoral theology and rich New Testament scholarship, favoured the covenant model of the doctor-patient relationship developed by thinkers such as Paul Ramsey and William May. This he combined with virtue ethics as a framework within which to develop and interpret an understanding and analysis of clinical ethics.[1] He noted the service done for clinical ethics by the four principles,[2] but also was aware of the need for interpretation and

---

1 Alastair V. Campbell, 'The Virtues (and Vices) of the Four Principles' (2003) 29 *Journal of Medical Ethics* 292.
2 The four principles are beneficence, non-maleficence, autonomy, and justice. See Tom L. Beauchamp and James F. Childress, *Principles of Biomedical Ethics* (3rd edn, Oxford University Press 1989).

application to give real-life meaning to the key concepts so as to explore the roles of professionals and patients in healthcare relationships. His ethics is for the clinical coalface and is informed by scholarship that is wide-ranging, compassionate, deconstructive, and hermeneutic (in the sense of moving between principle and application to find a reflective equilibrium that is both broad and humane in its treatment of suffering, vulnerability, and imbalances of power and knowledge in the clinic).[3]

This chapter examines a model of healthcare ethics that is sensitively human and cobbles together an ethics of care, virtue ethics, and the idea of a covenant. It reflects an ethos that is finely aware of, and richly responsive to, human beings at their points of need. It puts the professional-patient relationship at the heart of ethical healthcare, exploring issues raised by significant differences in knowledge, power, and interpersonal encounters discernible in healthcare settings. The relevant issues of power and knowledge reflect the technologies of modern medicine and the human engagement with which a more natural human science ('true ... to life as found and lived'[4]) must come to grips. Power imbalances and the need for educative and formative interaction that is neither coercive nor infantilising appear time and time again. These complexities of human inter-dependency affect the persona of a good health professional so that the idea of covenant should not nudge us toward a caricature of the health professional as godlike unless we have a participatory and incarnational form of that characterisation.[5] This is not an ethic based on superior knowledge and the dispensing of expertise and largesse from a superior position, but an ethic of the servant saviour sharing the vulnerabilities and weaknesses of flesh while aiming to displace vice with the mind of Christ and the father heart of God and to realise and inspire virtue. The lesser covenant partner – the patient – should be empowered and included in the healthcare relationship, that is, within a participatory and emancipatory model where the professional-patient relationship is aimed at restoring human wholeness to someone whose story is broken.[6] Patients are carefully introduced, within such a relationship, to the truth of shared and potentially tragic situations requiring mutual attention and virtue on both sides. Those qualities will sometimes not prevail against the cruelty of disease but even when cruel contingencies intrude, their mutual support in bearing a shared burden will mitigate many of the cruel events that cannot be prevented. As doctor and patient caught up

3 John Rawls, 'Outline of a Decision Procedure for Ethics' (1951) 60 *Philosophical Review* 177; Martha C. Nussbaum, *Love's Knowledge: Essays on Philosophy and Literature* (Oxford University Press 1990) 148ff.
4 Leon R. Kass, *Toward a More Natural Science: Biology and Human Affairs* (Free Press 1985) xii.
5 Alastair V. Campbell, 'Dependency: The Foundational Value in Medical Ethics' in K.W.M. Fulford, Grant Gillett, and Janet Martin Soskice (eds), *Medicine and Moral Reasoning* (Cambridge University Press 1994).
6 Alastair V. Campbell, 'Establishing Ethical Priorities in Medicine' (1977) 1 *British Medical Journal* 818; Howard Brody, '"My Story Is Broken; Can You Help Me Fix It?": Medical Ethics and the Joint Construction of Narrative' (1994) 13 *Literature and Medicine* 79.

in an illness journey, they can negotiate its triumphs and tragedies so that they conduct themselves with integrity. The Old Testament is full of awful events but the new covenant (as prophesied by Jeremiah and realised in Christ) promises an inclusive kind of other-regard or redemptive, restorative, and transformative love: *agape*.[7] When that informs our vision for human relationships, bioethics is able to transcend the debate between paternalism and autonomy, so as to deepen our understanding of the role of the good clinician by focusing not just on individuals and their autonomy, rights, and entitlements but moving to a relational conception of persons that notices how we can support each other. We are gently prised away from a somewhat artificial conception of power, exercised by self-standing individuals, and introduced to the servant model in which the professional is part of a clinical partnership that embeds the life-giving possibility of restoration to wholeness and a compassionate awareness of tragedy as beings who share mortality, vulnerability, and the sometimes cruel 'tuche' or 'encounter with the real'.[8]

The importance of conducting oneself well when we falter and the possibility of restoration allow physicians to use wisely increasingly powerful means of remedying the damage inflicted by illness. It also opens up the possibility of growth and change for both parties as part of a clinical relationship. In the clinic, both doctors and patients take on, in different ways, a response to suffering and learn to ameliorate the physical, personal, and even moral harm that illness sometimes causes. Good teaching and writing in medical ethics bring these features of human illness into view as part of a redemptive or transformative strand of ethical thought and a partnership model as we ask not only 'how shall I live ... [but also] how shall I live with mortality, the inevitability of death?'[9]

Campbell, writing on the foundations of medical ethics, suggests 'a more patient orientated medical ethics'[10] which should be interpreted in the light of the covenant model acknowledging a difference in authority and knowledge between the health professional and the patient and their shared journey through 'the land of Clinicum' and its many imbalances of power.[11] Within that new covenant, the weaker partner is not only helped but also enlightened and potentially given the means of being restored to a kind of human flourishing. This process is deeply felt but quasi-objective as it locates goodness in an '(open-ended) picture of human life'.[12] It also draws on humanity in community and an inclusive kind of love referred to as *agape*. The covenant model functions within a set of ideals – 'the ideal humanity', the ideal relationship between humanity and creation, and the

7 Campbell, 'The Virtues (and Vices) of the Four Principles' (n 1) 293.
8 Jacques Lacan, *The Four Fundamental Concepts of Psycho-Analysis* (edited by Jacques-Alain Miller, translated from French by Alan Sheridan, Penguin 1977) 53.
9 Campbell, 'The Virtues (and Vices) of the Four Principles' (n 1) 294.
10 ibid.
11 Grant R. Gillett, *Bioethics in the Clinic: Hippocratic Reflections* (Johns Hopkins University Press 2004) 70 and esp. 162ff.
12 Martha Nussbaum, 'Non-Relative Virtues: An Aristotelian Approach' in Martha Nussbaum and Amartya Sen (eds), *The Quality of Life* (Oxford University Press 1993) 259.

ideal relationship between healer and sufferer.[13] Because the shared enterprise is a phase in life's journey for the patient and contributes to the professional identity of the doctor (in that the illness journey creates the roles of professional and patient) an ethical analysis unpacks good ways of fulfilling those roles, and applies to both. Both human partners in the clinic are people for whom the covenant functions as a source of knowledge, shared power, and hope. It aims to realise, as far as possible, the potential for recovery (and sometimes discovery) of self as a dependent rational animal whose life is shaped by shared creatureliness – vulnerabilities, afflictions, and affections – emerging from a walk alongside others.[14]

Campbell identifies dependency as a foundational value in medical ethics, grounded in human creatureliness: 'To be a creature is to be born of others, to know ourselves through them, to depend on them and create dependency, to know the pain of losing them and finally to be the instance of that pain to others'.[15]

Human dependence, rationality, and creatureliness shape a distinctive set of virtues[16] so that a covenant model enunciates a conception of health and healthcare that is shared and holistic, encompassing mental, physical, and spiritual well-being. (That, no doubt, marked a point of real convergence between Campbell's view and that of Māori – the indigenous people of Aotearoa – when he came to New Zealand). Covenant, and its link to fragile humanity confronting mortality in the light of redemption, also marks the passing of an individual through a deeply engaging protocol rather than a light acceptance.[17] Bearing oneself properly in the face of human mortality does not mean foregoing the tendency to rage against the dying of the light, nor does it mean that we ignore '[t]he indignity of death with dignity';[18] there remains a sense in which the contemplation of death is always linked to '[t]he dread of oblivion, of their being only an emptiness in one's stead';[19] thus death 'is not an event in life'.[20]

William May, with whom Campbell shares the covenant model (based on the work of Paul Ramsey), notices that covenant offers more than a contractual model and reaches beyond the mortal span of a human life to carry a lingering promise of eternity and abiding love of the kind found in sacred narratives.[21]

---

13 Janet M. Soskice, 'Creation and Relation' in Kenneth W.M. Fulford, Grant Gillett, and Janet M. Soskice (eds), *Medicine and Moral Reasoning* (Cambridge University Press 1994) 20.

14 Alasdair MacIntyre, *Dependent Rational Animals: Why Human Beings Need the Virtues* (Open Court 1999) 1.

15 Alastair V. Campbell, *Moderated Love: A Theology of Professional Care* (London, SPCK, 1984) 96.

16 MacIntyre (n 14) 5.

17 Paul Ramsey, 'The Indignity of "Death with Dignity"' (1974) 2(2) *The Hastings Center Studies* 47.

18 ibid.

19 ibid 50.

20 Ludwig Wittgenstein, *Tractatus Logico-Philosophicus* (first published in 1921, translated by David F. Pears and Brian F. McGuinness, Routledge & Kegan Paul 1961) para 6.4311.

21 William F. May, 'The Virtues in a Professional Setting' in Kenneth W.M. Fulford, Grant Gillett, and Janet M Soskice (eds), *Medicine and Moral Reasoning* (Cambridge University Press 1994) 82.

Prudential arrangements and a contract/autonomy framework with an implicit (but unrealistic) equality between patient and doctor have both unfortunate associations with a 'let the buyer beware' ethos and the notion of justice associated.[22] The contract/autonomy framework also has limited horizons easily absorbed into bureaucratically framed value statements suggesting policies rather than a spirit of human restoration within a shared enterprise. Within that richer context, we can discern a sense of life in the midst of the trials of the clinic and its demands.[23] Healthcare and what it achieves is therefore diminished when seen within a 'value free' or individual interests framework,[24] but is restored when covenant ideals are recognised.

The virtues fostered by a covenant both supplement the four principles and highlight their deficiencies (or vices) by introducing further aspects of the clinical partnership, some of which allow the warmth and humanness of healthcare and the life of healthcare professionals to be acknowledged.[25]

Our shared humanity surfaces at many of these points: 'In Aristotle – for example, the concept of the intellectual virtues, of practical wisdom and of *eudaemonia* are key, while for Aquinas the goal of human flourishing provides an account of humanity in community'.[26] Both intellectual virtue and a clear eye on what, for the patient, constitutes flourishing are important in healthcare and a well-framed ethical vision allows both patient and doctor to see themselves and each other on a richer canvas, the colours of which highlight certain features of the clinic that a more functional view can miss. Campbell notes that human flourishing should guide clinical activity and healthcare policy, and he cautions us against well-meaning but ill-thought initiatives that do not proceed with the clear eye that can guide the perplexed when confronting the complexities of healthcare, particularly in relation to novel and exciting new technologies and challenges. A clear focus on human well-being, however imperfect or effaced, never loses sight of the ethical question: 'How, then, shall I live, and yet acknowledge the truth of my own mortality?' In bioethics, the four principles help us to structure our reasoning when faced with moral challenges and remind us of key questions illuminating what we do, always informed by the needs presented by different groups and individuals. It is obvious, for example, that a child needs more care and attention than a mature and reasonably healthy adult; and that an elderly and infirm person will not survive in a society that gives only the help needed by those whose faculties are unimpaired.[27] These questions of need and well-being lie at the root of well-directed ethical attention and illuminate an informed and humane healthcare praxis.[28] A more natural science highlights the humanity of

22 ibid.
23 ibid 78.
24 John McDowell, *Mind and World* (Harvard University Press 1994) 19.
25 Campbell, 'The Virtues (and Vices) of the Four Principles' (n 1).
26 ibid 293.
27 Campbell, 'Establishing Ethical Priorities in Medicine' (n 6) 820.
28 See Kass (n 4).

virtue, and the purposes informing a sense of life that acknowledges mortality and its contrast with eternity such that the passing of the seasons also conveys a sense of the uniqueness of every moment of every human life.

Virtue ethics (particularly that which goes beyond 'the virtues in practice') awakens us to a sense of life, an orientation we can impart to those who come after us and to whom our stories will be told. It directs us to the character shown by our actions, but also to the implications for society of our individual choices and shared policy decisions. Despite this being 'somewhat abstract'[29] as a perspective ... it gives us a glimpse into what many would regard as an adequate 'account of the moral life'.[30] A similar thought emerges from William May: 'The virtues reflect not only commitments to principles and ideals but also to narratives, the exemplary lives of others, human and divine'[31] so that a deep connection between lives well lived and personal flourishing, intuitively recognisable despite diverse realisations, informs healthcare ethics as part of the light that 'dawns gradually over the whole'.[32]

Campbell notes a necessary complementarity between principle-based ethics and virtue approaches because 'the four principles themselves, ... as the advocates of that approach readily concede, ... do not contain within themselves a criterion for ordering, if they conflict'.[33] The virtues, informed by clinical judgement and experience, are discerned by an educated intellectual eye for what all humankind share as creatures who indwell stories of worth. Virtues allow one to bridge the gap between abstract principle and a clinical situation in which the contingencies of life and the varieties of human affection and vulnerability play themselves out. Those intersections between contingency and human fragility produce events so diverse that they resist full schematisation or planning. Thus a succinct set of rules for acting according to a right understanding is impossible and an educated version of 'mother wit' is required in bioethics and clinical life.[34] These are aspects of human conduct that a trained pastoral caregiver can recognise, that resonate within clinical colleagues, and that inform an account of the virtuous clinician. Character, schooled by medical education (perhaps including a soupçon of ethics and informed by an appropriate responsivity to the patient), must guide the clinician where no calculus or formula can dictate what he or she should do, and clinical acumen – appropriately nuanced clinical judgement tempered by fine awareness and a rich sense of responsibility – is needed to refine and systematise professional conduct in ways that lead to good practice.

---

29 Campbell, 'The Virtues (and Vices) of the Four Principles' (n 1) 296, 293.
30 ibid 296.
31 May (n 22) 81.
32 Ludwig Wittgenstein, *On Certainty* (edited by Gertrude Elizabeth M. Anscombe and Georg Henrik von Wright, translated by Denis Paul and Gertrude Elizabeth M. Anscombe, Harper & Row 1972) para 141.
33 Campbell, 'The Virtues (and Vices) of the Four Principles' (n 1) 293.
34 Immanuel Kant, *Critique of Pure Reason* (first published in 1789, translated by Norman Kemp Smith, Macmillan 1929).

Covenant, care, well-being, and the teaching, informing role of the experienced professional enable an evolving transformation of character, both in our patients and apprentice healthcare professionals, that gives substance to a commitment that tends towards care and mutual trust between clinicians and patients, making healthcare practice a shared endeavour that mitigates suffering when the health of a dependent rational animal depends in part on the support and skill of another. Such endeavours pose challenges expressed by the question: 'How, then, should we live in the face of our own mortality?' The relevant skills rest on trust as 'the cornerstone of effective doctor-patient relationships' and enables one to cope with the massive contingency of the *tuche* (or intrusion of blind contingency) in which human beings confront the forces of nature (or of their own use of force). It may be that such force 'turns anybody who is subjected to it into a *thing*' and, at the limit, 'makes a corpse out of him'.[35] In medicine, we do not have the option of shrinking away from those forces but must confront them within a covenant or compact forged in the face of adversity. That covenant evinces benevolence, candour, compassion, trust, and responsivity[36] making us finely aware and richly responsible to each other so that we miss nothing and it fosters a mode of 'bearing up' conducive to both doctor and patient conducting themselves well.[37] We are changed by witnessing the patient's ordeal so that we are made stronger by entering into that shared experience.

Many aspects of covenant – including the need for trust – are multifaceted: the professional must be trustworthy and the patient must learn that he or she is able to trust so that the professional is changed by the clinical journey as is the state of being that the patient begins to recognise as the best that can be achieved, given the way that fate (or the real) has impinged on his or her humanity. The potentially and actually damaging touch of force or fate, which at the extreme may make a corpse out of him or her,[38] gestures at a journey that must be made on a path and towards an end not knowable from the beginning. In such a journey, the need for somebody to lean on is part of the human condition and it takes multiple forms.

The doctor is the expert, the captain of the ship, but remains answerable to the patient who stands in the place of the owner of the ship (or its commissioner for a given voyage). The ship and its crew are united in a single purpose – to serve the owner and to do their best with the resources they command to bring the enterprise through what may be a difficult passage. The overall aim is tied into their mutual covenant by a sense of eudaimonia – the harmony that underpins a life of well-being – and a healthcare service should focus on what can be achieved for the patient and its own healthcare workers as members of a community in the context of which the service is provided. This context of belonging and service

---

35 Simone Weil, 'The Iliad, or the Poem of Force' in Simone Weil and Rachel Bespaloff, *War and the Iliad* (translated by Mary McCarthy, New York Review Books 2005) 3.

36 May (n 22) 82.

37 Nussbaum (n 3).

38 Weil (n 36) 3.

out of which we should not fall must be skilfully melded with the need for the patient to stand forth as an individual realising a value that is unique and irreplaceable and that goes beyond the healthcare context. This uniqueness lifts every human being out of the anonymity of being merely one instance of a type to being a unique locus of value, an enigma whose self-disclosure adds something to creation in a way that no other person could. Humankind is present to us as a series of individual faces inscribed with a mark of incalculable value: 'Thou shalt not kill'.[39] These people, each named as a being-in-relation, are able to be greeted and addressed; they exist in the vocative – 'I not only think of what he is for me, but also and simultaneously, and even before, I *am* for him'.[40] Here ethics and spirit are intertwined in a way that becomes crystal clear at the end of life as we confront not only the end of an encounter but the potentiality of further encounters and of a lived story.[41]

The new covenant of Christian theology has an enduring or ongoing quality that is meant to take us beyond our mortality and the law of natural cause and effect. For a patient, possibly confronting their own mortality as we do in every illness journey, the healthcare relationship should intimate a value that endures despite the flesh which cannot. That is why Ramsey speaks of death with dignity as 'dehumanizing',[42] despite the attractive 'drag' in which it often appears.[43] Patients and healthcare professionals need to draw close to each other on their shared paths through the vast sea of humanity so that together and with shared purpose they can 'rage against the dying of the light'[44] because death is a mystery that confronts us in our humanity, stripped of any vestments of our fragile existence. As Wittgenstein remarked, 'Death is not an event in life ... eternal life belongs to those who live in the present'.[45] Death, we could say, lets us know that each present moment is precious and cannot be put into storage or frozen in time to retain its value. The moment one shares, as a doctor or nurse, with a living patient possibly confronting death, and the need to convey to that patient that one cares, draws on one's virtue as a person who can engage with another and impart a blessing that no mere physical remedy can provide. 'Death with dignity' and 'a good death' are phrases that can too glibly overlook the 'rage' we need others to feel on our behalf as we face death. We want them to feel anger and outrage because of their love for us and we think that we should also infuse that moment with our love for them and what is being lost. This fellowship in mortality and its final moment we see in the dying God who suffers as he completes

---

39 Emmanuel Levinas, *Basic Philosophical Writings* (edited by Adriaan T Peperzak, Simon Critchley, and Robert Bernasconi, Indiana University Press 1996).

40 Emmanuel Levinas, *Difficult Freedom: Essays on Judaism* (Athlone Press 1990) 7.

41 Grant Gillett, Maeve McMurdo, and Jing-Bao Nie, 'The Human Spirit and Responsive Equilibrium: End of Life Care and Uncertainty' (2015) 7 *Asian Bioethics Review* 292.

42 Ramsey (n 18) 53.

43 ibid 61.

44 Dylan Thomas, 'Do not go Gentle into that Good Night' in *The Poems of Dylan Thomas* (New Directions Publishing Corporation 1952) 239 as cited in Ramsey, ibid 48.

45 Wittgenstein, *Tractatus Logico-Philosophicus* (n 21) para 6.4311.

his momentous and painful task. The God who dies is not secure in the bright and immortal heavens but is exposed to the indignity of incarnation and is made complete in an experience that every human being must face and that no other Gods enter into.

Doctors, as all healthcare professionals, also experience and are affected by a lifetime of sharing moments of human mortality and learn to care in those moments, even though it is not we ourselves who are mortally touched by the dying of the light. Shared, witnessed moments of mortality – of ending the refrain as contingency strikes home – punctuate our stories as they interweave the narratives of our medical lives with the lives of others. This interweaving changes us, creating traumata, and leaving scars – touches of the real to which we have bound ourselves in a calling that is demanding in ways that others are not subject to. Healthcare professionals are entrusted with a sacred task of readying ourselves and others to be there when moments of fragility happen and to become better people through such experiences rather than hardening ourselves against their effects. A covenant in which we are softened and made more caring rather than hardened by the wounds of human life underpins the vocation of healing and goes beyond successive contracts to deal with what we understandably try to avoid. Healthcare professionals put themselves at risk when they say, and mean, 'I will be there', 'I will not abandon you'. We cannot be everything our patients need as they face their mortality but, by being part of the journey at the place of need, we make the touch of mortality more bearable. It is the nature of the human soul to have that need and we can try to help others meet it. Our students, as they head towards being doctors and nurses, should understand that being somebody who can be leaned on comes with the territory. It is not negotiable. Even if any conceivable healthcare contract or policy limits the self-giving of professionals, and such contracts are seen as the norm, most of us come to see that a caring relationship can go beyond what a contract can ask of anyone.

The language of contracts is entitlement, autonomy, interest, benefit, harm, and duties, but the medical life is conducted in a domain where 'we all need somebody to lean on'. The uncertainty associated with that is a scary thing to deal with by yourself and none of us should think we can do so. Levinas's hospitality and infinity as marks of the human condition introduce the enigmatic domain of healthcare where we are drawn into relationships. Putting limits around ourselves does not just build fences that keep others out – it accepts that our caring has, and must have, boundaries so that we do not get 'burnt out' or stray into areas where our caring is no longer professional. Professional life is marked by the serendipity of life in general but is also channelled by skills that enable the constantly changing healthcare world to be structured according to ethical constancies worked out within enduring values, such as hospitality and our lives in the community. The warmth evinced by welcoming those who arrive unexpectedly at our door, even if they have apparently little to offer us, softens the hard edges of contingency for the disabled, the widow, and the orphan. That warmth can be shown by every healthcare professional (maybe even the hospital cleaner). No human being exists completely apart from hospitality, even if its reality is dim and far off. In all mythologies, we are visited by mysterious strangers and hospitality is required of us. Odin, for instance, walks among us as a blind beggar reminding us (from a Northern rather than Middle-Eastern source) that the fellow traveller with whom we walk for a while on an otherwise bleak road should be welcomed not dismissed. One never knows whether the traveller may, in fact, warm our hearts and explain our own sacred texts to us as a messenger of the Gods, or perhaps even as 'the God' himself (to follow Kierkegaard).

The healthcare relationship seen as a covenant suggests certain virtues found in the stories which take care of us. Healthcare is full of such stories in which the human spirit is nurtured and valued and these stories richly inform the ethics of medicine. In truth, without such stories, healthcare itself is much less than what it should be – a cluster of professions orientated to the skilled restoration of wholeness for someone whose story is broken. That calling creates demands far beyond anything we can turn into duties or general principles. The spirit of the healing professions therefore makes one a lifelong student of the human condition and a fellow traveller on shared journeys with those who suffer. As such, we are both surprised and inspired by the people we meet. We learn to address each other's needs with a freshness and openness that evinces a 'sense of life'[46] – the sense of what life is, that life is really worth something, and a sense of what human beings 'can least live without'.[47] Virtue tends to nurture that fragile something in the face of both natural challenges and human indifference, and virtue is evident in the people we need to meet on our illness journeys who, through their sense of life, can help us want to get better.

Some bring to bioethics a hard-edged analytic rationality that seems to offer and demand reasons for everything, but which does not bring into the view the values underpinning those reasons. Most pointedly, it may miss the reasons of which reason knows not but which are attuned to what matters to human beings, especially those whom mortality has in its unrelenting grasp. The physician's covenant is shared with all the healthcare professions as we enter into it and are educated by it and it makes the unreasoned reasons constituting the love of humanity more salient to us by strengthening among us a sense of life that should be present in every healthcare setting.

46 Nussbaum as in (n 3) 174.
47 ibid 174.

Part III
Healthcare ethics in disciplinary contexts

4 Healthcare ethics and theology

Robin Gill

Practical theology at Edinburgh

For 16 years, Alastair V. Campbell and I were close colleagues in the Department of Christian Ethics and Practical Theology at New College, Edinburgh University. We both became senior lecturers there and were both applying for chairs at other universities in the 1980s (at a time of economic stringency when these were not plentiful and personal chairs at Edinburgh were still uncommon). We both had to wait a while, yet in 1988 I was appointed to the newly established William Leech Professorial Fellowship in Applied Theology at Newcastle and in the following year Campbell was appointed to a specially created Personal Chair in Biomedical Ethics at Otago. In the 1990s, he moved to the new Chair of Ethics in Medicine at Bristol and I to the new Michael Ramsey Chair of Modern Theology at Kent. This was a point of transition for both of us – firmly into healthcare ethics and more distant from practical or pastoral theology for Campbell, and into healthcare ethics while remaining primarily in applied theology for me. (The adjective 'practical' has been used widely in Scottish theology departments whereas 'applied' or 'pastoral' are more commonly used in England – all are used interchangeably in this article.)

We were both members together of the well-resourced medical ethics committee of the British Medical Association until Campbell was appointed in Singapore. Our paths have crossed at many points, so it is a pleasure and a privilege to contribute to this volume of essays in his honour. He has been an important figure in the development of healthcare ethics in New Zealand, the UK, and Singapore. As it happens, we are also both ordained ministers in national and established churches – the Church of Scotland for Campbell and the Church of England for me – and, perhaps as a result of this, we have been committed to a theological approach to healthcare ethics, sometimes called 'theological realism', but more about that in a moment.

Within the Department of Christian Ethics and Practical Theology at Edinburgh under Professor James (Jim) Blackie's leadership, there was a new emphasis upon interdisciplinary and interprofessional involvement and away from the so-called 'hints and tips' approach to ministerial training. It should be explained that, unlike many other denominations, the Church of Scotland has typically required those called to its ordained ministry to train within universities rather than seminaries, taking two university degrees, only the second of which is in theology. As a result, practical theology, traditionally taught by a senior Church of Scotland minister with extensive parish-based experience, was a required subject in its four oldest universities. In contrast, Blackie's parish ministry was not extensive but he came with a new vision learned from observing medical training. In this vision, students were expected to learn professional skills, for example how to preach, from their parish placements rather than from the staff of the department.

Campbell was appointed to the department in the mid-1960s precisely because he had a doctorate in pastoral care and counselling and could bring insights from secular psychology and psychiatry into his teaching of practical theology. I was appointed to the department in 1972 (the first non-Presbyterian) because I had postgraduate degrees in both theology and sociology. Blackie, a very successful chaplain at Edinburgh University before his appointment to the chair in 1965, was instrumental in this development. At the same time, we were also expected to contribute to separate modules on Christian ethics – Campbell on healthcare ethics and I on social ethics.

Sadly Blackie died aged only 54 in 1976. In an editorial in the *Journal of Medical Ethics* at the time, Campbell wrote:

> Jim Blackie's ... personal influence extended far beyond his own department, faculty and city. He was held in particularly high regard by members of the medical and nursing professions. His advice was often sought on medical matters and his scholarly yet practical approach made contact with him both a stimulating and helpful experience ... he rapidly established a style of open and productive relationships with all sections of the University – an approach which he subsequently used to transform the academic department of which he became head. Under his direction education for ministry in Edinburgh became 'experience-centred'. His students were constantly encouraged to allow insights from the social sciences and from practical experience to challenge and enlighten the formal components of the divinity curriculum ... Above all, he was a realist and a pragmatist, in the best sense of those terms.[1]

This realist/pragmatic and interprofessional approach is well in evidence in Campbell's first book, *Moral Dilemmas in Medicine* (1972) – a compact paperback that was widely used in courses in ethics for nurses in the 1970s and, in its later editions, also in medical education. It does contain a few (but only a few) mentions of theology, but typically they are negative accounts of approaches to Christian ethics that he does not support himself, especially Roman Catholic pro-life approaches based on natural law. Even his depiction on the title page – 'Lecturer in Christian Ethics, University of Edinburgh. Lecturer in Ethics, RCN

---

1 Alastair V. Campbell, 'Editorial' (1976) 2 *Journal of Medical Ethics* 155.

Institute of Advanced Nursing Education (Scotland)' – makes no mention of his role in practical theology. In the Introduction he writes simply as follows:

> My intention is to provide a short introduction to some of the major theories of moral philosophy and to relate these to contemporary moral problems. I have organised the material under a set of broad topic headings and have listed references to other literature in moral philosophy and medical ethics. In this way I hope to have laid the foundations of a short course in ethical theory in relation to medicine, which may be used both by the medical and nursing educators and by individuals interested in teaching themselves more about the subject.[2]

Moral philosophy (Campbell's first degree was in philosophy) rather than theology is the discipline followed in this book designed for healthcare educators – whether they are religious themselves or not.

Two years after Blackie's untimely death, Duncan Forrester (1933–2016) was appointed to the Chair of Christian Ethics and Practical Theology at Edinburgh. He too was ordained into the Church of Scotland, had been a university chaplain (at Sussex) and had interdisciplinary qualifications – in his case in both politics and theology. But he was less pragmatic than his predecessor and more sympathetic to the theologically driven political actions of Karl Barth. Duncan soon founded the Centre for Theology and Public Issues at Edinburgh that did indeed bring in professionals from a wide variety of disciplines, yet it had a specific aim of attempting to show how specifically theological insights could contribute relevantly to public issues. While Campbell continued his largely secular role as founding editor of the *Journal of Medical Ethics*, his books under Duncan's leadership became more theological in tone, especially his influential *Rediscovering Pastoral Care* (1981) and his two books concerned with healthcare professionalism: *Moderated Love: A Theology of Professional Care* (1984) and *Paid to Care? The Limits of Professionalism in Pastoral Care* (1985). This can also be seen clearly in his contribution to one of the seminars at the Centre for Theology and Public Issues where he argues against a purely libertarian view of autonomy:

> [J]ustice and injustice must always be seen in terms of respect for God's creation, responsibility for our community and love of neighbour, whether near or distant... Material prosperity, individual choice and the possession of private property are not ultimate goals in a Christian scale of values: each must serve the end of love, through the enhancement of the whole community (with special attention to its vulnerable members) and through a concern and respect for all of nature. Those with power over people and material things are merely 'stewards', answerable for the good or evil which

---

2 Alastair V. Campbell, *Moral Dilemmas in Medicine: A Coursebook in Ethics for Doctors and Nurses* (Churchill Livingstone 1972).

may come from their treatment of God's creatures... A society like ours which tolerates increasing child poverty and inadequate facilities for the frail and handicapped is becoming like a society which tolerates falsehood – it will eventually lose all sense of the meaning and worth of the non-material, allowing health and truth to become merely aspects of the individual's advantage over others.[3]

So theology for Campbell now becomes less something to critique than itself a critique (albeit within 'a Christian scale of values') of some forms of secular, individualistic ethics. He continued this critique of pure libertarianism even when he moved fully into academic healthcare ethics, as can be seen in his book *Health as Liberation: Medicine, Theology and the Quest for Justice* (1995). In some forms of liberation theology he found an antidote (for Christians at least) to rigorously secular libertarianism. Increasingly, he also became impatient with a dispassionate style of healthcare ethics that is too 'dominated by the dilemmas of acute medicine and by the preoccupations of the relatively affluent and health'[4] – rather than, say, by a more passionately held (often religious) sense of a lack of justice in healthcare between richer and poorer nations.

Another vehicle for specifically theological reflection was his seminal reference book, *A Dictionary of Pastoral Care.*[5] This book was so successful for the theological publisher SPCK that 15 years later it invested heavily in a much-expanded version, edited now by Wesley Carr and retitled *The New Dictionary of Pastoral Studies* (2002). This new version included an updated version of Campbell's original entry on 'pastoral care'. Both versions are indicative of his continuing commitment to theological realism and his suspicion of fideism. Interestingly, in neither version of this dictionary does he contribute entries on medicine or health. It is specifically in his role within practical theology that he contributes, even though by 1989, and for the rest of his academic career, he had formally moved out of a theological department.

In the 1987 version of this entry, pastoral care is defined as 'that aspect of the ministry of the Church which is concerned with the well-being of individuals and of communities'.[6] But in the 2002 version the scope of this definition is expanded considerably, becoming 'activities of the Church which are directed towards maintaining or restoring the health and wholeness of individuals and communities in the context of God's redemptive purposes for all creation'.[7]

3 Alastair V. Campbell, 'Health, Justice and Community: A Theological View' in Alison J. Elliot (ed.), *Inequalities in Health in the 1980s* (Occasional Paper 13, Centre for Theology and Public Issues, Edinburgh 1988) 28.
4 Alastair V. Campbell, 'Secularised Bioethics and the Passion of Religion' (2003) 1(1) *New Review of Bioethics* 117.
5 Alastair V. Campbell, 'Pastoral care, Nature of' in Alastair V. Campbell (ed.) *A Dictionary of Pastoral Care* (London, SPCK 1987) 188–190.
6 ibid 188.
7 Alastair V. Campbell, 'Pastoral Care' in Wesley Carr (ed.) *A New Dictionary of Pastoral Care* (London, SPCK 2002).

So, perhaps surprisingly as we shall see, 'the Church' (undefined but with a capital C) still remains the *locus* for pastoral care, but 'ministry' is dropped, 'maintaining or restoring' is added, 'health and wholeness' replaces 'well-being', and the whole is now set into 'the context of God's redemptive purposes for all creation'. With his philosophical training Campbell is ever exact in his definitions, so we can be sure that each of these changes represents a theological shift in his thinking.

In his original entry he had four sub-headings: providers, recipients, aim, and limits. Under the first, he insists that 'a theological understanding of pastoral care must begin with a full account of the ministry of the whole Church. The basic discipleship of *all* Christians entails caring for others as though they were Christ.'[8] And here he cites the parable of the sheep and the goats and the parable of the good Samaritan, as well as the New Testament commands to love God and neighbour. Under the second, he insists that the recipients of pastoral care should 'not be defined by religious boundaries', noting that 'Jesus rejected the company of the religiously respectable in favour of those who were not so secure in their social status and religious faith'. Under the third, he also insists that pastoral acts 'have a moral and a symbolic dimension, making them forms of proclamation or of moral guidance and support without the necessity for a translation into some special religious language'. And under the final heading, he warns that 'the pastoral ministry of Christians is carried out in a complex world in which numerous agencies are operating for good and for ill. A confidence in the omni-competence of pastoral care must be avoided.' As a result, it may 'often' be appropriate to refer those in need 'to other persons or agencies better qualified to act'.

From all of this, it is not at all difficult to see how his developing interest in healthcare ethics has already shaped his understanding of pastoral care: caring for all those in need whether they are religious or not; avoiding specifically religious language and labels; and referring those in need to those 'better qualified to act'. However, at this stage he is still fairly confident that church-based ministry is the focus of pastoral care.

In the revised entry 15 years later, this confidence seems to have been eroded. By this stage, of course, he had been long away from actively teaching those training for ordained ministry. However, there may be more than this involved. The following telling sentences have been added under the 'limits' sub-heading:

> The Church has frequently colluded in the injustices of society, and individual Christians often lose vision and hope as they struggle with their own weaknesses and doubts. This means that ecclesiastical triumphalism and delusions of omni-competence must be both eschewed in a spirit of true Christian humility.[9]

8 Campbell (n 5).
9 Campbell (n 7).

Note the words 'frequently' and 'often' here. Having made these strong statements he returns to the words of the earlier version, reminding readers that 'if we are honest, we are closer to Good Friday than to Easter morning, vulnerable, afraid ... wounded healers'. The term 'wounded healers' occurred frequently in his writings on pastoral care.

Another significant change is that by 2002 he clearly recognises that the emphasis upon pastoral counselling 'which dominated the American literature' (and in which he trained himself while writing his doctorate at Berkeley) has now waned. In addition, pastoral care is now seen less in terms of individual ministry within the Church than in the social terms of the Kingdom of God and God's creation. In short, his vision of pastoral care, like that of one of his former students Stephen Pattison,[10] has become distinctly less ecclesial. While key notions in practical theology – such as liberation, justice, stewardship, and humility – remain significant elements in his Christian critique of some forms of purely secular and often individualistic healthcare ethics, his move away from the Department of Christian Ethics and Practical Theology at Edinburgh has been accompanied by a vision that is decreasingly ecclesial and, perhaps, less confident about what he had earlier termed 'the difficult path between practical relevance and theological integrity'.[11]

Joseph Fletcher and Paul Ramsey

In order to understand the theological path that Campbell has trodden, it is necessary to trace the pivotal role that theologians of the previous generation played in both the US and the UK in the development of modern healthcare ethics – a role that is not always fully appreciated. In the US, especially, there was a considerable clash of visions between Joseph Fletcher and Paul Ramsey in the early 1960s and an ongoing clash between James Childress and Stanley Hauerwas today. All four of these theologians have been highly influential within healthcare ethics but their visions are radically at odds. In the UK, leading theological figures in the development of modern healthcare ethics were perhaps, until recently at least, less polarised. This may have been because of the key role of establishment Anglicans, such as Archbishop John Habgood, Professor Canon Gordon Dunstan, Dean Ted Shotter, and high-profile hospital chaplains in central London like Canon Norman Autton. All these figures gained the respect of leading doctors and their royal colleges in the capital city (just as Blackie and then Campbell did in Edinburgh) and influenced the way that healthcare ethics was gradually introduced into medical training. Of course sharp differences remained among the religiously active, especially on pro-life issues, but these key establishment Anglicans ensured that these differences did not translate into public policy

10 Stephen Pattison, *A Critique of Pastoral Care* (3rd edn, London, SCM Press 2000); *Pastoral Care and Liberation Theology* (Cambridge University Press 1994).
11 Alastair V. Campbell, 'The Nature of Practical Theology' in Duncan B. Forrester (ed.) *Theology and Practice* (London, Epworth 1990) 20.

in England and Wales – as the Church of Scotland did similarly in Scotland. Only in Northern Ireland did this happen more ambiguously given its sharp religious tensions, where, for example, medically induced abortion remains largely, and uniquely, illegal in the UK.

The clash over healthcare ethics between Joseph Fletcher (1905–91) and Paul Ramsey (1913–88) in the US is particularly instructive. They represented radically different ecclesial, ethical, and theological positions – Fletcher as a liberal Episcopalian committed to a personalist style of ethics that he later termed 'situation ethics' and Ramsey as a more conservative Methodist committed to a form of deontological ethics based on biblical norms.

Joseph Fletcher was an ordained Episcopalian priest who had taught social ethics at the Episcopal Theological School (ETS) at Cambridge, Massachusetts, since 1944 but became famous for the publication of his book, *Situation Ethics*, in 1966. He retired from ETS in 1970, severed his connection with the Episcopal Church, and spent the next 8 years working explicitly as a humanist Professor of Bioethics at Virginia University.

Those working in Christian ethics and, especially, in healthcare ethics at the time that *Situation Ethics* was published would have known his earlier book, *Morals and Medicine*. The latter is much more sober in style than *Situation Ethics*, lacking its jokes, provocations, and fanciful examples. Yet it was still a polemical work, written to provide a counter to traditional Roman Catholic moral theology on healthcare ethical issues, stating in the Preface that to his knowledge 'nothing of this kind has been undertaken by non-Catholics as yet'.[12] His challenges to Catholic teaching were made directly on the issues of contraception, artificial insemination, sterilisation, and voluntary euthanasia.

Many other non-Catholics, especially in Anglican and liberal Reformed denominations, were to echo the points that he made in this early book on the permissibility of contraception and artificial insemination. In fact, the Lambeth Conference of Anglican Bishops in 1930 had already made a tentative reversal of their complete rejection of contraception at their conference 10 years earlier. However, on sterilisation and voluntary euthanasia, Fletcher already held positions yet to be adopted by many Christian denominations – accepting voluntary euthanasia as 'a means of ending a human life enmeshed in incurable and fatal physical suffering'[13] and (just as controversially) involuntary, punitive sterilisation 'as a means of social justice' when 'it may sometimes be necessary to deprive a criminal – say a rapist – of the power of procreation'.[14]

He was yet to use the term 'situation ethics' in *Morals and Medicine*, but this approach was clearly emerging as can be seen from this paragraph from the Preface:

---

12 Joseph F. Fletcher, *Morals and Medicine: The Moral Problems of the Patient's Right to Know the Truth, Contraception, Artificial Insemination, Sterilization, Euthanasia* (Princeton University Press and London, Victor Gollancz 1955) xi.
13 ibid 208.
14 ibid 169.

The bias of my ethical standpoint, apart from its frame of reference in Christian faith, is probably best pin-pointed as personalist. It is not naturalist, humanist, utilitarian, or positivist. As will be seen, by personalism I mean the correlation of personality and value; the doctrine, that is, that personality is a unique quality in every human being, and that it is both the highest good and the chief medium of our knowledge of the good.[15]

However, by the early 1960s, he was using the term 'situation ethics' to depict his approach and was linking it to act-utilitarianism as well as to secular humanism. He also dropped many of the Latin tags used in *Morals and Medicine*, raised the level of caricature and provocation, and added rather weak jokes and fanciful examples to *Situation Ethics*, making such claims as this:

There are at bottom only three alternative routes or approaches to follow in making moral decisions. They are: (1) the legalistic; (2) the antinomian, the opposite extreme – i.e. a lawless or unprincipled approach; and (3) the situational.[16]

Pedants will at once notice the sloppy use of 'alternative' here to denote three rather than two things. Ethicists will note no mention of consequentialism. And attentive readers of the rest of the book will puzzle about whether he really did eliminate legalism from his own thinking in the extraordinary examples that he deployed. A year later he continued to write stridently: 'Law ethics is still the enemy, by far … [its] suffocation is bad faith, and irresponsible'.[17]

However, to focus upon these features is to miss the central message of *Situation Ethics* – a message that has continued to attract followers and that does resonate strongly with parts of the New Testament. In summary, it is simply this: love should indeed direct our moral behaviour to each other, and love properly understood cannot readily be captured by moral laws. For Jews, Christians, and Muslims alike, love (or compassion) derives from a conviction that God first loves (or shows compassion to) us, so we in turn should show love (or show compassion) to each other *and* (some of us would add) to the rest of God's creation:

Christian situation ethics has only one norm or principle or law (call it what you will) that is binding and unexceptionable, always good and right regardless of the circumstances. That is 'love' – the *agape* of the summary commandment to love God and the neighbour. Everything else without exception, all laws and rules and principles and ideals and norms, are only *contingent*, only valid *if they happen* to serve love in any situation.

15 ibid xii.
16 Joseph F. Fletcher, *Situation Ethics: The New Morality* (Philadelphia: Westminster Press and London: SCM Press 1966) 17.
17 Joseph F. Fletcher, *Moral Responsibility: Situation Ethics at Work* (Philadelphia: Westminster Press and London: SCM Press 1967) 241.

Christian situation ethics is not a system or program of living according to a code, but an effort to relate love to a world of relativities through a casuistry obedient to love. It is the strategy of love. This strategy denies that there are, as Sophocles thought, any unwritten immutable laws of heaven, agreeing with Bultmann that all such notions are idolatrous and a demonic pretension.[18]

He put the first word here in italics because he wanted to emphasise that a non-Christian may have a norm that is different from 'love' or *agape*. Such a person would, in his view, still be a situationist but not a Christian situationist. (Once he became a secular humanist himself, he might have changed his mind on this point.) For him 'the *Christian* is neighbour-centred first and last'.[19] Some recalled that it was precisely because he was so neighbour-centred as a young man that he became an Episcopalian priest. His early ministry, so it has been argued, was driven more by this ethical conviction than by theology. If that is so then, despite all the hyperbole of *Situation Ethics*, there was at its heart a strong moral passion.

Paul Ramsey was clearly appalled by *Situation Ethics* and wrote a lengthy refutation of it in 1967 in his *Deeds and Rules in Christian Ethics*. Here he argues that it is flawed by 'fabricated sensationalism',[20] individualism, and arbitrariness:

Reading a number of Fletcher's cases one is struck by an unexpected *arbitrariness* of the judgement or decision the author regards as valid. From what he says about a given case one expects him to lean in the same direction in another case that is not too different from the first; yet, unpredictably, in the second case he recommends the option (or one like it) that was refused in the first instance where it seems that this would have been equally appropriate.[21]

To Ramsey's horror, Fletcher did make an explicit commitment to some form of moral relativism in *Situation Ethics*, as can be seen here:

It is necessary to insist that situation ethics is willing to make full and respectful use of principles, to be treated as maxims but not as laws or precepts. We might call it 'principled relativism'. To repeat the term used above, principles or maxims or general rules are *illuminators*. But they are not *directors*. The classic rule of moral theology has been to follow laws but to do it *as much as possible* according to love and according to reason… Situation ethics, on the other hand, calls upon us to keep law in a subservient place, so that *only* love and reason really count when the chips are down![22]

18 Fletcher (n 15) 30–31.
19 ibid 31.
20 Paul Ramsey, *Deeds and Rules in Christian Ethics* (New York: Charles Scribner 1967) 208.
21 ibid 208.
22 Fletcher (n 15) 31.

Fletcher returned to the issue of relativism at several points in *Situation Ethics*, aware perhaps that this was its most vulnerable feature. At one point he claimed that 'the situationist avoids words like "never" and "perfect" and "always" and "complete" as he avoids the plague, as he avoids "absolutely".'[23] Or again: 'No twentieth-century man of even average training will turn his back on the anthropological and psychological evidence for relativity in morals. There are no "universal laws" held by all men everywhere at all times, no consensus of all men.'[24]

He was, at least partially, aware that 'to be relative, of course, means to be relative *to* something. To be "absolutely relative" (an uneasy combination of terms) is to be inchoate, random, unpredictable, unjudgeable, meaningless, amoral.'[25] Yet he still faced an obvious problem: dogmatic claims about relativism (such as those in the previous paragraph) are mightily curious. If someone, for example, claims that 'everything is relative', then that person might expect someone else to ask whether that claim itself is relative and, if it is, how it can then be trusted. This is a running problem in *Situation Ethics* because it made so many dogmatic claims about situationism.

His own 'solution' to this dilemma was to make another dogmatic claim: 'There must be an absolute or norm of some kind if there is to be any true relativity.'[26] But note the word 'true' in this claim. Later he avoided this word and used instead the term 'the highest good' (as he did in *Morals and Medicine*), resorting at this point to a Latin tag for greater emphasis:

> Nothing is intrinsically good but the highest good. The *summum bonum*, the end or purpose of all ends – love. We cannot say anything we do *is* good, only that it is a means to an end and therefore *happens* in that cause-and-effect relation to have value.[27]

So for Fletcher there was a 'highest good' (that is, love) beyond anything that we actually do. In most other places in *Situation Ethics*, he claimed love to be the highest good only for specifically Christian situationists. Here, however, love seems to be the highest good for all people regardless of their situation. This is not the most comfortable position for a professed situationist.

Ramsey also argued strongly against Fletcher's alignment with act-utilitarians:

> [A]nyone who proposes to effect a coalition between Christian ethics and utilitarianism in propounding a situation ethics should make it abundantly clear that he is making common cause with a beleaguered sect among contemporary utilitarians, namely, the act-utilitarians. It is difficult to tell whence comes the resulting rule-less and un-principled version of Christian

23 ibid 43–44.
24 ibid 76.
25 ibid 44.
26 ibid.
27 ibid 129.

ethics – whether from the mistaken belief that the freedom of *agapé* is unbinding or from the act-pragmatism that is begged.[28]

Ironically Ramsey himself (and Hauerwas more recently) was sometimes faced with the criticism of being too 'sectarian' himself, albeit for rather different reasons, as he showed when arguing in a different context:

> My thesis is that ... we will no longer be able to speak and act if there is a closer identification between Christian social ethics and the policy making of the Secular City that was asserted in the Middle Ages. In the *contents* of ecumenical ethics there needs to be some way to tell some difference between the spiritual and the temporal power. Yet I fear that to propound this thesis even in an age that is assertedly post-Christian will only brand the author as one who believes the church to be a spiritual cult with no pertinent social outlook.[29]

Ramsey's own strong sense of Christian distinctiveness and theological independence is well in evidence in one of his most fascinating and enduring contributions to healthcare ethics, his 1970 book *Fabricated Man*. Here he anticipated (only sometimes correctly) future developments in human genetics, including the possibility of human reproductive cloning. While listening carefully to some of the medical scientists of his time, he also offers them a strong and repeated warning that 'we should not play God before we have learned to be men, and as we learn to be men we will not want to play God'.[30] For him the biblical concept of 'wisdom' calls for radical caution when faced with possibilities of genetic science applied to human beings:

> The question [is] whether man is or will ever be wise enough to make himself a successful self-modifying system or wise enough to begin doctoring the species. When concern for the species replaces care for the primary patient, and means are adopted that are deep invasions of the parameters of human parenthood as it came to us from the Creator, will we not be launched on a sea of uncertainty where lack of wisdom may introduce mistakes that are uncontrollable and irreversible?[31]

Applied to other areas of healthcare ethics, such as sterilisation, abortion, and euthanasia, Ramsey's understanding of theological 'wisdom' precluded him from adopting the radical positions espoused by Fletcher. Over the next two decades

---

28 Ramsey (n 19) 225.
29 Paul Ramsey, *Who Speaks for the Church? A Critique of the 1966 Geneva Conference on Church and Society* (Nashville: Abingdon Press 1967).
30 Paul Ramsey, *Fabricated Man: The Ethics of Genetic Control* (New Haven: Yale University Press 1970) 151.
31 ibid 124.

these two theologians remained deeply polarised, separately and very differently influencing the next generation of theologians contributing to healthcare ethics, including Campbell and myself.

Continuing theological tensions in healthcare ethics

James Childress and Stanley Hauerwas are two of the most significant present-day American Christian ethicists who have made a substantial impact upon healthcare ethics. Like Paul Ramsey, Hauerwas is a Methodist with strong fideist convictions. Childress, in contrast, is a Quaker who has long collaborated with the secular utilitarian, Tom Beauchamp, in their seminal textbook now in its seventh edition, *Principles of Biomedical Ethics*.[32] I have written extensively before about the strengths and weaknesses of the Beauchamp/Childress eirenic approach to healthcare ethics[33] and Hauerwas's determinedly theological approach,[34] so I will not repeat all that now. In summary, I concluded that the four-principle approach of Beauchamp and Childress does offer a useful heuristic basis for teaching healthcare ethics in introductory modules to medical practitioners, but on its own and without considerable additional engagement with virtue ethics it lacks depth (as later editions of *Principles of Biomedical Ethics* have tended to acknowledge). I have also concluded that Hauerwas's immensely stimulating theological contributions to healthcare are far too prone to hyperbole – painting a picture of Christian communities embedded in distinctive virtues that is considerably at odds with the empirical realities of church congregations that emerge from a serious study of sociological data.

I doubt if Campbell would dissent from either of these conclusions. On the Beauchamp/Childress approach, especially, he has written as follows:

> I conclude that virtue ethics and the four principles are 'partners in crime' when it comes to the final justification of our moral intuitions. Each captures different dimensions of our moral universe, but one is not better than the other in settling finally how we make correct moral judgments. The principles help us to structure our reasoning when faced with novel moral challenges and they remind us of key questions to be explored. Virtue ethics directs us to the character of the decision maker, but also to the implications for our whole lives and for society of individual choices and policy decisions.[35]

In two of his most important contributions to healthcare ethics – *Suffering Presence* (1986) and *Naming the Silences* (1990) – Hauerwas engages positively with Paul

---

32 Tom L. Beauchamp and James F. Childress, *Principles of Biomedical Ethics* (7th edn, New York: Oxford University Press 2013).

33 Robin Gill, *Health Care and Christian Ethics* (Cambridge University Press 2006) 102ff.

34 Robin Gill, *Theology in a Social Context: Sociological Theology Volume 1* (Farnham, Ashgate 2012) 207ff.

35 Alastair V. Campbell, 'The Virtues (and Vices) of the Four Principles', (2003) 29 *Journal of Medical Ethics* 292, 293.

Ramsey at several points but only twice, and disparagingly, with Beauchamp and Childress. With Ramsey he displays an unsurprising affinity (even their polemical and discursive style of writing is similar) but with the Quaker Childress he displays very little indeed:

> [E]ven though religious thinkers have been at the forefront of much of the work done in the expanding field of 'medical ethics', it is not clear that they have been there as religious thinkers... Jim Childress [and others] have done extensive work in medical ethics, but often it is hard to tell how their religious convictions have made a difference for the methodology they employ or for their response to specific quandaries. Indeed it is interesting to note how seldom they raise issues of the meaning or relation of salvation and health, as they seem to prefer dealing with questions of death and dying, truth telling, etc.[36]

He is particularly critical of Childress's collusion with what he sees as the utilitarianism of Beauchamp in the first edition of *Principles of Biomedical Ethics* when arguing that rational, autonomous suicide can be ethically justifiable. Hauerwas insists that, from a Christian perspective of God-given life, their conclusion is 'deeply misleading' and 'reveals the insufficiency of autonomy ... as a basis or ideal for the moral life'.[37]

Of course Hauerwas has a point here and it does appear that in later editions of *Principles of Biomedical Ethics* Beauchamp and Childress modified their earlier claims about suicide and autonomous rights. Yet Hauerwas is not always clear about the different audiences that public theologians need to address. Recently I have argued at length that it matters a great deal whether a theologian is addressing fellow Christians (the typical audience for Hauerwas), or professionals drawn from a wide range of religious and secular positions (the audience of Beauchamp and Childress), or even law-makers in a pluralistic society.[38]

So, to give one example, many Christian couples may have very serious reservations about aborting a viable foetus of their own, however inconvenient an unplanned or disabled baby might be. They might also choose not to have certain tests where abortion is the expected outcome if a particular disability is detected. Yet they might still conclude that some level of medically supervised abortion should be retained or made legal in a pluralistic society in order to avoid the horrors of unsafe illegal abortions. Or again, a theologian who sits on a public ethics committee (as Campbell and I have done many times) may conclude that insisting upon a single theological, ethical, or even philosophical perspective is counter-productive in a pluralistic society. The theologian in such a context who insists upon speaking about God (let alone Jesus) may be just as irritating to others as the philosopher who reduces everything to utility.

36 Stanley Hauerwas, *Suffering Presence: Theological Reflections on Medicine, the Mentally Handicapped, and the Church* (University of Notre Dame Press 1986).
37 ibid 102.
38 Robin Gill, *Moral Passion and Christian Ethics* (Cambridge University Press 2017).

Perhaps there is a proper time and place for 'witness' (Hauerwas's preferred term) and a proper time and place for restraint in the interests of mutual, rational engagement – especially for those theologians who wish others to be ethical whether they are religious or not. Inappropriate 'witness' – like enforced prayer for non-believers – might actually do more harm than good in a pluralist society. If you do not agree with this last statement, then just think for a moment about the many encounters you have had with fervent (and, indeed, courageous) members of the Jehovah's Witnesses. Did you find them even remotely convincing? Or did you find them just irritating?

Another point to note in response to Hauerwas is that Childress is not alone in seeking to work, when possible, with secular utilitarians. Charles Camosy is a particularly interesting example of a Catholic theologian who sought to do just this in his book *Peter Singer and Christian Ethics: Beyond Polarization*[39] and in the subsequent theological conference, with Singer present, of the Oxford McDonald Centre for Theology, Ethics and Public Life. John Perry, who organised this conference, argues that utilitarianism has clear Christian roots and ongoing affinities with versions of Christian ethics based on 'wellbeing' or *eudaimonia*. Perry maintains that – shorn of its single-mindedness, quasi-mathematical certainty, and proposals such as infanticide – what is left of Singer's utilitarianism *is* compatible with Christian ethics.[40]

At a more personal level, I have long cooperated with the humanist moral philosopher Richard Norman at the University of Kent on healthcare ethics and professional ethics more widely. Chairing the university's main research ethics and governance committee for more than a decade, with a remit that extended to every faculty and across all disciplines, it was essential for me to establish that careful ethical consideration of their projects is required of *all* those who do research on human or animal participants, regardless of their own particular religious, ideological, or philosophical convictions. Because Norman and I shared a common commitment to virtue ethics, we were able to work together quite readily and to set aside our metaphysical differences (with him self-identifying as an atheist and me as a Christian) while we did this work. This did not preclude us from having quite separate public debates about these differences (debates that were very popular with our students). Distinguishing carefully between different audiences was again important here.

In a recent book edited by Richard and the Anglican theologian Tony Carroll (to which I contributed), the two editors defended such cooperation across divisions as follows:

> Dialogue between believers and atheists, if it is oriented towards mutual learning, should help both sides to move beyond their ideologies and

---

39 Charles Camosy, *Peter Singer and Christian Ethics: Beyond Polarization* (Cambridge University Press 2012).

40 John Perry (ed.), *God, the Good and Utilitarianism: Perspectives on Peter Singer* (Cambridge University Press 2014).

idolatries. Such dialogue can enable both positions to recognise that other options are possible... It can help to temper tendencies towards fundamentalisms of both religious and secular varieties. It can increase awareness of the complexity and diversity of religious and non-religious perspectives, and ... correct a misleading picture of a simple polar opposition between religion and non-religion.[41]

My own conviction is that such cooperation is also important between Christian ethicists who disagree with each other. I believe that theological realists, such as Campbell and Childress, do have a significant role to play in public healthcare ethics and that they need not abandon their theological commitments to do so as Fletcher apparently did (I am still not exactly sure why or even to what extent he did). But they are also under no obligation to follow Hauerwas's advice to talk about 'salvation' within public healthcare ethics. I also believe that fideists such as Ramsey and Hauerwas have an important role especially within Christian communities. While I do not share all their ethical conclusions (any more than I share all those of Fletcher) I do find them to be important stimulants to deeper ethical and theological reflection. Together and separately, I believe that theologians can continue to make significant contributions to healthcare ethics today.

41 Anthony Carroll and Richard Norman (eds), *Religion and Atheism: Beyond the Divide* (London and New York: Routledge 2017) 256.

5 In that (hard) case

Could ordinary talk in clinical care have an extraordinary moral importance?

Roger Higgs

Introduction

As the medical school Dean came down the corridor, he was smiling. When top academics smile at their heads of department, it usually means they have thought of a foolproof way of saving money – perhaps by retiring your senior people, or maybe closing the whole department. So I was on high alert. Then the Dean said: 'I think the GP part of you would like this one, Roger.'

As a physician he was sending me to the surgical wards to see a young woman with severe abdominal pain who had been unsuccessfully investigated by the surgeons every which way for nearly a fortnight. I introduced myself and as I sat down on her bed, I asked, 'When did the pain begin?' She answered, 'When my husband took my son back to Nigeria.'

Before that episode with the Dean, when Alastair V. Campbell was the founding editor of the *Journal of Medical Ethics* and he and I had worked together in the early editions, we decided to write a book.[1] This became *In That Case: Medical Ethics in Everyday Practice* (*ITC*), about day-to-day moral choices in medicine, based around a case in general practice. The first chapter was called 'Choices': it addressed the paternalism with which the story of the case began, and examined what we thought respecting a patient's autonomy really meant.

The encounters we described in the book were by no means routine (and the outcome was tragic) but, although clinical practice has changed greatly since we wrote, giving proper respect to the autonomy of patients and clinicians in clinical practice remains far from easy. Some interactions seem so difficult that we can reasonably call these 'hard' cases. I want to look at some ideas about how doctors and patients talk to each other, and ask whether simple talk like the Dean's described above can change outcomes, even to the point of unlocking what might seem to be a hard case; or when talk is conducted differently, whether it may lead to the hardening and locking up tight of an interaction that might otherwise have been successful.

---

1 Alastair V. Campbell and Roger Higgs, *In That Case: Medical Ethics in Everyday Practice* (London: Darton, Longman & Todd 1982).

ITC's approach is different from what this essay, partly because although it followed the story of a mother and her child it did so into the home, onto the ward and then into social service and police departments, using imagined witnesses, each from a different point of view. We tried to make it as three-dimensional as possible, a 'thick' case around which clinical practice and a variety of different modes of thinking could meet and coalesce. It tried to translate the complexity of the insights and the talk of all these different disciplines into ordinary prose in its discussion of important moral arguments and of the way they could illuminate medical care in a structured way.

As an aside, it was great fun to write with Campbell, as we moved back and forth between creative writing and academic thought. We finished with several days holed up in a cottage near Dunsinane, till the final version came over the hill, waving branches. Unlike the protagonists at the end of *Macbeth*, it neither hoped to spawn (nor stifle!) a rich and royal line, but we thought the book was the first of its kind. In resoundingly celebrating Campbell and what he brought to *ITC*, I want to follow some of its inspiration down into the present day. I am interested in whether the practice of medical ethics is working at its best, now, for ordinary people meeting in medical care. Personal as well as professional lives have altered greatly since then.[2] Medical ethics is now a fully established discipline, but how engaged in current medical practice is that discipline? How have the ideas we looked at in *ITC* been received? Our hopes for a thriving culture of multidisciplinary discussion have spluttered and remained just about alive, but the central issue that consumed much of our thought – the relationships in the meeting between patient and clinician – continue to hold attention and often perplex. So I have chosen to focus on that area and look at examples of those meetings that for some reason refuse to go well, or get stuck. This is what I mean here by *a hard case*.

The hardness of hard cases

Medical practice is hard, both to learn about and to deliver well. Being seriously ill is also very hard, disappointing to become or to discover, and difficult to respond to in the best way. Doctors are very busy, in almost all situations, and have to make complex decisions, often in the absence of good information, about disparate problems that can be deeply disturbing if they are allowed to be so and which are often covered by rules or frameworks that have implications in themselves and often are a poor fit for the problem at hand. Patients may arrive in distress, in pain or confused by what is happening to them, often to the extent that they cannot be coherent about what has happened, let alone think clearly about options; wielding this thing called autonomy may seem beside the point. So it is not surprising that meetings between sick individuals and their clinicians

2 Roger Higgs, *The Medical Paradigm: Changing Landscapes* (London, Royal College of Physicians 2003).

can on occasions become difficult. Each side has expertise,[3] one in the practical science of medicine and the other in the personal history, but ideas and aims may not agree and expectations of each other may not turn out well. Personalities may clash and things go wrong in so many ways. To get to grips academically with all the possibilities requires much more than an essay: maybe not even a book so much as a library. In reducing the focus to cope with this enormous territory, I want to focus on two areas, often overlapping: where symptoms are *not easily explained by medical investigations*, in the broadest sense (often called in jargon 'medically unexplained symptoms', or 'MUS' for short); and where clinician and patient become *embattled*.

Unsurprisingly, when these two types of hard case conjoin, the results may become even harder. As well as no solution or explanation being forthcoming, either or both parties may retire perplexed but also hurt in yet new ways. Patients may refuse to go back to the same or indeed to any doctor. Doctors may make sure they avoid that type of problem or person in every way they can. Whether such cases are common or not, the spectrum of unconstructive outcomes may, in the extreme, pass through mere confrontation to become sadder and harder, all the way through bitterness to litigation, early retirement or breakdown.

Some personal background

It may help to say why this topic became of interest to me. I was in the middle of coping with serious illnesses in my family, and in the previous decade by chance I had become a reluctant but intrigued witness to a whole range of different clinical interactions. Some of these interactions were brilliant, and some extraordinarily helpful and creative. Others were shockingly bad, and as such impossible to forget. That I was a declared medical colleague in the room undoubtedly made it harder for some medics we met, although it enabled me to spread some explanation on troubled waters later; but it did not seem to stop the clinician sometimes being thoughtless, rude, unengaged or simply spiteful.

So in some sense I do have an axe to grind; but that is because we have to chop wood. On the one side, it often seems harder than it should be for an ill person to make a clinician see what their problem really is, or to have a dialogue with or question the decisions of busy doctors; and much too easy for both sets of people to become grumpy and seem 'difficult' to each other, as a straightforward case threatens to become a hard one. On the other hand, medical practice becomes steadily more complicated with every breakthrough, and busier and more stressful because of competing demands and rising medical and interpersonal standards. Doctors are people and we all have preferences, about how we want to lead our lives, about situations or personalities we would rather not meet, and about problems or discussions we would rather not have. But while life outside medicine, in the parts of countries where I spend my

---

3 David Tuckett *et al.*, *Meetings between Experts* (New York, Tavistock Publications 1985).

time, especially urban Britain and rural France, is not amazingly easy, people meet and greet, problems get solved and everyone moves on. Why do things often seem so much less satisfactory in medical encounters? Whose job is it to look for answers?

Is this the business of medical ethics?

At first glance, these hard cases seem to contain a legitimate question for medical ethics. Harm is being perpetuated and new harms created. One or both parties may see their ability to make decisions, to choose actions that seem appropriate to them (and to avoid other things that they do not) curtailed or thwarted. The personal and institutional costs of the processes may well become enormous, both in terms of time and money. Beneficence and benevolence both may sink beneath waves of resentment and frustration. We have ticked the boxes of those famous four principles without going any further.

But objections to my interest here may be raised from a number of points of view. At one end of the spectrum, is what I am saying not all too obvious? What I may be seizing on is likely to be second-class or even bad medicine, and we do not need to discuss the morality of that, just as we do not need to agonise in our ethics writing about giving patients the wrong dose of a drug or removing the wrong kidney. The sort of hard cases I have outlined may sometimes contain things that are so clearly out of order that all we need to do is identify them, and then ring the regulatory body or talk to a lawyer. But although either action may satisfy the often-quoted motivation of 'making sure it never happens again', neither seems to address the woes of patient or clinician, or to solve the original problem.

At the other end, an argument might be advanced that this is just how things are. Medical ethics thinkers do not get involved when patients cannot work or doctors get tired. People fail to get satisfactions in all sorts of ways. The supermarket checkout person is unengaged or too chatty, the driver in front is always doing it wrong. That is life. Get over it and move on. My argument is that it need not be so in medicine. I have been lucky enough to see amazing social changes in my lifetime. My gay friends no longer, in the UK anyway, live in fear of persecution. We no longer, officially, tolerate barriers of gender, race or religion for aspiring individuals in the workplace. We may see these either as incivilities to be reduced in liberal society in a number of ways, or important evils to be expunged. Either way we may be conscious of how much more needs to be done, or be bothered that the 'Trump tendency' (after USA President Donald) – that is, when people in power intervene to make things worse – seems unpleasantly common. But on the simplest day-to-day level, however grim the news may be, I go to sleep happy that women and men can walk home alone and unmolested after midnight past my house in south London, and keep at bay the cynic in my head who may whisper in the small hours that there is no moral progress in the world.

Ethics and the everyday

To reach improvement in our society, we have to name the problem and suggest remedies. Consultations in practice are sometimes not as good as they should be and people are coming to harm on both sides of that meeting when that does not need to happen. It is, in part at least, a moral problem to be examined and addressed. In doing so I want to try to stay close to the people who are experiencing the hardness – that is, the clinicians, patients and relatives who feel the frustration and pain of finding themselves stuck or unable to progress to a creative solution – and look at what medical ethics can offer in unravelling or even healing such hard cases.

The Dean's case

What stood out about the case as originally presented to me by the Dean was that he thought he had somehow broken through the impasse presented by a young woman with undiagnosed abdominal pain by enabling her to remember that it started when her child was stolen from her. I returned to this example, 'thin' and unsubstantiated as it was, because it suggested that he had found some way of interacting with a distressed patient on a physically focused ward that could move on to an understanding of why she felt so ill. We do not know if this 'worked': if this led to a continued improvement of her symptoms. He clearly could not bring back her child, but he thought they had made important progress together. He was a charming and thoughtful physician, but not, I think, seductive or a fantasist. From my experience, dealing with grief is usually a long process, often impossible to assuage. Mothers who have lost a child report that, rather than get better, the feelings get worse as the years pass by. It is not hard for others to imagine the yawning deadening pain of the loss that gets bigger as the child is no longer there, year on year, missing every bedtime and flattening each birthday into a scream of loneliness. Nevertheless, something happened on that ward with the Dean that could be called helpful.

How was this achieved? He reported three actions. He introduced himself; he sat down; and he asked an ordinary question.

Introducing oneself with ordinary speech

To someone who has never experienced receiving or working in healthcare, this seems a bizarre idea: what is the big deal about introducing oneself? Yet to an experienced patient, it may seem revolutionary and is part of the instruction given to neophytes learning about communication skills in medicine and nursing. With the advent of uniform scrubs, the situation has become worse: it is often obscure why different people wear different clothing or colours. Even as a relative sitting by, I was at a loss when a colleague asked, 'Well, who has she been seen by?' Name may mean less than expertise or position, but the anxiety of a conscious patient may increase as it is clear that something is about to be done. If the patient has been in hospital for more than a short time, the space round the bed has become home: would any of us accept people barging into one's home without asking, or saying who they were or why they were there?

Four themes emerge. The first is that for some reason clinicians, especially doctors, feel it is satisfactory to economise on ordinary polite actions and speech, ostensibly in the name of saving time. If this raises anxiety or disorientation, it is clearly counterproductive. The second is distancing, as an intentional act by doctors to retain an 'objective' viewpoint and not get too emotionally invested and drained: this is completely understandable, but the possibilities of a normal human relationship, within which important information might be exchanged, are reduced. The third is unfamiliarity. One of the insights in medical ethics in another context was that a patient with whom discussion was to occur was a moral stranger: how can we make decisions for someone else about whose values and way of seeing the world we are completely ignorant?[4] But behind that idea lies the simple question of how to treat someone who actually *is* a stranger. Each society has slightly different rules, whether it is shaking the hand in France, saying 'Excuse me' on a New York street or closing both eyes fractionally when confronting a cat! That clinical medicine as a whole so often feels the lack of need to abide by these sorts of simple rules when meeting someone begins to extract a theme. Once he had introduced himself, the Dean asked his ordinary question. The medical part could wait – and should await the ordinary conversational introductions that people are used to. Ordinary speech is mandatory for us at certain points in any conversation, and without it defences start to build, with the thought intruding that this person has no need to come down to my level; and if I trust him or her with confidences, I have only myself to blame.

Levelling with the patient

Many things that are heard do not have to be spoken. Ward rounds are still almost universally conducted with the clinical group standing up as the patient lies in bed. In ambulatory reviews, a patient may enter the room and the clinician may remain seated. Neither is the way we usually act. The message is clear. The psychic echoes for newcomers are of facing adults with power over them (teachers, work superiors, police) and the effect is infantilising. Trust is likely to be the last emotion to be felt in this situation.

For the Dean, something had to change. The young woman, without the negative tests and her time sitting thinking on the ward, would probably have kept the story about her family to herself. Nevertheless, at some stage in the clinical journey of a patient whose case has become hard, someone professional needs to step back and try to look at things in a different, maybe an 'ordinary',

---

4 Hugo T. Engelhardt Jr, 'Personhood, Moral Strangers, and The Evil of Abortion: The Painful Experience of Post-Modernity' (1993) 18 *Journal of Medicine and Philosophy* 419–421.

light. The helter-skelter pace of clinical throughput needs to slow down for trust to be rebuilt, to allow the patient to express other concerns, to talk 'sideways' as it were, for the professional to look for and to hear something new, taking it seriously and without immediate dismissal. The Dean created something special for his patient, probably a moment where at last she felt safe, perhaps even the first time in her own helter-skelter life too that someone had seemed to want to listen thoughtfully to her 'inner voice' and then hear her out, rather than reach for a form to order some more tests or arrange another appointment.

So he 'sat down on her bed'. Whether this was in accord with usual practice or not, it was a very powerful way of saying that he was there for her and the time was at least partly hers, to use and define as she wished. Professionals have a hard time seeing how it is that many of their normal rituals (for walking patients, for instance, the distant calling system, the unfamiliar room and the large desk with the computer that maybe holds information that the newcomer is not party to) create a communication moat of medieval proportions that it is very hard to cross. The Dean, on the other hand, sat down on his patient's bed in the same way perhaps as she had sat down with her son, before the child was stolen away. Maybe that too helped to bring her loss to mind. But without looking behind it, the key statement, made without words, was: I am on your level now, so we can level with each other. It was respect, not just in theory but also in practice.

Respecting respect

ITC spoke quite a lot about respect: and nowadays it trips off the tongue easily for many who talk about the important principles of personal care, in health and elsewhere, in the couplet of 'respecting autonomy'. No one should doubt the importance and extraordinary power of this concept in reshaping medicine in the last half century. If students remember nothing else of their ethics teaching, it is this, backed both by law and (usually but unusually!) the practice of many doctors outside their *alma mater*. It defines what should be done in difficult clinical situations, and it sets limits to what can be researched with patients. But in moral discussions the focus is usually on the noun and its implications. When the verb 'respect' comes into play it is often to enable lip service to be played to 'autonomy' while its strong implications have regretfully to be denied in some (possibly important) way. But 'respect' is a verb about action, about doing something. It is a 'giving' interpersonal verb, and no one should be exempt from its giving or receiving any more than they are to be deprived of water or air. So in 'respecting' autonomy the word is doing two things at once: reminding us of the importance of allowing the individual freedom to choose, and defining everyone's roles and responsibilities in a response that has to be delivered in the interaction if the choices are to be real ones. This should hold wherever the interaction happens – emergency work, specialist or general practice – and however much a protocol has to be followed. This is a great deal easier to write than to deliver, especially day after day, night after night, patient after patient. It requires special skill and a particular view of what sort of professional you are trying to be.

No one of course can ever be fully clear about any other individual's 'real' intentions, and although there are attitudes that we may come across in healthcare students that would prevent someone being an effective physician, nevertheless we have to accept that doctors and nurses will have a range of attitudes. Some of these we might like to change, but we cannot, and quite possibly should not. We need to respect a professional's autonomy too. What matters is that the consultation is effective and that the patient believes his or her views are being attended to. This is what makes the ordinary speech even more important, as a surrogate or a *marker* of a positive interaction, however on their guard the individuals may still feel.

Attending to attention

There is of course an extensive literature in general practice manuals and the teaching of professionalism and communication skills on how such respect should be given to a patient's agenda, and the importance of attending to her narrative, her ideas, her understanding and expectations. Paying attention starts from the beginning of the process. A clinician coming to the waiting area and shaking hands while introducing themselves is always a good start. Some open-ended questions are vital: gazing at a computer screen and firing questions may kill a developing relationship stone dead. There is a person to be met and a proper relationship, however brief, to be made. When ordinary people meet, talk in an ordinary way is the way in which progress is normally made. It is the provisional thesis of this piece that this type of exchange in medical care is in shorter supply than it should be. But can this really unearth deeper issues?

How thick is your case and how deep the anxiety?

The story of the 'case' the Dean gave to me is in one sense ridiculously simplified. It leaves us all unsatisfied. Speculating on what we do not know could take up the rest of this essay. In *ITC*, we suggested that complexity was part of human life and should be sought when we are making moral assessments if we possibly can. The whole structure of *ITC* was intended to show the many different facets of a judgement that could and should be brought into play, to show how 'thick' a case could be. Compared with this, the Dean's case is diaphanously thin. But it is what we have, and it comes for a reason.

The Dean had later indicated that he thought his patient would not have been in that situation 'if she had seen a decent general practitioner' instead of coming straight to the hospital's Accident & Emergency Department. In A&E she would have had some sort of triage, but would quickly have been seen by surgeons in some guise or other. But would any 'decent general practitioner' have discussed the young woman's family situation rather than packing her and her abdominal pain off quickly to hospital? The GP thinker and academic, Marshall Marinker, was fond of saying that the GP's job was to marginalise danger, just as the specialist's was to marginalise ignorance.[5] Even if the first doctor knew about the family situation and if the pain had come on gradually, no one would have wanted any more delay than was actually necessary before this patient saw a surgeon.

But the Dean asked an ordinary question in an ordinary way. It is unlikely that it had not been asked before, although the anxiety surrounding her pain and her admission may have made it impossible for her to answer her surgeons as she did the Dean. Immediately we trip up on one of the ways that medical encounters are different from others. We may be anxious about the car's flat battery or that our internet is not working, but the implications of those sorts of questions do not distress us deeply; and it certainly is not usually in the back of our minds that the person we are seeing *may* make the matter worse. But most people, statistically speaking, are not driven to their doctor by serious illness but by the *fear* of serious illness: and there is intrinsic to medical practice the extra possibility that the intervention will in some way create further harm. That anxiety may add to the original worry to mean that, whether anxiety really was part of the original presentation, it is now, as the consultation starts. Together with the concern doctors may feel to get the diagnosis right and to cope with their workload, this all means that tension could be very high in such an interaction. Good communications have to be established in the space between the participants to reduce this tension, as surely as asepsis has to be addressed before an operation.

Assuming, as here we must, that the Dean had come closer to the cause of the pain than his colleagues, we must also acknowledge that the story he uncovered is not that unusual, in the sense that as human beings our bodies often hurt when we are distressed: that sort of pain, in the world as it is now, may take us into medical care. Many studies have born witness to the fact that sizeable proportions of patients seen by physically orientated specialists are also grappling with anxiety or depression, and mechanisms have been proposed. Socially induced pain exists, may be severe and may resist resolution.[6] It may well be that work has to be done in a special place and in a special way to get beyond presenting symptoms, seen from the clinician's angle. But if the Dean did indeed get to an important point, how, in addition to setting the discussion up so well, did it go so well? Were he and his patient just lucky?

The nose

The Dean's schedule was clearly quite relaxed. For most of today's hard-pressed National Health Service staff, task follows task like frightening white water rafting. Busy and focused professionals, following a protocol and adhering to

5 Catherine Foot *et al.*, *The Quality of GP Diagnosis and Referral* (London: King's Fund 2010).
6 Zhansheng Chen *et al.*, 'When Hurt Will Not Heal: Exploring the Capacity to Relive Social and Physical Pain' (2008) 19(8) *Psychological Science* 789.

best practice, still need a second sense to enable them to 'smell', as it were, something else that is going on. To stay with the metaphor, the key thing is to sniff and to want to know what is being smelt. To explain this more fully, consider another incident at the beginning of my training, far from general practice.

As a resident in an infectious disease unit, part of my job was to be on alert for serious conditions: young people with certain types of meningitis, for instance, can be overwhelmed with septicaemia even as one's talking to them, so we often took the history as we were preparing to do a lumbar puncture. One night a policeman arrived in A&E acutely unwell with dramatic neck stiffness and no obvious injury or other neurology: classic meningitis territory. As I assembled my lumbar puncture kit, I asked him the routine questions about other contacts with infectious diseases. 'Like what, doctor?' 'Like a nasty flu or hepatitis'. 'What's hepatitis?' 'A liver infection that makes you go yellow.' 'Well, I've just run over a Chinaman.' I stopped what I was preparing. I realised I was seeing not a dangerously ill but a desperately frightened young man, rigid with fear and remorse at what he had done in a car chase, facing censure or charges and pretty likely to lose his job. As he began to talk, his body relaxed.

However horrid his experience and however unpleasant his throw-away racism, in the heat of the moment, we landed on a childish association that allowed him to 'come out of hiding', challenge my jargon and tell me what was really wrong. There may seem no logic in this, but it does underline the fact that old sayings like 'I was rigid with fright' express something of how our bodies behave under stress. People really do waste away with grief, worries often really are headaches, being in love still does make a lover tremble and sweat. None of this goes away in the age of microsurgery and genetic engineering. And when people do not understand it in themselves, they may come to the doctor.

Whether clinicians include these ideas as part of their differential diagnosis system, however, is a great deal less certain. Perhaps the most common, weight loss in grief, is not part of the usual medical student's 'causes of weight loss' list. That 'decent GPs' understood was due to their personality, their training or wrought from a lot of careful listening. There has been an acknowledgement recently that emotional intelligence is a real and separate thing from the sort tested by IQ assessments, and it in turn can be improved by teaching those who are naturally less skilled but can be persuaded to learn.[7] That it is usually hard to find such teaching within the standard medical school curriculum is a problem needing to be addressed. But there are some big caveats.

Not 'either/or' but 'both/and'

Although it would be foolhardy for a doctor to make a primary diagnosis of anxiety in someone with severe abdominal pain, for a patient the circular effect

---

7 Daniel Goleman, *Emotional Intelligence: Why It Can Matter More Than IQ* (London, Bloomsbury Publishing 1996).

of symptom, then distress, then associations (say, memories of others with the symptom or a TV programme) make it all deeper and wider.[8] The odd thing is that at the point of entering medical care there is often a sudden change: all emotional or psychological aspects may be discounted. Also, once a person has had a positive diagnosis, say of cancer or heart disease, the anxiety caused by further symptoms is not only completely reasonable but also very hard for an individual to handle without help. But patients understand that for their symptoms to be thought to be (and worse, to be labelled) 'psychological' would mean not to be taken seriously and so to be shown the door. Understandable as this may perhaps be on a surgical ward, it is ultimately self-defeating. On the most basic assessment, *all* symptoms must be felt 'in the mind', and to leave that part of our natures uncared for is simply bad medicine. Skilled and sensitive clinicians are perfectly able to handle both aspects of an interaction. But what should happen if they are not?

Minding the mind

Apart from the 'decent GP', the small number of mind doctors, psychiatrists, rightly have a special training, but over my clinical lifetime this has become focused mostly on serious psychotic illness using closed systems of thinking and regulated care on the same model as somatic medicine. So while patients wonder what a symptom 'means' for them, and become more skilled at thinking about the role of their distress in bringing it on, specialists in the mind have turned almost completely away from open questions or interpretation, and what the symptom means to the patient has come to have no meaning at all: in discussion in the profession, even if it presents clues to help clear up a problem, it is usually ignored.

So it is not surprising that clinicians in somatic medicine develop a narrow focus and become distressed themselves when the dial points elsewhere. If the patient's symptoms indicate distress, who is there to help the physician, let alone the patient? As one doctor expressed it to me, 'I don't want to ask ordinary questions about their lives, as this would open up a can of worms and I don't know what to do to get them back in the can!' In a complex and highly charged atmosphere where a life is at risk, a focus is needed that can easily be disturbed by emotional factors: the hand trembles, the eye blurs, mistakes are made. A cool brain is needed. This is not the time to talk about experiences, families, or anxieties real or imagined. To add to that, although support and supervision are in place in many other professions, doctors are still largely on their own in this regard and, if they get distressed or things go really wrong, there is little between them and the law.

8 Roger Higgs and Anne Stephenson, *Psychological Issues in General Practice*, (Boca Raton, Taylor & Francis 2011).

The profession and the pedestal

All sick people must want their doctors to be as powerful as possible when coming to their aid: but for physicians, given their expectations of themselves and their necessary anxiety in their daily work, it seems likely that they see themselves powerful or protected in other ways too. In 1984, just after *ITC* was published, I heard Nicholas Kraemer, the conductor of an opera called *Beauty and the Beast* (Ross Griffel M 2013) performed in the grounds of an Italian monastery, explain on TV his take on the meaning its creator had given to this tale.[9] In his view, the Beast could only be helped by Beauty when she had been able to come off her pedestal, which he likened to what we all experience to be the pedestal from which doctors and police work. His insight was that this descent from the pedestal was (in the opera) and could be (in real life) *transformative* in some circumstances, Although clearly needing to use the power of their knowledge and position most of the time, Kraemer suggested the possibility that in certain instances or situations it is only by voluntarily surrendering something, coming off their pedestal, that doctors may transform the 'beastiness' of their patient and create the possibility of a 'beautiful' cure.

Fanciful or not, as Balint observed in his ground-breaking discussions with GPs faced with difficult patients 60 years ago, a doctor has the 'urge to prove to the patient, to the whole world and above all to himself, that he is good, kind and knowledgeable and helpful'.[10] That self-belief is strongly defended psychologically in a number of ways. One is the use of jargon that confirms membership of the special group. That language is not just for internal use but is turned outwards and colours the whole of the doctor's views of his work and where the boundaries lie. Balint thought that every doctor has a 'vague, but almost unshakeable, belief of how a patient ought to behave when ill', which compels him to convert his patients to his own standards and beliefs. This will be satisfactory much of the time, but when symptoms are to be explained differently or there is a clash within the consultation that requires resolution by normal interchange between two people, on a level, discussion from a pedestal in a style of talk that is not shared simply will not do.

Ordinary questions

As I replayed in my mind the interviews I had witnessed that had seemed so unsatisfactory, it was suddenly clear that the paucity of ordinary talk in those interviews was the mark of something wrong that went near to the heart of this issue. Ordinary talk is a sign: not necessarily of the presence of empathic thinking but, in the context of medical interactions certainly, its *sine qua non at certain*

---

9 Margaret Griffell, *Operas in English: A Dictionary* (Westport Connecticut, Greenwood Press 1999).

10 Michael Balint, *The Doctor, His Patient, and The Illness* (London, Churchill Livingstone 1957).

points in the interview. In gauging the moral health of the interaction, the normal temperature is the presence of ordinary talk.

In what way is talk *ordinary*? Discussion of 'registers' in studies of speech may seem a little clumsy and out of date now philology has been taken so far from different directions. How it is expressed of course varies from culture to culture. But broadly most languages have an official or high version that is reserved for high-status interaction, law courts or official work, and coarse or low speech that is for very informal occasions, while normal discussion between strangers or near-strangers is in a style that is demotic and can be considered 'ordinary'. Ordinary talk is not based on professional jargon but depends on what is ordinarily spoken in the cultural and geographical area in question. If a musician played or a speaker gave a presentation and the audience did not clap at the end, there would be a clear gap and a negative message would be being conveyed. This is the sort of absence I believe there to be when ordinary talk goes missing in a medical encounter.

The sort of ordinary questions that bring rewards are worth noting. 'What's happened to you?' 'Are you feeling unsafe?' 'What are you most afraid of?' 'Have you felt like this before?' 'Am I asking you the right sort of questions?' There is the sense that there is a thread waiting to be pulled. In a similar way, the young policeman asked me to step outside my jargon, and so stopped my manic medical behaviour and enabled us to confront, together, the tragedy that had just occurred. Clinical history taking has been refined over so many years. But it does seem odd not to use ordinary speech when it reaches places that standard medical questioning cannot.

The deeper content of ordinary talk

We should remind ourselves what is there in ordinary talk. Greeting is so important because it contains an acknowledgement not only of the other person's presence and importance but also of their relevance, of their potential impact on the greeter; and so begins a relationship, even of the most trivial or superficial sort. It contains an acknowledgement of equality and shared values within the context: the other person's right to be there, say, or that we both are happy with them behaving as they are. The action of shaking hands may have originated in showing that we are unarmed, but it too carries the values that circulate around equality. Suddenly we are using very big concepts that may seem too heavy for the fragility of chat in a chance human meeting. Am I really signing up to the ideas of the Enlightenment merely by grinning at someone and saying hello? Is that not freighting ordinary talk with more than it can carry?

Questions of scale and scope

When starting out it might have seemed that a bad-tempered or inattentive clinician was something quite petty, even trivial. My claim is that, unfortunately, small things can make a great difference. It comes to mind that the word 'trivial' has its origins in the Latin for crossroads, where the Roman saw three possible ways forward. (The word presumably 'went downhill' because it was at the crossroads where people met to gossip – itself a word with more august origins.) But the original concept indicted that here and now there were decisions to be made about direction, and it is my contention that the trivial things in human interaction, when there is a problem, show us that there is something to examine.

Perhaps we are expecting too much: we cannot turn good scientists into great communicators overnight. Clinicians would not be doing their job if they were not at least minimally altruistic: I should not ask to remodel human beings who are doing their best. Two things should be said to that. Professional skills courses have been developed in medical curricula to do just that very thing: and my concern here is that such courses are not taking ordinary talk seriously. Technical skill and detailed medical knowledge may not always be at a premium as they are now: looking to the future, if computers could take over most medical work, it is not the human and interactive tasks in medicine that appear to be vulnerable.

Doctors may be no less rude or thoughtless than the people they are dealing with, but given the importance of good communication when meeting a sick and anxious person, it seems odd that this is not brought under control. My argument is that ordinary talk, what happens normally when people meet, seems to be associated with taking seriously ordinary concerns (the important content of politeness); that its absence sometimes in clinical practice seems associated with bad feelings and attendant behaviours, and is possibly part of the reason some interactions of the sort I have described become difficult. If I am right, why do doctors go short on ordinary talk? Why does putting on a white coat or a set of blue scrubs suddenly change language? Does the barista in the lunch break get the same treatment? If not, why not?

Medical pathology

We can immediately say that a highly technical area will have its own talk: when this talk has to be done at high speed to achieve results, there is bound to be a problem in interaction with other domains. Time is of the essence. But also all power corrupts. Doctors have high social status at present, training is arduous and competition to join and to succeed is intense. All these contribute to the 'corner cutting' we have outlined. But is there more?

All professions or ways of life, however meritorious, have their dark side. Sometimes this is about preserving the integrity of the group from intrusion by non-members (who have not taken the right steps to learn the codes), but sometimes it is caused by 'invasion' or 'contamination' by the very problem or group that the profession is set up to deal with. Bent coppers, lawless briefs and mad psychiatrists are not just the stuff of fiction. News in hot summers is often about serious fires, and some of these turn out to be started by off-duty firemen. In response to these sorts of concerns, professions raise the barriers high against such contamination. One taboo is becoming a patient: it is unusual for doctors to phone in sick. When I was recovering from a cancer operation in my own hospital, several colleagues passed me by with a look of horror on their faces as I took my drip stand for a walk down the corridor. As one senior nurse joked to me, I had 'gone over to the other side'. When a person is ill, they are excused duties like washing up or going to work, and it seems in some way as if in exchange doctors have excused themselves the ordinary duties of ordinary talk.

Fanciful or not, it is clear that most doctors have high views of their work, so high that they tolerate both the burdens of stringent moral values and, in the UK at least, an immense amount of legal shaping of their activities. The 'system' demands dedication, and there is no such thing, in management terms, as too much work for a doctor to do. But no one is a robot, and so there are limits. Rather than break down, one strategy may be to save time on ordinary talk and its associated behaviours.

Back to medical ethics

It will have been clear by implication, I hope, how medical ethics may practically contribute to the examination of the questions I have raised, simply samples of what could and should be considered. Such a survey of what may be lost when ordinary talk is not allowed or is not attended to is in many ways superficial and certainly not adequate. But recognising the rarity of opportunities to negotiate in ordinary ways in the context of medical care raises one final concern within the practice of medical ethics itself.

One of the important contributions medical ethics has made in medical care has been to focus on the idea of arguments: that we should be explicit about our *reasons* for doing things, so that the pros and cons of a particular approach or action may be discussed. One of the clear contrasts with one of our older academic siblings, philosophy, is that debates in medical ethics usually have time limits: medical care demands a conclusion, because something has to be done. Law in practice has to come to a conclusion too: but here there is a winner or a loser, even if there is opportunity for appeal. But in ordinary life, the lives involved in ordinary talk, things are often very different. Even if one set of arguments for or against a medical action has prevailed, very often the contrary or 'losing' options *remain in force*, morally speaking. In ordinary life, such contrary arguments would still have force to modify behaviour, say, or to mitigate the less humane sides of a decision. Ordinary talk may be transformative, as we have seen, but also may remind us of our ordinary actions and obligations *as human beings*. Interpersonal understanding, 'the benefit of the doubt', offering respect or challenge and give and take – even informal mediation – are all part of that world. If ordinary talk and its extraordinarily powerful effects are to be reclaimed for medical care and patients, the young people in medicine who have already begun to make these sort of moves must be backed by the powerful thinking and arguments of medical ethics: and people who work in that field in turn must preserve their own integrity and ability to talk about ordinary talk in ordinary ways that will make a difference. Medical practice may be a bit harder, but the cases themselves will surely be less so. I owe it to that mother, to the Dean and to Campbell to say so.

6 Human tissue

A story from a small state

Margaret Brazier and Sheila McLean

Introduction

When we began our careers in the Faculties of Law at Manchester and Glasgow Universities, modern medical law was barely more than an embryo. As the years passed, medical law grew and developed alongside its twin, medical ethics, or, as it came to be styled, bioethics. Interactions and collaboration between the lawyers and the bioethicists were useful, exciting and at times heated. Among the army of bioethicists, Alastair V. Campbell stands out as a scholar of huge intellect and a man of great compassion. We have both been fortunate to work with him. His ability to communicate complex ideas and recognise that, in matters of heated controversy, rationality alone is not enough was a source of support to both of us. Working with Campbell was always fun: he knew when the time had come to pause and open the chilled white wine or fine whisky.

Campbell's scholarship covers an immense range of bioethical debates. As Gareth Jones says in his essay (Chapter 13) in this collection, Campbell's work on the significance of the human body contributes originally and forcefully to the many debates that touch on our attitudes to bodies and human tissue. Human tissue, its uses and misuses, is a vexed question in relation to which both of us have worked with Campbell in translating ethical debate into law and public policy. Addressing some small part of the human tissue story from the UK seemed a suitable tribute to our friend and colleague.

In 2018, the question of how the law should regulate cadaver organ donation is once again being debated in that small state in the north of Europe, the UK. At the time of writing, within the UK, three separate statutes govern transplantation, retention and use of human tissue: the Human Tissue Act 2004 (England and Northern Ireland, and Wales except in relation to cadaver organ donation for transplant); the Human Transplantation (Wales) Act 2013; and the Human Tissue (Scotland) Act 2006. Wales has introduced a system of soft 'opt out'. The Scottish government has confirmed that it will bring forward legislation to move to soft 'opt out' in Scotland.[1] A consultation to amend the law in England is

1 Scottish Government, 'Organ Donation and Transplantation' (Scottish Government RiaghaLtas na h-Alba govscot, 8 January 2018) <www.gov.scot/Topics/Health/Services/OrganDonation> accessed 5 June 2018.

under way closing on 6 March 2018.[2] As we note later, the proposals for a change in England have not met with universal support.

One factor is common across the UK, as is the case globally: there remains a large gap between the supply and demand for organs and many patients still die awaiting a transplant.[3] Nor is the transplant deficit the only problem caused by a shortage of donated human tissue. Medical schools find it hard to obtain sufficient bodies for anatomical dissection. Researchers complain that crucial research is impeded by lack of tissue.

As Jones (Chapter 13) explains, transplantation is far from the only beneficial use to which the dead body and its parts may be put. Medical students need corpses to dissect and learn from. Doctors need organs to develop new surgical procedures and train junior doctors. Human tissue is central to research. These other uses of human remains are what have so often given rise to fear, distrust and hostility, muddying the waters of debates on the regulation of organ donation for transplantation. In England in particular, debates on organs for transplant have sometimes been obscured by concern and controversy about other uses of the dead body and its parts.

Failure to understand the perspective of the family and the crucial importance that many people attach to the manner in which the dead are laid to rest has again and again opened up a chasm of misunderstanding between science and popular opinion. Campbell's scholarship brings new dimensions to philosophical reflection on the body.[4] His work in helping to frame public policy in addressing how the law should regulate uses of human tissue set him a challenging task in seeking to reconcile divergent opinions and bring together ethics and humanity.

In our essay, we first examine briefly why for centuries the treatment of the corpse has been a source of controversy and occasionally criminality and violence in the UK. Then we will look at the organ retention scandals at the turn of this century and their aftermath – events in which Campbell and both authors were heavily involved. We will seek to understand why the bodies of the dead remain a matter of public concern, especially in England, and how that concern affects today's debates on organ transplantation and any change in the law from 'opt in' to 'opt out'. Finally, we reflect on the role of academics, such as Campbell, in shaping and informing policy.

Contested bodies: the spectre of the body snatchers

As the twentieth century approached its end, evidence emerged into the public domain that throughout the UK pathologists had routinely retained human tissue

2 Department of Health and Social Care, 'Introducing "Opt-Out" Consent for Organ and Tissue Donation in England' (GOV.UK, 12 December 2017) <www.gov.uk/government/ consultations/introducing-opt-out-consent-for-organ-and-tissue-donation-in-england> accessed 5 June 2018

3 NHS Blood and Transplant, *Organ Donation and Transplantation: Activity Report 2016–17* (Department of Health, London 2017).

4 Alastair V. Campbell, *The Body in Bioethics* (Abingdon, Routledge, 2009).

and organs (and, in the case of stillborn infants, whole bodies) without consent from the deceased or their families. In many, but not all, cases the organs were retained for good ends, including medical research and training. Many families were outraged.[5] In the case of retention of organs from babies and small children, parents accused doctors of stealing their children's organs, desecrating bodies.[6] Outrage was not confined to retention of organs from children. In particular, certain faith communities abhorred the retention of any parts of the body given the strict rules relating to burying the body intact. While unauthorised organ retention took place both south and north of the Scottish border and across the Irish Sea in Northern Ireland, and resulted in the establishment of public bodies to address the practice, it should be noted that popular outcry was at its most vociferous in England and Wales. In the next section, we deal more fully with the 'organ scandals' of the turn of the century. First, echoing Jones, we emphasise how the treatment of the dead has for centuries been a cause of controversy and public concern in the UK. In her seminal book, *Death, Dissection and the Destitute*, historian Ruth Richardson has shown how the history of the treatment, or mistreatment, of the corpse influences popular conceptions of organs and tissue to this day.[7]

Jones sets out some of the history of dissection in continental Europe, and how doctors began to learn more about the human body and its ills via the growth of the 'anatomical renaissance'. Sawday recounts how, in great cities across Europe, the public flocked to watch the surgeons at work in the anatomy theatres.[8] Enthusiasm for science and dissection among the elite in Europe was not always shared by the less educated and poorer people who were more likely to end up on the dissecting table. In England and Scotland, such fears were particularly deeply embedded: many ordinary people feared that, were their mortal remains eviscerated by the anatomists, their bodies would not be resurrected on the Day of Judgment. After initial scepticism of the anatomical renaissance on the part of the College of Physicians, English and Scottish doctors wanted to be able to emulate their European peers, and needed corpses to dissect. In 1506, King James IV of Scotland came to their aid and granted the Guild of Surgeons in Edinburgh a number of corpses of executed criminals, an example later followed in England by the Scottish King's brother-in-law, Henry VIII. The number of bodies so provided still fell well short of the demands of the anatomists and the source, the bodies of convicted criminals, tainted the image of dissection for centuries. The attempt in the 'Murder Act' of 1752 to meet demand for corpses for dissection by allowing judges to impose an additional penalty of dissection after

---

5 Margaret Brazier and Emma Cave, *Medicine, Patients and the Law* (6th edn, Manchester University Press 2011) 545–551; Alastair V. Campbell and Michaela Willis, 'They Stole My Baby's Soul: Narratives of Embodiment and Loss' (2005) 31 *Medical Humanities* 101.

6 Campbell (n 3) 96.

7 Ruth Richardson, *Death, Dissection and the Destitute* (2nd edn, Chicago University Press 2000) 409.

8 Jonathan Sawday, *The Body Emblazoned: Dissection and the Human Body in Renaissance Culture* (Manchester University Press 1995).

hanging in the case of especially horrid murders as 'a further Terror and Mark of Infamy' once again failed to balance supply and demand.[9]

In bridging the gap, a new breed of criminals emerged: the notorious 'body snatchers'.[10] Sometimes known as the 'Resurrectionists', gangs took bodies from the grave to sell to the anatomy schools. In London, Bishop and Williamson eventually decided on a more direct approach. Rather than wait for a grave to rob, they murdered their victims, usually people who were poor and destitute, and unlikely to be missed. In Edinburgh, Burke and Hare skipped the grave-robbing stage and moved straight to a lucrative business of killing the poor and unloved and selling their bodies. There can be little doubt that, in London and Edinburgh, anatomists connived in grave robbing and were unlikely to be unaware of the murderous practices of some of the body snatchers.[11] The impact of the use of dissection as the supreme penalty for crime coupled with the criminal activities of the body snatchers tarnished the reputation of the very science the anatomists sought to promote.[12]

By 1800, senior doctors and Parliamentarians saw the urgent need for reform. After several versions of an Anatomy Bill had been debated and failed to reach the statute book, the Anatomy Act 1832 became law *inter alia* repealing the Murder Act and seeking to distance the study of anatomy and the process of dissection from the taint of criminality. But as Richardson so eloquently describes, the new 1832 Act was perceived as the means for doctors to grab the bodies of the poor and indigent.[13] The Act allowed for donation of bodies – what today we might describe as an 'opt-in' system. It also allowed for bodies to be taken on the authority of the person in lawful possession of the dead body where no wishes had been expressed by the deceased – that is, 'opt out'. For the unfortunate paupers incarcerated in a workhouse, that person would be the master of the workhouse. Ordinary people feared that few workhouse inmates would have expressed any wishes about the fate of their corpse and, even if they had, those wishes might well be simply ignored. For much of the populace, the Anatomy Act constituted legalised body snatching. In a series of riots, the anatomy school in Sheffield was burned to the ground.[14]

The anger and deep distress expressed by many ordinary people over the centuries about dissection were often sneered at by more educated people and those deeply committed to advancing the science of medicine. Popular beliefs about the resurrection of the body and cultural customs surrounding respect for the corpse were dismissed as mere superstition. It may be noted, however, that very few of the educated elite chose to donate their bodies to science.

---

9 Margaret Brazier and Suzanne Ost, *Medicine and Bioethics in the Theatre of the Criminal Process* (Cambridge University Press 2013) 20; Richardson (n 7).

10 Richardson (n 7) 75.

11 ibid 57, 137.

12 Brazier and Ost (n 9).

13 Richardson (n 7) 220.

14 ibid 260.

Organ retention in the twentieth century: England and Wales

In the days of the anatomical renaissance and the battles surrounding the Anatomy Act, the possibility that organs might be taken from the dead and transplanted into another individual whose own kidney, heart, liver or other organs were failing was distantly considered by some scientists and surgeons, including the (in)famous John Hunter.[15] It was not until the mid-twentieth century that organ transplants became reality. Qualms about the legality of removing organs for transplant were met by legislation first to 'legalise' corneal transplants (Corneal Grafting Act 1952), and later, in the Human Tissue Act 1961, to provide for lawful removal and donation of human organs from the dead. The 1961 Act provided that a person in lawful possession of the dead body (probably the hospital authority when the person died in hospital) could authorise 'removal of any part of the body [of the deceased] to be used after his death for therapeutic purposes or for purposes of medical education or research' providing that either:

(1)   Before his death, the deceased had expressed a request that his body be so used after his death; or if;

(2)   After 'having made such reasonable enquiry as may be practicable', he had no reason to believe that the deceased had expressed an objection to his body being so used or that the surviving spouse or any surviving relative so objected.

Note that the 1961 Act made no reference to *consent* and applied not just to donation of body parts for transplant but also to donation for medical education and research.[16] Initially the Act provoked little comment and such academic commentary as there was focused largely on the loose language of the Act, the absence of any redress for breaches of the rules and the failure of the legislation to facilitate transplantation.[17] Much later, when the organ retention 'scandals' entered the public domain, the 1961 Act (together with a raft of other statutory and common law rules relating to dead bodies) was soundly condemned as both complex and obscure.[18] In the decades following the passing of the 1961 Act, very different approaches to the Act were taken by transplant teams seeking agreement from families to remove organs for transplant, and other doctors, especially pathologists, retaining organs and tissue after post-mortem examinations for medical research and education. Transplant teams interpreted the Act so cautiously that potential donations were lost. Many other doctors,

---

15 Wendy Moore, *The Knife Man: The Extraordinary Life and Times of John Hunter, Father of Modern Surgery* (Bantam Press, London 2005) 217.

16 Peter D.G. Skegg, 'The Use of Corpses for Medical Education and Research: The Legal Requirements' (1991) 31 *Medicine, Science and the Law* 345.

17 Gerald Dworkin, 'The Law Relating to Organ Donation in England' (1988) 33 *Modern Law Review* 353.

18 Bristol Royal Infirmary Interim Report, *Removal and Retention of Human Material* (UK 2000) 20.

including pathologists, were unaware that the Act applied to their activities when after a post-mortem examination they retained organs for research or teaching purposes.[19]

Evidence of a widespread practice of organ and tissue retention first came to public knowledge during the Inquiry established in 1998 to investigate the paediatric cardiac service at Bristol Royal Infirmary.[20] Over a long period of time, organs and tissue had been taken at, or after, post-mortem examinations from children's bodies and used 'for a variety of purposes, including audit, medical education and research, or had simply been stored'. The interim Inquiry report noted that this had become an 'issue of great and grave concern', generating an outcry not confined to the Bristol parents.[21] Giving evidence to the Inquiry, Professor R.H. Anderson commented on the many collections of children's hearts elsewhere, including the largest collection at Liverpool's Alder Hey Children's Hospital. Parents in Liverpool exploded with anger and a further independent confidential Inquiry was set up by the English Department of Health, chaired by Michael Redfern QC, and directed to investigate the removal and disposal of human organs and tissue following post-mortem examinations at Alder Hey.

The report of that inquiry, the Redfern Report, revealed long-standing practices of removing and retaining children's organs without the consent or even knowledge of parents. In some cases, all the infants' organs were removed and what was returned to their families was an 'empty shell'. As in Bristol, some organs and tissue were simply stored and not put to good use. In some instances, the whole foetus or stillborn infant was kept and stored in pots.[22] The report also catalogued subsequent mishandling of requests for the return of children's organs and other mismanagement that exacerbated public anger in Liverpool.

In January 2001, the Chief Medical Officer (CMO) for England published a census surveying the extent of organ retention since 1970 across the NHS in England and Wales.[23] The census established that practices whereby pathologists simply took and retained human organs and tissue after post-mortem examination were routine and often failed to comply with the Human Tissue Act 1961. Adequate and free consent from the bereaved family was rarely obtained or thought necessary. In some cases, families signed forms agreeing to donate 'tissue' not contemplating that tissue might mean whole and/or multiple organs. They thought that tissue meant a few slivers of cells.[24] The CMO's census showed that organ retention was not limited to children.

19 Retained Organs Commission, *Remembering the Past: Looking to the Future* (UK, Department of Health 2004).

20 Bristol Royal Infirmary Inquiry, *The Report of the Public Inquiry into Children's Heart Surgery at the Bristol Royal Infirmary 1984–1995* (UK, National Archives 2001)

21 Bristol Royal Infirmary Interim Report (n 18).

22 Royal Liverpool Children's Inquiry, *Report of the Royal Liverpool Children's Inquiry* (London, House of Commons 2001)

23 Department of Health, *Report of a Census of Organs and Tissues Retained by Pathology Services in England* (London, The Stationery Office, 2001).

24 Margaret Brazier, 'Retained Organs: Ethics and Humanity' (2002) 22(4) *Legal Studies* 550.

Across the whole of the UK, families, backed by a sympathetic media, demanded information as to whether their relative had been the subject of organ retention. In many, but not all, cases families called for the return for burial or cremation of any organs and tissue still stored, and new laws to ensure that in future no body parts could be taken without consent.

We do not dispute the value of human organs and tissue to medicine and human good. Tests on organs and tissue may benefit the immediate family, for example by revealing a propensity to suffer from genetic disease. Much medical research is dependent on access to human organs and tissue. Research into at present incurable neurodegenerative diseases such as motor neurone disease needs donated brains. Medical education requires such material.

Why then did the disclosure that doctors had been collecting organs and tissue for good ends in many cases result in public outcry and media frenzy? Seeking to address that public outcry, in January 2001, the Secretary of State for Health for England, who described the Redfern Report as the most shocking he had ever read,[25] established a special health authority, the NHS Retained Organs Commission (ROC), to manage the process in England and Wales by which NHS trusts provided information to families about organ retention, oversee the process of organ return, act as an advocate for families to develop a new regulatory framework for organ and tissue retention, and advise on new legislation. Brazier chaired the ROC and Campbell was the vice-chair. Public meetings were held in most major cities in England and in Cardiff. Often the meetings were volatile, highly emotional and very occasionally frightening.

The reasons for the reaction to news of 'modern' organ retention and its depiction as the return of the 'body snatchers' are complex. At ROC meetings, as Campbell himself has written, it became clear that for many families who learned that they had not buried or cremated their child or other relative whole and intact, the distress of finding that they had not laid their dead, especially a dead child, to rest was overwhelming.[26] The physical remains of the person they had loved, the body, was all they had left and that had been taken from them. A number of families, including orthodox Jews, Muslims, Hindus and some Christians, regarded it as a religious imperative to bury or burn the body intact.[27] Such families, had they been asked to consent to retention, would have refused to consent. However, for other families who expressed fury on learning the fate of a relative's body, what angered them was the loss of control over their relative's burial or cremation, made worse in some instances by what was perceived as deceit. Some relatives said publicly that had they been consulted they would have agreed to doctors retaining the organs of their dead relative. Some had even offered to consent to donation for transplant to be told that the deceased's organs were not suitable for

25 BBC news, 'Parents Await "Shocking" Report' (BBC News, 30 January 2001)<http://news.bbc.co.uk/2/hi/health/1143466.stm> accessed 5 June 2018.

26 Campbell (n 4).

27 Sheelagh McGuinness, 'Respecting the Living Means Respecting the Dead Too' (2008) 28(2) *Oxford Journal of Legal Studies* 297.

transplant, but not told that the organs would be retained for other purposes.[28] Families condemned a lack of respect, feeling that someone whom they loved 'had been treated as a mere convenience, treated with contempt'. In those cases where it was not possible to discover what had happened to the retained organs and those where enquiries showed that organs had simply been stored in pots and not put to any use, anger was particularly acute. Family support groups sprang up in many cities, most notably in Liverpool, PITY II (Parents who Inter Their Young Twice), and in Bristol, the National Committee on Organ Retention (NACOR).

Doctors and scientists struggled to understand the outcry. Physician and philosopher Ray Tallis recounts how Alder Hey Hospital was 'besieged by bereaved parents' and its 'doctors and managers were demonised'. Tallis graphically describes the initial response of much of the media, which had a field day carrying banner headlines such as 'BASEMENT OF HORRORS', 'most gruesome chapters in the history of the National Health Service'.[29] At ROC meetings, doctors and scientists had reason to feel under attack but failed to understand why families should be so angry. Save for a few rogue clinicians, doctors retaining organs believed that they were doing good, often considering that in not giving full and frank information to relatives they were acting to save families from distress.[30] Doctors had little if any understanding of the Human Tissue Act, an Act which we have already noted was vague and obscure.

Distressed families and the medical professionals had little understanding of the others' point of view. Faced with what they saw as disdainful dismissal of their grievances, labelled irrational and delusory, families' anger and suspicion increased and angry demands were made for 'justice', which in essence expressed the belief that the 'guilty medics' should be prosecuted. Confronted by the spectre of the jailhouse door, some scientists and doctors fought back, claiming that many relatives were either sublimating their own emotions of grief, and maybe guilt, at the death of a relative or were simply out to get compensation, or both.[31]

ROC meetings became the forum in which the opposing parties met. Efforts were made to try and establish dialogue, efforts in which Campbell played a leading role. His ability to convey difficult concepts with clarity, so evident in his writing, was present in his work to seek reconciliation. His background as a pastor further enabled him to appreciate the hurt of those whose concerns were rooted in faith.

It was against this background of conflict that work began to prepare new laws to replace the Human Tissue Act 1961 in England, Wales and Northern Ireland. In the event, the ROC played a relatively minor role in the drafting of what was to become the Human Tissue Act 2004. The Department of Health, after the

28 Royal Liverpool Children's Inquiry (n 22).
29 Raymond Tallis, *Hippocratic Oaths: Medicine and Its Discontent* (London, Atlantic Books 2004) 186.
30 Alastair V. Campbell *et al.*, 'Human Tissue Legislation: Listening to the Professionals' (2008) 34(2) *Journal of Medical Ethics* 104.
31 Tallis (n 29).

Secretary of State's initial full-blown support of the Liverpool families, became worried about the backlash from medicine and science and may have considered that the ROC had become too much of an advocate for the families.

Organ retention: Scotland

The publicity given to organ retention in England and Wales naturally raised concerns in families in Scotland whose children had died. Several 'pressure groups' of parents were formed and lobbied long and hard for a public inquiry to be set up in order to discover whether or not organs and/or tissue had been retained without their agreement or knowledge. The then Minister for Health and Community Care, Susan Deacon MSP, declined to hold a public inquiry, but agreed to establish an independent review group, chaired by one of us (McLean) to inquire into past practices, including organs or tissue potentially retained by the prosecution where such retention was deemed to be in the interests of justice. In the course of the review group's inquiries, it was also asked to produce a separate report on the possible retention of bones that were used in research to identify levels of absorption of Strontium-90, a known carcinogen, following the atmospheric testing of so-called 'dirty' bombs. While this issue was less controversial and less well publicised, it also arguably provided some of the most important information gleaned from retained tissue and was influential in shaping the Partial Test Ban Treaty in 1963.[32] In passing, a fascinating fact about Strontium-90 is that it is named after the small hamlet of Strontian on the west coast of Scotland where it was first identified. Professor Lenihan, one of the researchers involved in the Glasgow arm of the project, described it as follows, 'The Glasgow work ... has involved a lot of careful scientific studies and has produced a unique collection of data – reviewed along with projects on many other aspects of the fall-out problem ...' He further noted that at the close of the 'second international conference on strontium metabolism ... a piper will play the 'Lament for the Children' to signify the end of an earnest and humane scientific endeavour'.[33]

In November 2001, the review group presented its final report on organ retention to the Minister for Health and Community Care. For the review group, the critical issue throughout its inquiries was the question of the involvement of parents (in particular) in what happened to their children even after their death. Very few cases in Scotland involved the removal and retention of organs or tissue from adults. It was parents who seemed most distressed and most active in pursuing their concerns. As a general proposition, it was agreed that failure adequately to involve families by a full discussion of options, conducted in circumstances conducive to the sympathetic disclosure of information and

32 Independent Review Group on Retention of Organs at Post-Mortem, 'Independent Review Group on the Retention of Organs at Post-Mortem: Report on Strontium 90 Research' (March 2002) <www.sehd.scot.nhs.uk/scotorgrev/Strontium%2090%20Report/roos90.pdf> accessed 5 June 2018.
33 ibid 9.

by a person in whom the family had confidence, amounted to a singular, and distressing, abdication of responsibility. It was taken as read that parents have an interest in what happens to their children even after death and the distress evidenced by many of those who gave evidence to the review group reinforced that commitment. One bereaved father explained that he felt that he should have protected his daughter during her brief life and that the doctors who removed tissue had denied him the chance to protect her in death.

An audit of all hospitals was conducted, which concluded that some 5,960 organs were currently held in Scottish hospitals, although this number does not clarify whether or not appropriate permission was either sought or gained from families. Nor would it include organs or tissue retained briefly by hospitals and subsequently disposed of. For example, if examination of a brain was required for diagnostic purposes, the organ would need to be retained for around 6 weeks before analysis could be carried out.

Despite the distress – and sometimes anger – of the families and individuals who gave evidence to the review group, as was the case in England and Wales, many indicated that, had they been asked for permission for retention of organs or tissue for purposes such as research, they would almost certainly have agreed. It was the failure to recognise their legitimate interest in the body and body parts of their deceased children that they objected to – not the legitimate pursuit of medical research and education. While it may be tempting to say 'they would say that, wouldn't they?', support for this proposition came when the review group's preliminary recommendations were first presented to the families and involved organisations at a public meeting.

In order that bereaved families were able – should they so wish – to reclaim retained organs or tissue, the review group initially recommended that any organs or tissue currently held in hospitals should be retained for a period of 5 years. This would allow families to make appropriate enquiries and to reach a conclusion as to what they wished to do with the organs or tissue. During that time, it was proposed that no research could be conducted without explicit permission being granted by the family. The review group was requested by families and associated groups to vary this recommendation in order that medical research was not completely stultified. Rather, the families suggested, non-destructive research should be permitted within that period of time, and the review group modified its recommendation accordingly.

One further point about the review group's recommendations that attracted some interest (and was adopted by the equivalent Inquiry in Ireland) was the terminology to be used. Whereas 'consent' is the terminology generally used as the trigger that permits subsequent action, the review group – after presentations *in camera* by members of the group – concluded that, while in common parlance and generally well understood, the concept of consent was flawed in this area, admittedly on somewhat legalistic but – the group believed – important grounds. By and large, the rights or – perhaps more accurately – responsibilities that parents have in respect of their children are delimited by the requirement that their decisions are 'in the best interests' of their children. How, the review group asked, could the removal of organs or tissue be 'in the child's best interests'? To be sure, such actions may be in the interests of other children whose illnesses or disease might ultimately be treatable when the organs or tissue of deceased children are available for medical research, but that scarcely fulfils the 'best interests' of the particular (deceased) child. On the other hand, in line with the review group's commitment to placing authority where it belonged – that is, with the parents – some alternative language was needed to locate power where it was appropriate. Ultimately, the review group settled on the language of 'authorisation' rather than 'consent'. Authorisation was felt to be a strong word that seemed to encapsulate the rights and responsibilities of parents without stretching the requirements currently attached to the more common concept of consent.

Following a consultation process, the review group's recommendations were incorporated into law in the shape of the Human Tissue (Scotland) Act 2006. Although the review group's remit did not include transplantation, the Scottish government took the opportunity to review and revise the outdated legislation concerning transplantation as well as the removal and retention of organs. Somewhat surprisingly, to this author (McLean) at least, the concept of authorisation was carried through the legislation not only in terms of the removal and retention of organs at post-mortem but also into the transplantation arena. The review group's choice of the term 'authorisation' has much to commend it in terms of legal analysis. In England, the outcry about the taking of organs without consent and the repeated demands for the authorities to appreciate that consent is 'such a simple word' made the use of any alternative term impossible.[34]

The Human Tissue Acts 2004 and 2006

The reader of the 2004 Act who comes to the statute with a primary interest in transplantation and no knowledge of the turbulent events that led to its passing will be astonished to find very little direct reference to transplantation. In a welter of complex provisions, transplantation seems to get lost. Transplantation is just one of twelve scheduled purposes within the Act. There are few direct references to transplants. The only provisions of the Act that are primarily concerned with transplants are those sections continuing the ban on sales of organs for transplant. On its face, the Act is dominated by provisions regulating the removal, storage and uses of what is described as 'relevant material'. In *Mason and McCall Smith's Law and Medical Ethics*, the Human Tissue Act 2004 is described as 'rushed into service as the result of the widespread unauthorised retention of tissues following post-mortem examinations'.[35] As a result, the Act, unlike its Scottish counterpart and the 2013 Welsh Act, does nothing to help enable transplants or commend transplantation. The question of a move to opt out relating to organ donation for

---

34 Margaret Brazier, 'Organ Retention and Return' (2003) 29 *Journal of Medical Ethics* 30.
35 Graeme T. Laurie *et al.* (eds), *Mason and McCall Smith's Law and Medical Ethics* (10th edn, Oxford University Press 2016) 595.

transplants (while raised briefly in parliamentary debates on the Human Tissue Bill) was barely canvassed.

Reasons for this apparent 'neglect' of the need for organs for transplant is, as Laurie *et al.* indicated, to be found in the Act's origins as a reaction to the organ retention 'scandals'. Given that the excoriated 1961 Act was founded not on consent but no objection, considering opt out would have been inflammatory. The focus of the Act appears to be directed at responding to questions about human materials kept and used for research and education. The 2004 Act regulates not simply the retention and use of whole bodies and the removal, retention and uses of organs or substantial parts of organs post-mortem, but all 'relevant material' defined as 'material other than gametes that consists of or includes human cells' (section 53). It embraces a much broader range of human material than the 2006 Scotland Act. Embryos outside the human body, nails and hair are excluded from the scope of 'relevant material'. Blood, faeces, urine and the smallest sliver of tissue are included. In a further marked difference from the 2006 Scottish Act, the 2004 Act extends beyond retention and uses of human tissue after death to regulate (albeit with a somewhat lighter touch) the retention and use of relevant material from the living: surgical tissue. For those purposes covered by the 2004 Act, appropriate consent must be obtained. In relation to materials from a dead adult, that means consent either from (1) the deceased ante-mortem, or (2) from his nominated representative, or (3) from a person who stood in a qualifying relationship to the deceased before his death.

In relation to the living, the original Bill provided that the patient must give appropriate consent to any retention and use of material removed in the course of surgery. If a woman had a hysterectomy and any parts of the excised uterus were kept, be it for audit, education, research or any other purpose, her explicit consent would have had to be obtained. Scientists expressed grave anxiety that the burdens of such a process would mean medical education and research would grind to a halt and, in its final form, the 2004 Act dispensed with the requirement for explicit consent for a number of purposes of medical education and training and further provides that regulations may permit research on anonymised material from the living approved by a research ethics committee.

Whatever the trigger for new legislation, the breadth of the definition of 'relevant material' in the 2004 Act, the extension of its provisions to surgical tissue from the living and the lack of focus on, or any highlighting of, donation for transplant purposes, especially the absence of consideration of opt out in relation to transplantation, are by no means wholly consequences of its origins in the organ retention controversy. When the first draft of the Bill was discussed with family support groups, representatives were bemused to be told that urine and faeces were within the Act, treated in theory no differently from a child's heart or a husband's brain. Nor did they think that lumps and bumps removed in surgery were of great import.

The driver for the massive framework of the 2004 Act may have been a valiant attempt at internal logic and consistency. One set of principles founded on the right of the individual or, after his death, his 'family' to control retention and use of his body and bodily material should apply to all such uses and the consequent requirement for explicit appropriate consent. If such a claim to control of separated body parts and material is a right, then treating donation for transplant as different is hard to justify. This approach takes no account of the evidence that, for some people at least, the purpose to which the bodily material is to be put affects their judgement about their willingness to accept infringement on the integrity of the body.

As we have already noted, in Scotland, the Parliament seized the opportunity not only to review the law surrounding removal and retention of organs and tissue at post-mortem but also to revise the somewhat unsatisfactory provisions of the Human Tissue Act 1961. In a much more reader-friendly statute, by utilising the concept of authorisation, the legislators firmly based the use of tissue and organs after death in the hands of those most closely related to the deceased. Part 1 of the Human Tissue (Scotland) Act concerns transplantation, Part 2 deals with the removal and retention of tissue or organs at post-mortem and Part 3 deals with organs or tissue no longer required for the purposes of justice.

Section 3 (1) of the Act indicates the purposes for which part(s) of a deceased person may be used as follows:

(a)   transplantation;
(b)   research;
(c)   education or training;
(d)   audit.

This is subject to the caveat that removal and use will only be lawful when properly authorised. Authorisation may be provided by an adult (in writing), by a young person over the age of 12 (again in writing) and can be likewise withdrawn. When a child dies before reaching the age of 12 years, '(1) A person who immediately before the death of a child who died under 12 of age had parental rights and parental responsibilities in relation to the child (but who is not a local authority) may authorise removal and use of a part of the body of the child for one or more of the purposes referred to in section 3(1).

(2)   Authorisation by virtue of subsection (1) –
      (a)   must be—
            (i)   in writing and signed; or
            (ii) expressed verbally,

by the person who gives the authorisation in accordance with that subsection' (section 10).

As we have seen, the Scottish legislation focuses exclusively on the use of organs and tissue post-mortem, presumably because the legislators were satisfied that any body parts or tissue removed during surgical procedures would be legally regarded as 'abandoned', although doubtless, were the relevant individual to request their return, they would – in theory at least – be able to comply. Equally, no elision of human organs tissue with, for example, faeces is made.

Transplantation revisited

Whatever the differences in detail and emphasis between the Human Tissue Act 2004 and the Human Tissue (Scotland) Act 2006, both statutes unequivocally adopt a central principle of opt in: that organs may only be taken for transplantation with appropriate consent or authorisation from the deceased or a nominee or a qualifying relative. Organs cannot be taken without explicit permission. The deceased or his family must take some positive step to give organs for transplant. Campbell describes the system as 'Gifts from the Dead'.[36] The trouble is that not enough gifts are donated to meet the demand for organs. In an attempt to bridge that 'fatal gap', Wales opted to introduce opt out. But note that opt out in Wales applies only to donation for transplant. Donation for other purposes within the Human Tissue Act 2004 will continue to require appropriate consent. The Welsh Assembly would appear to regard transplantation as different from other uses of parts from the dead. It does seem that the use of body parts for transplantation purposes is less contentious than removal of body parts for other reasons such as education and research.[37] Apart from those for whom faith or culture dictates that a body should be buried whole, anecdotal evidence suggests that a considerable majority of people in the UK favour the use of body parts in transplantation, which can save many lives and restore people to health, and would in theory be willing to donate. This 'evidence', however, is not necessarily borne out in practice. If it were, then the vast majority of the people in the UK would have signed the Organ Donor Register (ODR) and, although the number of people on the ODR rose from 22.5 to 23.6 in 2016–17, there are still insufficient donors to meet the shortfall between supply and demand[38] and in 2016–17, 457 patients died while on the active waiting list for a transplant.

This number of potentially preventable deaths has led some to argue that the current consent/authorisation approach is deeply flawed. Rather, it is argued, it should be presumed that people would wish to donate (which would be in line with the purported majority who say they would be willing donors). Given this, organs should be available for transplantation unless the individual has expressed his or her wish *not* to become a donor: what is known as an opt-out, or sometimes presumed consent, model.

Wales introduced a system of 'soft opt out' for cadaver organ donation in December 2015. On 28 June 2017, the Scottish government announced that similar legislation would be introduced in Scotland at some point before the

---

36 Campbell (n 4) 95.
37 Francisca Nordfalk *et al.*, 'From Motivation to Acceptability: A Survey of Public Attitudes towards Organ Donation in Denmark' (2016) 5 *Transplantation Research* 5.
38 For details, see NHS Blood and Transplant, 'Statistics about Organ Donation' <www.sehd.scot.nhs.uk/scotorgrev/Strontium%2090%20Report/roos90.pdf> accessed 5 June 2018.

next election for the Scottish Parliament,[39] an undertaking confirmed in January 2018.[40]

In October 2017, a spokeswoman for the UK Prime Minister told reporters that the government was paying close attention to whether changes in the law in Scotland and Wales resulted in increased donation rates and would consider such a change in England.[41] The Prime Minister has subsequently expressed her intention to move to an 'opt-out' system in England. Since December 2015 in Wales, organs for transplant may be removed from the deceased patient unless there is evidence that the deceased objected to donation. Her consent will normally be 'deemed' from her silence. The early evidence from Wales suggested that, if extended to the UK as a whole, opt out might result in more organs becoming available for transplant and narrow the gap between supply and demand, thus saving lives. However, the recent statistics of transplant activity in the UK make any judgement about how far presumed consent in Wales has resulted in a significant rise in cadaver donations uncertain.[42] The impact of opt out in across Europe is much debated. Nonetheless, in the autumn of 2017, the momentum for change looked strong. In Scotland, a commitment to move to an opt-out system had been made and the consultation process expected to result in change in the law in England was under way. The possibility of similar reform of the law has been under consideration in Northern Ireland. The UK might again have a more uniform law on cadaver transplantation.

In England, however, proposals were to meet with unexpected opposition. Dr Chris Rudge, the former medical director of UK Transplant and chair of the Organ Donation Committee, told journalists he was 'horribly opposed' to the proposals.[43] Hugh Whittall, the director of the Nuffield Council on Bioethics expressed misgivings.[44] Why, one must ask, has 'opt out' received such a sceptical response?

At worst, many might say, an opt-out system would do no harm and, matched to better systems to identify potential donors, should 'do good'? Why then did most of the UK drag its feet and not opt to opt out? Why should Dr Rudge, a

39 Bryan Christie, 'Scotland Plans to Move to Opt Out System for Organ donation' (2017) 358 *British Medical Journal* 3298.

40 Scottish Government (n 1).

41 Peter Walker, 'Organ Donation: Presumed Consent Could Be Adopted in England (*The Guardian*, 30 June 2017) <www.theguardian.com/society/2017/jun/30/presumed-consent-organ-donation-could-be-adopted-england> accessed 5 June 2018

42 John Fabre, 'Too Soon to Assess Effects of Deemed Consent to Organ Donation in Wales' (2017) 357 *British Medical Journal* 1.

43 Sarah-Kate Templeton, 'Ex-transplant Chief Chris Rudge: My Doubts About New Donor Plan' (*The Sunday Times*, 8 October 2017) <www.thetimes.co.uk/article/ex-transplant-chief-paul-rudge-you-wont-get-my-organs-p7tbjf03t> accessed 5 June 2018.

44 Nuffield Council on Bioethics, 'Nuffield Council on Bioethics Raises Concern over the Lack of Evidence to Support Government's Planned Move to Opt-Out Organ Donation' (Nuffield Council on Bioethics press release, 23 February 2018) <http://nuffieldbioethics.org/news/2018/nuffield-council-bioethics-raises-concern-lack-evidence-support> accessed 5 June 2018

champion of transplant medicine, not welcome opt out? Part of the answer is that the question of organs for transplant cannot be separated from that much broader question about how the bodies of the dead should be regarded and treated. A number of ethicists support a move to opt out only as a second preference to a mandatory duty to donate: conscription of organs. For example, John Harris has declared:

> ... the complaint of those who object to actions that violate the physical integrity of the corpse are *scarcely rational.* Illusions are fine, but whether the State and the Courts should give judicial or official support to these illusions is more doubtful, particularly when to do so might deprive others of life saving therapies. (Our emphasis)[45]

Either, it is further argued, there is a moral responsibility to assist others after death, or the state has some quasi-proprietary rights over deceased bodies and their parts. The good that may follow the potential increase in availability of organs for transplantation outweighs any purported interest that the person while alive, or their families after death, might claim. Many British bioethicists take a robust stance. The interests of bereaved families cannot outweigh the need to save lives. 'Donation' of cadaver organs for transplant and also tissue for research, education and other purposes should be mandatory. The dead have no interests, the corpse is just a 'thing' and the interests of grieving relatives are to be subordinated to the needs of the sick requiring a transplant.

Finally, there is the question of efficacy. Were a move to an opt-out system be shown conclusively to increase organ donation significantly, some of those opposed to it might reconsider their position. However, as Whittall has said, 'We fully endorse the aim of increasing the rate of donated organs, but we are concerned that making a legislative change based on poor evidence risks undermining public trust in the organ donation system, and could have serious consequences for rates of organ donation.' [46] While in some countries that operate an opt-out system – most notably Spain – report increased rates of donation, this, it is argued, is more likely a result of vastly improved service provision rather than the opt-out system *per se.*[47]

Contrast Campbell's views on human bodily material. In his scholarly work and contributions to policy making, Campbell has always espoused the view that human tissue is not to be treated as simply a 'thing'.[48] Reflecting on the relationships between us and our own bodies, between us and the bodies of

---

45 John Harris, 'Law and Regulation of Retained Organs: The Ethical Issues' (2006) 22 *Legal Studies* 527.

46 Nuffield Council on Bioethics (n 44).

47 Nuffield Council of Bioethics, *Human Bodies: Donation for Medicine and Research* (Nuffield Council of Bioethics 2011).

48 Alastair V. Campbell, 'Why the Body Matters' in John Coggon *et al.* (eds), *From Reason to Practice in Bioethics: An Anthology Dedicated to the Works of John Harris* (Manchester University Press 2015).

others and the natural world we inhabit, Campbell declares that 'No account of bioethics can possibly be accurate if it ignores this aspect of our bodily existence.'[49] He advances a complex and nuanced evaluation of the body and its parts in society and ethical debate. He recognises that human bodies, living or dead, and their parts, cannot simply be perceived as 'things'. Campbell writes of the dead body:

> From a scientific perspective the human dead body – or 'cadaver' – is easily viewed in an impersonal way, as a source of knowledge of the causes of death or the effectiveness of therapy through autopsy, or as a source of benefit to others through the harvesting of organ and tissue. Such an objectified view of the body is however a universe of meaning removed from the perceptions of the bereaved family of the dead person. For them the body of the deceased represents all that they cared for and all that they have lost.[50]

Rudge's concerns about 'opt out' resonate with Campbell. Declaring that if the proposals to change the law were implemented he would opt out, Rudge declared that 'organ donation should be a present and not for the state to assume they can take my organs without asking me'. Hugh Whittall's concerns focused on the evidence for change. There was as yet no evidence that the system in Wales had resulted in more organs being available for transplant. Crucially, no change should be made until 'we are confident that it won't undermine people's trust in the [transplant] system in the long term'.[51]

We would not presume to try and read Campbell's mind in the current debate on opt out. However, it seems unlikely that Campbell would be comfortable with an opt-out system that may result in organs being removed without a positive decision to make the gift of organs by the deceased or his family. Indeed, he has written '[i]deally ... we should be holding on to the concept of gift when considering how life can come from death'.[52] Plausibly, we *ought* to donate far more of our generous pensions to those in need. Few would argue that unless we opt out of larger donations the money may be taken from our bank accounts. Campbell, we suggest, would also have concern for the family who, as he eloquently says above, sees the body not as a thing, a resource, but as the symbol of the lost loved one. Campbell's focus on the bereaved is supported by the empirical research of Sque, Payne and MacLeod Clark who suggest that donation by the family might better be described as a sacrifice than merely a gift.[53] Of course in soft opt-out, the impact on the bereaved family will be considered,

---

49 Campbell (n 4) 125.
50 ibid 1.
51 Nuffield Council on Bioethics, 'Ethics Think Tank Expresses Concern over Premature Move to an Opt-Out Organ Donation System in England' (17 December 2017) < http://nuffieldbioethics.org/news/2017/ethics-tank-expresses-concern-premature-move-optout-organ > accessed 5 June 2018
52 Campbell (n 4) 114.
53 Magi Sque *et al.*, 'Organ Donation: Gift of Life or Sacrifice?' (2006) 11(2) *Mortality* 117.

but if that compassionate approach means that, even if the deceased has not signed the register to object to donation, organs are not taken, what is the point of changing the law? Numbers of deceased donors are rising; overall consent/ authorisation rates are rising. Perhaps the focus should be on ever-better practice, not law reform that might re-ignite controversy. The foreword to the latest NHS Blood and Transplant activity report makes two pertinent points. First, the high demand for organs in black and Asian communities is noted, communities in which religious and cultural values may create concerns about removing parts from the body. Second, the sheer human impact on families asked to consent to or authorise donation is evidenced in the comment that, faced by delay and lengthy processes in finding suitable recipients, some 'donor families' withdraw consent because they can no longer cope with the time involved.[54] For any family having to sit at the bedside of a relative already declared dead but ventilated and still looking alive, is a nightmare. For certain faiths, the imperative to bury or cremate the person swiftly may mean delay is further disincentive to donation. For many years, the British Medical Association was firmly opposed to the opt-out system, claiming (as Campbell does) that donation for transplantation should be altruistic: a gift. Its relatively recent conversion to supporting a 'soft' opt-out system may be a pragmatic response to the continuing problems confronting transplantation medicine in fulfilling its life-saving agenda. In the absence of evidence that such pragmatism will result in an increased number of organs for transplant without any backlash threatening the success of transplant programmes, should the gift principle advocated by Campbell be maintained?

Conclusion

While many may believe that academics sit quaintly in their ivory towers and think great thoughts, a picture that may have been true many years ago, increasingly they are involved in helping to shape policy at a number of levels. Campbell is a classic example. Not only has he established three separate ethics centres in Bristol, England; Dunedin, New Zealand; and Singapore but also his involvement in the ROC, as well as his chairmanship of the Ethics and Governance Council of UK Biobank – and many other public services – shows the extent to which Campbell's skills and expertise have helped to develop important social policy. Policy making is not straightforward. Bochel and Duncan, for example, postulate that making policy 'rarely proceeds in ... an orderly fashion', because making policy 'involves many different actors, and it involves conflict over aims, goals and values'.[55] The fact that this is so makes Campbell's contributions of particular significance if shaping and generating policy are to proceed in a principled and reasoned manner. In his published work, Campbell writes with eloquence and

54 NHS Blood and Transplant, *Organ Donation and Transplantation: Activity Report 2016–17* (London, Department of Health 2017).
55 Hugh Bochel and Sue Duncan, 'Introduction' in Hugh Bochel and Sue Duncan (eds), *Making Policy in Theory and Practice* (Bristol, Policy Press 2007) 3.

engages with complex intellectual debate. But he has also striven to make ethics accessible and to demonstrate the importance of shaping society in line with ethical principles and human need. His is a vital contribution. Seeking to attain a balance between a precautionary approach to scientific and medical advances and the desire not to stultify progress is no easy task. For many years, both in his academic and his public service endeavours, Campbell has helped generations of students and regulators walk that difficult line. He has listened to people who have lived through the experience of organ retention, surrogacy and many other dilemmas that are debated in those ivory towers. Recognising that there may be profound ideological and other differences between individuals and groups, Campbell has provided leadership in logic, tolerance and intellectual debate.

Part IV

Healthcare ethics in cultural contexts

7 'Where our common language lies'

Virtues, embodiment and faith in global bioethics

Michael Campbell and Jing-Bao Nie

Introduction

Global Bioethics must respect the whole diversity of world views of ethics, both religious and non-religious. In the last analysis we do have to negotiate about 'reasonableness' of arguments to determine where our common language lies; and it is often true that when we enter the ream of religion we simply talk past each other. But I also suggest that we could too readily dismiss some religious insights as of little use to the field as a whole, because they depend on a faith element. In response I would say that faith of some kind (not necessarily religious) is a feature of all ethical commitment, and that we can learn from each other by listening to and respecting some ignored religious and cultural apperceptions of goodness.[1]

Alastair V. Campbell has been an influential voice in bioethics since its inception. He has consistently celebrated the breadth of bioethics and stressed the humanistic character of the discipline. In his work, he continuously reminds us to take care not to lose sight of the fact that the practical problems and technical language, which are the bread and butter of medical and political decision making, are subservient to the more nebulous and non-technical demands of ethics and political philosophy. Bioethical issues raise important questions not only about the rightness of certain courses of action but also concerning the qualities of relationships, the admirability of attitudes, the aspirations for our society and, at its broadest, our conception of what it means to be human.

Within bioethics, moral, legal and political concerns all jostle with one another. In the context of single particular problem, there will always be a myriad of points of view. Patients and family members, doctors and nurses, chaplains, hospital managers, policymakers and the general public may each have a stake in the discussion of a relevant issue. Each of these individuals inhabits a different position and each will bring their own perspective, informed by their unique experiences, to bear. Adding to this confusion, globalisation has opened up bioethics to a range of voices speaking different languages, and speaking from different (sometimes

---

1 Alastair V. Campbell, 'Presidential Address: Global Bioethics – Dream or Nightmare' (1999) 14(3) *Bioethics* 183, 186.

radically different) cultures and traditions.[2] And there exists significant internal moral plurality and cultural diversity within every culture.[3]

We must be careful neither to overstate nor to underplay the differences between people confronting similar situations. On the one hand, although we must find a common language if we are to solve practical questions, we must not let this aspiration fool us into thinking that the differences between people can always be bridged. On the other hand, we must avoid the tendency to overplay these unbridgeable distances, as sometimes happens when a foreign culture is idolised for some perceived untranslatable wisdom or inscrutable otherness.

In charting a course between these twin dangers, three aspects of Campbell's work are especially helpful. The first concerns the role of virtues in ethics. The second concerns the importance of narrative and experience. The third concerns the role of embodiment and our relation to the environment. Each of these elements can only be appreciated fully in its relations to the others. In what follows we will sketch out these ideas, as well as the connections between them, albeit in a rough and programmatic way. First, however, it will be helpful briefly to describe the background against which Campbell is writing. Campbell's work goes against the grain of the prevailing 'principlist' conception of bioethics. In the next section, we outline this view and show how a conception of bioethics in these terms makes it difficult properly to appreciate the nature and significance of moral difference.

Moral disagreement and diversity: the limits of principlism

Bioethics is concerned with ethical aspects of the development and deployment of biomedicine. Points of disagreement concerning these issues are among the most emotive faced by society, and command significant popular attention. (Consider, for instance, the Charlie Gard case, where the fate of a single unfortunate infant in the UK drew the attention of figures as diverse as the Pope and Donald Trump.[4]) These conflicts are unsettling precisely because they test the limits of our ability to build consensus and so threaten to cause irremediable splits within society. In such cases, it is very tempting to think in terms of 'competing sides' and 'right' and 'wrong' positions, and for bioethicists it can be alluring to think that they might be able to 'beat' their opponents by 'defending' their position. The allure of this way of thinking leads philosophers, writing in the media, to 'shoot from the hip' – to offer an immediate response

---

2 Campbell (n 1).

3 Jingbao Nie and Alastair V. Campbell, 'Multiculturalism and Asian Bioethics: Cultural War or Creative Dialogue' (2007) 4 *Journal of Bioethical Inquiry* 163.

4 Charlie Gard was born with mitochondrial DNA depletion syndrome, a rare and often fatal genetic disorder. He became the subject of a protracted legal battle concerning the rights of his doctors to overrule his parents' requests for treatment. For an intervention by a medical ethicist in the case, see Julian Savulescu, 'Is it in Charlie Gard's best interest to die?' (2017) 389(10082) *The Lancet* 1868.

to a case based on little more than a rudimentary consideration of the facts.[5] The metaphors of conflict are seductive and self-reinforcing. Soon, bioethics becomes a war of words, fought in broadsheets and journals by antagonists arrayed under different banners (deontologist vs. utilitarian vs. libertarian, etc.). And thus, the most pressing goal of bioethics comes to reflect the resolution of conflict, ideally through the provision of reasons that all rational parties are bound to accept. On this understanding, the multitude of different voices in bioethics must seem like a threat, for the more (and more diverse) perspectives that we introduce into our conversation, the more remote must seem the prospect of consensus.

Without denying the importance of questions of policy, we suggest that to focus on these questions without attending to the broader context within such conflicts arise is deleterious to our understanding of both the nature of these problems and their importance to bioethical enquiry. It is parallel to the mistake that sees the primary aim of medicine to be bringing about the speedy physical recovery of patients, when, as Campbell and Roger Higgs point out, 'a large part of professional work [in medicine] is educative and supportive, mobilizing the patient's resources to meet the irremediable features of an illness or disability'.[6] For a truly inclusive, global bioethics, we need a framework in which 'the richness of human cultures [can] blend together in a common understanding of the obligations and the opportunities of human inventiveness and moral agency in healthcare'.[7] 'Human inventiveness' in this context is not merely confined to technical advancement but can include inventing such things as new ways of living together, or of living with illness. A view of moral debate in terms of trading reasons and reaching agreement will struggle to make sense of the notion of voices as blending together, or of the process of moral thought as at root a creative one.

A focus on conflict resolution lends an urgency to these issues, which, while appropriate in certain circumstances, can if left unchecked lead to a constriction of moral thought. Our search for a common language for bioethical 'problem solving' can make us unable to appreciate fully the diversity of voices and approaches in bioethics. The effects of such a constriction of moral thought are apparent in the principlist approach, according to which some set of principles forms the core of bioethical reflection.[8]

We can see this by considering the work of David Wong. According to Wong, morality can be understood in terms of the naturalistic functions that it serves, which include securing harmony within a group. On his account, moral differences between societies are to be accounted for by differences either in the

---

5 James Rachels, 'When Philosophers Shoot from the Hip' (1991) 5 *Bioethics* 67.
6 Alastair V. Campbell and Roger Higgs, *In That Case: Medical Ethics in Everyday Practice* (London: Darton, Longman & Todd 1982) 32.
7 Campbell (n 1) 183.
8 Principlists will typically include other elements of moral thought, such as virtues, as extra components to be welded onto the picture. See Tom L. Beauchamp and James F. Childress, *Principles of Biomedical Ethics* (7th edn, Oxford University Press 2013) ch 2.

application of fundamental moral principles or else in the weight that they put on these principles. Wong's position is interesting because it is a form of principlism that aims to accommodate the fact of widespread and persistent disagreement among people. He thus treads a path between unfettered universalism on the one hand and unfettered relativism on the other. In this view, there are certain universal constraints on morality that are derived from the conjunction of 'human nature' and the 'functions of morality' (that is, securing individual flourishing and enabling interpersonal cooperation).[9] A range of different moral systems are consistent with these general constraints, and so long as a system meets them and is 'internally coherent' then it may be 'true':[10]

> The moral norms accepted within a group specify the way that they go about determining the correct balance of reasons given an agent or agents, given an action, and given a situation ... [T]he moral norms that emerge and get accepted within a group establish the truth conditions for moral statements as made by its members, but the truth conditions are subject to the universal constraints on adequate moralities that spring from human nature and the functions of morality.[11]

This allows Wong to accommodate variation between moral outlooks while at the same time imposing limits on what can count as a legitimate ('true') moral system. In this way, he aims to respect the diversity of ethical world views without precluding the possibility of critiquing, or rejecting, other moral outlooks. Wong's view is complex and nuanced, and we cannot go into a full discussion of it here. All that is important for our purposes is that he represents moral differences in terms of different weights that are attached to a common set of reasons or principles. This comes out starkly in his remarks on abortion:

> The complexity and ambivalence over the priorities to be given in case of conflict among plural values is reflected in our own moral traditions. For example, the source of disagreement in the United States over the moral permissibility of abortion seems not so much to be a difference in the ultimate moral principles held by opposing sides as partly a difference over the applicability of a commonly held principle requiring the protection of human life and partly a difference over the relative weight to be given in the circumstances to another widely held principle requiring the protection of individual autonomy.[12]

9 See David B. Wong, *Natural Moralities: A Defense of Pluralistic Relativism* (Oxford University Press 2006) xv.

10 ibid xiv. Note that Wong is happy to predicate truth both of moral statements and of 'a morality'. He endorses Harman's slogan that 'there is no single true morality'.

11 ibid 71.

12 ibid 20, 77. Wong's interest is not in applied ethical issues *per se* but rather in broader issues surrounding the status of moral judgements. But his characterisation of the nature of moral thought inevitably leads to this distortion when it is applied to particular issues. The broader

Wong is not alone in treating the issue of abortion in this way. A view of bioethics that privileges moral principles is inexorably drawn to phrasing the argument between pro- and anti- abortion camps in terms of a conflict between a principle of non-maleficence (to protect human life) and a principle of autonomy (to respect the woman's control over her body).

The difficulty with such an account is that, by phrasing the abortion controversy in these terms, the issue is disconnected from the lives of those who are directly and indirectly affected by it. On this account, there is no reason to think that the woman whose body is in question would have any special insight into the nature of the ethical issues surrounding abortion: her role is relegated to insisting on her autonomy, and the force of that insistence in this case depends on the relative weight that we attach to the principle of autonomy over that of the protection of human life. Moreover, by seeing this as one instance of the phenomenon of 'respecting autonomy', we presume that we can understand what is at stake for the woman by analogy with other contexts where we insist upon our bodily autonomy. And that closes off the possibility that this case might be *sui generis*: that the considerations relevant to settling the ethical significance of the act might have no analogue in other parts of human life. In this way, on the principlist view, the experiences of those involved in the abortion debate – primarily the pregnant woman but also the father and the medical professionals who are called upon to assist in the procedure – are marginalised in moral thought.[13]

For Wong, intercultural and interpersonal moral disagreements are analogous. Differences between moral cultures, insofar as they are intelligible and worthy of attention, can be represented in terms of the different weights that they attach to values within a common range. For instance:

> Different forms [of moral thought] may be partly distinguished according to distinctive emphases that are given to a particular sort of reason. The feeling of a debt of gratitude for a kindness or a gift is something we all know, but in Chinese and Japanese societies that feeling is greatly magnified, corresponding to a difference in the priority given to this sort of reason relative to others.[14]

But this account underplays the extent of cultural difference and just how radical, and unsettling, confrontation with another culture can be. The magnification of the concept of gratitude in Chinese and Japanese cultures may mark not a difference in degree from its Western analogues but rather a difference in kind, such that one cannot grasp the idea of such gratitude simply by imagining an

---

lesson here is that attention to the actual nature of practical moral problems is necessary if one is to formulate an adequate theory of what morality is.

13 On the danger of marginalising certain experiences in moral thinking, see for instance Alastair V. Campbell and Michaela Willis, 'They Stole My Baby's Soul: Narratives of Embodiment and Loss' (2005) 31 *Medical Humanities* 101.

14 ibid 199.

intensification of the feeling of gratitude as experienced by the typical American or British person. The point of stressing this difference as one of kind is to hold that the difference between gratitude and its dictionary equivalent in Chinese or Japanese (e.g. in Japanese: 感謝 *kansha*) cannot be understood along the lines of the difference between someone who merely likes football and a devoted fan, which may be thought to be a matter of different intensities of interest in the same thing.[15] As any emigrant will tell you, integrating into another culture can be deeply existentially unsettling, and one is often left with, as Wittgenstein remarks, the feeling that genuine understanding of another culture will always be impossible:

> We also say of a person that he is transparent to us. However, for our observation it is important that a person can be a complete enigma to another. One experiences this when coming into a foreign country with altogether foreign traditions; and, what is more, even given mastery of the country's language. One does not *understand* the people. (And not because of not knowing what they are saying to themselves.) We cannot find our feet with them.[16]

A principlist such as Wong may want to accommodate these kinds of differences as well, but to do so will threaten a picture of moral differences as representable in terms of divergent opinions surrounding a common core of principles. Once we dig into the details of what it means to understand another, we will see that 'moral disagreement' is in fact a label for a whole range of different problems. The simplest cases can be represented in terms of divergent opinions over a particular proposition, as for instance when one person thinks that stealing a loaf of bread can be justified and another thinks that it cannot. But other cases abound. Some conflicts arise because one person sees a moral problem where another sees none (e.g. whether masturbation or suicide raise moral problems). Others arise when two people operate with different moral concepts and do not know how to translate from one set to another (e.g. one speaks of duties, the other of virtues). Yet others arise when two people simply have different experiences and despite a common repertoire of words cannot make sense of each other.[17]

The diversity of these cases resists easy characterisation. To be sure, one may be able to represent any putative difference in terms of principles. But, as Campbell

---

15 Although even in the case of football this account may strain plausibility when one considers the life of a football fanatic; see Peter Winch, 'Can We Understand Ourselves?' (1997) 20 *Philosophical Investigations* 193.

16 Ludwig Wittgenstein, *Philosophical Investigations: The German Text, with a Revised English Translation* (3rd edn, Elizabeth Anscombe (tr), Oxford, Blackwell 2001) II xi 225e. The final phrase in German is '*Wir konnen uns nicht in sie finden*' – literally, 'we cannot find ourselves in them'.

17 See Cora Diamond, 'Moral Differences and Distances: Some Questions' in Lilli Alanen, Sara Heinämaa and Thomas Wallgren (eds), *Commonality and Particularity in Ethics* (St. Martin's Press 1997) 197–223.

shows, a representation in these terms is often (although not always) unenlight-ening.[18] The real underlying factors that explain the difference lie much deeper, in (as we might put it) different ways of seeing the world. Thus, while principles have a role to play in the explication of moral difference, they must be subordinated to the unsystematic demand to do justice to the other's point of view.

This opacity of others to us (and us to them) is not only a bad thing: it is what gives language its creative power, as well as life (much of) its interest. Understanding and being understood is a challenge only because – and only to the extent that – it carries risks. By seeing differences between cultures in terms of difference balances within a set of accepted principles, we defuse the threat of moral difference, but only at the expense of denuding moral difference of its genuinely creative power. Accordingly, we need a richer account of both moral difference and of the nature and goal of moral confrontation if we are to do justice to the creative possibilities inherent in interpersonal relationships.

Three necessary virtues: humility, integrity and faith

In the last section, we explained principlism and suggested that it gives an inad-equate account of the moral differences between people. We also showed that this distortion has knock-on effects for understanding what is at stake in deliberation of moral issues. Another way to put our complaint is that, for the principlist, conflicts occur between positions rather than people. The role of the individual is to apply general moral principles to specific situations, using reasoning that any rational person could at least understand, if not agree with. A person's moral thought is distinctive only in terms of variation within the scope that such a pic-ture allows: hence, with respect to the application of principles or of their relative weights. Such a view sidelines the role of the individual in moral thought.

As Campbell has argued, virtue ethics provides a necessary corrective to attempts to understand differences between individuals as simply variation in principles or disagreement over facts. As he puts it, 'we need an account of char-acter, not just of right and wrong decisions, in order to give a full account of the moral life'.[19] Virtue ethics achieves this through its focus on the ethical (on the way in which assessments ramify throughout a person's life) and in its related emphasis on critical categories that apply simultaneously to thought and action, such as justice, humility and wisdom. Questions concerning the kind of person one ought to be are only partially answered by reflection on how to act, since one's personality also includes such things as one's patterns of thought, one's demeanour and one's bearing. As Iris Murdoch put it:

> When we apprehend and assess other people we do not consider only their
> solutions to specifiable practical problems, we consider something more

18 Alastair V. Campbell, 'The Virtues (And Vices) of the Four Principles' (2003) 29(5) *Journal of Medical Ethics* 292.
19 ibid 296.

elusive which may be called their total vision of life, as shown in their mode of speech or silence, their choice of words, their assessments of others, their conception of their own lives, what they think attractive or praiseworthy, what they think is funny: in short the configurations of their thought which show continually in their reactions and conversation.[20]

The introduction of virtue ethical considerations into our picture of moral deliberation is the first step in the rehabilitation of the individual in moral thought. Disagreement occurs between individuals and is one stage (perhaps the last) in a relationship. As such, it is beholden to the standards that the context imposes on it. The requirement is only part of the broader requirement that one's response to the other be appropriate. It is not sufficient simply to say something – for, if it were, we could always get away with offering truisms. Sometimes appropriateness of response means foregoing either making a proposal or offering a principle.[21] Sometimes it means something else besides trading arguments entirely.[22] Thus, at heart, question of conflict between individuals is that of whether or not we can insist that another person sees or does things in our way. The virtues provide a framework that help us in negotiating our relationships with others, settling what differences can be tolerated and what not, and what ought to be done once we have decided that someone's behaviour is intolerable. This is at heart a matter of forming and re-evaluating one's own integrity and sense of self.

The nature of our virtue ethical account depends therefore on our conception of the self, as well as what virtues we choose to privilege.[23] In this context, it is worth noting that the virtues that Campbell typically appeals to in his account of the important characteristics for medical professionals are different from those characteristically discussed in contemporary secular virtue ethics.[24] As opposed to the typical emphasis on the virtues of agency such as courage, benevolence and justice, Campbell stresses virtues such as humility, integrity and faith.

Humility, integrity and faith are all necessary if we are to handle the challenges of moral difference. Of these, humility must be *primus inter pares*, for it enables us to listen to another non-judgementally, and so understand (even if we cannot share) the outlook of an individual whose perspective may be radically different

---

20 Iris Murdoch, 'Vision and Choice in Morality' (1956) 30 *Proceedings of the Aristotelian Society Supplementary* 32, 39.

21 This is part of the background on which the principle of autonomy gets its sense.

22 Situating moral thought in this broader context will include offering what Campbell and Higgs call a 'four dimensional' account of a person, one that takes into account temporal aspects of life such as growth and change. Campbell and Higgs (n 6) 55.

23 These two are related, in that one's conception of the virtues will influence one's conception of the self, and vice versa.

24 We should also be careful not to make medical ethics overly focused on medical practitioners. On the virtues appropriate to patients, cf. Alastair V. Campbell and Teresa Swift, 'What Does it Mean to be a Virtuous Patient? Virtues from the Patient's Perspective' (2002) 5(1) *Scottish Journal of Healthcare Chaplaincy* 29.

from our own. Humility in this sense is the suspension of judgement, an ability to accept that one's own understanding of a situation may not be the only one possible, or the best. But we also need integrity if we are to resist being taken in by illusions either in the outlooks of others or our own. Without integrity, humility would degenerate into an uncritical deference to others' points of view. Finally, we need faith because we need to believe that it is genuinely possible to achieve mutual comprehension and consensus, despite the apparently recalcitrant disagreement between people.

On Campbell's account, these virtues are not essentially connected to action, consistency or adherence to principle. Rather, they are a matter of the adoption of a certain type of attitude. Consider his definition of integrity:

> To possess integrity is to be incapable of compromising that which we believe to be true ... To possess integrity is to have a kind of inner strength which prevents us from bending to the influence of what is thought expedient, or fashionable or calculated to win praise; it is to be consistent and utterly trustworthy because of a constancy of purpose. Yet the honesty conveyed by the word integrity is not to be confused with inflexibility and dogmatism, with the refusal to recognize error in oneself and the inability to perceive and respond to change in things around one. The person of integrity is first and foremost a critic of self, of tendencies to self-deception and escape from reality, of desire for a false inner security in place of the confrontation with truth which integrity demands.[25]

Here we see a dual role for the concept of integrity. On the one hand, only a person of integrity is able to comport themselves appropriately when they confront someone whose perspective is radically at odds with their own. Integrity enables one to stand firm to one's convictions without conflating this firmness with belief in the superiority of one's own way of life. What marks out the person of integrity is in fact a deep suspicion of themselves, and of their ability to understand who they are and the position from which they speak. On the other hand, possessing integrity enables one to care for another by revealing oneself as a fellow suffering human being. Integrity in this sense is a matter of acknowledging one's own fallibility and vulnerability:

> It is out of the consistency and depth of the caring person's own character that help is given to another. Because he or she has known within self the sense of failure and lostness which the other feels, the steadfastness and wholeness offered is grounded in human reality. The carer and cared for are not on two sides of a divide which must be bridged by some form of expertise on the part of the one who cares ... [C]are is grounded in mutuality, not in

25 Alastair V. Campbell, *Rediscovering Pastoral Care* (London: Darton, Longman and Todd 1986) 12.

expertise; it is possible because we share a common humanity with all the splendour and all the fallibility which that implies.[26]

Embodiment and an elusive common human nature

From the above quotation we see how reflection on the virtues brings us to facts concerning our embodiment, since the caring relation that integrity enables is only possible between embodied beings who are finite and suffer similar fates. We are not simply rational agents, pursuing our life plans through deliberation and action. Our physical forms do not only enter into our lives through the realisation of our projects. Indeed, so pervasive are facts of our embodiment in defining our form of life that to even speak of an interdependence or relationship between a person's mind and the human body is misleading, in that it implies that these two might in principle be separated, whereas we have (at least for now) only vague and fantastical ideas of what such a separation would be like.[27] This confluence of mind and body comes out most clearly in intimate relationships:

> Intimate relationships never concern merely a meeting of minds or of Lockean self-valuing pools of consciousness! The physical body of the person loved is fully part of the love that parent feels for child or wife for husband.

Loving relationships demonstrate the way in which our values are intimately connected to our natures as embodied creatures. Our bodily existence both enables and constrains the expressive possibilities open to us. The limits of these expressive possibilities are brought into poignant relief in the death of a loved one. Here too, embodiment plays a role, in bringing out our powerlessness in the face of death. Here acts, which used to be part and parcel of our ordinary relationships, take on a new, more poignant, meaning:

> This embodiment of the person does not suddenly disappear in death, though, of course, it soon becomes necessary to let go of the body and live only with the memory and mental images of the person now dead. A mother cuddling her dead child, a husband kissing the cold brow of his wife's dead body, are not acts which deny the death of the person. They are part of the story of human lives shared and of the pain which comes from parting.[28]

In this way, the body of the deceased becomes more than mere remains and takes on a symbolic role. The poignancy of acts of caring for the body of the deceased

---

26 ibid 15.
27 The transformation to our form of life effected by technologies that separate us from the physical realm are part and parcel of modern science fiction. See for instance, the movie *Ghost in the Shell* 攻殻機動隊 (1995) directed by Mamoru Oshii.
28 Campbell and Willis (n 13) 103.

reflects the juxtaposition of the meaning of these gestures in this context with their meaning when they occur in our everyday lives. As Campbell urges, these gestures need not depend on a denial of the reality of death, or confusion between the deceased person's 'real self' and their physical form. Rather, they can be a part of a recognition of the nature of our form of life, our natures as 'earthbound'.[29] This notion can be developed, through imaginative elaboration, into arguments for and against certain bioethical positions, for instance concerning our treatment of human body parts. Campbell himself connects this concept to the notion of respect for persons, and thence to an argument against the creation of a market in organs.[30]

It is beyond the scope of the paper to go into the details of such practical arguments here. Rather, we are concerned with a more general question – namely, how facts to do with our biological natures relate to the contours of moral thought and the possibility of mutual understanding. On the one hand, we all share a common human form and fate, and our thought, however varied it may be, is shaped by and must be answerable to these non-optional facts of human life. On the other hand, while this commonality may provide us with a route to comprehension of others, it can provide no guarantees of common understanding. First of all, the ways in which our thought develops are not constrained by these facts, and radically different perspectives on human life and ethics remain possible. Second, human nature changes over time, and it is only tenuously something that we have in common. Technological change threatens not only to alter the nature of human flourishing and our status as embodied beings but also to widen inequalities in our forms of life.[31]

In one sense, technology is only exacerbating natural trends within human nature. Human beings have always used experiences to distinguish themselves from others, and have created divisions based on the range, nature and quality of experiences available to a person. On a personal level, we use experience both to distinguish ourselves from others as well as to build relationships and foster solidarity. This tension between the private and the shared recurs, with variations, throughout human life. It manifests in the conflicting impulses for solidarity and solitude: to live in the town or to leave for the countryside. Each of us has our own point of view and we each speak from our own history. At the same time, each of us is a member of a community, dependent on others from birth and never fully free from needing, and being needed by, others. In each successful interaction, even in sharing such mundane things as commiserations over the

---

29 Alastair V. Campbell, *The Body in Bioethics* (Routledge 2009) 125.

30 ibid 27. Note, however, that arguments employing such concepts need not be conservative; see for instance, Emson's argument in favour of organ reclamation at death on the grounds that our bodies are only ever 'on loan from the biomass' in Harry E. Emson 'It is Immoral to Require Consent for Cadaver Organ Donation' (2003) 29 *Journal of Medical Ethics* 125.

31 Already we see gulfs opening up between those who live large parts of their lives online or in front of screens and those who do not. Consider, in this respect, controversies surrounding whether access to the internet should be considered a basic human right.

weather or enjoyment of the wine, we affirm that our experiences are not ours alone, but can be shared by an indefinite range of others.

But as the nature of experience changes, the nature of this indefiniteness changes as well. And in this sense the technological advancements of the last half century represent a fundamental step-change in the modes of human existence. One of the effects of modern technology is to untie our experience from the natural world around us. The creation of cyberspace has not only shifted the ways in which we attend to and interact with the natural world around us but also created entirely new spaces in which we can move and with which we become entangled. In this way, as we replace physical sharing with its virtual analogues, we radically widen the circle of people with whom we may communicate while simultaneously narrowing the base of that communication.

The effects of this step-change on our ethical thought may be far-ranging, but we should not suppose that they are uniformly deleterious. It would be folly to try to proselytize for some bygone, more 'authentic' mode of existence, or to try to impose some particular vision of human well-being on future generations. Within a short space of time, such proselytizing is likely to seem silly and old-fashioned.[32] As Campbell urges, 'human flourishing is a "fragile and altering phenomenon", and it would be foolish to try to fix it for future generations'.[33]

However, that is not to say that we ought to be indifferent towards changes in the conditions of human existence, or that we can find no principles for governing our responsibilities towards future generations. In this context, Campbell advocates for a 'precautionary principle', which calls for us to take whatever steps we can to maintain, as far as possible, the conditions that enable each generation (and each individual) to formulate and pursue their own conception of what is important.[34] But the tolerance implicit in this principle need not preclude us from taking steps to ensure that the values or insights peculiar to our generation are preserved to be passed down to future generations.

The negative aspects of technological change include the danger that, by disconnecting ourselves from an appreciation of our embodied natures, technological change can foster negative aspects of our personalities, such as the hubristic urge to sweep away anything that might stand in the way of our egoistic satisfactions. We see the distorting effects of technology in such things as the rise of online abuse (so-called 'trolling'). It is an open question how we should respond to the moral challenges that such technologies pose.[35]

---

32 Witness, for instance, the debates on obscenity that were carried out in the UK in the 1960s.
33 Campbell (n 18) 296.
34 ibid.
35 Note that both the nature of the challenge and the appropriateness of proposed responses can only be ascertained with a firm grasp on the facts. In this way, conceptual and empirical questions interrelate, and philosophers must work hand in hand with both qualitative and quantitative researchers, and policymakers. See for instance, the mixture of approaches in Campbell and Swift (n 24).

For the moral philosopher, there is a standing obligation to challenge what society considers to be normal and to create space for people to consider a different vision of what is important in human life. But it is one thing to create such a space and another to attempt to fill it. One move in philosophy is to attempt to legislate conditions for what constitutes an authentic mode of existence. Another move is to show any such picture to be optional. Even if we cannot show one way of life to be objectively the best, we can offer suggestions as to what ways of life are better, or worse (or, at least, what is at stake in the choice of one). In the context of the rise of technologically enabled virtual lives, Campbell stresses the importance of our embodied natures, as a means to help us accept the 'limits on our powers as human' and develop 'equanimity in the face of human mortality and vulnerability'.[36] He appeals to memory as one concept that may bridge the apparent gap between the conditions of modern life and our embodied natures. After all, when memory is the imaginative reliving of a state of one's past, then it is more than just the recollection of the details of a past event. The body's role in memory is as intimate as its role in experience, as in the act of tracing out a scar to relive a traumatic experience. Memory in this way provides us with a way to remind ourselves of our location within the world, as existing not only at a point in space but in a particular place:

> The gift of memory can take us back to a physical place of our ancestors – a place transformed no doubt by all the rapid change of our era, so not the place they knew – yet still a place where we can reconnect to earth and, for a time, leave cyberspace. This may seem somewhat mystical, but in fact it relates wholly to the corporeal, to the embodiment of persons and their physical location on earth. For those millions of us who no longer know ourselves as a people of the land – what the Maori call *tangata phenua* – this is a major challenge.[37]

In this way, we see how ethical questions concerning the important facts of human life relate to the broader question of how we conceptualise our relationship to the natural world around us. Any philosophy that marginalises ethical questions concerning these matters is in danger of being self-defeating, in two senses. First, our lives will remain a mystery if we exclude environmental relations from our understanding. After all: 'Every moment of our lives is lived in (mostly unconscious) total dependency on our environment. Thus we are only in a very restricted sense separate beings.'[38]

Second, and more practically, concern for the environment is of fundamental importance for our survival as a species. Unless we find a sustainable way of

36 Campbell (n 18) 296.
37 ibid 117–118. This can be fruitfully read next to Campbell's claim that 'friendship alters the rhythms of time, introducing a cross-rhythm to the onward drives of purpose and desire', in Campbell (n 25) 93.
38 Campbell (n 29) 14.

living, and a way of articulating the rationale behind it, then we are in danger of planetary disaster. These two points meet in a view of ethics that stresses that embodiment is a matter of re-establishing one's connection to the environment:

> [T]he ultimate issue for ensuring respect for the body in bioethics is not the resolution of our inner disunity or the celebration of a common humanity within our rich diversity, important though these clearly are. It is the restoration of the sustaining relationship between our bodies and the (massively re-engineered) natural world.[39]

The environment's standing as an object of concern is intimately connected to its being an object of contemplation. Unlike animals or other humans, the environment is unable to draw itself to our attention and, as such, is easily overlooked. In environmental ethics in particular, beauty must be a symbol of morality, where a symbol is something that 'participates in the reality towards which it points'.[40] Those who can see beauty in the natural world are thereby enabled to find an ethics that locates the human within its surroundings, which does not privilege the satisfactions of what Murdoch called 'the fat, relentless ego'.[41] The cornerstone of such an outlook is a contemplative awareness of one's surroundings. This contemplative frame of mind is nurtured as much by poetry as by science or philosophy.[42] Consider the following *haiku* by Myoe:

> The winter moon comes from the clouds to keep me company.
> The wind is piercing, the snow is cold.[43]

Yasunari Kawabata chose this poem in his Nobel Prize acceptance speech as an example of 'the deep quiet of the Japanese spirit'. Praising the poems' 'warm, deep, delicate compassion', he says:

> Seeing the moon, he becomes the moon, the moon seen by him becomes him. He sinks into nature, becomes one with nature. The light of the 'clear heart' of the priest, seated in the meditation hall in the darkness before the dawn, becomes for the dawn moon its own light. [...] Winter moon, going behind the clouds and coming forth again, making bright my footsteps as I go to the meditation hall and descend again, making me unafraid of the wolf: does not the wind sink into you, does not the snow, are you not cold? [...] When we see the beauty of the snow, when we see the beauty of the

---

39 Campbell (n 29) 125.
40 A phrase of Paul Tillich's, quoted in Campbell p.20.
41 Iris Murdoch, *The Sovereignty of Good* (London: Routledge 2013) 51.
42 It is a noteworthy feature of Campbell's work that he often appeals to poetry in elaboration of his points.
43 Quoted in Yasunari Kawabata, 'Japan, the Beautiful and Myself' in Allén Sture (ed.), *World Nobel Lectures, Literature 1968–1980*, (Singapore, Scientific Publishing Co. 1993).

full moon, when we see the beauty of the cherries in bloom, when in short we brush against and are awakened by the beauty of the four seasons, it is then that we think most of those close to us, and want them to share the pleasure. The excitement of beauty calls forth strong fellow feelings, yearnings for companionship, and the word 'comrade' can be taken to mean 'human being'.[44]

We can compare this to what Raimond Gaita writes about his interactions with his childhood friend Hora, also a friend of his father. When Gaita was young, Hora would take him sailing and tell him stories, usually 'stories of men and women who had been persecuted or ridiculed for their beliefs or who had resisted tyranny'. Here is how Gaita now describes the effect this had on him:

[W]hen I try to understand why the inspiring examples of a few men and women should count against the folly and much worse of millions (as it then seemed), when I try to understand why those stories have nourished me throughout my life, I know the answer must include the way Hora was so distinctively present in their telling, his openness to the world and the quality and many tones of his laughter. And, strange though it may sound – indeed, I fear that it may sound obscurantist – it must include his sensuous love of the sun and the water, and how, in between stories, he plunged into the reservoir from the boat, swimming sideways, forwards and backwards, splashing and whooping. From none of that can I abstract the distinctive quality of his humanism. In that virile, sun-drenched, summer-coloured humanism I found food to nourish hope. The physical details I have dwelled on express the embodied nature of our at-homeness in the world.[45]

Kawabata and Gaita both share a conception of ethics as emerging from the harmony between an individual and their environment. The insight of the people depicted in the passages (the nameless priest and Hora) is connected to their being a part of, rather than apart from, their surroundings. In this respect, the visions in these passages are similar, although in another respect they are as different as the winter and the summer.[46] They gesture at different ways of becoming at home in the world: on the one hand, through the virtues of active restraint (silence, stillness); on the other, through those of joyous abandon (storytelling, swimming).

These cases are instances of beauty in its ethical aspect. Here we have two different 'apperceptions of goodness': two figures whose lives are oriented around their distinctive perceptions of value, and whose perceptions of value arise from

---

44 ibid.
45 Raimond Gaita, *After Romulus* (Melbourne: Text Publishing 2010) 19–20.
46 Compare Wittgenstein: 'If white turns into black some people say "Essentially it is still the same". And others, if the colour becomes one degree darker, say "It has changed *completely*"'. Ludwig Wittgenstein, *Culture and Value* (G.H. von Wright (ed.), Peter Winch (tr.), University of Chicago Press 1984) 42ᵉ.

their sense of connection to the natural world. Hora is convinced that 'even in the most appalling circumstances, there has been a handful of men and women who redeemed humanity by the nobility of their vision and their courage to be true to it'. The truth of these claims is in their power to move us, for us to see them as insights rather than illusions. Kawabata's priest finds, in the coincident rhythms of her ritual and the passage of the moon, a sense of security that makes her 'unafraid of the wolf'.

Similarly, Campbell stresses a conception of beauty that is at odds with that promulgated in cultures that conflate well-being with status, and so tie value to appearance:

> Against this false picture of how fulfillment is to be found, we must assert the essential fragility of human beauty, something discovered in the lights and shadows of our life together as changing, vulnerable and mortal beings. Our shared experiences of birth, intimacy and death are where hope of a human future, however uncertain, is to be found. This is the 'beauty that binds', rather than the beauty that divides us from one another in a hopeless race to be the best (or at least not amongst the worst).[47]

How far can we follow the thoughts of Kawabata, Gaita and Campbell here? How far can we understand and share in this vision of nature and man's relation to it? With this worry, we return to the phrase 'where our common language lies' in its unsettling ambiguity. For although we may speak the same language, we may not yet understand each other. And although a dictionary may tell me what words mean, it cannot tell me what another means by their words. Our common words, the tools that we use to make sense of the circumstances in which we find ourselves, may conceal from each of us deep unclarities within oneself as well as deep differences between oneself and others.[48] For we are only imperfectly aware of the consequences of our words, and our grasp over meaning, even in the case of sincere speech, is only ever partial. We are seduced by the ease of ordinary life into assuming that we have control over our words. But, in fact, misunderstanding may arise at any moment.[49]

Where our common language lies?

Throughout this essay, we have argued that bioethical reflection can be appropriate only if it is based on a suitable understanding of the experiences of those

---

47 Campbell (n 29) 91.
48 This is one of the problems of the modern predilection, in meta-ethics, to speak of morality in terms of classes of reasons. Reasons are conceptually articulated and shared items. Accordingly, to take them as a common coinage is to underplay the vast gulf that there may be between people, even those who appear to speak the same language.
49 See Stanley Cavell, *Must We Mean What We Say?* (2nd edn, Cambridge University Press 2002) 52.

involved in bioethical problems. Language and experience stand in complex relationship, each transformed by its relation to the other. On the one hand, in learning to speak, people learn to describe their experiences, allowing them to give voice to parts of their lives that would otherwise remain mysterious to others. But, as Wittgenstein reminds us, the development of language does not only enable us to describe experiences but alters them as well.[50]

We use words to bring ourselves into relationships with others. Some of the simplest, but most powerful and unsettling, of those relationships are those that involve the communication of experience (of joys and sufferings, hopes or anxieties). This communication can work in the background of shared sympathy or can be used as a means to foster it. But we can also use words to hide what we really feel, as when we retreat to commonplaces in order to avoid an uncomfortable situation.

In his early work *In That Case*, Campbell and Higgs use a single story of a woman called Angie and her family in order to describe the communicative and experiential aspects involved in medical decision making.[51] Campbell and Higgs show how there are a number of different and conflicting languages that people employ to understand the behaviour of others: from the purely technical language of the emergency room doctor, to the more nuanced language of the GP, to the language that the patient herself uses and many others. Each of these languages is useful for certain ends. In some cases, the aim is a form of understanding corralled to the service of a practical goal (in the case of the doctor in the emergency room, this may be, for instance, the restoration of normal functioning of the circulatory system). In others, such as Angie's own way of talking, there is no practical goal that governs the appropriateness of her uses of language, beyond the obscure end of 'self-understanding'.[52]

There is no reason to think that these various different languages could ever be subsumed into a single unified way of talking. Moreover, it is at least practically impossible (and may simply be impossible *sans phrase*) for any individual to master all of them. Our attention is partial: if we inspect the trees, we cannot take in the sweep of the forest. Indeed, it is not even clear whether it would be desirable to see from all points of view at once: would it be possible for medics to do their jobs properly if they saw each patient through the eyes of the patient's loved ones?[53]

As we have seen, these issues are made even more complicated when we consider differences of natural (rather than technical) language and associated differences of culture. Taken together, these difficulties may make us think that

---

50 Cf. Wittgenstein (n 16) II xi 229.
51 Campbell and Higgs (n 6) *passim*.
52 Indeed, in one of the cases described in the book, a patient objects precisely to the way in which their communication with medical professionals is always relegated to certain practical purposes: see the case of Ken, discussed on ibid 60–61.
53 This is one instance of the more general challenge to reconcile the professional and humanistic aspects of medicine; see for instance, Alastair V. Campbell, *Paid to Care? The Limits of Professionalism in Pastoral Care* (London: SPCK 1985).

the task of finding a common language is an impossible one. Here is one way our confidence in reason may seem to give way. Given the disparities in human life and culture, how can legitimate convergence on issues of common concern ever be possible? Perhaps the only way to attain consensus is through ignoring some voices, or belittling or marginalising some experiences. People can be indoctrinated. In this case, reason would achieve its ends through unreasonable means. And, since we are not infallible, there is always the danger that we might have slipped into such illegitimate modes of persuasion without realising it. In the context of global bioethics, this danger comes out in the 'promotion of a lowest common denominator, homogenized bioethics', which, like Auden's vision in *The Shield of Achilles*, replaces the dream of consensus with the nightmare of conformity.[54]

Once we concede that reason is vulnerable to unreasonable forces in this way, then another fear raises its head – namely, that reason is in fact epiphenomenal, incapable of moving us on its own and only able to rationalise the interplay of power structures. Reason would then be, in Wittgenstein's image, a knob that appears connected to the mechanism but is in fact mere decoration.[55] In bio-ethics, this is the fear that the best a thinker can do is 'bless the battleships'. After all, as Campbell observes, bioethics rarely threatens the profits of biotechnology companies and other vested interests.[56]

This brings us, then, to Campbell's claim that, alongside reason, ethics always involves faith. Ethics depends on beliefs that cannot be proven, two of which are especially important: belief in the possibility of mutual understanding and belief in the possibility of meaningful change. We must have confidence both that it is possible to formulate a framework in which each person is heard and in which justice is done to each point of view, and also that, having imagined it, we could then put it into practice. Without faith in this sense, there would be no reason to do the work of ethics: formulating and critiquing theories, creating conceptions of the good, trying to get things right in the service of making things better. Faith in this sense need not be understood as a kind of hope, or an ungrounded belief, so much as a way of acting. To have faith in this sense is to be faithful, to pursue goodness despite all the myriad 'despites': the confusion of tongues, 'the folly and worse of millions' and so on.

Of course, we must not confuse faith in this sense with dogmatism. Conviction in the correctness of one's views can hinder as much as help, and much that is done by people acting in good conscience is in fact positively harmful. But although our belief in the possibility of improvement must go beyond the evidence, it is not entirely ungrounded. When scepticism threatens to overwhelm us, we can return to instances of goodness as reminders that it is possible to find

---

54 See Campbell (n 29); Alastair V. Campbell, *Moderated Love: A Theology of Professional Care* (London: SPCK 1984) 115.
55 Wittgenstein (n 16) §270.
56 Alastair V. Campbell, 'Public Policy and the Future of Bioethics' (December 2008) *Asian Bioethics Review* 24.

common ground in simple acts of kindness. For every Charlie Gard there is a Martha Tolputt.[57] And, whatever the prospects for intellectual consensus there remains, prior to language, the possibility of care born of the simplicity of being with another. This care of companionship is based on our awareness of our shared form and fate, including our mutual difficulties in understanding each other and ourselves. It provides a necessary corrective to the tendency to over-intellectualise:

> Words are often the enemy of care, for they seduce the carer and cared for into playing verbal games, concealing still further the wholeness they might be able to seek together, if they did not fear the simplicity of silence ... [C]are as integrity must therefore be, first and foremost, that presence of one person with another which precedes all words.[58]

Conclusion

The intelligibility of the aspiration for a truly global bioethics depends crucially on how we are to understand both what bioethics is and what it might become. If our aspiration is to reach unforced agreement on questions concerning how things ought to be, then the variety of ways of life in the modern world must seem threatening. We have suggested that, rather than facing this threat head-on, it is more profitable in the first instance to turn away from it, towards ensuring, first of all, that we listen to others and try to make sense of their point of view. To do this we need, above all 'a willingness to risk new ways of learning about others and new ways of sharing with others'.[59] Only after we have satisfied this demand might we permit ourselves to return to more practical questions.

The advantages of taking this detour are two-fold. First, it enables us, as bioethicists, to provide a forum for a range of different voices to be heard. This is a good in itself and not only for its incidental benefits. Second, once we have schooled ourselves in these quieter virtues, then when we return to points of practical contention the issues may appear in a different light.[60]

---

57 Martha Tolputt was born with severe brain damage due to her mother suffering a concealed placental abruption. She lived only 5 days and her case generated no significant media attention. However, her parents were very grateful for the care that they received from the NHS. As Ed Tolputt, her father, put it: 'You – the doctors and nurses of the NHS – gave life to Martha. You gave her 5 happy days, surrounded by care and love and laughter. That Sophie and I can think back on Martha's life with deep pride and natural sadness, without the invasion of blame or resentment, is something for which we are immeasurably grateful.' See Ed Tolputt 'Our Daughter Lived Five Days. We Thank the Doctors and Nurses Who Made It Possible' <www.theguardian.com/commentisfree/2017/jul/30/thank-you-doctors-and-nurses-who-cared-for-our-daughter> accessed 17 September 2017.
58 Campbell (n 25) 16.
59 ibid 105.
60 Of course there can be no guarantees here; because there is no one problem of moral difference, there can be no one solution either. Here we must trade the security of *a priori* philosophizing for the uncertainty of conversation.

Medicine must find a place in society. But as society and medicine both change, this place will change in turn. As social and technological developments transform our self-understanding, we must continue to search for 'fresh imaginative associations that do greater justice to our complexity as persons and to the depths of experience' and relate them, as best we can, to the practical issues that we face.[61] In this ongoing and open-ended activity, Campbell's work remains a source of inspiration.

Acknowledgements

The lead author's work was supported by the following grant: Operational Programme Research, Development and Education (OP VVV/OP RDE), 'Centre for Ethics as Study in Human Value', registration No. CZ.02.1.01/0.0/ 0.0/15_003/0000425, co-financed by the European Regional Development Fund and the state budget of the Czech Republic.

61 Campbell (n 25) 25.

8 On the open seas

Pluralism and bioethics in Europe

Richard Huxtable

Introduction

Back in 1999, years before he was to enjoy the first, let alone the third, of his retirement celebrations, Alastair V. Campbell referred to the challenge of 'establishing a viable medical ethics in our pluralistic and confused age'.[1] Almost two decades on, we allegedly live in a 'post-truth' world, and pluralism and confusion continue to surround medical ethics and its (more expansive and inclusive) sibling bioethics. As I explore in this chapter, there is even confusion about the pluralism that can be detected *within* the field of bioethics.

At the time he was writing, Campbell was inaugural director of the Centre for Ethics in Medicine at the University of Bristol, UK. Appointed 'to one of the first British chairs in medical ethics',[2] Campbell established the centre in 1996,[3] welcoming a young Richard Huxtable among its first PhD students that same year. Having previously studied and worked in the US and Scotland, Campbell had founded a similar centre in New Zealand before coming to Bristol, and he would go on to create one more in Singapore.[4] The title of the Bristol centre (Centre for Ethics *in* Medicine) was deliberate, conveying the sense that ethics would not only be drawn from *within* the domain (medicine) but also be brought into that domain from *without*. 'Medical ethics', if conceived narrowly, could be reduced to (or mistaken for) professional medical ethics, in the sense of the ethics of doctors; 'ethics in medicine', however, not only afforded room to the values of the various healthcare professions and professionals but also invited a broader account of ethics to be brought to bear on the medical endeavour.

These points – about pluralism, confusion, and ethics coming from both within and without a particular domain – resonate with the topic under consideration in this chapter: that of so-called 'European bioethics'. Lenoir, a former chair of the European Group of Ethics in Science and New Technologies, has

---

1 Alastair V. Campbell, 'Making Sense of MacIntyre' (1999) 25 *Journal of Medical Ethics* 282.
2 Duncan Wilson, *The Making of British Bioethics* (Manchester University Press 2014) 196.
3 One British newspaper reportedly sought to reassure its readers that, despite the identical spelling of their names, this Alastair Campbell was not the notorious 'spin doctor' working for the then Prime Minister, Tony Blair.
4 He has not (yet) created a fourth, at least at the time of writing.

suggested that 'bioethics ... is everything that Europe is about: sharing common values while respecting European cultural diversity; promoting research and innovation while ensuring respect for these values; providing honest and understandable information to the public...'.[5] Yet, this assessment presumes that we can identify both 'Europe' and 'bioethics' in isolation, before they combine to form something distinctive that might legitimately be dubbed 'European bioethics'.

Some commentators have suggested that there is indeed something identifiable and distinctive about bioethics within the different territories in which it is practised and theorised, Europe included. The territories with the relevant unifying features all range in size. At the modest end of the spectrum lie regions, states or even whole countries; for example, Campbell has remarked that 'there is clear emergence of regional identities, especially in Asia'.[6] Distinctive identities can also be detected at the other end of the spectrum, at – and even beyond – the level of continents. Cheng-Tek Tai, for example, summarises the stereotypical caricatures of Eastern and Western bioethics: 'In Western society, patient autonomy is emphasized, but in the East, especially those regions influenced by Confucian teachings, an individual is regarded as a smaller self within a larger self, specifically the family'.[7] In such an account, Western bioethics is individualistic and particularly influenced by American contributions, not least the four principles of respect for autonomy, beneficence, non-maleficence, and justice articulated by Beauchamp and Childress;[8] Eastern bioethics, meanwhile, is more collectivist or communitarian.

In order to ascertain the veracity of such caricatures, we need first to locate and identify the relevant unifying, constitutive elements. I will begin the search for 'European bioethics' by looking at these terms in isolation. Neither is easily pinned down but, perhaps surprisingly, bioethics seems the more readily discernible, because this can be viewed as an interdisciplinary field of inquiry in which ethics in and of the biosciences is explored. The geographical boundaries of Europe, meanwhile, are not so easily drawn, which leads me to look away from the landmasses and towards the 'idea(s)' of Europe. On doing so, an apparently united European bioethics comes into view, which can be explained both in terms of what it is not (e.g. it is allegedly not American or Asian bioethics) and what it is (because distinctive values and approaches appear to emerge). But such accounts carry risks of reductionism and abstraction. I go on to argue that, beyond any unifying elements, Europe and European bioethics are also marked

5 Noëlle Lenoir, 'Biotechnology, Bioethics and Law: Europe's 21st Century Challenge' (2006) 69(1) *The Modern Law Review* 1.
6 Alastair V. Campbell, 'Medical Ethics, Then and Now: A 40 Year Perspective' in Richard Huxtable and Ruud ter Meulen (eds), *The Voices and Rooms of European Bioethics* (Abingdon, Routledge, 2015) 14.
7 Michael C. Tai, 'Western or Eastern Principles in Globalized Bioethics? An Asian Perspective View' (2013) 25 *Tzu Chi Medical Journal* 64.
8 Tom L. Beauchamp and James F. Childress, *Principles of Biomedical Ethics* (7th edn, Oxford University Press 2013).

by diversity and fragmentation because there are different world views, different values, different times, and different influences to consider.

In light of these arguments, I close by following Campbell in suggesting that it might be better to talk, not of 'European bioethics' but of 'bioethics *in* Europe'. In doing so, we can affirm the presence of particular ideas emerging from particular areas, while also recognising the wider plurality of values and approaches that will be held in such areas. Although the empirical hypothesis deserves to be tested, pluralism looks likely to exist wherever bioethics occurs in the world. Whether we should go further and hold that bioethics *should* be an ethically pluralistic pursuit remains to be seen, but I cautiously conclude that there may be a case for so arguing.

In search of European bioethics

Capturing 'European bioethics' is challenging because neither of its two constitutive terms is easy to pin down. Starting with 'bioethics', the origins of which are somewhat contested,[9] Campbell points out that this literally 'just means the "ethics of life"'.[10] Bioethics' gaze is often fixed on medicine and healthcare, but its remit is wider than either 'medical ethics' or 'healthcare ethics', as Reich's definition further indicates: 'the systematic study of the moral dimensions – including moral vision, decisions, conduct, and policies – of the life sciences and health care, employing a variety of ethical methodologies in an interdisciplinary setting'.[11]

The final clause of Reich's definition indicates the inter- and multi-disciplinarity of bioethics. As a sub-group of ethics, bioethics is evidently a philosophical endeavour, thus encompassing normative ethics (exploring what we should do or who we should be), applied ethics (relating such work to specific fields), meta-ethics (analysing the concepts involved), and descriptive ethics (investigating actual moral beliefs and practices).[12] However, bioethics cannot be reduced to a field of philosophers – nor, indeed, to a 'club of clerics'.[13] Rather, as the reference to descriptive ethics implies, practically orientated disciplines will also contribute, including law[14] and, increasingly, the

---

9 Mark A. Rothstein, 'The Role of Law in The Development of American Bioethics' (2009) 20(4) *Journal International De Bioethique* 73.

10 Alastair V. Campbell, *Bioethics: The Basics* (Abingdon, Routledge, 2013) 1.

11 Warren T. Reich, *Encyclopedia of Bioethics, Vol. I,* (New York, Macmillan, 1995) xxi.

12 Wibren van der Burg, 'Law and Ethics: The Twin Disciplines', (2010) *Erasmus Working Paper Series on Jurisprudence and Socio-Legal Studies No. 10-02* <https://papers.ssrn.com/sol3/papers.cfm?abstract_id=1631720> accessed 31 July 2017, 5.

13 Paul Schotsmans, 'Bioethics Past, Present and Future: A Personal and Narrative Perspective from the European Continent' in Richard Huxtable and Ruud ter Meulen (eds), *The Voices and Rooms of European Bioethics,* (Abingdon, Routledge, 2015) 18.

14 Richard Huxtable, 'Friends, Foes, Flatmates: On the Relationship between Law and Bioethics' in Jonathan Ives *et al.* (eds), *Empirical Bioethics: Practical and Theoretical Perspectives* (Cambridge University Press 2017) 67.

social sciences.[15] As such, bioethics seems to be an endeavour that is both critical *and* practical.[16]

Bioethics therefore provides a meeting place for various disciplines, which are themselves potentially heterogeneous.[17] Whether bioethics is itself a discipline is a moot point. Dove detects 'some degree of consensus today that bioethics comprises a discipline, a profession, as well as a social movement'.[18] Bioethics certainly has many of the features of a discipline:[19] it involves 'a specific body of knowledge and particular cognitive skills',[20] deploys particular methodologies, approaches, and commitments, and offers specific training courses and specialist journals, such as the *Journal of Medical Ethics* (of which Campbell was, of course, the founding editor). Yet, bioethics should beware of the risks associated with disciplines, such as exclusivity, narrow(-minded)ness, and insularity.[21] In such a vein, Pinker has infamously claimed that bioethics has 'become a professional guild that all too often impedes sound ethical concerns rather than advancing them',[22] arguing that bioethics should not wield its power conservatively and prohibitively but should 'Get out of the way'.[23]

Bioethics' status as a discipline has nevertheless been contested, on the basis that it lacks the required unity.[24] Bioethics not only draws on diverse disciplines but also occurs in diverse settings, as its work can be seen in the activities of professional regulators (like the General Medical Council), trade unions (like the British Medical Association), pressure groups (like Dignity in Dying), and academics.[25] Perhaps the better view, says Chadwick, is simply that bioethics is a 'multidisciplinary *field of study*'.[26] This interpretation is taken by the International

---

15 Jonathan Ives *et al.* (eds), *Empirical Bioethics: Practical and Theoretical Perspectives* (Cambridge University Press 2017) 67.

16 Roger Brownsword, 'Bioethics: Bridging from Morality to Law?' in Michael Freeman (ed.), *Law and Bioethics: Current Legal Issues 2008, Volume 11* (Oxford University Press 2008) 15.

17 Tomas J. Silber, 'Bioethics: An Interdisciplinary Enterprise' (1982) 21(1) *Journal of Religion and Health* 24.

18 Edward S. Dove, '*Review: Richard Huxtable and Ruud Ter Meulen (eds), The Voices and Rooms of European Bioethics*' (2017) 25(1) *Medical Law Review 25(1)* 175.

19 Michel Foucault, *Discipline and Punish: The Birth of the Prison*, Alan Sheridan (trans), (New York, Vintage 1977) 223.

20 Henk ten Have, 'Introduction: Bioethics And European Traditions' in Henk ten Have and Bert Gordijn (eds), *Bioethics in a European Perspective* (Dordrecht, Springer 2001) 2.

21 Daniel Callahan, 'Bioethics as a Discipline' (1973) 1(1) *The Hastings Center Studies* 66.

22 Steven Pinker, 'Steven Pinker Interview: Case Against Bioethocrats and CRISPR Germline Ban' (2015) *The Niche* <https://ipscell.com/2015/08/stevenpinker/> accessed July 31 2017).

23 Steven Pinker, 'The Moral Imperative for Bioethics' (2015) *Boston Globe.* <www.bostonglobe.com/opinion/2015/07/31/the-moral-imperative-for-bioethics/JmEkoyzl TAu9oQV76JrK9N/story.html> accessed 31 July 2017.

24 Nicolette Priaulx, 'The Troubled Identity of the Bioethicist' (2013) 21(1) *Health Care Analysis* 6.

25 Cf. José Miola, 'The Interaction of Medical Law and Medical ethics' (2006) 1(1) *Clinical Ethics* 23.

26 Ruth Chadwick, ' "Getting Ethics": Voices in Harmony in Bioethics' in Richard Huxtable and Ruud ter Meulen (eds), *The Voices and Rooms of European Bioethics* (Abingdon, Routledge 2015) 33.

Association of Bioethics, of which Campbell was a founding board member and later President, which holds that 'bioethics is the study of the ethical, legal, social, philosophical and other related issues arising in health care and in the biological sciences'.[27] The idea that bioethics is a field seems sufficient for our purposes, because it captures the sheer variety of people and perspectives involved in the endeavour.

'Bioethics' might now be in view but the other term, 'European', first requires an account of Europe. Any intuition that this is a more readily graspable idea than 'bioethics' must be dispelled. It is tempting to begin the search by looking to the landmass – or, rather, landmasses – that make up Europe. Named after Europa, a princess of Phoenician origin who was abducted and raped by Zeus and taken to Crete,[28] Europe is a continent that is located at the westernmost part of Eurasia, which borders Asia in the east. Yet, quite which landmasses and states combine to make up Europe will depend on when and where you look.

The relevant boundaries and constitutive countries that combine to form Europe have changed over time and no doubt will continue to do so. Even at the present time, however, the countries included under a 'European' banner will depend on which European grouping you have in view. The European Union, for example, does not include such ostensibly European countries as Norway, Switzerland, and Iceland, and – following the tragedy of the Brexit vote – the UK will soon be departing.[29] Russia is also not a member, although we should note that its landmass straddles both Europe and Asia. A Russian medical ethics group nevertheless *is* included as an associated member of the European Association of Centres of Medical Ethics (EACME).[30] Even more expansive – albeit rather less pertinent to bioethics – is the geographical reach of the Eurovision song contest, which has included Australia since 2015. Given the temporal and geographical variations, we are unlikely to get far if we restrict ourselves to Europe's landmasses. Instead, we can look to the idea – or ideas – of Europe, in the hope that this focus will give us more purchase on 'European bioethics'.

The idea(s) of a united European bioethics

ten Have suggests that Europe 'is not merely a distinct geographical entity but rather a political and cultural concept'.[31] In historical context, Europe has become an 'idea'. Echoing the Cartesian body/mind distinction that underpins many accounts of personal identity, we can perceive the distinctive identity of Europe,

---

27 International Association of Bioethics (IAB) 'Introduction' (2017) <www.bioethics-international.org/work-progress/> accessed 31 July 2017.

28 ten Have (n 20) 3.

29 What Brexit might Mean for Bioethics Remains to Be Seen. See Jonathan D. Moreno, 'Bioethics after Brexit' (2016) *Huff Post Blog* <www.huffingtonpost.com/jonathan-d-moreno/bioethics-after-brexit_b_10756608.html> accessed 31 July 2017.

30 European Association of Centres of Medical Ethics (EACME) 'Members' (2017) <www.eacmeweb.com/members.html> accessed 31 July 2017.

31 ten Have (n 20) 3.

and European bioethics, by looking not to the 'body' or landmasses of Europe but instead to the 'mind' or idea(s) of Europe.[32] Viewed in this way, says Bayertz, we might understand Europe 'as a part of the world with a genuine historical and cultural identity, including a common set of values'.[33]

Both Bayertz and ten Have acknowledge that Europe's identity is difficult to pin down, with Bayertz admitting that 'it is by no means clear which elements are included in this cultural and moral identity, how they are to be interpreted, or what their respective weight is'.[34] Despite this, these authors and others detect something distinctive in Europe and, by extension, European bioethics. ten Have suggests that the distinctive identity of Europe and European bioethics might be discerned by looking for particular processes (approaches to bioethical theorising) and products (values).[35] Bayertz further proposes that the emergent values and approaches can be depicted either in negative and functional terms or in positive and substantial terms.[36]

The *negative and functional* depiction distinguishes Europe from elsewhere, pitting it as a rival to some perceived threat or enemy, from which it can be demarcated.[37] Among the 'threats' to which European bioethics is apparently alert are developments in biotechnology, globalisation, and marketisation,[38] while the 'enemies' of – or, more benignly, alternatives to – European bioethics are said to include American bioethics and Asian bioethics.[39] European bioethics is thus distinguished from, for example, the aforementioned principlism of American bioethics and, in particular, its alleged preoccupation with respect for individual autonomy. Campbell has recently suggested that bioethics has 'narrowly escaped from American capture, a threat coming from the sheer extent of the subject in the USA, and it has become truly global, though risks of Western dominance remain'.[40] The extent of American bioethics and the risks to which Campbell referred were borne out by Borry *et al.* in 2006, in their retrospective quantitative study of articles published in nine leading peer-reviewed bioethics journals.[41]

---

32 Accepting, if only for the purposes of this metaphor, that the two are distinct. See Alastair V. Campbell, 'Why the Body Matters: Reflections on John Harris's Account of Organ Procurement' in John Coggon *et al.* (eds), *From Reason to Practice in Bioethics: An Anthology Dedicated to the Works of John Harris* (Manchester University Press 2015) 131.

33 Kurt Bayertz, 'Struggling for Consensus and Living Without It: The Construction of a Common European Bioethics'. (2004) <www.uni-muenster.de/imperia/md/content/philosophischesseminar/mitglieder/bayertz/texte/consensus.pdf> accessed 31 July 2017.

34 ibid.

35 ten Have (n 20) 7.

36 Bayertz (n 33) 5.

37 Bayertz (n 33) 4.

38 Bayertz (n 33) 8–9.

39 ten Have (n 20) 8; Bayertz (n 33) 5–6; Richard Huxtable, 'Introduction: All of the Future Exists in the Past?' in Richard Huxtable and Ruud ter Meulen (eds.), *The Voices and Rooms of European Bioethics* (Abingdon, Routledge 2015) 7.

40 Campbell (n 6) 12.

41 Pascal Borry *et al.*, 'How International is Bioethics? A Quantitative Retrospective Study' (2006) 7(1) *BMC Medical Ethics.*

Although (as Campbell also suspected) the contribution of West European countries appeared to be increasing, the authors found these (apparently international) journals to be 'clearly dominated by English speaking countries, and especially by the USA'.[42] Campbell has also lamented,[43] like others,[44] the 'myopia of American bioethics', which is evident in at least some books emerging from the US that purport to address bioethics globally but which significantly fail to look beyond American shores. Implicit in these complaints is the idea that there is something out there beyond, and distinct from, American bioethics. On a negative account, then, European bioethics offers something different.

Of course, in order to discern the distinct offerings of European bioethics, a more *positive and substantial* depiction of the relevant approaches and values is needed. According to Bayertz, this depiction 'consists in identifying one crucial idea, principle or value, or several ideas, principles or values, which are constitutive for the European identity'.[45] Such a depiction starts to emerge from the negative account by implication: for example, by distancing itself from the individualism of American bioethics, European bioethics appears more invested in the community at large.[46] But many scholars have gone further, by seeking explicitly to identify the relevant constitutive ideas. Bayertz, for example, cites freedom, individuality, and rationality as distinctively European ideas, which he traces back to Greek and Roman antiquity, with their emphasis on rationality; Christianity, with its concern for equality and dignity; and the Enlightenment, which contributes such values as toleration, human rights, and democracy.[47] European bioethics then builds on these European ideas to develop its idiosyncratic approaches and values. For Bayertz, dignity is a – even *the* – fundamental value of European bioethics, emerging from such roots as Greek and Roman philosophy, Judaeo-Christian accounts of humans as created *imago dei*, and Enlightenment philosophers like Kant.[48] Similarly, for ten Have, European values include, again, human dignity, as well as freedom, tolerance, equal opportunity, social justice, and solidarity, while European approaches involve reference to historical background, the development of substantive moral viewpoints, and a particular interest in the society rather than the individual.[49]

Others have made strikingly similar observations about the processes and products they consider characteristic of European bioethics. In a volume emerging from the 25th anniversary conference of EACME in 2012, 'distinctive values, concepts and approaches' were discernible.[50] These included an interest in character and virtue ethics,

---

42 ibid 5.
43 Alastair V. Campbell, '"My Country 'tis of Thee": The Myopia of American Bioethics' (2000) 3 *Medicine, Healthcare and Philosophy* 195.
44 Jonathan Ives, 'Review: The History and Future of Bioethics: A Sociological View by John H. Evans' (2014) 43(3) *Contemporary Sociology* 362.
45 Bayertz (n 33) 2.
46 ten Have (n 20) 8.
47 Bayertz (n 33) 4.
48 Bayertz (n 33) 10, 32.
49 ten Have (n 20) 8.
50 Huxtable (n 39) 7.

a concern with justice (and associated issues of power and powerlessness), and the promotion of solidarity, all of which further reinforce the idea that European bioethics is often orientated away from the individual and towards the community at large.

One of the contributors to the EACME volume, Schotsmans, suggests that 'it is only when the turn to empirical bioethics and to care (and also to nursing) ethics was made, that distinctively European bioethics developed'.[51] Beyond these approaches, he also points to particular values, going so far as to assert that 'two concepts have guided the majority of continental European approaches to bioethics: the concept of personhood as an integrative concept and the strong belief in the value of solidarity as the basis for a just health care system'.[52] He suggests that these concepts are captured well in a 1990 European project, which involved 22 partners from many European Union (EU) countries and sought to articulate 'four important ideas or values for a European bioethics and biolaw'.[53] The four values were respect for autonomy, dignity, integrity, and vulnerability; Campbell, who was in attendance, offered the participants a fifth, which generated spirited discussion but sadly did not make the final list.[54]

The European four principles are evidently not those of the 'Georgetown mantra'.[55] Although autonomy features in both lists, a 'more comprehensive' notion of autonomy is apparently offered by the European principles, one which is not merely concerned with the 'liberal sense of "permission"', but expresses the thicker 'principle of the self-legislation of rational human beings taking part in the same human life world'.[56] The authors recognise that this and the other principles will be 'institutionalised in various ways in the different European countries',[57] but they propose that 'the wide presence of the basic ethical principles in European ethics and law [means] we may promote them as the basis for future initiatives in bioethics and biolaw'.[58]

The idea(s) of a fragmented European bioethics

The recurrence of particular ideas – like dignity, solidarity, and justice – in the preceding section suggests there may be something distinctive about Europe and, by

51 Schotsmans (n 13) 20. See also Jonathan Ives, 'Methodology and Myopia? Some Praise, a Problem, and a Plea', (2016) 46(5) *Hastings Center Report* 47.

52 Schotsmans (n 13) 22.

53 Jacob D. Rendtorff, 'Basic Ethical Principles in European Bioethics and Biolaw: Autonomy, Dignity, Integrity and Vulnerability – Towards a Foundation of Bioethics and Biolaw' (2002) 5 *Medicine, Health Care and Philosophy* 235.

54 The only published account of this fifth principle comes in a footnote from Engelhardt, in which he thanks Campbell for his 'spirited introduction' to the 'principle of bunnahabhain', which is said to encompass 'four constitutive principles: those of haleness, wholeness, hope, and heteronomy': Hugo T. Engelhardt. 'Autonomy: The Cardinal Principle of Contemporary Bioethics', in Peter Kemp *et al.* (eds), *Bioethics and Biolaw, Vol II: Four Ethical Principles* (Copenhagen, Rhodos 2000) 44.

55 Campbell (n 6) 13.

56 Rendtorff (n 52) 236.

57 ibid.

58 ibid 241.

extension, European bioethics. But neither Europe nor European bioethics is necessarily as united or uniform as the previous accounts implied. In his review of the collection emerging from the 2012 EACME conference, Dove lamented the lack of 'a unifying core that brings the '"European-ness" together'.[59] This could be a failing of the volume (although, as we saw, some unifying themes were suggested), but it could also say something about the very idea of European bioethics. Only a major empirical study could begin to capture the relevant points of convergence and divergence in European bioethics, but even that could only offer a snapshot in time and such a study would, in any case, require some prior account of the parameters of Europe. In the absence of such data, however, there are already indications that the ideas of Europe and European bioethics are fragmented, because there are different world views, different values, different times, and different influences to consider.

Starting with the *different world views*, attempts have been made to map the various bioethical models operating in Europe. In 1999, Dickenson noted that an *imperial* concept of justice, which sees this as a gift of the emperor, operates in some Eastern European states, although she focuses most on three other models.[60] First, she suggests that Southern Europe favours *deontological codes*, in the sense of professional ethics, rather than Kantianism as such.[61] In this model, in which 'the paramount values … are the professionalism of physicians and the dignity (rather than the rights) of patients',[62] a patient has a positive duty to heed the doctor and maximise his or her health and welfare. Second, Western Europe adopts a *liberal, rights-based* approach, in which the patient has a negative right to reject medical opinion and pursue his or her own notion of welfare. The Netherlands is said to exemplify a strong version of this model, the UK a weaker one.[63] Finally, Nordic Europe prefers a *social welfarist* model, in which 'it seems to be assumed that conflicts can be resolved in the public health care system precisely because it is a public health care system, with the virtues of universality and solidarity built in'.[64]

Dickenson suggests that her typology highlights 'important differences which can otherwise be too easily ignored, particularly by those outside Europe', but she admits that the models are 'caricatures', which risk over- and under-specification.[65] Like the proposers of the European four principles,[66] Dickenson appears to derive her models from some of the dominant legal messages emerging from the relevant territories. Of course, the law can be an important source of bioethical values and approaches, but it is only one such source.[67] Yet, her central thesis – that there are different ethical models in operation in Europe – still

---

59 Dove (n 18) 179.
60 Donna L. Dickenson, 'Cross-cultural Issues in European Bioethics' (1999) 3(4) *Bioethics* 250.
61 ibid 251.
62 ibid 252.
63 ibid 249.
64 ibid 254.
65 ibid 255.
66 Rendtorff (n 52).
67 And, of course, law will not only (or even straightforwardly) *receive* values because it will also *provide* values.

stands if we look elsewhere, such as to the philosophical traditions of different European countries.[68] Bayertz argues that there is not, and has never been, a uniform European 'ethical culture': for example, 'One can roughly distinguish a consequentialist and need-oriented type of moral reasoning in countries like Great Britain, the Netherlands and Scandinavia from a deontological and value-oriented type of reasoning prevailing in France or Germany'.[69]

As Bayertz notes, the different 'traditions have a strong influence and shape the philosophical and public debates' in different European countries.[70] But he concedes that there is a risk of 'oversimplification',[71] suggesting that 'If Europe has ever been a unity at all, it has always been a unity-in-diversity, or even a unity-in-controversy'.[72] Diversity is also apparent if we look to – and within – only a single territory. Even an apparently united territory can comprise a variety of ways of life and world views. The United Kingdom of Great Britain and Northern Ireland (UK) is a good example. Great Britain comprises Wales, Scotland, and England; with the inclusion of Northern Ireland, these countries form the UK. The four countries differ – as do their legal systems to varying extents – and the differences mount up once we bring in the other states that make up the British Isles, such as the Channel Islands and the Isle of Man. Despite this variety, there have been suggestions that a dominant bioethical approach (or approaches) can be detected in this broad territory: for example, Schotsmans opines 'that the bio-ethics scene in the UK occupies the mainstream of bioethics, as it is understood and practiced in American, Australian and Asian bioethics centres',[73] while Bayertz refers to the idea that Great Britain is utilitarian in its thinking,[74] and Rendtorff refers to the tension in the UK between the latter school of thought and human rights perspectives.[75] Certainly, there are bioethicists working in the UK or Britain who espouse principlism,[76] as well as those with consequentialist orientations[77] and those with human rights leanings.[78] But this is not the whole story: there are also feminist ethicists[79] and, as Campbell exemplified,[80] virtue ethicists, and so on.

---

68 Leaving open the question about the extent to which the laws in the different jurisdictions are derived from these different philosophical traditions.

69 Bayertz (n 33) 22.

70 ibid.

71 ibid.

72 ibid 13.

73 Schotsmans (n 13) 18.

74 Bayertz (n 33) 22.

75 Rendtorff (n 52) 239.

76 E.g. Raanan Gillon, 'Ethics Needs Principles – Four can Encompass the Rest – And Respect for Autonomy Should Be "First Among Equals"' (2003) 29 *Journal of Medical Ethics* 307.

77 E.g. John Harris, *The Value of Life: An Introduction to Medical Ethics* (London, Routledge and Kegan Paul, 1985).

78 E.g. Deryck Beyleveld and Roger Brownsword, *Human Dignity in Bioethics and Biolaw* (Oxford University Press 2001).

79 E.g. Sorcha U. Chonnachtaigh, 'Ethical Commentary: A Necessarily Feminist Critique of the Judgments' in Stephen W. Smith *et al.* (eds), *Ethical Judgments: Re-writing Medical Law* (Oxford, Hart Publishing 2016) 248.

80 Alastair V. Campbell, 'The Virtues (and Vices) of the Four Principles' (2003) 29 *Journal of Medical Ethics* 292.

Given the different world views detectable between and within different European states, it is unsurprising that there can be *different values* in play. As an example, Horn's empirical research into doctors' views on honouring advance directives found significant differences between, on the one hand, English and German doctors, who sought to respect the autonomous decisions of their patients, and, on the other hand, French doctors, who 'defended a physician-centred approach focusing on physicians' responsibilities to guarantee that individual choices are in accord with socially accepted values'.[81] Sometimes the difference in values might appear to be only one of degree, although that difference can still be considerable. Looking back to the law, English law affords some respect to the sanctity of human life, but considerably less than obtains in the law of Italy, and arguably more than is evident in Dutch law, given that the latter has long tolerated assistance in dying.[82] Such findings might still only tell us something about the values of biolaw, rather than those featuring in the broader field of bioethics but, even if we stick with biolaw, the variation of values is notable. Bayertz notes, for example, that the European Convention on Human Rights and Biomedicine – to which not every EU state is even a signatory – is silent on such contested issues as embryo research and assisted dying, presumably in view of the diverse European views thereon.[83]

It is also not necessarily the case that there is consensus on those issues that the aforementioned Convention *does* cover; rather, the convention is a product of a political compromise, says Bayertz, precisely because there is no consensus between and within member states.[84] The purportedly European values that are captured in such documents, such as 'dignity' and 'solidarity', permit of multiple interpretations. European law allows for national variation, because member states are afforded some discretion in their enactment of the rules. As Bayertz puts it, 'the *setting* of standards is one thing, the *enacting* of standards quite another'.[85] A similar variability can be seen in academic bioethics, where a single term or concept can attract numerous readings, as is readily apparent in the literatures on the aforementioned 'dignity' and 'solidarity', since even scholars working within a single territory disagree about how the concepts are to be understood.[86]

Then there is the temporal dimension to consider, because bioethical approaches and values can differ at *different times*. Returning to the UK, Wilson's

81 Ruth Horn, ' "Why Should I Question a Patient's Wish?" A Comparative Study on Physicians' Perspectives on their Duties to Respect Advance Directives' (2016) 24 *European Journal of Health Law* 3.

82 Ruth Horn *et al.*, 'European Perspectives on Ethics and Law in End-of-Life Care' in James L. Bernat and Richard Beresford (eds), *Ethical and Legal Issues in Neurology: Handbook of Clinical Neurology* (Edinburgh, Elsevier 2013) 155.

83 Bayertz (n 33) 17–18.

84 ibid 18.

85 ibid 28.

86 E.g. Charles Foster, *Human Dignity in Bioethics and Law* (Oxford, Hart 2011); Ruud ter Meulen, 'Solidarity, Justice, and Recognition of the Other' (2016) 37(6) *Theoretical Medicine and Bioethics* 517.

excellent book, *The Making of British Bioethics*, traces some of the evolutions and revolutions in that territory. Wilson, a historian, interviewed some of the pioneers of British bioethics, Campbell included, and one of the themes he explores is the retreat from medical paternalism towards the requirement that patients and research participants should provide informed consent.[87] Wilson's book takes a cue from the sociologist Reubi, who (in Wilson's words) has 'demonstrated how specific factors shape what counts as '"bioethics" in different times and places'.[88] Reubi cited Singapore, where Campbell directed his third bioethics centre, as an example. According to Reubi,[89] bioethics emerged there as part of a 'will to modernize': bioethics' presence was designed to create confidence in the safety and standards of the Singaporean biomedical research sector. Recalling our earlier observations about bioethics as a field, Reubi further notes how bioethics in Singapore is 'an assemblage of knowledge, experts and techniques', performing various social and political roles.[90] As Wilson puts it, Reubi's 'insight prevents us from mistakenly identifying bioethics as a monolithic entity with a single perspective and mode of inquiry'.[91]

The changes that come over time can also be traced at local and regional levels within a single country. Bristol's Centre for Ethics in Medicine, for example, has always been dedicated to enquiry, education, and engagement, but the emphasis of its work has shifted slightly with its different directors.[92] Founding the Centre in 1996, Campbell initially emphasised the educational endeavour and, in his (individual and collaborative) research, virtue ethics was prominent.[93] ter Meulen, the second director, sought to encourage European research, with his own research exploring such (apparently) European values as justice and solidarity.[94] Since I became director in 2015, public and professional engagement activities have come to the fore,[95] as has multi-disciplinary empirical bioethics research,[96] while my own research in bioethics explores such notions as pluralism and compromise.[97] The Centre's collaborative work has also evolved over time, with the first phase marked by both national and

---

87 Wilson (n 2). Of course, this particular theme has played out elsewhere in the world.

88 ibid 7.

89 David Reubi, 'The Will to Modernize: A Genealogy of Biomedical Research Ethics in Singapore' (2010) 4 *International Political Sociology* 142.

90 ibid 144.

91 Wilson (n 2) 8.

92 I should emphasise that these are subjective and selective impressions, which also should not be taken to imply that the 'identity' of a Centre is formed entirely by its director.

93 E.g. Teresa L. Swift *et al.*, 'Living Well Through Chronic Illness: The Relevance of Virtue Theory to Patients with Chronic Osteoarthritis' (2002) 47(5) *Arthritis and Rheumatology* 474.

94 E.g. ter Meulen (n 85).

95 University of Bristol, '2015/16 Engagement Award winners announced' (2016) <www.bristol.ac.uk/news/2016/september/engagement-awards.html> accessed 31 July 2017.

96 Ives *et al.* (n 15).

97 E.g. Richard Huxtable, *Law, Ethics and Compromise at the Limits of Life: To Treat or Not to Treat?* (Abingdon, Routledge 2012).

international collaborations, the second by European collaborations in particular, and the third looking increasingly to colleagues in Asia, such as in South Korea, Japan, and Singapore. All these transitions further illustrate, in the words of de Vries *et al.*,[98] how 'bioethics is a plural noun and its plurality is multiple' – not only between and within countries, as Wilson notes,[99] but even within a single bioethics centre.

The Bristol Centre also exemplifies how bioethical work, wherever it occurs, will be subject to and informed by *different influences*. Maybe it is noteworthy that the aforementioned three directors are, chronologically, a Scottish theologian-philosopher, a Dutch psychologist-philosopher, and a Welsh healthcare lawyer.[100] Also notable is the fact that Campbell and ter Meulen came to the UK from New Zealand and the Netherlands, respectively, with Campbell then moving from the UK to work in Singapore. Although such individuals will seek and gain new insights from the contexts and cultures in which they come to work, ideas will also travel with them. The transfer of ideas can be a very positive phenomenon, but it further complicates the notion of a united European bioethics. As Bayertz says, 'ideas have spread all over the world and have developed deep roots in major parts of it. If freedom, individuality, and rationality are constitutive for the European identity, then at least North America and Australia have long become 'European'. It is hard to see how a distinctive European identity could be based on such ideas or values'.[101]

Pluralism and bioethics in Europe (and beyond)

Although there may be some common ideas, the picture of European bioethics that emerges is one of what Bayertz called 'unity-in-diversity',[102] because both Europe and bioethics encompass a variety of places, people, and perspectives. In trying to understand each term, we have been looking to the land – literally in the search for Europe, and metaphorically in the depiction of bioethics as a field. But rather than remain on the land, perhaps we should (metaphorically) take to the oceans.[103] Populated by diverse crews, a bioethics fleet traverses the globe 'on

---

98 Raymond de Vries *et al.*, 'Social Science and Bioethics: The Way Forward' in Raymond de Vries *et al.* (eds), *The View from Here: Bioethics and the Social Sciences* (Oxford, Blackwell Publishing 2007) 2.

99 Wilson (n 2) 8.

100 This sounds like the feedline of a joke; although I might regret this, I leave it to the reader to supply his or her own punchline.

101 Bayertz (n 33) 4.

102 Bayertz (n 33) 13.

103 Captain Campbell is no stranger to watery metaphors, having written about 'the good ship NHS' (Alastair V. Campbell, 'Clinical Governance: Watchword or Buzzword?' [2001] 27 *Journal of Medical Ethics Suppl* 54) and been described as 'A Scotsman on the High Seas' in a paper presented at a conference marking his first retirement (Soren Holm, 'A Scotsman on the High Seas: Alastair Campbell and the Birth of Global Bioethics'. Presentation at a 1-day conference celebrating the retirement of Alastair Campbell [Bristol, 1 August 2003]).

a willing course',[104] its vessels weighing anchor in different ports, where crew and cargo are refreshed and replenished. The ships' anchors attach to different areas of the seabed deep beneath, each area offering a relatively secure foundation, albeit one that erodes and shifts over time. The ship might sometimes remain in roughly one geographical spot, but it will be buffeted by different winds at different times, with the waters that surround it surging and swelling, ebbing and flowing.

Rather than suggesting that bioethics is all at sea, this metaphor hopefully captures the stability and change that is characteristic of bioethics, and thus of European bioethics. Bioethics in a given territory might owe a debt to particular tenacious historical ideas, but ideas will change and travel, both from and into that territory. On this account, bioethics is pluralistic, and this might be the case wherever it is theorised or practised. ten Have suggests that, just as there are various approaches to continental philosophy, in continental bioethics 'many schools and approaches flourish in practice and literature: applied ethics, hermeneutical ethics, casuistry, clinical ethics, narrative ethics, care ethics. But this situation seems not too different from North America'.[105] He sees (American) principlism as dominant in the US, but is surely right to suggest that, even there, 'also a variety of approaches exists'.[106]

Similar points can be made about the other alleged 'enemy' of European bioethics, Asian bioethics. Just as Western approaches cannot be reduced to a liberal emphasis on individual rights and freedoms, Nie rejects the 'specious idea of an Asian bioethics', which trades on a stereotype of Asia as communitarian, collective, or family-oriented.[107] That stereotype might not be distinctive to Asia: we saw earlier that a communal emphasis is also apparently characteristic of European bioethics, so (to echo Bayertz) perhaps Europe is Asian – or Asia is European. In any event, the implicit (and sometimes explicit) cultural homogenisation of the stereotype is simplistic in the extreme. According to Nie and Campbell:[108]

> nowadays no country or area in Asia (or anywhere else in the world for that matter) is truly mono-cultural... The "golden age" of cultural purity, like its near relation, "ethnic purity" – if it ever existed in human history at all – has long since gone, and can never be restored.

Asia – like Europe, the US, or in theory any territory on the globe – is diverse in its ethical approaches and values. Campbell draws a simple but compelling

---

104 To invoke the Campbells' beloved band, Runrig.
105 ten Have (n 20) 7.
106 ibid.
107 Jingbao Nie, 'The Specious Idea of an Asian Bioethics' in Richard Ashcroft *et al.* (eds), *Principles of Health Care Ethics* (2nd edn, London, Wiley 2007) 143.
108 Jingbao Nie and Alastair V. Campbell, 'Multiculturalism and Asian Bioethics: Cultural War or Creative Dialogue?' (2007) 4 *Journal of Bioethical Inquiry* 164.

conclusion: we should 'abandon the notion of "Asian Bioethics"' and instead 'should discuss what might be important features of "Bioethics *in* Asia"'.[109] Substitute Asia(n) for Europe(an) and the point stands: there is no European bioethics, only bioethics *in* Europe.

These arguments need not leave us with a bioethics of everywhere and there-fore, potentially, nowhere. In his review of the EACME 2012 volume, Dove complained that some of the arguments therein were 'more global than European in nature'.[110] But, referring back to the earlier observations of Campbell and the findings from Borry *et al.*, there may be a risk of 'American capture', if bioethics is aggregated into a global endeavour in which context is irrelevant.[111] Instead, as Campbell explains, we should recognise that we are everywhere dealing with the same field of inquiry, but that the 'context can add new dimensions, raise new questions or help to shift perspectives'.[112] I interpret Campbell as arguing that bioethics should be open to the different people in different places who offer different perspectives – so bioethics and bioethicists in Europe might offer some-thing distinctive – but that we should not be reductionist because plurality is rife in bioethics, wherever its work is occurring.

It is tempting to infer from these remarks that pluralism is the bioethical condition. But such an inference needs unpacking, which I can only begin to attempt here. The sort of pluralism I have in mind walks a tightrope between universalism (or objectivism) and relativism (or particularism or subjectivism). First, however, there is an empirical claim. In different (particular) locales, there are likely to be dominant, historically informed ideas, but there will also be a wider plurality of values and approaches. When we widen our search, we are likely to find that the same is true in many, maybe all, contexts. That hypoth-esis could be tested but, if we assume (on the evidence we have) that this is a global phenomenon, then ethical pluralism is a universal feature of bioethics *in fact*. This is an empirical claim about the wide field of bioethics, rather than any individual bioethicists: an individual or group can be monistic, absolutist, and so on, in outlook, but the field as a whole is ethically pluralistic in the sense that it is ethically diverse.

The reader might retort 'so what?' This empirical claim appears rather banal, because the same can be said of many fields or endeavours (recall, for example, the heterogeneity of the individual disciplines that populate bioethics). But behind it, second, lurk more complex prescriptive or normative questions. What, if anything, *should* flow from the fact of ethical pluralism in the sense of ethical diversity?[113] Indeed, regardless of the fact of ethical diversity, *should* bioethics (globally) embrace ethical pluralism? These questions engage with a different

109 Alastair V. Campbell, 'Commentary: Autonomy Revisited – A Response to H. Haker' (2011) 269 *Journal of Internal Medicine* 381.
110 Dove (n 18) 179.
111 Campbell (n 6) 12; Borry *et al.* (n 41).
112 Campbell (n 108) 381.
113 Mindful that this risks blurring the much-discussed distinction between facts and values.

interpretation of 'ethical pluralism' – 'the view that there are many different moral values', which are not 'reducible to one super value'.[114]

Strictly speaking, this account of ethical pluralism says nothing of universalism and particularism: for example, one can believe, as a universal proposition, that there are many ethical values. But Wolf thinks ethical pluralism has important implications for both universalism and particularism:[115]

> In understanding and interpreting moral disagreements, pluralism offers an alternative to the relativist position that my views are right for me and your views are right for you, as well as to the absolutist position that only one of us can be right ... If, as pluralism says, there is a plurality of values or principles or reasons for favoring and disfavoring things that does not form a complete well-ordered system, then it seems reasonable to expect that the realm of moral facts will contain pockets of indeterminacy.

Bioethics might not be able to resolve the indeterminacy,[116] but (to return to the seafaring metaphor) it may be able to offer ways of navigating choppy waters, if it adopts a pluralistic outlook.

De Castro indicates towards this conclusion, when he sets out on the tight-rope between the relative and universal:[117]

> In a world characterised by increasing cross-cultural encounters and ethical pluralism, we cannot abandon the drive for universal acceptance and understanding. However, the universality of our ideals cannot be found in a single standard that is common to all outlooks, but, rather, in a collage of cultural informed perspectives built upon an ever increasing aggregate of shared experiences.

Hongladoram has some difficulty with the ambivalence in de Castro's position but still detects something of value in de Castro's pluralistic 'collage'. Like Wolf, Hongladoram talks of disputes occurring at different 'levels':[118]

> the way to move beyond the universalism/relativism debate is to allow for different ways in which a bioethical practice (such as informed consent) can be justified, while at the same time allowing for different ideas in which the first-order judgment (such as how informed consent is actually done in the field) could be compared.

114 Elinor Mason, 'Value Pluralism' in Edward Zalta (ed.), *The Stanford Encyclopedia of Philosophy* (2015) <https://plato.stanford.edu/archives/sum2015/entries/value-pluralism/> accessed 31 July 2017.

115 Susan M. Wolf, 'Two Levels of Pluralism' (1992) 102(4) *Ethics* 788.

116 Nor, for that matter, can philosophy as such, according to Wolf (n 114).

117 Leonardo de Castro, 'Is there an Asian Bioethics?' (1999) 13 *Bioethics* 234.

118 Soraj Hongladarom, 'Universalism and Particularism Debate in "Asian Bioethics"' (2008) 1 *Asian Bioethics Review* 11.

What this might entail for bioethics is some form of proceduralism (which will not be welcomed by everyone in bioethics), as is confirmed by Hongladoram's suggestion that 'bioethics can be nothing more than this constant process of discussion and negotiation'.[119] An open willingness to hear the different perspectives – not just, for example, those emanating from American principlism – will be key to that negotiation. As Campbell has suggested, 'Global Bioethics must respect the whole diversity of world views of ethics, both religious and nonreligious.'[120] Here, as we might expect from his work, Campbell (writing with Nie) perceives a role for the virtues: 'we can make our own history by learning from history and responding to our inevitable multiculturalism with humanity, compassion, wisdom and prudence'.[121]

Conclusion

The arguments above combine to suggest that bioethics should be pluralistic: values and approaches, plural, should be drawn upon in order to address bioethical problems, wherever they arise. In doing so, we are likely to find some regional variations but, on stepping back, also substantial overlap, which might offer a promising basis for exploring, and perhaps even resolving, real dilemmas. So, the conclusion seems to be, bioethics is and should be pluralistic in outlook.

The normative claim is complex and invites further thought (indeed, in keeping with the recent argument, it needs further discussion and negotiation). Leaving aside that particular claim, the central thrust of this chapter was as follows. I argued, first, that the ideas of Europe and European bioethics can be glimpsed, both (negatively) as ideas that are distinct from those that might be found elsewhere, and (more positively) in various distinctive values and approaches. Second, however, I argued that any perceived unity should not be inflated, because across Europe (whatever its geographical boundaries) and, by extension, European bioethics, there is what Campbell has described as 'variation from society to society and epoch to epoch'.[122]

Finally, this pluralism was seen to be characteristic of bioethics as such, with the implication being that – following Campbell – it is more accurate to talk of 'bioethics in Europe' (for example), rather than 'European bioethics'. This looks like a viable empirical claim, and might even lead to a normative one – bioethics, wherever it is theorised or practised, should be pluralistic. That, however, is a more challenging claim, meriting further work. For now, I hope to have conveyed that, in the manner of Campbell's own academic voyage, the good ship(s) bioethics should continue to traverse the globe, picking up and depositing different perspectives, people, and produce in different ports.

119 ibid 11–12.
120 Alastair V. Campbell, 'Presidential Address: Global Bioethics – Dream or Nightmare?' (1999) 13(3/4) *Bioethics* 189.
121 Nie and Campbell (n 107) 166.
122 Campbell (n 79) 294.

9 Healthcare ethics in New Zealand

Lynley Anderson and Nicola Peart

Introduction

Alastair V. Campbell was Professor of Biomedical Ethics and Director of the Bioethics Research Centre at the University of Otago in Dunedin, New Zealand, from 1990 to 1996. This was a time of radical change in the ethical landscape of health care in New Zealand, following the release of the *Report of the Committee of Inquiry into Allegations Concerning the Treatment of Cervical Cancer at National Women's Hospital and into Other Related Matters* in 1988. Judge Silvia Cartwright was appointed as the Chair of the Committee of Inquiry in 1987 following publication of an article in *Metro* magazine, revealing shocking abuse of the doctor-patient relationship in the context of research that had disastrous consequences for some of the women participants.[1] This article and the report of the Cartwright Inquiry had far-reaching consequences for health care and health research in New Zealand.

Campbell was completing a sabbatical year at the University of Otago Medical School when the *Metro* story broke. He was by then known in New Zealand for his inspirational work in medical ethics. The Cartwright Inquiry called him as an expert witness and his evidence played a vital role in the Committee's findings and recommendations. The recommendations were wide-ranging and covered both healthcare delivery and the conduct of health research, as well as medical education and regulation of the profession. The core value underpinning all the Committee's recommendations was the importance of respect for patients and research participants in the healthcare setting. During his 6-year tenure at the University of Otago, Campbell had a profound influence on the implementation of the Cartwright Inquiry's recommendations and the development of healthcare ethics in New Zealand.

We begin by explaining Campbell's introduction to New Zealand and his contributions to the Cartwright Inquiry, following which we explore his wide-ranging influence on healthcare ethics in the post-Cartwright era during his time in New Zealand. We conclude by providing a brief overview of significant

---

1 Sandra Coney and Phillida Bunkle, 'An Unfortunate Experiment at National Women's' (1987) June *Metro* 47.

changes affecting healthcare ethics since his departure to demonstrate and evaluate Campbell's legacy.

Campbell's introduction to New Zealand

Campbell first visited New Zealand in 1985, when he was a senior lecturer in the Department of Christian Ethics and Practical Theology at the University of Edinburgh. He came to Dunedin on a Thomas Burns Memorial Lectureship to give a series of lectures to the Theological Hall, Knox College, where training for the Presbyterian Ministry took place in conjunction with the Faculty of Theology at the University of Otago. Campbell had a strong interest in medical ethics and had published several books on the subject, including *Moral Dilemmas in Medicine* and *Medicine Health and Justice*.[2] He was also the founding editor of the *Journal of Medical Ethics*. During that visit, Gareth Jones, Professor of Anatomy at the University of Otago Medical School, invited Campbell to visit the school, where there was by then a growing interest in medical ethics. Professor Geoffrey Brinkman, the Dean of the medical school in the early 1980s, had initiated a series of public seminars on ethical issues in medicine involving academics from across the university and affiliated institutions, including Mrs Gwennyth Taylor from the Department of Philosophy, Professor Peter Skegg, newly appointed to the Faculty of Law, and the Rev. Peter Marshall, Master of Knox College.[3] The Faculty of Medicine's curriculum committee had also established a working party[4] to explore integration of bioethics teaching into the undergraduate medical curriculum. The working party discussed its views with Campbell during his visit to the medical school and received his strong support for their recommendation that ethics be taught as an integral part of the curriculum in all years.[5]

The working party was also seeking support for the establishment of a University of Otago Bioethics Resource Centre.[6] Campbell advised the working

---

2 Alastair V. Campbell, *Moral Dilemmas in Medicine: A Coursebook in Ethics for Doctors and Nurses* (Churchill Livingstone 1972); Alastair V. Campbell, *Medicine, Health and Justice: The Problem of Priorities* (Churchill Livingstone 1978).

3 See the letter from Gwennyth Taylor to Nicola Peart published as an appendix to Nicola Peart, 'Health and Disability Research Ethics Committees in New Zealand: Will the Current System Prevent Another "Unfortunate Experiment"?' in Mark Henaghan and Jesse Wall (eds), *Law, Ethics, and Medicine: Essays in Honour of Peter Skegg* (Thomson Reuters 2016).

4 The working party on the teaching of medical ethics was chaired by Professor Gareth Jones and its membership included the Dean and senior staff from the Faculty of Medicine as well as Professor Peter Skegg, the Rev. G.P. Fitzgerald and the Rev. Peter Marshall.

5 Letter from Professor Geoffrey L. Brinkman to the working party members (11 March 1985); Alastair V. Campbell 'Teaching Medical Ethics Symposium. Reflections from New Zealand' (1987) 13 *Journal of Medical Ethics* 137. See further in this volume Neil Pickering, Lynley Anderson and Peter Skegg, 'Healthcare ethics education at Otago and the Master of Bioethics and Health Law' (Chapter 10).

6 Letter from Professor Geoffrey L. Brinkman to Dr Robin Irvine, Vice-Chancellor, University of Otago (2 April 1985). Brinkman first raised the possibility of establishing a Bioethics Centre with the Vice-Chancellor in November 1982.

party that such a centre, led by a director, would be the best way to raise the status of bioethics at the university. Ideally, the director would be a medical doctor with a degree in moral or ethical philosophy, but the working party realised that such a person might be difficult to find. Instead, their aim was to appoint a moral philosopher with experience in the medical setting.[7]

Recognising the contribution that Campbell could offer the medical school and the wider university, Campbell was invited to spend a sabbatical year at the University of Otago as a visiting professor to enhance awareness and discussion of biomedical ethics, and to assist in developing ethics teaching in the medical curriculum and in the setting up of a bioethics centre.[8] His visit from September 1986 to August 1987 as the Visiting Professor in Biomedical Ethics was sponsored by the Education Committee of the Presbyterian Synod of Otago and Southland, St John's College Trust Board of the Anglican Church of New Zealand, the Roman Catholic Diocese of Dunedin, the Alexander McMillan Trust, the Otago Hospital Board, and the University of Otago.[9] This cross-sectoral support indicates the widespread interest in medical ethics at the time and the growing appreciation of its importance to the healthcare sector.

The sponsors had high expectations and Campbell did not disappoint! He advised, initiated, and evaluated medical ethics teaching in the undergraduate medical curriculum. Because ethics teaching was to be integrated throughout the curriculum, he also ran workshops and a symposium on biomedical ethics to improve the expertise and confidence of all teaching staff in handling ethical issues. He spent time at the Christchurch and Wellington Clinical Schools of Medicine of the University of Otago to advise on ethics teaching in the clinical years. He also held a short-term visiting professorship at the University of Auckland's medical school to advise on ethics teaching.[10]

To improve public awareness of ethical dilemmas facing healthcare providers and society as a whole, he gave public lectures and facilitated public meetings. He contributed to conferences and courses run by professional organisations and gave lectures to health professional and non-health professional groups, such as within the chaplaincy and theological education. As healthcare providers got to know him, they started calling on him to discuss ethical issues in their clinical work.[11] His expertise and experience in pastoral theology and medical ethics were seen as valuable to clinical discussion. He was also involved in the appointment of Grant Gillett, a neurosurgeon and ethicist, to a half-time senior lectureship in medical Ethics, the first such appointment at the University of Otago.

7 ibid.
8 Alastair V. Campbell, 'Report to the Faculty of Medicine, University of Otago' (21 August 1987) (Campbell Report).
9 ibid.
10 The Universities of Otago and Auckland are the only New Zealand universities with a medical school. Otago's Faculty of Medicine has a clinical school in Dunedin, Christchurch, and Wellington.
11 Campbell Report (n 8).

Meanwhile, discussions on the establishment of a bioethics centre and the appointment of a director continued, with significant input from Campbell. By June 1987, it was apparent that there was cross-disciplinary support for a bio-ethics centre and that the University of Otago was seen as the ideal place for such a centre, given the wide range of people within the University with interest and experience in ethical issues.[12] The functions that the centre was envisaged to perform included sponsoring seminars, both within the university and for the general public; providing a consultation and resource service for medical professionals; commenting on current legislation and advising on law reform proposals; creating a forum for bringing together different disciplines; coordin-ating and encouraging research within applied ethics; and producing a newsletter on current developments in bioethics within and beyond New Zealand.[13]

The appointment of a suitable director remained an issue. Finding the right person was crucial to the success of the centre. Campbell's wife, Sally Campbell, knew that her husband was at a crossroads in his career and suggested that a move away from Christian ethics in a Faculty of Theology to bioethics in a med-ical school might be of interest to her husband. Following Campbell's return to Edinburgh, formal discussions between the university and the Presbyterian Synod of Otago and Southland resulted in the establishment in 1988 of the Otago Bioethics Research Centre and a Chair in Bioethics, which was to be offered to Campbell.[14] Jones was appointed as the first director of the centre in 1988 and held that position until Campbell arrived in 1990 to take up the chair and the directorship of the centre.

Campbell's contribution to the Cartwright Report

Metro magazine published an article in June 1987 entitled 'An Unfortunate Experiment at National Women's'.[15] This 16-page article described a research study into cervical cancer at New Zealand's largest women's hospital that ran from 1962 until about 1982, in which Dr Herbert Green, a consultant obstetrician and gynaecologist at the National Women's Hospital, withheld standard treatment from women presenting with carcinoma in situ (CIS) without their knowledge or consent. Green did not accept the prevailing international view that CIS was a precursor to invasive cervical cancer and that early detection through cervical

---

12 Minutes of a meeting to discuss a proposal to set up a Bioethics Centre on 10 June 1987. The working group members were Professor D.G. Jones (Department of Anatomy, Convenor); Dr B.L. Brookes (Department of History); Professor A.V. Campbell (Visiting Professor in Biomedical Ethics); Rev. V.J. Hunt (Faculty of Theology); Professor R.D.H. Stewart (Dean, Dunedin Division, Faculty of Medicine); and Professor P.D.G. Skegg (Faculty of Law).

13 D. Gareth Jones, 'Proposal to Establish a Bioethics Research Centre' (22 August 1988) 3. The Centre was to be called the University of Otago Bioethics Research Centre.

14 The Presbyterian Synod of Otago and Southland contributed $20,000 towards the estab-lishment of the Chair of Biomedical Ethics: letter from L.E. Williams, Clerk of Synod, to Professor John Hunter, Dean of the Faculty of Medicine (28 April 1988).

15 Coney and Bunkle (n 1).

screening could save lives. His hypothesis was that invasive cervical cancer was a separate disease and that CIS was harmless and did not need to be eradicated.[16] Rather than giving the women the standard treatment of a full cone biopsy, which carried a risk of morbidity, or performing a hysterectomy, he decided to observe the natural progression of their disease, giving only limited treatment (including punch biopsies with incomplete excision of the abnormality), even when the pathology reports were 'conclusive for malignancy'.[17] Many women were not told that they had CIS, nor did they know that their treatment departed significantly from internationally accepted treatment for CIS. In common with many doctors at the time, Dr Green believed that doctors, not patients, should decide on appropriate treatment.[18]

In 1966, Green sought and was granted approval for his research proposal from the National Women's Hospital's medical committee, despite concerns about patient safety raised by some of his colleagues outside the committee. As the study progressed, concerns about adverse consequences on some of the women mounted, but these were largely ignored and the study was not halted.[19] A paper published 3 years before the Cartwright Inquiry evidenced the scientific and ethical flaws in Green's study.[20] Subsequent analysis of patients diagnosed with CIS between 1955 and 1976 showed a marked increase in patients developing invasive cervical cancer between 1964 and 1974, while others suffered persistent disease and a few women died.[21]

The *Metro* article shocked New Zealand and provoked an immediate response. As Campbell observed in 1989:

> The response to the *Metro* article was dramatic and virtually instantaneous – in marked contrast with the virtual absence of any reaction from the medical profession to the technical articles upon which it was based.[22]

Society's strong reaction went well beyond the unethical conduct of a single doctor. The inability of Dr Green's colleagues to halt the study as soon as they became aware of his misconceived hypothesis rocked society's confidence in the

---

16 ibid 48.
17 ibid 49.
18 ibid 50.
19 ibid 53. Dr W.A. McIndoe, Dr M.R. McLean and later Dr R.W. Jones expressed concern. See Dr W.A. McIndoe's Memorandum of 14 December 1973 and Dr M.R. McLean's Memorandum of 10 May 1974 in *The Report of the Committee of Inquiry into Allegations Concerning the Treatment of Cervical Cancer at National Women's Hospital and into Other Related Matters* (Government Printing Office, 1988), Appendices 5 and 6 respectively (Cartwright Report).
20 William McIndoe *et al.*, 'The invasive potential of carcinoma in situ of the cervix' (1984) 64 *Obstetrics and Gynecology* 451.
21 Cartwright Report (n 19) 210.
22 Alastair V. Campbell, 'A Report from New Zealand: An "Unfortunate Experiment"' (1989) 3 *Bioethics* 59, 60.

whole of the medical profession. At the request of the Superintendent-in-Chief of the Auckland Hospital Board, the Minister of Health responded promptly by appointing Judge Silvia Cartwright on 10 June 1987 as the Chair of the Committee of Inquiry to investigate the allegations made by the authors of the *Metro* article.[23] Her report, commonly referred to as 'the Cartwright Report', was released a year later, in July 1988.

Campbell played a pivotal role in this Inquiry. He was called as the first of many expert witnesses. His role was to provide evidence about the ethics of conducting a health research study. He assisted the Inquiry in determining that the research proposal Green submitted for approval to the hospital's medical committee in 1966 was an experimental study that did not comply with scientific or ethical research standards at the time. The hypothesis that CIS was not a premalignant disease could not be proved and it could not be disproved without putting the participating women at serious risk of harm. The absence of consent was a clear breach of ethical standards, first articulated in the Nuremburg Code in 1947 and subsequently in the Declaration of Helsinki 1964.[24] Yet, the proposal had received approval from the hospital's medical committee and was allowed to continue for many years despite increasing evidence that Green's theory was fundamentally flawed. Judge Cartwright was firm in her conclusions:

> The fact that the women did not know they were in a trial, were not informed that their treatment was not conventional and received little detail of the nature of their condition were grave omissions. The responsibility for these omissions extends to all those who having approved the trial, knew or ought to have known of its mounting consequences and its design faults and allowed it to continue.[25]

Events at National Women's Hospital highlighted a wider problem within the practice of medicine generally. Campbell explained to the Cartwright Inquiry that until the end of World War II the ethics of medical practice was a relatively undeveloped subject.[26] The medical profession had been confusing ethics with etiquette. Ethics was thought to require courteous behaviour towards each other and non-interference in each other's work. There was a strong commitment to clinical freedom and collegial loyalty.[27] However, Campbell emphasised that this commitment did not override the primary duty to the patient. Furthermore, during the period of the Green study, there had been significant developments in

---

23 Cartwright Report (n 19) 4. The Committee of Inquiry was appointed on 10 June 1987, within days of the *Metro* article appearing.
24 ibid 67–8.
25 ibid 69.
26 ibid 127.
27 Dr Green's personality and belligerent reponse to comments and criticism made it more difficult for colleagues to question the ethics of his research: the Memoranda of Dr McIndoe and Dr McLean (n 19). Ronald W. Jones, *Doctors in Denial: The Forgotten Women in the 'Unfortunate Experiment'* (Otago University Press 2017).

the doctor-patient relationship. No longer was the doctor seen as the sole decision maker as regards 'his' patient and:

> ... a wholly autonomous and authoritative judge of 'what is in the patient's best interests'. In its place there has come the recognition that patients themselves are usually the best judges of this, provided they are properly informed of the options available.[28]

However, as some of the clinical witnesses said in their evidence to the Committee of Inquiry, it was not easy for clinicians to recognise the responsibilities attached to clinical freedom, particularly in 1966.

Campbell also told the Inquiry that there had long been an ethical obligation on clinicians to seek peer review in all situations of uncertainty and to maintain realistic self-scrutiny.[29] Peer review meant not only discussing topics informally. It required formal structured reviews of cases and research proposals to increase awareness, identify problems, learn from mistakes, and make improvements. The Cartwright Inquiry concluded that the National Women's Hospital's medical committee had failed Dr Green by not reviewing his research proposal carefully in 1966 and not taking note of the concerns that had already been raised. Even after publication of scientific papers in the 1980s identifying the flaws in Green's study and the adverse consequences for some participants, the hospital took no steps to halt the study formally or to locate and treat its participants.[30] It was not until the *Metro* article was published in 1987 that the hospital initiated a review of the study. The Cartwright Inquiry was highly critical of the inadequacy of peer review and the lack of processes to deal decisively with issues relating to competence.[31]

Of greatest concern to the Committee of Inquiry was the failure to obtain informed consent from the women prior to their enrolment in the study. As Campbell wrote in 1989:

> ... patients were not party to the unusual treatment regimen being pursued and were often falsely assured that there was no cause for concern. Such things are now labelled as 'paternalistic' and are rightly seen as serious affronts to the dignity and autonomy of patients.[32]

He questioned why in the 1980s even the most well-meaning healthcare professionals still had such difficulty in treating their patients as self-determining adults. He postulated that it might be in part the fault of the ethos of professionalism and its 'Hippocratic tradition' and in part the difficulty of explaining

28 Cartwright Report (n 19) 128.
29 ibid 130.
30 ibid 131.
31 ibid 70.
32 Campbell, 'A Report from New Zealand' (n 22) 62.

to patients the complexities and uncertainties of diagnosis and treatment. This failure was clearly a breach of ethical codes and arguably also a breach of a legal duty. However, New Zealand's 'no fault' accident compensation scheme meant that there was little case law on consent to medical treatment.[33] The Cartwright Inquiry thus concluded that there was a need to spell out the consent requirement in legislation.

The need to establish ethics committees in hospitals had been recognised since the 1970s, but the initial committees lacked independence and did not necessarily include anyone with ethical expertise. The National Women's Hospital's ethical committee was no exception, even in 1988. It also had no written ethical principles for clinical research or an application form. Campbell gave details of the recommended composition of ethics committees, explaining that professional members are needed to assess the validity of the research design and the potential usefulness of the outcome, but that they had to be balanced by lay members whose impartiality puts them in a better position to question the protection of research participants.[34]

Campbell's evidence to the Cartwright Inquiry is reflected in the findings and recommendations. Aside from recommendations specific to the women involved in Green's study, the Cartwright Report made recommendations that called for a fundamental change to the doctor-patient relationship from a doctor-centred approach to one where the patient was central, in regard to both treatment and research. To protect the interests of patients, the report recommended a statement of patients' rights, including a stipulation that fully informed consent to treatment and research was essential; the development of treatment protocols and quality assurance programmes; the ethical and scientific evaluation of significant shifts in treatment or management of disease; and the appointment of a health commissioner to deal with complaints and grievances from patients, to increase health professionals' understanding of patients' rights, and to refer concerns about breaches of patients' rights to a tribunal for a ruling and sanction. The report also recommended the establishment of an independent patient advocacy service and independent ethics committees with equal lay and professional representation.[35]

The Cartwright Inquiry's findings and recommendations went well beyond one doctor, one study, or even one hospital. As Dr Charlotte Paul, one of the medical advisers to the Inquiry, observed shortly after the report was released, public distrust in the medical profession as a whole was an unavoidable consequence of the Inquiry.[36] Commentators have described it as a 'public scrutiny of

---

33 The Accident Compensation Act 1972 established a state-funded compensation scheme for anyone who suffered a personal injury by accident, but in return injured persons were precluded from bringing civil proceedings for compensation for the injury: section 5.

34 Cartwright Report (n 19) 146.

35 ibid ch 11.

36 Charlotte Paul, 'The New Zealand Cervical Cancer Study: Could it Happen Again?' (1988) 297 *British Medical Journal* 533, 538.

medical practice, research, education, and institutions in New Zealand', which was of a depth and breadth unprecedented in New Zealand.[37] It changed the social contract between medicine and society, and provided further impetus for the appointment of Campbell to the Chair in Bioethics and the establishment of the Otago Bioethics Research Centre. When Campbell took up his appointment in 1990, New Zealand was in the midst of implementing the recommendations of the Cartwright Report.

Campbell's influence post-Cartwright

The Cartwright Inquiry had opened up a Pandora's box of legal and ethical issues. Society was ready for change and Campbell was perfectly placed to play a leading role in assisting to bring about that change. The year he spent as a visiting professor had paved the way for what was to come and his expertise was by then well known throughout the country. On arrival in April 1990, he was able to hit the ground running and contribute to the implementation of the Cartwright recommendations and the aspirations of the university and the Presbyterian Church for the newly established bioethics centre.

The Otago Bioethics Research Centre

Much of Campbell's work was achieved through the Bioethics Research Centre. At his insistence, the fledgling centre was sited in the academic wing of the Dunedin Public Hospital. This positioning was strategic. Not only did it give tangible recognition to the financial commitment of the Otago District Health Board to the director's position, it also made centre staff readily accessible to hospital clinicians, many of whom came to the centre for advice and an opportunity to discuss difficult cases. The Cartwright Inquiry had demoralised the medical profession. As Charlotte Paul subsequently observed, 'doctors found themselves cut off from their moral roots – the internal morality of medicine'.[38] They could not trust their own moral story. By offering an open door, Campbell was able to help restore confidence in and among health professionals bruised from the Inquiry.

The hospital location also facilitated attendance of centre staff at multidisciplinary clinical team meetings. Campbell was often called upon to provide ethical advice on the care of newborns in the neonatal intensive care unit and on other cases involving significant moral dilemmas, such as end of life and withdrawal of life-prolonging treatment. His strengths were to listen, find compromise, guide, facilitate, and build bridges. He sought to find common ground, leaving people

---

37 Jing Bao Nie and Lynley Anderson, 'Bioethics in New Zealand: A Historical and Sociological Review' in John F. Peppin and Mark J. Cherry (eds), *Annals of Bioethics: Regional Perspectives in Bioethics* (Swets and Zeitlinger 2003) 352–53.

38 Charlotte Paul, 'The Cervical Cancer Study' in Joanna Manning (ed.), *The Cartwright Papers: Essays on the Cervical Cancer Inquiry, 1987–1988* (Bridget Williams Books 2009) 93.

at ease with the direction to be taken. Such support was invaluable to the staff, and to patients and families.

One of the centre's main roles was to educate students and staff and encourage public debate. To that end, Campbell led the implementation of ethics teaching throughout the undergraduate medical curriculum and established several post-graduate courses, such as the Master of Bioethics and Health Law.[39] He started a journal club where staff members presented papers for discussion, usually to an academic audience. Public lectures were held in the university lecture theatres within the hospital, thereby encouraging hospital staff to attend and engage in public dialogue. The Cartwright Inquiry had raised public awareness of ethical issues and there was a demand for public involvement and discussion about moral dilemmas in medicine. Most popular were the 'hypotheticals' (often chaired by Campbell or Gillett), when a panel was presented with controversial medical cases, such as withdrawal of life-prolonging treatments or human embryo research. The panels were made up of a mix of people (consumer groups, doctors, nurses, and others – often with diametrically opposed views) and their discussions provoked lively debate and attracted large audiences.

The relevance and importance of the centre's work to the growing field of bioethics, and the potential to increase the centre's contribution regionally and nationally, led to a gradual expansion of its staff. Campbell and Gillett were joined by Barbara Nicholas, and later by John McMillan, Alex Lautensach, Katherine Hall, and Lynley Anderson. Campbell was also acutely conscious of New Zealand's bicultural environment and the need to accommodate Māori values, customs, and perspectives in bioethics.[40] In an attempt to foster the development of cultural competency in health care, he welcomed Māori scholar and nurse, Irihapeti Ramsden, to spend time at the centre. Ramsden was by then a leader in cultural safety.

One of Campbell's noted skills was his ability to engage people across trad-itional discipline boundaries. Building on the links he had established during his earlier visits, he actively pursued collaborations with the Faculties of Law and Theology, and the Departments of Philosophy and History, as well as various medical specialties. This multidisciplinary involvement was also reflected in the bioethics summer schools. They were, and still are, biennial events organised by the bioethics centre to provide an opportunity to bring together people from across the country for discussion and learning about current ethical issues.

Campbell's work in New Zealand and that of the Bioethics Research Centre generally were noted internationally. Campbell took every opportunity to inform the world about developments in New Zealand.[41] Although a small country, at

39 Campbell's contribution to education at Otago University is addressed in this volume by Pickering *et al.*. (n 5).

40 Alastair V. Campbell, 'Ethics in a Bicultural Context' (1995) 9 *Bioethics* 149.

41 His publications list many articles about New Zealand, including Alastair V. Campbell, 'Teaching Medical Ethics Symposium. Reflections from New Zealand' (1987) 13 *Journal of Medical Ethics* 137; Max Charlesworth and Alastair V. Campbell, 'Bioethics in Australia and New Zealand: 1989–1991' in B. Andrew Lustig and others (eds), *Bioethics Yearbook, Volume*

the bottom of the world, there were valuable lessons to be learned from the Cartwright Inquiry and the responses to it. Despite such remoteness, the bioethics centre attracted international visitors and hosted the International Association of Bioethics conference in 1993.

Ethics committees

Campbell's recommendations to the Cartwright Inquiry about the need for independent ethics committees and their composition were actioned almost immediately. A mere 3 months after the release of the Cartwright Report, the Department of Health issued a national Standard for Hospital and Area Health Board Ethics Committees, directing each board to establish an ethics committee.[42] Their remit was wide-ranging. Committees were expected to review health research and treatment protocols, ensure that the rights of subjects were upheld and that they were protected from harm, foster awareness of ethical principles within service delivery, and consider any matter of ethics relevant to the board's statutory role.[43] To ensure competence and impartiality, the committees had to have an equal number of lay and professional members, as Campbell had recommended. The committees were also to be chaired by a lay member.[44] Mrs Gwennyth Taylor held the chair of the Otago area health board ethics committee from late 1988 until Campbell took over on his arrival in April 1990. He chaired the committee until he left for Bristol University in 1996.

Ethics committees in the major centres reviewed a wide range of health research protocols, mostly emanating from tertiary institutions. But their remit was wide enough to review research from anyone wanting to conduct health research in their region. These committees were also called upon to give opinions on clinical matters, such as the withdrawal of life-prolonging treatment and innovative treatments. If such matters ended up in court, the opinion of an ethics committee was a relevant factor to the court's decision.[45]

Campbell's national reputation on ethical issues was such that he was co-opted onto a number of national ethics committees. He was appointed almost immediately to the Health Research Council Ethics Committee – the major funder for health research in New Zealand. He was also one of the founding members of

---

2: *Regional Developments in Bioethics: 1989–1991* (Springer 1992); Alastair V. Campbell, 'Bioethics in New Zealand: 1991–1993' *Bioethics Yearbook, Volume 4: Regional Developments in Bioethics: 1991–1993* (Springer 1995); Alastair V. Campbell, 'Ethics in a Bicultural Context' (1995) 9 *Bioethics* 149; Alastair V. Campbell, Voo Teck Chuan and Jacqueline Chin, 'An International Perspective' in Manning (n 38).

42 Department of Health, 'Standard for Hospital and Area Health Board Ethics Committees Established to Review Research and Treatment Protocols' (1988) 1.2.

43 ibid 1.1.

44 For a description of the development of ethics committees in New Zealand before and after the Cartwright Inquiry, see Nicola Peart, (n 3).

45 *Auckland Area Health Board v Attorney General* [1993] 1 NZLR 235 (HC); *Re G* [1997] NZFLR 362 (HC); *Auckland Healthcare Services v L* [1998] NZFLR 998 (HC).

the Interim National Ethics Committee on Assisted Reproductive Technology (INECART), established in 1993 and replaced in 1995 by the National Ethics Committee on Assisted Human Reproduction (NECHAR). Similarly, when the Health Research Council established the Gene Technology Advisory Committee in 1995 to assess clinical trials involving gene technology, Campbell was the appointed ethicist. These latter appointments reflected his interest in new technologies.

Healthcare services

New birth technologies were of particular interest to Campbell. He frequently expressed concern about the 'legislative vacuum' and absence of nationally agreed ethical guidelines regarding reproductive technology in New Zealand.[46] It was left to INECART and NECHAR to develop guidelines on complex ethical issues, such as authorising surrogacy arrangements. Campbell was firmly of the view that it was inappropriate for an ethics committee to be ruling on the admissibility of surrogacy applications and formulating policy on assisted reproduction.[47] This legislative vacuum lasted until New Zealand finally adopted the Human Assisted Reproductive Technology Act in 2004.

In 1991, a year after Campbell took up his appointment, the government announced radical restructuring of the publicly funded health system.[48] Area health boards were replaced by regional health authorities responsible for purchasing health services for their regions from the public and private sector. Hospitals became crown health enterprises (CHEs) run by boards of directors and drawing on business and health sector expertise. CHEs were also expected to make a profit. The government would define core health services that it would fund.

Unsurprisingly, this commercially driven model of health service delivery met with a lot of criticism, from Campbell among others. Although the primary objective of the reform was 'to secure, for everyone, access to an acceptable level of health care',[49] it was, in reality, a means of reducing public expenditure and encouraging growth of the private health sector to which the wealthier members of society could escape if they could not get treatment in the public sector.[50]

A National Advisory Committee on Core Health and Disability Support Services (the Core Services Committee) was established in 1992 to develop a list of core health services that the regional health authorities were obliged to offer. This committee commissioned Campbell and Gillett to prepare discussion papers

46 Alastair V. Campbell, 'Bioethics in New Zealand: 1991–1993' (n 41); Alastair V. Campbell, 'Dangerous Liaisons: Ethics, Politics and Health Care' (Valedictory Lecture, University of Otago 1996).
47 Campbell, Valedictory Lecture (n 46) 5.
48 Ministry of Health, *Your Health and the Public Health* (Minister of Health 1991).
49 Message from the Hon. Simon Upton, Minister of Health, ibid 1.
50 Campbell, Valedictory Lecture (n 46) 9–11.

on three ethical areas central to resource allocation: 'Justice and the right to health care'; 'Defining effectiveness and benefit'; and 'Autonomy revisited'. The Core Services Committee published the three papers in 1993 to encourage and inform public debate,[51] and subsequently hosted workshops to test the responses of a wide range of groups of people to the ethical issues raised in resource allocation. Campbell developed and delivered the material for the workshops, led the discussions, and reported to the committee on the overall effectiveness of the initiative.[52] The difficulty, as Campbell soon discovered, was that the government was unwilling to define an acceptable level of care, 'since this would drive expenditure by entitlement, instead of controlling the level of entitlement by capping budgets'.[53] And so the 'core' was abandoned in favour of guidelines for prioritising levels of need for a clinical service, on the basis of which a booking service would be devised.[54] Campbell was highly critical of this change because it removed resource allocation from ethical scrutiny and 'allow[ed] the party in power to dismiss criticism of their policy as merely party political'.[55]

Statement of patients' rights

In response to the Cartwright Inquiry's recommendation, Parliament eventually adopted a Code of Health and Disability Services Consumers' Rights in 1996, issued as a regulation under the Health and Disability Commissioner Act 1994. This code lists ten consumer rights and corresponding duties of healthcare providers applicable to treatment, research, and education. It also gives consumers a right to complain to the health and disability commissioner in the event of a perceived breach of the code. While Campbell endorsed the statement of rights, with its strong emphasis on patient choice and informed consent, he disapproved of the term 'consumer'.[56] Not only was it conceptually incongruous to characterise a patient as a consumer, it also implied some serious ethical problems in the approach to health care. In his valedictory lecture in June 1996, Campbell said:

> Although the advocates of patients' rights do not seem to realise this, it gives credence to a market driven approach to health care and appears to encourage the government to take a laissez-faire approach to what is provided and received, intervening only when forced to it by public pressure or when fiscal reasons require it.[57]

---

51 *Ethical Issues in Defining Core Services* (National Advisory Committee on Core Health and Disability Support Services, July 1993).
52 Alastair V. Campbell, 'Ethics Workshops on Public Participation in Discussing Ethical Issues in Defining Core Services' (1994).
53 Campbell, Valedictory Lecture (n 46) 10.
54 ibid 10.
55 ibid 10–11.
56 ibid.
57 ibid 4.

Unfortunately, his comments fell on deaf ears. However, the substantive rights set out in the code and its complaints process are undoubtedly one of the positive outcomes from the Cartwright Inquiry. The code has been pivotal in changing the relationship between healthcare providers and their patients, and between health researchers and research participants.

Campbell's legacy

When Campbell left, Jones described his time at Otago as revolutionary. He arrived in an uncharted environment and flourished, setting up most things for the first time and nourishing them to maturity. His expertise in pastoral theology was decisive in providing him with an entrée into decision making. Campbell's involvement was seminal and his influence was always felt.[58] Central to all his work was respect for the patient and the practical implementation of ethics in the clinical setting.[59] His remarkable influence was widely felt and his expertise relied on by many, including patients, health professionals, educational institutions, and the wider community.[60]

The development of bioethics and of the bioethics centre did not stand still following Campbell's departure for Bristol in 1996. The foundations he helped lay have had a lasting influence on healthcare ethics to the present day. The bioethics centre has now grown to more than eight full-time equivalent academics and two support staff. The teaching roles have expanded to an integrated programme throughout the medical curriculum and comprehensive programmes within all health professional schools at the University of Otago, including pharmacy, physiotherapy, dentistry, and oral health. Undergraduate and postgraduate bioethics papers, courses, and programmes have also developed since Campbell's time with diplomas and Master's and PhD degrees now available.

Public lectures and weekly seminars in the bioethics centre continue with contributions from centre staff, affiliated staff from elsewhere within the university, and international visitors. The advantage of modern technology means that these events now reach a national audience. Space issues forced the centre to move to a building opposite the hospital. While this move has reduced the ease of accessibility between centre and clinical staff, other avenues have been established to encourage contact.

Centre staff continue to play a major role in regional and national ethics committees. They are represented on the University of Otago Human Ethics Committees, the Health Research Council Ethics Committee, and the National Ethics Advisory Committee, which is responsible for drafting national guidelines

---

58 Gareth Jones, 'Alastair V. Campbell: Pastoral Theologian and Bioethicist' (1996) 5(2) *Otago Bioethics Report* 1.

59 One of the books he co-authored with Grant Gillett and Gareth Jones while at Otago was *Practical Medical Ethics* (Oxford University Press 1992), now in its fourth edition under the title *Medical Ethics* (Oxford University Press 2005).

60 Jones (n 58).

for ethics committees.[61] Staff of the bioethics centre are also members of committees established by the Human Assisted Reproductive Technology Act 2004.[62] Centre staff serve on the Australian and New Zealand Council for the Care of Animals in Research and Teaching, the New Zealand Medical Association, the Gene Technology Advisory Committee of the Health Research Council, the Professional Conduct Committee of the New Zealand Medical Council, and the New Zealand Psychologists Board.

Campbell's contribution to the development of regional ethics committees in New Zealand has endured, although in a disturbingly reduced form. The 14 regional ethics committees established in 1988 have been replaced by four national Health and Disability Ethics Committees (HDECs). The four HDECs have joint responsibility for review of health and disability research conducted anywhere in New Zealand and there is an HDEC meeting almost every week of the year. While this change has the advantage of speedy access to ethical review, the local flavour and input have been lost.

Of greater concern is the significantly reduced scope of review. The HDECs review only the ethics of research, not the scientific validity. They merely have to be satisfied that the science has been appropriately peer-reviewed.[63] This more limited focus means that there is no need for a wide range of scientific expertise on the committees. Whereas previously the regional ethics committees had up to six professional members and an equal number of lay members, the HDECs have a maximum of eight members, with equal representation from the professional and lay communities. The separation of scientific review from ethical review provoked a great deal of criticism, in particular by those involved directly or indirectly in the Cartwright Inquiry.[64] Furthermore, HDECs only review health research that carries more than a minimal risk of harm and do not review student research at Master's level or below.

The greatly reduced scope of HDEC review has left significant gaps in the ethical review landscape. The universities of Otago and Auckland have filled those gaps by establishing an extra committee structured to review health research not covered by HDECs. But gaps remain, leaving some researchers without ready access to ethical review processes.[65]

---

61 For example, National Ethics Advisory Committee, *Ethical Guidelines for Intervention Studies* (Ministry of Health 2009, revised in 2012) and National Ethics Advisory Committee, *Ethical Guidelines for Observational Studies* (Ministry of Health 2006, revised in 2012).

62 The Human Assisted Reproductive Technology Act 2004 established two committees: the Advisory Committee for Assisted Reproductive Technology, which drafts ethical guidelines for application by the Ethics Committee for Assisted Reproductive Technology, which grants approval to applicants seeking to access assisted reproductive procedures.

63 'Standard Operating Procedures for Health and Disability Ethics Committees' (Ministry of Health 2012, revised in 2014) accessible at <www.ethics.health.govt.nz>

64 Grant Gillett and Alison Douglass, 'Ethics Committees in New Zealand' (2012) 20 *Journal of Law, Medicine & Ethics* 266; Charlotte Paul, 'Research Participants Need Protection' *Otago Daily Times* (New Zealand, 12 October 2011) 9; Martin Tolich and Barry Smith, *The Politicisation of Ethics Review in New Zealand* (Dunmore Publishing 2015) ch 4.

65 For example, the School of Nursing at the Otago Polytechnic.

The reason for the radical change in the ethical review system was driven primarily by economic incentives. When New Zealand's National Party came to power in 2008, one of its responses to the global recession was to encourage innovation through industry-sponsored clinical trials. Such trials were seen as providing economic and educational benefits in addition to health benefits.[66] It was claimed that pharmaceutical companies had withdrawn from New Zealand out of frustration with the ethical review process. The new national system of HDECs was designed to make ethical review simpler and more efficient. However, with reduced scientific expertise on the HDECs, there is reason to question whether trial participants are sufficiently protected from harm.

The vulnerability of participants in industry-sponsored clinical trials was a concern of Campbell's in the 1990s, when ethical review was arguably more robust. His concern then related to compensation for research participants in such trials.[67] They are not covered by the accident compensation scheme and pharmaceutical companies were reluctant to articulate the grounds and nature of compensation that they would provide in the event of an adverse event.[68] The HDECs are now required to ensure that participants in commercially sponsored trials receive compensation at least to the level of the accident compensation scheme.[69] Leaving aside the limits on accident compensation, equating adverse events in treatment with those in a clinical trial ignores a fundamental distinction between the two. As Joanna Manning, Professor of Law at the University of Auckland points out, medical treatment is intended to benefit the particular patient, while clinical research is intended to produce generalisable knowledge rather than benefiting the research participants, and thus exposes participants to an increased risk of harm.[70] Assuring research participants that they will receive compensation to the level of the accident compensation scheme is unlikely to assuage Campbell's concerns about the vulnerability of research participants in commercially sponsored clinical trials.

Conclusion

Campbell had a profound influence on New Zealand's healthcare ethics in the 7 years he spent here. His contribution was remarkable, all the more so because it was so extensive. He arrived at a time of seismic change in New Zealand's ethics landscape. It gave him the opportunity to facilitate and influence the development of a new social contract between medicine and society, one in which

---

66 Health Committee, *Inquiry into Improving New Zealand's Environment to Support Innovation to Clinical Trials* (Report 1.6F, June 2011) 11, 19.
67 Campbell, Valedictory Lecture (n 46) 7–9.
68 Nicola Peart and Andrew Moore, 'Compensation for Injuries Suffered by Participants in Commercially Sponsored Trials in New Zealand' (1997) 5 *Medical Law Review* 1.
69 Standard Operating Procedures (n 63) para 147.
70 Joanna Manning, 'Compensation for Research-related Injury in Commercially-sponsored Clinical Trials in New Zealand' in Mark Henaghan and Jesse Wall (eds), *Law, Ethics, and Medicine: Essays in Honour of Peter Skegg* (Thomson Reuters 2016) 177.

autonomy of the patient and research participant stood central and where public engagement in bioethical issues was possible and encouraged. His departure in 1996 for Bristol was a loss to New Zealand but, by the time he left, he had trained and encouraged others to continue the work that has ensured his legacy endures.

Acknowledgement

The authors would like to acknowledge Professor Linda Holloway who read and provided comment on the manuscript.

Part V
Healthcare ethics education

10 Healthcare ethics education at the University of Otago – and the Master of Bioethics and Health Law

Neil Pickering, Lynley Anderson and Peter Skegg

This chapter is in two parts, both of which relate to Alastair V. Campbell's influential role in healthcare education during his years in New Zealand. The first, and longest part, by Neil Pickering and Lynley Anderson, examines Campbell's influence on the teaching of ethics to medical undergraduates at the University of Otago. The second part, by Peter Skegg, reports on experience with the Master's degree in Bioethics and Health Law that Campbell played a key role in introducing.

I: Campbell's influence on medical undergraduate ethics teaching at the University of Otago

This account is based on three sorts of sources. First, there are published sources, such as books and articles. Second, there are non-published resources, such as letters and internal medical school documents retained as personal and Bioethics Research Centre ('the Centre' or 'the BRC') records. Third, two of the authors conducted an oral history interview with Professors Gareth Jones and Grant Gillett on the contribution of Campbell to the development and teaching of medical ethics in the undergraduate medical curriculum at the University of Otago. The proposal to conduct this interview was reviewed within the Centre and approved, and subsequently this approval was confirmed by the University of Otago's human ethics committee.[1]

In summary, Campbell, through his dedication to teaching as well as his ability to build bridges and include everyone in discussion, acted as midwife and then as the chief nurturer of the nascent undergraduate medical ethics programme, seeing it through its early years and some major curriculum changes that took place in the early 1990s. The work he started has been carried on by others, and the principles he embraced remain those that guide the continued development of ethics teaching in medicine at Otago.

Campbell had three periods of extended stay in Otago, each of increasing duration: the first in 1985, then again for a year in 1986–7 and then for 6 years from

---

1 Letter from G. Witte to N. Pickering (7 August 2017).

1990 to 1996. The following text will be divided into three, each part reflecting one of Campbell's visits and the wider context of medical undergraduate teaching of ethics around it.

Campbell's 1985 visit and early planning for medical undergraduate teaching of ethics

Campbell first visited the Otago Medical School in 1985 while on a Thomas Burns Memorial Lectureship to give a series of lectures at the Theological Hall, Knox College.[2] Although Campbell was not in Dunedin in relation to biomedical ethics, he already had a considerable reputation in the field by this time. He had written more than one monograph on the topic, and had been the first editor of the United Kingdom-based *Journal of Medical Ethics* (*JME*) (1975–80).[3]

It so happened that this first visit to Dunedin coincided with a number of significant developments related to bioethics more generally, and to the teaching of medical ethics to undergraduate medical students in particular. Within the Otago Medical School, as early as 1982, a steering group had been set up, seeking support from the university for the establishment of what was referred to then as 'The University of Otago Resource Centre for Bioethics' (although support for this was not forthcoming at the time).[4] Over the next 3 years, this steering committee ran a series of seminars on ethical issues and constituted a working party for a number of other organisations (including the Royal Society of New Zealand, the New Zealand Law Society, the Medical Council of New Zealand, the Medical Research Council of New Zealand,[5] and the New Zealand Medical Association) to propose that a New Zealand committee on bioethics be set up to advise the government.[6] In 1985, the steering committee numbered among its members Professor Geoffrey Brinkman (Dean of the Otago Medical School), Associate Professor Chris Heath (Associate Dean Undergraduate Studies, Faculty of Medicine), Rev. Gerald Fitzgerald (Holy Cross College, Faculty of Theology), Dr David Green (Pharmacology), Professor Gareth Jones (Anatomy), Rev. Peter Marshall (Master of Knox College), Professor Patrick Molloy (Cardiothoracic Surgery), Professor Peter Skegg (Law), and Mrs Gwen Taylor (Philosophy).[7]

Alongside the steering committee, the faculty board curriculum committee (FBCC) had set up a working party to 'explore how formal teaching in bioethics

2 L. Anderson and N. Peart, *Healthcare Ethics in New Zealand* (Chapter 9 in this volume).

3 L.A. Reynolds and E.M. Tansey (eds), *Medical Ethics Education in Britain, 1963–1993* (2007) (Wellcome Witnesses to Twentieth Century Medicine, vol 31, Wellcome Trust Centre for the History of Medicine at UCL) 11, 86, Appendix 1, 98–100.

4 See letter from G.L. Brinkman to R.O.H. Irvine (2 April 1985).

5 In 1990 replaced by the Health Research Council of New Zealand: Health Research Council Act 1990.

6 Brinkman (n 4); letter from G.L. Brinkman to Gwen Taylor, Rev. G.P. Fitzgerald, Dr D.P.L. Green, Professor D.G. Jones, Rev. Peter Marshall and Professor P.D.G. Skegg (6 September 1984).

7 Based on the addressees of Brinkman (n 4).

may be incorporated into the undergraduate curriculum'.[8] The setting up of the FBCC working party (FBCC WP) followed from discussion at a conference at Lincoln College[9] in Christchurch in February 1985.[10] The Lincoln conference was a 3-day conference and the idea of Professor Geoffrey Brinkman.[11] Historian Dorothy Page describes the conference in her history of the Otago Medical School:

> [S]taff and some students from all three Otago Medical School campuses converged on Lincoln College to consider the question: 'Are we making the optimum use of our educational resources to train doctors for the 21st century?' … The conference participants, numbering almost a hundred staff and a small number of students, worked through discussion groups, with regular plenary sessions, to debate medical ethics, continuing education, the examination system, student boredom, curriculum models and curriculum overload.[12]

The conference is highly relevant in two ways to the development of medical ethics teaching at Otago and sets the backdrop for Campbell's later role in it. First, it specifically discussed medical ethics as a subject in the undergraduate medical curriculum. As Heath reports, 'There was support for … further exploration of the teaching of ethics',[13] and there seems little doubt that it would have inspired the work of the FBCC WP. Second, the Lincoln conference began discussions on curriculum reform that were ongoing and indeed began to gather pace when Campbell was in Dunedin as director of the BRC from 1990–6, and which resulted in substantial development in the teaching of medical ethics.

Taking advantage of the fact that Campbell happened to be in Dunedin in 1985, Jones, who was Professor of Anatomy, invited Campbell to visit the medical school. Brinkman wrote to the steering committee members inviting them to meet Campbell while he was visiting the medical school, to 'take the opportunity to discuss with him the teaching of ethics'.[14] The meeting was scheduled for 26 March 1985. The next day, the FBCC WP terms of reference were established at a meeting of the FBCC.[15] The terms of reference were 'to advise the [FBCC]

---

8 Brinkman (n 4).

9 Lincoln College was part of the University of Canterbury at the time and became an independent New Zealand university in 1990.

10 Brinkman (n 4).

11 D. Page, *Anatomy of a Medical School. A History of Medicine at the University of Otago 1875–2000* (Otago University Press 2008) 255.

12 ibid 255.

13 ibid.

14 Letter from G.L. Brinkman to Rev. G.P. Fitzgerald, Dr D.P.L Green, Associate Professor C.J. Heath, Professor D.G. Jones, Rev. P. Marshall, Professor P.J. Molloy and Professor P.D.G. Skegg (11 March 1985).

15 The Report of the Faculty Board Curriculum Committee Working Party on the Teaching of Medical Ethics (26 May 1986) (FBCC WP Report).

on the need for, and the possible structure of, a defined course in medical ethics in the Faculty'.[16]

Having delivered the Burns lectures, Campbell returned to the UK. The FBCC WP continued to meet, and subsequently produced an important and ground-breaking report to the FBCC in May 1986. The authors of the report were D.G. Jones (Convenor, Department of Anatomy, Dunedin), J.R. Morton (Department of Surgery, Christchurch), T.M. Fiddes (Department of Obstetrics and Gynaecology, Dunedin), and R.B.H. Smith (Department of Medicine, Wellington).[17] The report is worth noting in some detail, because it provided the skeleton to which Campbell added the flesh when he returned in September 1986 for his 1-year visiting professorship.[18]

The report argues for formal ethics teaching to be introduced into the medical curriculum:

> Since medical ethics is not just a matter of personal conduct, but relates to political, economic and social issues as well, medical students require an understanding of their own values plus an understanding of the values of others within and outside the medical profession.[19]

Lying behind this justification, the FBCC WP report notes a number of changes supporting the development of ethics teaching. These included technological change, the increasing emphasis on patient decision making, and awareness of medical problems in the community. It should be noted that this community awareness of medical problems preceded the publication in 1987 in *Metro* magazine of Coney and Bunkle's exposé of the 'unfortunate experiment' at National Women's Hospital in Auckland[20] and the subsequent Cartwright Inquiry,[21] but may refer to the fall-out from the Milan Brych affair a decade or more before. Brych, a refugee from Czechoslovakia,[22] was appointed Registrar to the Radiotherapy Department at the Auckland Public Hospital on 1 July 1971[23]

16 ibid 1.

17 ibid.

18 Professor D.G. Jones, Professor G.R. Gillett and Associate Professor L. Anderson, Interview with Professor Alastair V. Campbell, *Oral History of the contribution of Professor Alastair Campbell to the development and teaching of undergraduate medical education at University of Otago* (1 August 2017).

19 FBCC WP Report (n 15) 2.2.1.

20 S. Coney and P. Bunkle, 'An Unfortunate Experiment at National Women's' (1987) June *Metro* 47.

21 *The Report of the Committee of Inquiry into Allegations Concerning the Treatment of Cervical Cancer at National Women's Hospital and into Other Related Matters* (Government Printing Office 1988), Appendices 5 and 6 respectively (Cartwright Report). For more detail on this Report, see Anderson and Peart (n 2).

22 RM Lowenthal, 'Snake Oil, Coffee Enema and Other Famous Nostrums for Cancer – a Recent History of Cancer Quackery in Australia' (2005) 29 *Cancer Forum* 150, 150.

23 R.D. Wright, 'Report: Committee of Inquiry Under Section 13(3) of the Hospitals Act 1957' (Melbourne Cancer Institute 6 June 1974) 20 <www.moh.govt.nz/notebook/nbbooks.nsf/0/DF4B23A3B69BF16B4C256863008270C1> accessed 9 October 2017.

and later promoted to Medical Officer Special Scale.[24] He claimed to practise immunological therapy on cancer patients, although he gave widely varying private accounts of his therapy to different people and refused on numerous occasions to clarify in more public forums what this treatment was.[25] He was eventually struck off the medical register in 1977.[26]

The FBCC WP report also suggests that, while ethics teaching was already taking place, it was ad hoc, driven by individuals who happened to have ethical interests, rather than planned and coordinated. Indeed, the report notes fears – voiced by Brinkman – of a 'perceived downgrading of attitudes to the teaching of ethics in the undergraduate curriculum compared with the mainstream subjects'.[27] That is to say, the fear was that even the existing ad hoc teaching was under threat from other subjects crowding it out.

The FBCC WP also carried out some research. This research included a questionnaire that was sent to all members of the Faculty of Medicine asking for 'their views regarding the teaching of medical ethics within the medical curriculum'.[28] The FBCC WP carried out a review of medical ethics teaching in medical schools around the world, and reported on a 1984 New Zealand Medical Council Statement and the discussions on teaching medical ethics at the Lincoln conference.[29]

Visiting Professor 1986–7

The FBCC WP report was still working its way 'through numerous committees', as Jones had predicted,[30] when Campbell returned to New Zealand in September 1986 to take up a 1-year visiting professorship. The Otago Medical School was keen to have his views on the report. Professor John D Hunter (who replaced Brinkman as Dean of the medical school on the latter's retirement in 1986) wrote to interested members of the faculty that 'Divisions and individuals may have the opportunity to discuss various aspects with Professor Alastair Campbell when he visits each Division'.[31] Campbell's views were clearly positive. He recognised the significance of the work of the FBCC WP in his Report to the Faculty of Medicine on his visit, noting that the 'preparatory work for [formal teaching in medical ethics within the undergraduate medical curriculum] had already been done' by the time he arrived in New Zealand for his year-long visit.[32]

---

24 ibid 36.
25 ibid 33ff.
26 Lowenthal (n 22).
27 FBCC WP Report (n 15) 2.2.2. See also 2.2.3.
28 ibid 2.2.5.
29 ibid.
30 Letter from D.G. Jones to P.D.G. Skegg (30 May 1986).
31 Memorandum to all interested members of Faculty from J.D. Hunter (Dean of Faculty) (17 September 1986).
32 A.V. Campbell, 'Report to the Faculty of Medicine, University of Otago' (21 August 1987) 1 (Campbell Report).

In addition to the justification for teaching and the research mentioned above, the FBCC WP report contained a proposed curriculum, with suggestions for teaching sessions in the 5 years of the medical curriculum: the 2 pre-clinical years, the 2 clinical years, and the trainee intern (TI) year. As Campbell later noted, the plans of the FBCC WP independently expressed a principle established in the UK by an Institute of Medical Ethics working party:

> Medical ethics is not a new subject to be added to the curriculum, but a vital aspect of all medical practice, the implications of which should be made explicit throughout medical education.[33]

A comparison of the curriculum suggested by the FBCC WP in its 1986 report[34] and the actual experimental curriculum, taught during 1987 and described by Campbell in his report[35] and his *JME* article,[36] suggests that nearly all the ideas the FBCC WP had put forward were put into action. It also suggests that ethics teaching was introduced simultaneously in every year of the medical course rather than being rolled out gradually.

It is worth noting that, from an international perspective, the FBCC WP report and the proposed curriculum were put together prior to the publication in the UK of the landmark Pond Report.[37] The FBCC WP does not make any mention of ideas to be found in the previously published *New England Journal of Medicine* Special Report on the Dartmouth College Conference in the United States, which sought to lay out a curriculum for medical ethics teaching in the United States.[38] The Pond Report did not suggest a model curriculum.[39]

Campbell was then present in Dunedin when the proposed 'experimental' curriculum was put into effect for what he describes as a trial run, starting in February 1987.[40] Campbell's role with respect to the proposed curriculum was its initial implementation.[41]

Jones recalls: 'As the medical curriculum matured that was very much Alastair … we just set something up and then he was the one who was putting the flesh on to all the bones'.[42]

---

33 Institute of Medical Ethics (IME) Bulletin, (August 1–9) 1986 cited in A.V. Campbell, 'Teaching Medical Ethics Symposium. Reflections from New Zealand' (1987) 13 *Journal of Medical Ethics* 137, 137.

34 FBCC WP Report (n 15).

35 Campbell Report (n 32) Appendix A, 10–11.

36 Campbell (n 33).

37 K.M. Boyd (ed.), *Report of a Working Party on the Teaching of Medical Ethics* (IME Publications 1987) (The Pond Report), chaired by Sir Desmond Pond.

38 C.M. Culver *et al.*, 'Basic Curricular Goals in Medical Ethics' (1985) 312 *The New England Journal of Medicine* 253.

39 R. Gillon, 'Medical Ethics Education' (1987) 13 *Journal of Medical Ethics* 115.

40 Campbell (n 33) 137.

41 Letter from D.G. Jones to P.D.G. Skegg (28 September 1989).

42 Jones, Gillett and Anderson (n 18).

At the close of his year-long visit, and following the experimental implementation of the programme suggested in the FBCC WP report, Campbell reflected:

> I have no doubt that the Working Party Report on the Teaching of Medical Ethics in the Undergraduate Medical Curriculum contained a viable and totally relevant scheme. ... [T]he general approach of the Report, which stresses the interweaving of ethics in all years of the course, is one which is gaining wide international recognition. ... It remains, then, for the Report's recommendations to be implemented in appropriate ways in all three centres.[43]

Whatever the actual role of Campbell's recommendation in subsequent planning, 3 years later, at the start of 1990 (the year of his return to New Zealand as director of the BRC), a curriculum very similar to the one given a trial run in 1987 was in place.[44] However, Jones's preamble to the description of the curriculum notes:

> In April 1990, Dr Alastair Campbell will take up a full-time position as Professor of Biomedical Ethics. Thus in 1990 we will be able to implement a full program of medical ethics teaching – something which has hitherto not been possible.[45]

From the following description of medical ethics teaching in the pre-clinical, clinical, and TI years at the University of Otago, it seems clear that the most significant area in which a full programme of medical ethics teaching had not as yet been possible was in the clinical years – as the description notes, 'In 1990 it is hoped to strengthen the ethics content of years 4 and 5'.[46] It was in part to achieve this that the University of Otago set about luring Campbell back to Dunedin.[47]

Director of the Bioethics Research Centre

Campbell's role in the conception, development, and directing of the BRC is detailed elsewhere in this volume, and will not be repeated in any detail here.[48] In summary, he strongly supported its conception, applauded the appointment of a half-time senior lecturer to it (Grant Gillett, in 1988), and then took up the challenge to be its director in 1990.

Medical undergraduate ethics teaching was then, and is now, a central responsibility of the Centre, which continues to promote and coordinate teaching in

---

43 Campbell Report (n 32) 7.
44 D.G. Jones, 'Medical Ethics Teaching University of Otago' (15 November 1989) 1.
45 ibid.
46 D.G. Jones's letter to P.D.G. Skegg (n 41) reference to 'years 4 and 5' reflects the fact that the clinical years at Otago then (as now) are usually the fourth and fifth years of the medical student's time at university.
47 D.G. Jones, 'Alastair V. Campbell: Pastoral Theologian and Bioethicist' (1996) 5(2) *Otago Bioethics Report* 1, 1.
48 See Anderson and Peart (n 2).

medicine and its development (to paraphrase Campbell's report).[49] Campbell argued that, in order to survive, the relatively new discipline of medical ethics 'must be pursued in a scholarly manner'[50] and saw the Centre as the means to ensure that this happened. In this, he echoed a view stated in the FBCC WP report:

> We wish to see the teaching of medical ethics to undergraduates as part of a wider academic emphasis on this discipline. If it is viewed in a narrow teaching context, it will probably not survive for more than a few years.[51]

Conversely, the FBCC WP report intimated that the presence of a successful bioethics centre would ensure the university's support of medical undergraduate ethics teaching. As Jones observed, Campbell recognised the significance of academic excellence to the success of the BRC and of medical undergraduate teaching.[52] Campbell embodied this excellence in his own work, and supported it in those working around him.

Campbell's tasks and achievements during his tenure as director of the BRC were many and various. A number of them relate directly to medical undergraduate teaching, and these will be noted here.

One major (and early) task was to make sure that the medical undergraduate teaching of ethics fitted with a new set of goals and objectives. These goals and objectives were the result of work by a working party set up by the FBCC to draft new objectives for the undergraduate medical curriculum and chaired by Professor Barry Baker.[53] It met from May 1987 to December 1988.[54] The goals and objectives had been ratified by the board of the Faculty of Medicine in June 1989. From March to November 1988, a task force with nominated people from pre-clinical departments (and interested others) met and drafted objectives for the intermediate level (pre-clinical years) of the medical curriculum. This latter draft was circulated for comment in 1989, prior to Campbell's arrival. Campbell's views were sought soon after he arrived.[55]

In her history of the Otago Medical School, Page records that:

> In 1989, the Faculty Board adopted a revised set of Goals and Objectives, which addressed Knowledge, Skills and Attitudes in some detail and emphasised the application of the principles of scientific method, teamwork, communication skills, lifelong learning, health promotion and ethics.[56]

49 Campbell Report (n 32) 6.
50 ibid 8.
51 FBCC WP Report (n 15) 5.2.
52 Jones, Gillett and Anderson (n 18).
53 Letter from A.B. Baker to A.V. Campbell (9 May 1990).
54 ibid.
55 ibid.
56 P.L. Schwartz, C.J. Heath and A.G. Egan, *The Art of the Possible: Ideas from a Traditional Medical School Engaged in Curricular Revision* (Otago University Press 1994) 90–91, cited in Page (n 11) 258.

The most explicit and focused reference to ethics was the general objective under attitudes attitudes that students 'should be able to apply the principles of ethics to medical practice',[57] which was underpinned by eight intermediate objectives. But goals and outcomes with implicit ethical dimensions are detectable throughout the document.

Page remarks that the new set of goals and objectives 'was the only tangible outcome from all the work of the energetic and conscientious committees that were set up to give form to the enthusiasm for curricular reform that had been expressed at the Teschemakers conference'.[58] This conference (or workshop), held at Teschemakers north of Dunedin in April 1986, had been in turn inspired to some degree by the Lincoln conference of 1985.[59] But whereas Lincoln had focused on ideas and concepts, Teschemakers had made concrete recommendations, with a focus on attitudes and the curriculum, as well as propositions (novel ideas). From the ethical point of view, however, even if the curriculum changes recommended at the Teschemakers workshop were in abeyance, the presence of overt ethical dimensions in the goals of the medical curriculum can be seen as an important setting in stone of the place of medical ethics teaching, as Campbell had hoped would be the case at his departure in 1987. Moreover, while the goals and objectives were only a paper exercise, they set the stage for greater curriculum change over the next 6 years.

According to the Australian Medical Council, curriculum development is about 'continuous renewal'.[60] However, the medical ethics teaching introduced in 1987 was integrated into the existing course, which had been in place for some time, and for which change was still in the future. The primary feature of this course was that it was divided into pre-clinical and clinical phases. The first of these phases was in the second and third years[61] when, after a science-based first year, all students remained in Dunedin for a primarily discipline-based classroom-taught course. Students attended classes in anatomy, physiology, biochemistry, and preventive and social medicine and, in the third year, medical decision analysis. The second (clinical) phase (fourth, fifth, and sixth years) saw students separated into three groups. One group attended the clinical school in Wellington, one in Christchurch, and one group remained in Dunedin. At each of the clinical schools, students rotated through various departments during each

---

57 General and Intermediate Objectives to be achieved by the end of Sixth Year, Faculty of Medicine, University of Otago (September 1992) 15.
58 Page (n 11) 258.
59 ibid 257–8.
60 2004 AMC Report, cited in Page (n 11) 263.
61 Most students then (as now) started medical school after being selected from among those completing an initial year of health science study. The first two (pre-clinical) years of medical school were thus their second and third years of university study, and were referred to as 'Med 2' and 'Med 3'. The subsequent 3 years of study (the clinical years and the trainee intern year) were their fourth, fifth, and sixth years of study. At the time of writing – 2017 – the pre-clinical years are now referred to as Early Learning in Medicine (ELM) and the clinical years as Advanced Learning in Medicine (ALM).

year – called 'runs'. The courses run by each clinical school had similarities to one another but also differences. All students were (and still are) expected to meet the criteria set by the fifth-year common exam.

Ethics teaching was integrated into this existing discipline-led structure. The general idea was to find ethical matters to teach that were relevant to whatever medical science teaching the student was receiving. For example, in the second year, issues related to bodies and human materials were considered within the anatomy course (such as the use of cadavers for dissection), the use of animals in research was considered in physiology, genetic engineering within the biochemistry course, issues of resource allocation within the preventive and social medicine course, and so on.[62]

But in light of the new goals and objectives, change to the discipline-based course was perceived as necessary. Thus:

> In 1992, the Faculty Board set up a working party to make recommendations on the courses to be taught and skills to be acquired in each semester of second and third year. ... The working party was instructed to ensure that the course had a substantial component of self-directed learning, fewer timetabled hours, and a greater degree of vertical integration (between pre-clinical and clinical years) and horizontal integration (between courses in any year).[63]

The subsequent recommendations for change to the second and third years were put into practice between 1994 and 1997. Page says the reform amounted to a 'change from a discipline-based course to an integrated system-based course'.[64]

The move from a discipline-based to an integrated curriculum forms the backdrop to the latter half of Campbell's tenure as director of the BRC. Ethics was to find itself with a major role in the new arrangements. This role was pre-eminently in the patient, doctor, and society (PDS) course, which was deliberately targeted at 'attitudes and skills, such as critical appraisal, communication, ethical reasoning and awareness of professional development'.[65] But ethics was also to find a role throughout the reformed second- and third-year curriculum, most notably in the systems integration (SI) course, in which small groups of students worked on issues raised by a series of cases, bringing together the basic medical sciences, in clinical contexts, with ethical, legal, and personal/professional elements.[66]

The Centre's Teaching and Research Plan 1995 confirms the impact the changes were having and were expected to have: 'The department [the Plan says, meaning the Centre] ... has a large role in the establishment of "Patient, Doctor

62 C. Maclaurin (ed.), 'The Teaching of Biomedical Ethics' (Proceedings of a Symposium, Palmerston North 18–19 August 1989) 13.
63 Page (n 11) 260–1.
64 ibid 261.
65 Page (n 11) reporting on Loten's report to the AMC in 1999, 261.
66 ibid 261.

and Society" (PDS) a new course in the pre-clinical years'.[67] Campbell and Kathy Peace (psychological medicine) were coordinators of PDS, and the Centre's role included a high degree of participation in its planning. In the light of this, the plan recognised the need to budget for and expand the Centre's resources in order to teach the new course. Although the BRC Teaching and Research Plan from 1995 suggests it was originally expected to be in place in 1996, the new curriculum did not actually start until 1997, the year after Campbell left.

The issue of resources was significant. For example, the hours of ethics teaching planned for the new medical undergraduate teaching course were considerably expanded from those in the old course. In the old arrangements, in the second and third years, in 1996 (the year of Campbell's departure) the Centre's staff were involved in 12 hours of lectures and roughly 40 hours of tutorials (many of these repeats of sessions for different groups). But in the new curriculum, in PDS alone, 19 lectures and 127 tutorial hours were planned. In addition, ethics teaching in SI and in other modules was expected, as was tutor training for ethical issues for which BCR staff wrote tutors' notes.[68] The issue of staff numbers was also a perennial one. It remained an issue through the reforms, and was commented on by the Australian Medical Council (AMC) when they visited again in 1999.[69] With respect to the 1994 review, the report for the 1999 visit notes that financial restraints had made it difficult to appoint the additional staff recognised as required in 1994, while at the same time:

> The extension of the role of the Centre in the ambitious reforms of the undergraduate curriculum in the Otago Faculty of Medicine has provided an even better model of the teaching of Medical Ethics than that praised in the 1994 AMC Report. It is a model which has aroused considerable interest in Medical Education and one which the Centre is keen to promote internationally.[70]

The new curriculum also demanded new forms of assessment. Under the old discipline-based teaching, bioethics had been assessed in the second year on the basis of a fairly traditional medical ethical essay. The essay titles reflect this – the choice for second-year students in 1989 and 1990 included: Is there a difference between the moral status of humans and other animals? Is autonomy a valid position for medical ethics? Can theology provide a rational and coherent basis for medical ethics? Why should a patient's consent to medical treatment be informed? Is there any such thing as 'the sanctity of life'? and Are there patients' rights as distinct from rights of other kinds? In the third year, there was a question in the end-of-course examination of the medical decision analysis course.[71]

67 Bioethics Research Centre 'Teaching and Research Plan 1995' (1995).
68 This information is from 'Staff Justification: Bioethics Research Centre' (1996).
69 See AMC Visit Report, 'Centre for Bioethics Research' [sic] (1999).
70 ibid.
71 D.G. Jones, 'Medical Ethics Teaching University of Otago' (n 44).

The approach represented by this traditional bioethics essay was not consonant with the new curriculum. For one thing, the essay topics were quite abstract and general. For another, though they reflected teaching alongside the biomedical sciences, they did not reflect clinical ethical issues, and it was these on which the new curriculum – particularly SI – was at least in part designed to focus. In 2017, the practice is to have ethics assessment in the second and third end-of-year written examinations, in the form of a short essay on an ethical issue arising in the context of a clinical case.

While the focus of development in Campbell's time as director of the BRC may have been mostly on the pre-clinical years of medical undergraduate teaching, the clinical years were not forgotten. In his report at the completion of his 1-year visiting professorship, Campbell recommended that more could be done with fourth- and fifth-year small groups, and that greater planning should be introduced to enable this to happen – with a suggestion that each group should have relevant small-group discussions as they rotated through the 'various firms'.[72]

Prior to Campbell's return in 1990, the fourth- and fifth-year ethics teaching in Dunedin consisted of some sessions in the clinical competencies course and others in clinical science contexts – for example, ethical questions around the discontinuation of treatment while studying the respiratory system. There were also 2 hours of lectures and case studies while the students were studying psychiatry.[73] In Christchurch, the ethics teaching in the fourth, fifth and sixth years was described at a symposium in Palmerston North. There were some formal ethics teaching sessions. For example, in radiology, there was a consideration of expensive investigations of patients nearing the end of their life; and in obstetrics and gynaecology, a tutorial on 'Ethics consent and communication'. Many other clinical areas lacked formal ethics teaching. The Wellington Clinical School reported that there were one or two sessions within each clinical teaching block with each of the principal departments in the fourth and fifth years, although no detail was given. There were no reports of what was happening in the sixth year at that time.[74]

It is, however, possible to infer that extending medical ethics teaching in the fourth, fifth, and sixth years proved something of a challenge. Dunedin – where the BRC and its team were based – is geographically very distant from Christchurch and Wellington. Furthermore, the three centres developed their clinical teaching in slightly different ways. Previewing Campbell's return, Jones remarked that he hoped it would enable the extension of teaching in the clinical years, suggesting that this was an identifiable lacuna prior to 1990.[75] Interestingly, however, it is possible to see that, in 2017, some of the suggestions put forward

72 Campbell Report (n 32) 12. The term 'firms' presumably refers to what are also called 'runs' or 'attachments'.
73 C. Maclaurin (n 62) 14.
74 ibid.
75 D.G. Jones, 'Letter to P.D.G. Skegg' (n 41).

by Campbell and his team were now in place – in particular face-to-face teaching by bioethically trained staff (in all three centres).

With respect to assessment for the fourth and fifth years, in 1991, Campbell suggested that fourth-year students should write a clinical case, which should first be presented by the student to their peers and discussed with a member of the clinical staff present, and subsequently submitted in written form for assessment by clinical staff.[76] In 1995, the suggestion was made that there should be an ethics 'long case' presentation.[77] That this suggestion was mooted in 1995, so soon after the 1991 suggestion, implies that either the 1991 proposal had not been put into practice, or that it had not worked out as hoped. Notwithstanding, in 2017, the proposed in-course essay assessment was introduced in all three clinical schools, and in many ways closely aligns with the 1991 suggestion (although the essay was a requirement of the fifth year, rather than the fourth). For this assessment, students choose a case from their experience during the clinical years, provide a brief summary, identify the ethical issues arising from it, and make recommendations about how the ethical issues should be dealt with, backed up with arguments.

A third approach to extending ethics teaching in the clinical years has not been adopted: this was for workshops for clinical staff in all three clinical schools to improve clinical ethical teaching. This third route suggests that it was envisaged that clinical staff would take on the ethics teaching in all three centres to some degree, supported by the BRC, but not necessarily with a staff member from the BRC present for all the teaching itself. This model was acted on for many years within the pre-clinical teaching in the SI course, but has not been put in place in fourth- or fifth-year teaching where, as mentioned above, either in-person teaching by ethicists or team teaching by ethicist and clinician has become the preferred model.

Campbell's departure in 1996 meant that he did not take part in the teaching of ethics in the new medical undergraduate teaching curriculum, which began in 1997. The evidence also shows us that the medical undergraduate teaching to which he contributed so much, both in his year as visiting professor and in his years as director of the BRC, was mooted and first planned by others. Yet, as is implicit in personal reminiscences of him, he had just the right mix of personality, skills, and academic excellence to turn these plans into reality. According to Jones, he flourished in this uncharted environment;[78] but it is also clearly the case that he was an essential part of the ecology that ensured the rooting and flourishing of medical undergraduate ethics teaching at Otago.

II: The Otago degree of Master of Bioethics and Health Law

As is apparent from the first part of this chapter, Campbell's influence on the teaching of medical undergraduates at the University of Otago was helped in

76 Letter from A.V. Campbell to A.G. Dempster (Acting Chairperson, Faculty of Medicine Curriculum Committee 28 March 1991).

77 Bioethics Research Centre (n 67).

78 D.G. Jones, 'Alastair V. Campbell' (n 47) 1.

part by the excellent relations he established with many members of the Faculty of Medicine. However, those good relations extended far beyond the confines of the medical school. The Otago degree of Master of Bioethics and Health Law (MBHL) is one outcome of those relationships and an element in Campbell's continuing legacy.

Proposals for the MBHL degree were debated in 1993–4 and the degree was introduced in 1995. In that and the following year, Campbell co-taught the one new paper (see below) that was created for the purpose of the degree. However, he returned to the UK before anyone graduated with the degree. This part of our joint chapter seeks to provide Campbell and others with an account of the Otago experience with what remains one of the few degrees of its kind anywhere in the English-speaking world.

First, however, it is appropriate to explain what was first proposed, and then adopted, for the new degree. The degree was provided for people who already had undertaken 4 years of university study and was expected to involve at least 12 months of full-time study, rather than simply an academic year – given that all candidates would be engaging in at least some areas of study they had not encountered previously. It was to involve both coursework and a thesis. The thesis was expected to involve both law and bioethics – although not necessarily in equal proportions – to be jointly supervised by academics in those fields.

The coursework for the MBHL made use of bioethics and law courses that had been introduced in the preceding years, plus a new paper entitled 'Issues in law, ethics and medicine' (BITC 403).[79] Its prescription was from the first as follows: 'Current issues in bioethics and medical law, considered with reference to theories about the actual and desirable relationship of law and morals'. It has included an examination of ongoing debates about, for example, the nature of law and ethics, the extent to which each draws upon (and is distinct from) the other, and issues about when it is ethical to enforce ethics by law, and ethical to breach the law. Most recently, it has also examined the role of human rights in healthcare, professional duties and patient choices, and conscientious objection. Alongside the examination of these matters has been scrutiny of leading medical law cases, where the facts have raised ethical as well as legal issues.

It was not until 1998 that anyone graduated with the MBHL degree, so this survey provides the opportunity to assess experience in the 25 years since the degree was first mooted and the 20 years since the degree was first awarded.

A major development was the provision of distance teaching for the degree, a development embraced wholeheartedly by bioethics but more reluctantly by law (given the pressure of numbers of would-be internal students). This development proved crucial to the ongoing success of the MBHL programme. With some courses, the distance teaching (where students elsewhere in the country

---

79 University of Otago papers are identified by a four-letter abbreviation and a number.

join seminars with Dunedin-based participants via audio-visual links) has been supplemented by intensive residential weekends. Many of those who have graduated with the MBHL degree in the past decade have been distance students.

Another significant development has been the provision of an entry and exit qualification. By no means all those who could benefit from, and contribute to, the standard bioethics and health law courses, or to BITC 403, have had the desire (or sometimes the ability) to embark on a significant thesis or dissertation. With others, their ability was not yet proven. A Graduate Diploma of Bioethics and Health Law (GDipBHL) was introduced first, and once the requirements of the national Committee on University Academic Programmes were met, so too was a Postgraduate Diploma of Bioethics and Health Law (PGDipBHL). Nowadays, most students are initially enrolled for one of the diplomas. Only those with a strong academic record who wish to embark on a significant research project are subsequently enrolled as MBHL students.[80]

For a significant minority of students, the PGDipBHL meets their needs, providing, as it does, recognition of their successful completion of the equivalent of a full year's coursework in health law and bioethics, including BITC 403.

The best of the theses or dissertations have been outstandingly good. Especially impressive have been some of the theses or dissertations by health professionals who have brought their new knowledge of law and bioethics to bear on their areas of professional experience. The product has been of a different order from anything that law or bioethics academics could achieve.

In the 20 years since the graduation of the first MBHL student (i.e. 1998–2017), 96 students have graduated with an MBHL degree. And more than 100 others have successfully completed the course (BITC 403) that was introduced for the purpose of the MBHL degree. Dozens of those who have completed the MBHL degree, and many of the others who simply completed BITC 403, have proceeded to careers where the degree and course have been directly relevant. The Director of Research at the Hastings Center may be the most prominent of them; another who audited BITC 403 in the first year it was co-taught by Campbell eventually returned to New Zealand as Director of the Bioethics Centre.

The MBHL has played a larger role in the Master's research portfolio of both the Law Faculty and the Bioethics Centre than was envisaged when it was introduced. The number who have graduated with MBHL since 2000 (92) is the best part of three times the number (34) who have graduated with the Otago degree of Master of Laws (LLM) in all areas of law during those years.

Prior to the introduction of the MBHL degree, the one Master's degree available to students in bioethics was that in health sciences (MHealSci). It was not until 2000 that the MHealSci could be endorsed specifically in bioethics. Since then, 18 students have graduated with MHealSci endorsed in Bioethics, less than

80 The regulations for these diplomas, and for the MBHL itself, are printed in the annual University Calendar: see <www.otago.ac.nz/study/otago628411.pdf> accessed 18 December 2017.

a quarter of the 92 who have graduated with MBHL during the same years. (Furthermore, a third of those MHealSci graduates included BITC 403 as part of their degree.) Mainly by way of the MBHL, the link with the University of Otago's Faculty of Law that Campbell fostered became a distinctive and ongoing element in the life of both the Bioethics Centre and the Faculty of Law.

The enrichment that the MBHL has brought to the lives and careers of those who have studied or taught it over more than two decades owes much to Alastair Campbell's key role in introducing the degree.

11 Healthcare ethics education in the UK

Gordon M. Stirrat and Julie Woodley

Introduction

Both authors of this chapter had the great privilege of working with Alastair V. Campbell throughout his stay in Bristol. It is therefore fitting that we begin by paying tribute to his outstanding contribution to healthcare ethics education in our city and beyond in his 7 years in the University of Bristol. Campbell came to Bristol from the University of Otago, Dunedin, in April 1996, as foundation Professor of Ethics in Medicine in the Department of Clinical Medicine and Director of the newly established Centre for Ethics in Medicine in the University of Bristol, the first in the UK to be nested within an acute Department of Clinical Medicine. In the all-too-short time until his first retirement in 2003, Campbell made a huge impact locally and nationally, while his international reputation went from strength to strength.

Healthcare ethics education in the UK

Healthcare ethics is, by definition, multi-disciplinary and multi-professional and medical ethics is a significant component of it. In *Medical Ethics Today*, the British Medical Association (BMA) emphasises 'that the aim of medical education is to provide doctors with the knowledge and skills needed to practise medicine within an ethical and legal framework'.[1] Given that 'doctors are confronted by ethical issues every day of their working lives – the medical training they receive must equip them with the skills and confidence needed to deal with these situations in an appropriate manner'.[2] This applies to education and practice in all healthcare professions.

Ethics and medical education

The development of ethics in medicine and its place in medical education in the UK has been well documented and much of it has been embraced by other healthcare disciplines.

1 British Medical Association, *Medical Ethics Today: The BMA's Handbook of Ethics and Law* (3rd edn, London, Wiley-Blackwell, 2012) 737.
2 ibid 739.

The Hippocratic Oath (*c.*400 BC) has been adopted and adapted as a guide to conduct by the medical profession throughout the ages. It also dictated the obligations of the physician to students of medicine and the duties of pupils to their teacher.[3] Major contributions also came from those such as Ibn Sina (Avicenna) and Maimonides in the tenth and twelfth centuries respectively. Thomas Percival (1740–1804), a physician in Manchester (now Royal) Infirmary, published the first modern code of ethics entitled 'Medical Jurisprudence or a Code of Ethics and Institutes adapted to the Professions of Physic and Surgery' in 1794 following a major dispute among surgeons. In it, the terms 'medical ethics' and 'professional ethics' were first used. An expanded version of this code, the first in the world, was initially published in 1803 which, in 1847, became the foundation of the first code of ethics of the American Medical Association.[4] Regrettably, save for in Percival's own hospital, it was ignored by the medical profession in the UK.

Over 170 years after Percival published his code, Pless found that there was no formal teaching on moral problems in UK medical schools and that discussions on ward rounds were very limited.[5] As Calman states, in his experience in the 1960s, 'there was very little medical ethics in the curriculum and what there was could be best described as the rules of etiquette for doctors'.[6] A General Medical Council (GMC) survey of medical education in the UK and Ireland in 1975–6 still found opposition to the formal inclusion of medical ethics in the curriculum; of the 34 schools that responded, nine had no plans to do so and four still believed strongly that it would be 'wrong to attempt any formal teaching since ethics is not a subject and cannot be taught by definition'.[7] One respondent felt it to be quite clear that a good clinical teacher would be constantly discussing ethical problems and thus saw 'no point whatever in having it as a separate subject in an already overcrowded curriculum'.[8] The same survey found that 25 of the responding schools now included ethics formally in the curriculum.[9] The way in which ethics was gradually included in the education of medical and other healthcare students has been the subject of several comprehensive reviews.[10]

3 The Editors of Encyclopaedia Britannica, 'Hippocratic Oath' in *Encyclopaedia Britannica Online* (2017) <www.britannica.com/topic/Hippocratic-oath> accessed 28 July 2017.

4 Thomas Percival, *Medical Ethics or A Code of Institutes and Precepts Adapted to the Professional Conduct of Physicians and Surgeons* (London, Lederle 1987).

5 Ivan B. Pless, 'Teaching Medical Ethics – Empirical or Rational?' (1967) 1 *British Journal of Medical Education* 290–3.

6 Lois A. Reynolds and Elizabeth M. Tansey (eds), 'Medical Ethics Education in Britain 1963–1993' (Wellcome Trust Center for the History of Medicine, UCL 2007) xxi.

7 Nuffield Trust, 'Basic Medical Education in The British Isles 2: The Disciplines and Specialties' (1997) <www.nuffieldtrust.org.uk/research/basic-medical-education-in-the-british-isles-2-the-disciplines-and-specialties> accessed 1 August 2017.

8 ibid.

9 ibid.

10 Kenneth M. Boyd (ed.), *Report of a Working Party on the Teaching of Medical Ethics* (London, IME Publications Ltd 1987); Reynolds and Tansey (n 6); Edward Shotter *et al.*, 'Fifty Years of Medical Ethics: From the London Medical Group to the Institute of Medical Ethics'

The main impetus for deeper consideration of difficult questions in medical ethics and law came from junior doctors and medical students. The way in which their energy was channelled and brought to fruition through the London Medical Group and its successor, the Society for the Study of Medical Ethics, which, in 1984, became the Institute of Medical Ethics (IME), has been well told elsewhere.[11]

In 1984, the IME convened a working party to review current practice in teaching medical ethics in UK medical schools that was published as the highly influential Pond Report.[12] Among its foundational proposals were that medical ethics should be taught at regular intervals throughout the medical course: clinical teaching of ethics should normally begin from clinical examples and small group discussion should be emphasised; interested medical teachers should be encouraged and assisted to undertake further study; multidisciplinary ethics teaching should be encouraged; care should be taken to ensure that teaching was not undertaken by those who held particular views or promoted a personal agenda; examinations and other assessments should have an ethics component; and elective courses should be arranged for interested students. Recognising that students also needed a reasonable understanding of medical law, in 1998, the IME produced a consensus statement on teaching medical ethics and law within medical education intended to be a model for the UK core curriculum.[13] Eight years later, a report commissioned by the IME found that, although medical ethics and law were represented in the curricula of the 22 of the then 28 UK medical schools that responded, significant concerns remained about the status, content, delivery and assessment of the teaching of ethics and law.[14] The consensus statement was updated in 2010 to provide outcome-based indicative core content of learning for medical ethics and law in UK medical schools that was consistent with the GMC's up-to-date guidance on undergraduate education.[15] (Stirrat *et al.*, 2010) The IME is currently undertaking a further comprehensive review of this core content of learning and its assessment that will be found at www.instituteofmedicalethics.org/.

Since the GMC's 1975–6 survey of medical education in the British Isles, it has become more proactive in its emphasis on medical ethics and law as it

---

(2013) 39 *Journal of Medical Ethics* 662; Gordon M. Stirrat 'Reflections on Learning and Teaching Medical Ethics in UK Medical Schools' (2015) 41 *Journal of Medical Ethics* 8.

11 Reynolds and Tansey (n 6); Shotter *et al.* (n 10); Stirrat (n 10); Michael Whong-Barr, 'Clinical Ethics Teaching in Britain: A History of the London Medical Group' (2003) *New Review in Bioethics* 1(73).

12 Boyd (n 10).

13 Consensus Group of Teachers of Medical Ethics and Law in UK Medical Schools, 'Teaching medical ethics and law within medical education: a model for the UK core curriculum' (1998) 24 *Journal of Medical Ethics* 188.

14 Karen Mattick and John Bligh, 'Teaching and Assessing Medical Ethics: Where Are We Now?' (2006) 32 *Journal of Medical Ethics* 181.

15 Gordon M. Stirrat *et al.*, 'Teaching and Learning Ethics: Medical Ethics and Law for Doctors of Tomorrow: The 1998 Consensus Statement updated' (2010) 36 *Journal of Medical Ethics* 55.

holds medical schools responsible for standards in medical education.[16] Between 1993 and 2016, these were set down in *Tomorrow's Doctors*, all the outcomes of which the graduates of each medical school were required to achieve.[17] This has been superseded by 'Promoting Excellence: Standards for Medical Education and Training.[18] The GMC has long stipulated that the graduate must be able to behave according to ethical and legal principles, and to know about and keep to the GMC's ethical guidance and standards.

Ethics and nursing education

The evolution of nursing ethics (and indeed ethical frameworks within other professions) owes much to the foundations laid down by the medical profession. Nursing ethics is 'the examination of all kinds of bioethical issues from the perspective of nursing theory and practice which in turn, rest on the agreed core concepts of nursing, namely: person, culture, care, health, healing, environment and nursing itself'.[19] It provides a very practical approach to clinical dilemmas and focuses upon the patient as a whole, taking into consideration relationships and environment. It encompasses the caring rather than the curing of the patient.[20] Nursing has always encouraged autonomous and collaborative care of both individual patients and their families and the communities they live in, and this ethos is strongly reflected within the teaching of nursing ethics.[21]

Nursing ethics takes advantage of the particularly close and continuing contact with patients and, while the medical profession is often deemed to have the last word in ethical dilemmas, nurses often act as advocates to protect the patients' autonomy, rights and freedom.[22] This advocacy is complementary rather than adversarial, thus promoting an interprofessional approach to ethical debate.

Ethics and dental education

Patrick noted that ethics and professionalism had formed part of the dental curriculum for the previous 35 years, and that the General Dental Council requires that they be included in the UK dental curriculum.[23]

16 Nuffield Trust (n 7).
17 General Medical Council, *Tomorrow's Doctors: Outcomes and Standards for Undergraduate Medical Education* (GMC, London 2009)
18 General Medical Council, 'Promoting Excellence: Standards for Medical Education and Training' (2015) <www.gmc-uk.org/education/standards.asp> accessed 27 July 2017.
19 Megan-Jane Johnstone, *Bioethics – A nursing Perspective* (4th edn, London, Churchill Livingstone 2004)
20 Janet L. Storch, 'Ethics in Nursing Practice' in Helga Kuhse and Peter Singer, *A Companion to Bioethics* (Blackwells 2009) 551–62.
21 Marsha D. Fowler, 'Why the History of Nursing Ethics Matters' (2017) 24 *Nursing Ethics* 292.
22 Kath M. Melia, 'The Task of Nursing Ethics' (1994) 20 *Journal of Medical Ethics* 7.
23 Alison C. Patrick, 'A Review of Teaching Ethics in the Dental Curriculum: Challenges and Future Developments' (2017) 21(4) *European Journal of Dental Education* 114.

The role of statutory and other bodies in healthcare ethics education

There are 12 statutory health and social care regulators in the UK responsible for the regulation of individual practitioners across these sectors. Their regulatory role encompasses education at all levels. Among them are the General Medical Council; the Nursing and Midwifery Council; the General Dental Council; and the Health and Care Professions Council that regulates a wide range of allied professions.

The British Medical Association is the trade union and professional body for doctors in the UK. It owns the *BMJ* that, in turn, co-owns the *Journal of Medical Ethics* with the Institute of Medical Ethics. Among the roles of its medical ethics department are to promote good practice and knowledge and understanding of medical ethics, and to provide advice to members on general or specific ethical issues. It also supports the medical ethics committee that publishes *Medical Ethics Today*, which includes detailed recommendations for undergraduate medical education and educational goals for teaching ethics and law.[24]

The Academy of Medical Royal Colleges and its constituent royal colleges play an important role in postgraduate education, training and assessment for foundation level doctors (i.e. the first 2 years of professional development following graduation from medical school), specialists and general practice. The Medical Schools Council works to improve and maintain quality in medical education often in collaboration with the GMC.

These bodies provide the frameworks for healthcare education but these need to be translated into real-world teaching and clinically relevant learning opportunities.

Current and persistent issues in teaching and learning healthcare ethics

Does teaching and learning of healthcare ethics translate into better ethical practice?

In the opinion of Pellegrino, 'it is hard to see how a discipline that aims to make ethical decisions more orderly, systematic and rational could be deleterious or how leaving everything to sentiment or feeling could be preferable'.[25] Thus teaching and learning of healthcare ethics and law should be at the heart of all stages in the education of healthcare professionals (HCPs) because they are integral to all healthcare and public health encounters and interventions.

In 2016, Sokol observed, 'probably for the first time in history UK trained doctors at all levels, and in all specialties, now receive formal ethics training at

24 British Medical Association (n 1) 739–745.
25 Edmund D. Pellegrino, 'Teaching Medical Ethics: Some Persistent Questions and Some Responses' (1989) 64 *Academic Medicine* 701.

medical school'.[26] This raises an important but uncomfortable question for those who teach the subject: has it made any difference?' Campbell *et al.* concluded that there was paucity of good evidence, conflicting findings and major design problems in the studies to that date.[27] Walpole considers it 'important and worthy that we continue to question how effective medical education is and how to improve it'.[28] While Sokol has 'become less certain over time of the effect of ethics teaching at medical school on the future behaviour of doctors, especially if it is delivered in the early years', he acknowledges 'that we do not know whether teaching ethics to medical students makes any long term difference to their clinical practice'.[29] Johnston and Houghton found that, as the course progressed, students in their medical school increasingly recognised that the resolution of ethical dilemmas required more than common sense, and that for students in the later years teaching of medical ethics and law had helped their ability to understand, appreciate and resolve difficult issues that would arise in practice.[30] A similar study from Cardiff University Medical School found that the great majority of students surveyed agreed or strongly agreed that the teaching of ethics and professionalism was an important part of a doctor's training and that learning about them would make them better doctors.[31]

Sokol quotes Andre as saying that teaching ethics is 'fundamentally an act of hope'[32] and concludes that 'the very presence of ethics in the curriculum is important. It sends a message that ethics is an intrinsic and valued part of medical practice. The teaching of ethics, even if its worth cannot be proved, is consistent with common sense and may reassure members of the public that the medical profession … has not lost its moral compass.'[33]

Ethics and professionalism

Professionalism is a way of behaving in accordance with certain normative values appropriate to one's occupation or vocation.[34] It 'is the keystone of the social contract between medicine and the public at large' – and it is what all HCPs

26 Daniel Sokol, 'Teaching Medical Ethics: Useful or Useless?' (2016) 355 *British Medical Journal* 415.
27 Alastair V. Campbell *et al.*, 'How can We Know that Ethics Education Produces Ethical doctors?' (2007) 29 *Medical Teacher* 431.
28 Sarah C. Walpole, 'Medical Students are Taking Medical Ethics Further and Wider, and They are Learning by Doing' (2016) 355 *British Medical Journal* 6415.
29 Sokol (n 26).
30 Carol Johnston and Peter Houghton, 'Medical Students' Perceptions of Their Ethics Teaching' (2007) 33 *Journal of Medical Ethics* 418.
31 Toni C. Saad *et al.*, 'A medical curriculum in transition: audit and student perspective of undergraduate teaching of ethics and professionalism' (2017) 43(11) *Journal of Medical Ethics* 766.
32 Judith Andre, *Bioethics as Practice* (UNC Chapel Hill Press 2002) 75.
33 Sokol (n 26).
34 Jeffrey J. Cohen, 'Viewpoint: Linking Professionalism to Humanism: What It Means, Why It Matters' (2007) 82 *Academic Medicine* 1029.

should be and do![35] Ethics deals with the moral principles or values that underpin professionalism. Supported by moral theories and arguments, it requires critical reflection about 'norms or values, good or bad, right or wrong and what ought or ought not to be done in the context of medical practice' whereas the law describes and defines standards of behaviour to which one is required to conform.[36]

The ability to make consistent ethical decisions is an essential part of professionalism.[37] The codes of practice promulgated by each of the regulatory authorities for HCPs are rightly dominated by professionalism but all have the ethics of 'How should I live?' and 'What should I do?' at their heart. Although the BMA's *Medical Ethics Today* is predominantly about medical professionalism, it too is underpinned by ethics and, for example, discusses both the teaching of ethics and law and the ethics of teaching.

Levenson *et al.* observed that:

> doctors do not become professionals by virtue of starting their first job as a qualified medical practitioner.[38] The process of becoming a professional begins in university and the task of sustaining professional behaviour continues for a lifetime.

Neither the skills necessary for critical analysis, reasoning and reflection nor an understanding of the ever-developing law arise spontaneously – they must be learned. These caveats apply to all HCPs. However, 'formal teaching of professionalism is only part of the issue' of how students can best prepare for the challenges of being a twenty-first-century professional.[39] 'Although professionalism can be nurtured and refined if the potential is there in the first place, teaching is unlikely to make much difference when an individual lacked the personal qualities, values and attitudes that are the foundation of professionalism'.[40] They doubt the feasibility and desirability of trying to select students for professional qualities before entry to medical school.[41]

The regulatory bodies set out ethical and professional standards of behaviour that apply to all students as they prepare to become HCPs. The GMC, for example, states that medical schools and the universities of which they are a part must have a process to make sure that only those medical students who are fit to practise as doctors are permitted to graduate with a primary medical qualification. Medical students who do not meet the outcomes for graduates or who are not fit to practise must not be allowed to graduate with

35 Michael E. Whitcomb, 'Professionalism in Medicine' (2007) 82 *Academic Medicine* 1009.
36 Raanan Gillon, *Philosophical Medical Ethics* (Chichester, Wiley 1985).
37 Louis Arnold, 'Assessing Professional Behaviour; Yesterday, Today, and Tomorrow' (2002) 77 *Academic Medicine* 502.
38 Ros Levenson *et al.*, *Understanding Doctors – Harnessing Professionalism* (London, King's Fund, 2008) 4.
39 ibid 5–6.
40 ibid 8.
41 ibid 6–7.

a medical degree or continue on a medical programme.[42] The GMC sets out the professional behaviour expected of medical students, areas of misconduct, the sanctions available and the key elements in student fitness to practise arrangements.[43] Among the other guidance documents is *Achieving Good Medical Practice: Guidance for Medical Students*.[44] Nursing and all allied health professions also have fitness to practise guidelines. For nurses it is part of the nursing code and for others it is incorporated within their codes of ethics.[45] Hickson *et al.* are right to assert that 'failing to address unprofessional behaviour simply promotes more of it'.[46] Thus it is mandatory that each school has clear and specific policies on how to deal with the few students who consistently and persistently display unprofessional conduct. While emphasising that no single strategy fits every situation, the model advocated by Hickson *et al.*, focuses on four graduated interventions – informal conversations for single incidents, non-punitive awareness interventions when data reveal patterns, leader-developed action plans if patterns persist, and imposition of disciplinary processes if the plans fail.[47]

In the UK, the GMC requires that medical students who are not able to complete a medical qualification or to achieve the learning outcomes required for graduates must be given advice on alternative career options, including pathways to gain a qualification if this is appropriate. Doctors in training who are not able to complete their training pathway should also be given career advice.[48]

There is a tendency in some UK medical schools to separate the organisation and delivery of the teaching of professionalism from that of medical ethics. We consider that they are so intertwined that such separation devalues both:

> Medical Ethics has become part of Bioethics. On one hand this has led to the subject being recognised as a rigorous academic discipline and progress in teaching and learning medical ethics and law could not have happened or continue without the close involvement of, for example, lawyers, social scientists, philosophers and theologians as well as doctors. On the other hand non-medical bioethicists sometimes fail to grasp clinical realities and

---

42 General Medical Council (n 18).

43 General Medical Council, *Professional Behaviour and Fitness to Practice* (2016a) <www.gmc-uk.org/Professional_behaviour_and_fitness_to_practise_0816.pdf_66085925.pdf> accessed 27 July 2017.

44 General Medical Council, *Achieving Good Medical Practice: Guidance for Medical Students* (2016b) <www.gmc-uk.org/Achieving_good_medical_practice_0816.pdf_66086678.pdf> accessed 27 July 2017.

45 Nursing and Midwifery Council, *The Code: Professional Standards of Practice and Behaviour for Nurses and Midwives* (2015) <www.nmc.org.uk/standards/code/> accessed 30 July 2017.

46 Gerald B. Hickson *et al.*, 'A Complementary Approach to Promoting Professionalism: Identifying, Measuring, and Addressing Unprofessional Behaviours' (2007) 82 *Academic Medicine* 1040.

47 ibid.

48 General Medical Council (n 18) 27.

clinicians feel inadequate, making them apprehensive about getting involved in formal ethics teaching.[49]

Thus it may be that, since clinicians tend to feel much more comfortable with thinking and talking about the more concrete aspects of professionalism, they wish to leave the more philosophical ethics to the 'experts'. In a survey of 32 ethics leads in UK medical schools, of the 20 who responded, only three had clinical backgrounds.[50] To encourage more clinicians to become involved in formal healthcare ethics teaching, we suggest that greater emphasis should be placed on 'teaching the teachers' and strategies to develop the careers of the increasing number of graduates who take a special interest in medical ethics as students.

Curricular issues

Each school of medicine, nursing, dentistry, etc. in the UK is currently still free to organise what, how and when to teach each element of the curriculum, as long as it can demonstrate that it complies with the required standards. The GMC's quality assurance mechanisms for medical education include detailed reports submitted by, and visits to, medical schools. However, in 15 of 22 UK medical schools that responded to a survey in 2004, it was possible for students to fail ethics assessments and still graduate.[51] That should not be possible today if the standards set down by the GMC are properly enforced.[52]

The 2010 indicative core content of learning for medical ethics and law in UK medical schools resulted from extensive consultation and was specifically formulated in line with the then current GMC guidance on undergraduate education.[53] It includes suggestions for the generic competencies to be aimed for as the course progresses.[54]

The teaching and learning of medical ethics, law and professionalism should be integrated vertically and horizontally throughout the whole undergraduate curriculum, beginning early and being reinforced throughout the course.[55] It is a shared obligation of all teachers and not the sole responsibility of designated teachers of healthcare ethics and law:

> It is important that medical (and other) educators do not confine ethical considerations to a few elements of a curriculum. It is not possible to divorce

49 Stirrat (n 10) 10.
50 Christopher Oldroyd and Lydia Fiavola, 'Ethics teaching on 'beginning of life' (2014) 40 *Journal of Medical Ethics* 849.
51 Mattick and Bligh (n 14) 184.
52 General Medical Council (n 18).
53 Stirrat *et al.* (n 15).
54 ibid 58.
55 Leveson *et al.* (n 38); Saad *et al.* (n 31).

any part of clinical practice from ethics, for even routine decisions presuppose moral judgements which doctors may or may not be aware of.[56]

The topic also needs to be specifically integrated with other complementary subjects such as the World Health Organization's recommendations on patient safety,[57] clinical communication,[58] medical humanities, psychology,[59] and 'there is a need for a coherent ethical and pedagogical framework to locate the appropriate roles of emotion in ethical deliberation and practice'.[60] Margetts has designed an applied law ethics toolkit for medical education in professionalism encompassing knowledge, skills and attitudes.[61] Legal knowhow in medical schools also 'needs to be cascaded to all staff, teachers, researchers and educationalists to tackle lack of knowledge and undeveloped skill and attitudes'.[62] This applies to the education of all HCPs.

It is for each institution delivering the pre- and post-qualification education of HCPs to determine the best context and method for teaching and learning ethics, law and professionalism in line with the guidance from the statutory bodies. However, clinical contact with patients from as early as possible in the course is fundamental because, to be useful, teaching and learning needs to be contextualised and the GMC requires that students have early contact with patients that increases in duration and responsibility as students progress through the programme.[63] In a small study on how medical students learn ethics, the single largest contributor to ethics learning experiences in Year 4 was observation during clinical encounters.[64] McCarthy and Fins recommend that:

> trainees should be taught to think beyond evidence-based treatments. By examining the legal, historical, and ethical precedents regarding seemingly mundane interactions with patients, they will be prepared to have more thoughtful interactions with their patients amidst the flurry of activity on the hospital wards;

---

56 Saad *et al.* (n 31).
57 World Health Organization, *Patient Safety Curriculum Guide for Medical Schools* (2009) <www.who.int/patient safety/activities/technical/medical_curriculum/en/index.html> accessed 18 July 2017.
58 Martin von Fragstein *et al.*, 'UK Consensus Statement on the Content of Communication Curricula in Undergraduate Medical Education' (2008) 42 *Medical Education* 1100.
59 Christine Bundy *et al.*, *A Core Curriculum for Psychology in Undergraduate Medical Education* (Higher Education Academy Psychology Network, UK 2010).
60 Lynn Gillam *et al.*, 'The Role of Emotions in Health Professional Ethics Teaching' (2014) 40 *Journal of Medical Ethics* 331.
61 J.K. Margetts, 'Learning the Law: Practical Proposals for UK Medical Education' (2016) 42 *Journal of Medical Ethics* 138.
62 ibid 140.
63 General Medical Council (n 18); Pirashanthie Vivekananda-Schmidt and Bryan Vernon, 'FY1 doctors Ethicolegal Challenges in Their First Year of Clinical Practice: An Interview Study' (2014) 40 *Journal of Medical Ethics* 277.
64 Carolyn Johnston and Jonathan Mok, 'How Medical Students Learn Ethics: An Online Log of Their Learning Experiences' (2015) 41 *Journal of Medical Ethics* 856.

and

the implications of ethical decisions should be discussed and dissected on ward rounds with the same rigor, enthusiasm, and attention to detail with which differential diagnoses are generated and treatments are rendered.[65]

The cultural pluralism among our students, teachers, fellow HCPs and patients further requires that students learn to work harmoniously with colleagues and care for patients who have a different world view. Campbell pioneered an interprofessional approach to teaching and learning ethics in the UK.[66] Hanson argued that teaching medical and nursing students health care ethics in an interdisciplinary setting is beneficial for them and that the benefits of interdisciplinary education, specifically in ethics, outweigh the difficulties many schools may have in developing such courses.[67] The GMC considers that an 'effective learning culture will value and support learners from all professional groups'.[68] Teachers need to become more 'savvy' about the effective use of digital technologies. Students continue to need clear guidance about the ethics of their use.

All regulatory authorities require that educational facilities and infrastructure be appropriate to deliver the curriculum. Thus it is the responsibility of each teaching establishment to provide adequate teaching and learning time and resources for healthcare ethics, law and professionalism.

Knight notes that, as healthcare ethics becomes increasingly broad and complex with more issues, settings and stakeholders, teaching and learning it in an increasingly constrained curriculum is more challenging.[69] It is, therefore, understandable that there continues to be resistance from those responsible for education in schools of medicine, nursing and allied professions to, as they see it, 'load more on to the curriculum'. In the context of medicine, Stirrat has previously suggested that the IME work with other cognate bodies to help medical schools properly to integrate these disciplines horizontally and vertically in the curriculum without overburdening it. Similar co-working could take place in other disciplines.[70]

Role models – good and bad

The GMC emphasised that every doctor who comes into contact with trainee doctors, medical students and other healthcare professionals in training should

65 Matthew W. McCarthy and Joseph J. Fins, 'Teaching Clinical Ethics at the Bedside: William Osler and the Essential Role of the Hospitalist' (2017) 19 *AMA Journal of Ethics* 528.
66 Alastair V. Campbell, *Moral Dilemmas in Medicine* (Churchill Livingstone, Edinburgh 1972).
67 Stephen Hanson, 'Teaching Healthcare Ethics: Why We Should Teach Nursing And Medical Students Together' (2005) 12 *Nursing Ethics* 167.
68 General Medical Council (n 18) 8.
69 Selena Knight, 'Ethics: Do We Still Need It? A Personal Perspective on Ethics in Practice' (2017) *Institute of Medical Ethics Annual Spring Education Conference 3rd February 2017* http://ime.datawareonline.co.uk/Resource-Centre accessed 30 July 2017.
70 Gordon M. Stirrat (n 10) 10.

act as a positive role model in their behaviour towards patients, colleagues and others. Students learn not only from their formal teaching but also from their experiences of observing and working with practising doctors as role models. As Pellegrino observed, 'courses in ethics cannot close the gap between knowing what is good and doing it' and (virtue) is 'best taught by good examples on the part of those we respect'.[71] *Medical Ethics Today* emphasises that, although many doctors (and other HCPs) are excellent role models and reinforce the lessons and principles that students have learnt throughout their studies, the example of how their tutors practise can be a far more powerful influence in the development of ethical, or unethical, practice than the edicts of formal ethics teaching; and senior colleagues may unwittingly give the impression that medical ethics gets in the way of good practice.[72] Indeed, two students in a medical school in the USA went as far as to assert that 'the chief barrier to medical professionalism education is unprofessional conduct by medical educators, which is protected by an established hierarchy of academic authority'.[73]

Medical Ethics Today emphasises that the potential for conflict between formal and informal learning underlies the tension that many medical students, motivated as they are to be 'good doctors', articulate in their response to the teaching of ethics.[74] One possible effect of this tension is the growth of cynicism and the erosion of ethical beliefs and conduct.[75] 'When there is a discrepancy between what students are taught about good ethico-legal practice and what they experience on clinical firms, anger, disillusionment, and cynicism may follow'.[76] In recognising the importance of professional culture and the working environment in contributing to burnout among HCPs, Lemaire and Wallace suggest that it can be one consequence of learners witnessing and adopting their teachers' maladaptive behaviours, which are often reinforced throughout their career.[77] These problems are not easily resolved and speaking out can require courage.[78] Singer argued that medical schools and teaching hospitals needed to develop formal guidelines for ethics in clinical teaching that highlighted the responsibility of teaching staff to serve as appropriate role models to medical students and to provide them with an opportunity to discuss ethical challenges; develop processes for reporting ethical concerns; provide access to individuals for medical students and their tutors to approach with ethical problems; and ensure that,

71 Pellegrino (n 25) 702.
72 British Medical Association (n 1).
73 Andrew H. Brainard and Heather C. Brislen, 'Learning Professionalism: A View from the Trenches' (2007) 82 *Academic Medicine* 1010.
74 British Medical Association (n 1) 758.
75 Gavin Yarney and Jason O. Roach, 'Witnessing Unethical Conduct: The Effects' (2001) 9 *Student British Medical Journal* 2.
76 Len Doyal, 'Closing the Gap Between Professional Teaching and Practice' (2001) 322 *British Medical Journal* 685.
77 Jane B. Lemaire and Jean E. Wallace, 'Burnout Damages More Than Just Individuals' (2017) 258 *British Medical Journal* 3360.
78 British Medical Association (n 1) 783.

when medical students express concern about ethical issues or decline to take part in certain activities for ethical reasons, this will not have any repercussions for them.[79] This should take place in a blame-free environment in which errors and difficulties are openly reported and discussed; and, instead of apportioning blame, which can lead to evasion and cover-up, systematic solutions should be found for the ethical challenges of medical education.

Assessment

The GMC has produced comprehensive criteria for the assessment of medical students and doctors in training. In summary, assessments must be fair, reliable, valid, mapped to the curriculum and carried out by a trained assessor with appropriate expertise in the area being assessed. Assessment strategies should be clear and comprehensive, setting out a school's philosophy about the value of assessment and how it selects assessment tools. Students' moral and ethical reasoning, attitudes and behaviour, as well as knowledge of laws relevant to clinical practice, should also be assessed in conformity with the standards set down by the GMC.[80] These criteria are relevant to all institutions responsible for the education of healthcare students.

In 2013, the IME produced a practical guide for the assessment of medical ethics and law to complement the core content of learning.[81] It provides examples of methods of assessment and some pointers for deciding what methods might be appropriate for particular learning outcomes.

In 2013–14, the GMC reviewed the assessment systems used in 31 medical schools across the UK.[82] They acknowledged that the assessment of professionalism is both critical and challenging, and suggest that 'it should be embedded in the values of the school from the beginning, and then continue to be assessed and monitored while being taught throughout the programme'.[83] In some schools, assessment and monitoring relied only on informal arrangements and many schools were not comprehensive or structured enough in their approach to teaching and assessing professionalism and some only assessed clinical assessments and placements.[84]

---

79 Peter A. Singer, 'Intimate Examinations and Other Ethical Challenges in Medical Education: Medical Schools Should Develop Effective Guidelines and Implement Them' (2003) 326 *British Medical Journal* 62.
80 General Medical Council (n 18).
81 Angela Fenwick *et al.*, *Medical Ethics and Law: A practical guide to the assessment of the core content of learning. A report from the Education Steering Group of the Institute of Medical Ethics* (London, Institute of Medical Ethics, 2013); Stirrat (n 15).
82 General Medical Council, *How are Students Assessed at Medical Schools across the UK?* (2016c) <www.gmc-uk.org/Assessment_audit_report_FINAL_pdf.pdf_59752384.pdf> accessed 26 July 2017.
83 ibid 12.
84 ibid 13.

Changing patterns of care and increased workloads

Education of healthcare professionals in the UK occurs within the context of our National Health Service (NHS). The authors have over 50 years' cumulative experience of working in the NHS to which we are totally committed. In common with all developed nations, funding of health and social care in the UK raises major financial, ethical and political issues. It is not within the scope of this chapter to consider these save inasmuch as they affect the education of all HCPs and, in particular, the teaching and learning of ethics and ethical practice.

According to the GMC, there is evidence that, when services are under pressure, time and resources for education are the first to be sacrificed.[85] Our experience suggests that ethical analysis, reflection and discussion among healthcare teams and with students and trainees are diminished by these pressures. Similar problems are present in other healthcare settings.

Junior doctors and other healthcare personnel in the NHS are experiencing alarming levels of stress and the GMC describes 'an unmistakeable state of unease within the medical profession across the UK that risks affecting patients as well as doctors'.[86] The report recognises that the reasons are complex and multifactorial and some are long-standing; but it suggests that 'at the heart of this are systems of healthcare across the UK that are struggling with the impact of a growing number of people living with multiple, complex, long-term needs'. It is an ethical and pastoral priority that all bodies responsible for the pre- and post-qualification education of HCPs prepare students and trainees to cope with stress and have effective strategies in place to prevent, reduce and treat its effects. This is only part of the solution because it is increasingly clear that effective interventions must be directed at professional and healthcare organisations as well as at individuals.[87]

When things go wrong

The general public and all HCPs working in our NHS were appalled by the dreadful events that occurred in Mid-Staffordshire NHS Foundation Trust between 2005 and 2009, and wondered how such things could have happened when 'the quality of care was subject to more inspection and regulation than ever before and doctors [and other HCPs] had unprecedented access to guidance on ethical practice'.[88] The comprehensive and detailed report by Sir Robert Francis

85 General Medical Council, *The State of Medical Education and Practice in the UK* (2016d) <www.gmc-uk.org/SOMEP_2016_Full_Report_Lo_Res.pdf_68139324.pdf> accessed 30 July 2017.

86 General Medical Council (n 83); Rachel Clark and Martin McKee, 'Suicide among Junior Doctors in the NHS' (2017) 357 *British Medical Journal* 2527.

87 Lemaire and Wallace (n 75) 183.

88 Wing May Kong and Bryan Vernon, 'Harnessing the LMG legacy: the IME's vision of the future' (2013) 39 *Journal of Medical Ethics* 671.

QC on this tragedy makes sombre reading.[89] In his Chairman's statement, he wrote that 'there was an institutional culture in which the business of the system was put ahead of the priority that should have been given to the protection of patients and the maintenance of public trust in the service'.[90] He thought that five things were needed: a structure of clearly understood fundamental standards and measures of compliance, accepted and embraced by the public and healthcare professionals, with rigorous and clear means of enforcement; openness, transparency and candour throughout the system; improved support for compassionate caring and committed nursing; strong and patient-centred healthcare leadership; and accurate, useful and relevant information.[91] We may argue that all these are already explicitly or implicitly contained in the ethical and professional guidance from our regulatory bodies but the fact that the tragedy occurred underlines the responsibility for those of us teaching medical ethics, law and professionalism to address the underlying problems.

Healthcare managers are another important professional group encompassed by these recommendations. The 1983 'Griffiths report' ushered in the era of 'managerialism' in the NHS but managers do not have an ethical or regulatory body equivalent to the GMC.[92] Francis recognised this anomaly and suggested the creation of an NHS leadership staff college 'supported by a common code of ethics and conduct for all leaders and senior managers'; but do ethical values, behaviour and attitudes not need to be inculcated from the earliest point in managerial training as occurs for HCPs?[93] He also proposed a registration scheme 'to ensure that only fit and proper persons are eligible to be directors of NHS organisations'[94] but we consider that this should apply to everyone training for management roles in the NHS. While we accept our responsibilities as educators of HCPs, we would have greater confidence that such tragedies could be prevented in the future if healthcare managers learned ethics and professionalism and were regulated in the same way as we are.

The way ahead

Massive changes have occurred in our society in general and in healthcare in particular since 1972 when Campbell produced his course book on ethics for doctors and nurses.[95] Although healthcare ethics education has, by and large, kept pace

89 Robert Francis, *Report of the Mid Staffordshire NHS Foundation Trust Public Inquiry* (2013) <http://webarchive.nationalarchives.gov.uk/20150407084231/http://www.midstaffs publicinquiry.com/report> accessed 31 July 2017.
90 ibid 3.
91 ibid 5.
92 Roy Griffiths, *NHS management inquiry* (Department of Health and Social Security, UK, 1983) <www.nhshistory.net/griffiths.html> accessed 31 July 2017; Brian Jarman, 'When managers rule' (2012) 345 *British Medical Journal* 345.
93 Francis (n 88) 8.
94 ibid.
95 Campbell (n 65).

with these changes, we must learn from our failures. It took Sir Robert Francis QC to remind us that we are still at the beginning, not the end, of a journey 'towards a healthier culture in the NHS in which patients are the first and foremost consideration of the system and all those who work in it'.[96] Let us pray that we are currently growing leaders like Campbell who will lead and guide us on that journey.

96 Francis (n 87).

12 Healthcare ethics education in Singapore

Anita Ho, Jacqueline Chin and Voo Teck Chuan

Introduction

Modern medicine requires highly skilled and knowledgeable practitioners to deliver services that may be accompanied by varying risks of harm. Even as medical advances are extending life, restoring functioning, and giving new hope to patients and families, and while medical information is increasingly accessible to lay persons, patients in most situations are bound to be anxious, vulnerable, and dependent on their healthcare providers. Inherent to clinical medicine is thus the need for patients' trust in healthcare professionals to deliver care competently and ethically.

The changing social and healthcare landscape exacerbates ethical and professional challenges for clinicians. In the face of an increasing commodification of healthcare, medical graduates may be tempted to find ways to increase their income, sometimes running the risk of putting 'profit before patients'.[1] Intersecting with information and technological advances, patients and families may demand more treatments, sometimes raising cost-benefit concerns and imposing additional challenges of balancing various professional duties.[2]

In this context of advancing technologies and an evolving social and healthcare landscape, medical education requires attention to the ethical, professional, and legal dimensions of how care is funded, organized, and delivered. There is now international consensus that ethics education should be an important part of any medical curriculum.[3] Medical trainees working within teams of healthcare providers are expected to be lifelong learners who continually acquire adequate and up-to-date knowledge, appropriate and effective skills, including those of teamwork, and caring and respectful attitudes towards all patients.

Based at the National University of Singapore (NUS) Yong Loo Lin School of Medicine, the Centre for Biomedical Ethics (CBmE) was founded in 2007 by

1 Alastair V. Campbell and Anita Ho, 'The Philosophy of Professionalism and Professional Ethics' (SMA News, June 2015) 24–25.
2 ibid.
3 World Health Organization, 'The Teaching of Medical Ethics: Fourth Consultation with Leading Medical Practitioners' (WHO 1995); World Medical Association, 'World Medical Association: Medical Ethics Manual' (3rd edn, WMA 2015).

Professor Alastair V. Campbell to lead the development of an integrated and longitudinal teaching programme in medical ethics for NUS undergraduate medical students. The programme aims to prepare trainees to develop the professionalism and the skills to address ethical dilemmas that arise in clinical medicine and research. With a focus on global ethical values in an Asian context, the CBmE also provides bioethics research degree programmes (at MSc and PhD levels) for graduate students. Its teaching responsibility gradually expanded over the years to include the provision of continuing education in clinical ethics for healthcare professionals, and training programmes in clinical, research, and transplant ethics for ethics committees in Singapore. This chapter will describe the evolving bioethics education and capacity-building projects of the CBmE, with a view to elucidating the educational philosophy, tenets, and factors that drive its mission and approach.

Virtue ethics as the cornerstone of medical ethics education

The NUS School of Medicine strives to nurture future clinicians who will be leaders in healthcare, academic medicine, and public service in Singapore. Bioethics education and associated training are regarded with utmost importance in supporting trainees who are on their path to become ethically responsible and responsive clinicians. Campbell, who had previously established two renowned bioethics centres at the University of Otago and University of Bristol respectively, brought his extensive research, teaching, and administrative experience to Singapore when he founded the CBmE. More than 10 years later, the CBmE remains the sole academic bioethics department in Singapore, building capacity across the nation and the region. In particular, Campbell's significant contribution to virtue ethics in bioethics provided the pedagogical foundation for Singaporean medical trainees to consider the core of their ethical and professional identity as they embark on their clinical training in the evolving social and healthcare landscapes.

In addition to understanding ethical concepts and principles, virtue ethics delves into a practitioner's moral character, offers suggestions to integrate reason and emotion, and attends to the context of decisions, including the changing healthcare environment.[4] Campbell's frequent question, 'Has medicine sold its soul?' became the title of one of his grand round presentations at the National University Hospital and reminds us to reflect on the purposes, expectations, and ideals of the profession. It highlights the need for medical educators and clinicians to think about the ethical core of clinical medicine, and how they can teach and role model virtuous characters and behaviour in the context of the changing healthcare landscape. It has helped our medical school to strengthen its focus on the values of medicine and the essential attributes of medical professionals and their deeper moral values and authenticity as trusted healers.

---

4 Alastair V. Campbell, 'The Virtues (and Vices) of The Four Principles' (2003) 29 *Journal of Medical Ethics* 292.

Undergraduate healthcare ethics education

Campbell sometimes talks about how he is an 'accidental bioethicist'. He studied philosophy and theology before a Harkness Fellowship took him to California to explore the relationship between religion and psychiatry. Upon his return to Scotland, he accepted an invitation to teach ethics to senior nurses. Eventually, he followed his heart – advice he continues to give his mentees regarding their professional endeavours – and devoted his career to medical ethics.

Ethics education for our NUS medical trainees is anything but accidental. It follows Campbell's advice that, for whatever profession we choose, it should be something we care deeply about, something we would help change as appropriate, and something we would do with integrity.

The NUS CBmE undergraduate longitudinal Health Ethics, Law and Professionalism (HeLP) curriculum prepares trainees to embrace such a professional path and attitude of lifelong learning. Established in 2008, it is designed to facilitate reflective practices and integrated learning throughout all 5 years of the Bachelor of Medicine and Bachelor of Surgery (MBBS) programme, thereby supporting medical students' professional identity formation in progressive phases of their training. Core elements of the HeLP curriculum include knowledge of ethical, professional, and legal foundations of clinicians' duties to patients, families, interprofessional colleagues, and other stakeholders. Other core elements envisage ways to 'habituate' ethical understanding in the practice setting of students' clinical postings, by learning through observing and reflecting on professional and unprofessional practices in everyday clinical encounters and how one might choose to act in similar circumstances.

As the NUS MBBS curriculum and medical pedagogy evolves, so does the HeLP curriculum, which is loosely 'pegged' to the rest of the school's academic programme to facilitate relevance and integration. In the last decade, developing a positive professional identity was increasingly recognized internationally as an important component of medical education.[5] In response, in 2013, a professionalism task force was formed to help design an integrated and explicit programme for enhancing professionalism in students through all stages of the medical curriculum. The multidisciplinary task force (pharmacology, surgery, obstetrics, medicine, emergency medicine, medical education, and ethics) sought ways to nurture important values that can then be articulated in a set of demonstrable behaviours by our students. In particular, the task force finalized the resulting list of 'professional attributes'. These are attitudes and behaviours organized into four domains: honesty and integrity; responsibility and participation; respect and sensitivity; compassion and empathy. The task force proposed specific mechanisms to

---

5 Hedy S. Wald *et al.*, 'Professional identity Formation in Medical Education for Humanistic, Resilient Physicians: Pedagogic Strategies for Bridging Theory to Practice' (2015) 90(6) *Academic Medicine* 753; Ian Wilson *et al.*, 'Professional Identity in Medical Students: Pedagogical Challenges to Medical Education' (2013) 25(4) *Teaching and Learning in Medicine: An International Journal* 369.

define professionalism in terms of these attributes in various student and faculty documents and guidelines. These attributes provide a foundational structure to develop granular curricular activities and professionalism-related guidelines; they also offer a broad framework to assess and record students' progress throughout the MBBS programme.

Other new national guidelines also required our HeLP curriculum to adapt accordingly. The Ministry of Health (MOH) in Singapore appointed the National Medical Undergraduate Curriculum Committee (NMUCC) to craft outcomes and minimum standards for our undergraduate medical curriculum.[6] The NMUCC recognizes that, whether trainees are preparing to become primary care physicians, specialists, clinician-scientists, or clinician-administrators and policy makers, they must be prepared to help build an inclusive healthcare system that will provide affordable, effective, and good-quality care. Recognising a changing healthcare landscape, the Singapore Medical Council also issued its revised ethical code and ethical guidelines in 2016 to update professional ethical standards accordingly.

With these recent developments in mind, the HeLP curriculum focuses on integrating identity formation and ethical reasoning in the pre-clinical years. In the clinical years, the curriculum expands to facilitate demonstration of the aforementioned professional attributes as related to care delivery and skills for engaging in structured analysis of various challenging clinical and public health issues. As the medical curriculum spirals upward, the HeLP curriculum tackles more complex ethical issues, keeping in mind that learners are expected to demonstrate a set of core competencies regarding healthcare professionals' clinical duties and interactions with patients and other stakeholders.

The modes of the HeLP teaching include didactic in-person lectures and e-lectures that provide the core background knowledge and information. To help learners apply these concepts to their training and real-life scenarios, case-based interactive and small-group tutorial sessions with simulated patients, clinician tutors, and ethicists are dispersed throughout the HeLP curriculum. These sessions are also tailored according to the basic science and clinical curricula, using cases that are linked to these particular domains.

While conceptual lectures in pre-clinical years are mostly delivered by academic ethicists, ethics education is increasingly interdisciplinary – clinical educators often teach or co-teach various formal ethics sessions in clinical years. Moreover, as ethics and professionalism are best demonstrated and role-modeled at the bedside, clinical educators are expected to provide relevant formal and informal training throughout students' MBBS journey. Enabling students to act on their growing ethical and professional understanding with competence, and supporting them in difficult and morally distressing situations, are challenges that call for coordinated efforts between medical schools and practice settings.

---

6 Ministry of Health, 'Outcomes and Standards for Undergraduate Medical Education in Singapore: Recommendations of The National Medical Undergraduate Curriculum Committee' (Singapore, Ministry of Health 2014).

Challenges: assessment and effectiveness

In medicine, clinicians are not simply technicians – they are considered members of a *profession*. To 'profess' is to make a public declaration or commitment according to which one's actions can be judged. This commitment is clearly spelled out in all the medical codes: to put the welfare of patients above personal advantage. Thus a medical professional is someone who can be trusted always to honour this commitment.[7]

However, the general acceptance of such commitment notwithstanding, there is widespread debate and uncertainty about what and how ethics and professionalism should be taught, and whether they can be assessed fairly and meaningfully.[8] Questions abound regarding whether we can truly 'teach' ethics and professionalism, and how we can assess learners' commitment during their undergraduate training. After all, there are few opportunities for highly supervised learners to explicitly showcase or violate such commitment, making independent assessment of students' long-term professionalism challenging. This raises the question of whether professionalism assessment should *presume* learners' professionalism unless they demonstrate problematic behaviours, and focus on providing reflective activities that can strengthen content knowledge and reinforce professional behaviours. In the HeLP curriculum, students are generally expected to demonstrate awareness and insight regarding various ethical and professional issues via formative and summative assessments (e.g. group case analysis presentations, modified essay questions, multiple choice questions, and objective structured clinical examinations) throughout the longitudinal programme. Interprofessional education is increasingly promoted at NUS via integrated classes where students from different disciplines (e.g., medicine and nursing) attend the same modules together; '360' assessment is also conducted by interdisciplinary clinical staff members who supervise the students.

This last point brings out another challenge and question regarding ethics education. Who is ultimately responsible for ethics education and character/identity formation in a medical school and team-care setting that is increasingly interdisciplinary? And how should formal ethics curricula in medical schools be assessed for their effectiveness in producing and nurturing ethical professionals, when the broader social environment and the hidden curriculum may also affect learners' understanding of compassionate and respectful behavior and their adoption of various behaviors?[9] While many of these clinical educators are not formal members of the HeLP teaching team, their clinical teaching and personal professionalism can all have impact on students' learning. We must also remember that what impacts patient care is not necessarily what we teach but what students learn.

7 Campbell and Ho (n 1).
8 A.V. Campbell, J. Chin, and T.C. Voo, 'How Can We Know That Ethics Education Produces Ethical Doctors?' (2007) 29(5) *Medical Teacher* 431.
9 Warren A. Kinghorn, 'Medical Education as Moral Formation: An Aristotelian Account of Medical Professionalism' (2010) 53(1) *Perspectives in Biology and Medicine* 87.

Ethics training for ethics committees

Soon after the first rollout of the undergraduate curriculum in 2008, the Ministry of Health in that year approached Campbell to invite the CBmE to apply for a project grant to support the training of hospital or clinical ethics committees (CECs) in the restructured hospitals. The appointment of a CEC with a specified interprofessional and layperson composition is part of the licensing terms and conditions for all hospitals in Singapore. The CBmE saw an opportunity here to understand and try to address any 'hidden curriculum' issues within the healthcare system – that is, the practice environment within which medical undergraduates receive training. It contacted the UK Clinical Ethics Network for advice on setting up a training programme for CECs – in particular, Dr Anne Slowther in London, and Professors Tony Hope and Michael Parker at the Oxford University Ethox Centre. The grant application was successful and, in October 2009, Campbell named the project 'CENTRES', an acronym for 'Clinical Ethics Network for Training, Research and Education'. The name conveys an aspiration of the project to nurture hospital settings as 'centres' for clinical ethics education within each hospital through the role and function of CECs, with support from the CBmE. However, there is at present still no role for the CECs in undergraduate education at the training hospitals.

This does not diminish the CENTRES project's importance in the overall scheme of professionalism education conducted by the CBmE. By 2010, all the public restructured hospitals' CECs were members of the CENTRES network. CENTRES conducted periodic surveys to analyse the needs of network members, and designed educational events to meet those needs. The first workshop was held in January 2010, concerning neonatal ethics dilemmas, and included participation from international leaders in the field. The second workshop focused on the role and function of CECs, and models and processes of ethical deliberation and consensus building dynamics in CEC work. Since then, CENTRES has organized more than 30 workshops on a variety of topics of interest to hospital ethics committees, including family decision making, reproductive care, medical futility, resource allocation, confidentiality, disclosure of medical errors, and migrant workers' healthcare. Typical workshops have been targeted at individual hospitals and their committees' particular needs.

CENTRES has been hosting an annual international clinical ethics conference since 2011, attracting significant interest from the local CECs and healthcare professionals. The conferences have been an opportunity to gather the ethics community together at a larger venue than is possible at workshops to discuss and deliberate on issues of mutual concern. The format has been well received: local and international experts give concise plenary lectures on a particular topic, following which attendees break out into smaller discussion groups to work through relevant case studies using ethics toolkits such as the ABC toolkit developed by the Singapore casebook team (see www.bioethicscasebook. sg), a collaborative project between the CBmE, the Oxford Ethox Centre and the Hastings Center. Afterwards, the groups reconvene to share and synthesize their thoughts. In 2017, CENTRES hosted the prestigious annual International Conference on Clinical Ethics Consultation (ICCEC) in Singapore, attracting 310 participants from 38 countries and 164 local participants. Bursaries were provided by Singapore hospitals, NUS and philanthropic organizations to 16 participants from low- and middle-income countries, enabling wide and vigorous discussions on the conference theme, 'Clinical ethics and change in health care', which addressed advancements and innovations in healthcare delivery, a rapidly aging population, and the effects of globalization, culture, and migration.

Online resources were developed in tandem with the above in-person events. The CENTRES website (www.centres.sg) was launched in 2010 and has been continually updated since then with relevant materials such as professional guidelines and law and educational materials from international sources. Videos of CENTRES events have been posted on the website, and a 'Topics' section is replete with cases, readings, and other documents derived from CENTRES activities that are relevant to various issues in clinical ethics support. In addition, a monthly newsletter (with over 50 editions) for network members keeps them updated on the latest developments in the field of clinical ethics. (The newsletter has been replaced with monthly electronic mailers that highlight developments in clinical, research, and transplant ethics due to the expanded remit of CENTRES, as described below).

Besides networking with local institutions to provide clinical ethics training and support, CENTRES aims to facilitate the adoption of uniform clinical ethics principles in Singapore towards the development of consistent nation-wide standards. In 2011, CENTRES published draft good practice guidelines for CECs based on the survey results of CEC practices and advice from the committee members. The resultant document was used as a foundation for the National Ethics Capability Committee (NECC)'s core competency framework for CECs, accepted by the Permanent Secretary of the Ministry of Health in May 2017.

Since 2015, CENTRES' remit has been expanded to include capacity building in research ethics and networking for Singapore's institutional review boards (IRBs). In light of this change, CENTRES now stands for 'Clinical Ethics Network+ Research Ethics Support'. In addition, it now has expanded responsibilities for delivering clinical ethics support to CECs in private healthcare institutions. To date, the network comprises 12 CECs from both public and private hospitals in Singapore. CENTRES also embarked on an initiative to foster an informal association of CEC chairs – the Committee on Clinical Ethics (COCE). Typically, CECs do not communicate with each other, focusing on their own institutional contexts. The purpose of the association is to improve communication and mutual support among Singaporean CECs, share challenges and best practices, and identify areas that need further development and training. A similar association for IRBs – a Committee on Research Ethics (CORE) – was simultaneously set up. In 2016, the remit of CENTRES was extended to include training sessions for transplant ethics committees (TECs) in the ethics of transplantation involving live donors. Training sessions are conducted biannually for both new and existing TEC members, and cover core knowledge such as international and local guidelines and law, skills such as interview techniques and weighing and balancing of ethical considerations, and issues raised by types of donations including minor donations and foreign donors and recipients.

National ethics competency frameworks: training the trainers

The popularity of the CENTRES clinical ethics workshops and conferences among hospital clinicians led the Ministry of Health to respond favourably to national ethics capacity building across the healthcare professions, an idea broached to the government by Campbell, the Dean of the Yong Loo Lin School of Medicine, Professor Yeoh Khay Guan and the previous Dean, Professor John Wong Eu Li. The Ministry set up the National Ethics Capability Committee (NECC) in 2014, chaired by the outgoing Director of Medical Services, Professor Kandiah Satkunanantham. Campbell was its Vice-Chair and the Committee's Secretariat was staffed by the CBmE through new funding. In early 2017, the NECC delivered its strategy and roadmap for healthcare ethics education to be provided through the medical, dental, pharmacy, nursing, and allied health professions and their representative bodies including the Academy of Medicine and the College of Family Physicians.

The CBmE's role is to train the trainers within the professions, as identified by their professional bodies, in healthcare ethics and pedagogical skills for facilitating ethical thinking in professional and interprofessional practice, with emphasis on core healthcare values of beneficence, prevention of harm, respect for persons, justice, and honesty as embodied in various national healthcare and professional ethics guidelines. In addition, the NECC strategy included competency frameworks for the training of specialized committees: hospital ethics committees, transplant ethics committees and institutional review boards (biomedical research ethics committees). In its roadmap, the NECC proposed that this training be undertaken by the CBmE CENTRES project, as mentioned earlier. The NECC approach was accepted by the Permanent Secretary of Health in 2017.

In sum, the outcome of this for CENTRES has been to design appropriate adult educational curricula to equip ethics trainers with the skills to teach healthcare ethics to fellow healthcare professionals. CBmE has also forged an important collaboration with the Singapore Medical Association to co-teach the identified trainers within the healthcare professions, and to look into achieving Ministry of Education accreditation of a NUS certificate and diploma in healthcare ethics in the future. The University has, through this work, recognized CBmE as an NUS department with a high societal impact and national role. Staff teaching hours committed to CENTRES training programmes would soon be logged for evaluation for promotion and tenure, in the same way as hours given to teaching NUS students.

Bioethics graduate education

The mainstay of the CBmE graduate programme in bioethics is the Master of Science and PhD in Medicine by research. Since 2008, students have earned PhD and MSc degrees based on research into diverse topics such as ethics literacy, palliative care ethics, ethical issues surrounding stem cell therapy, biobanking, and public health regulation of tobacco smoking. Methodologies of research range from philosophical, legal, empirical, and policy research methods. This raises the question of the appropriate expectation of a graduate with a degree in bioethics, and indeed the more fundamental question of whether bioethics is a discipline with methods and a theoretical grounding, or whether it is a field that applies multidisciplinary perspectives to problems in medicine and biology.[10] The growth of academic programmes in medical ethics and bioethics over the last 30 years or so has encouraged efforts to standardize core ethics, law, and professionalism curricula in medicine and nursing at the undergraduate level to offer greater consistency of preparation and skills training nationally and internationally.[11] But little has been done to standardize bioethics programmes in graduate education in professional schools, non-medical graduate programmes (such as philosophy or law) and post-professional education.

In Singapore, where a need is developing for more teachers of medical ethics, research ethics, and, more broadly bioethics, with appropriate credentials, this challenge is not lost on the CBmE. Should post-professional bioethics programmes for clinicians, scientists, and technology professionals be conceived along the lines of graduate education at this point of time? Should MSc and PhD programmes in bioethics be structured along 'tracks' in clinical ethics, research ethics, and public health ethics with curricula designed to train graduates in domain-specific skills? Should modules in biolaw, and philosophical and empirical methodologies be core requirements in bioethics training? Should training in one or more disciplines of law, philosophy, or social science methods be prerequisites for admission to graduate degree programmes by research? As the CBmE moves into the future, these challenges must be carefully navigated, with attention to international best practices. The strong collaborative networks established by Campbell with bioethics centres around the world will serve well to promote needed conversations in this space.

Conclusion

This discussion has explored the multifaceted role of the CBmE in bioethics education and capacity building under the mentorship and leadership of Campbell. It has raised many questions about ethics education, which continues to challenge and inspire the work of the CBmE. Solutions to address the pedagogical challenges it faces have been tenaciously pursued through the combination of scholarship, real-world experience, reflective judgment and collaborative thinking with clinical educators and healthcare practitioners. This approach has been the distinctive and enormous legacy of Campbell for bioethics at CBmE.

10 Lisa M. Lee and Frances A. McCarty, 'Emergence of a Discipline? Growth in US Postsecondary Bioethics Degrees' (2016) 46(2) *Hastings Center Report* 19.
11 Alberto Giubilini, Sharyn Milnes, and Julian Savulescu, 'The Medical Ethics Curriculum in Medical Schools: Present and Future' (2016) 27(2) *Journal of Clinical Ethics* 129.

Part VI

Health-related practices in ethical focus

13 The dead human body

Reflections of an anatomist

D. Gareth Jones

Introduction

On the surface, it may appear that the views of a scientist are an intrusion into this collection of essays, and yet that would be to underestimate the influence of Alastair V. Campbell. Getting to know Campbell during his initial visit to the University of Otago in the late 1980s convinced me, among others, that he would be of inestimable value to the Bioethics Centre, and this led to his invitation to become the Foundation Director in 1990. That came to be seen as a prescient decision that was to transform the bioethical landscape in the University of Otago.[1] During this time and afterwards, my many interactions with him, including working with him on the four editions of *Medical Ethics*,[2] convinced me that here was someone coming from a different disciplinary background from my own who understood the ethical issues confronting me in anatomy, and who thereby enriched my own writings at the interface of anatomy and ethics.

Campbell's own approach to the human body was succinctly expressed in his book, *The Body in Bioethics*, where he eloquently set out the importance of paying serious attention to the significance of the human body for bioethical debate.[3] In this, he sought 'to re-establish the importance of the human body in bioethics'.[4] His concern was to argue against viewing the dead body merely as a source of knowledge about the causes of death or the effectiveness of therapy, thereby removing it from the concerns and interests of the bereaved family. He had been closely involved in responses to the retention of organs by a pathologist at Alder Hey Children's Hospital in Liverpool,[5] and more specifically by his membership of the Retained Organs Commission.[6] He clearly demonstrates the limitations

1 D. Gareth Jones, 'Alastair V. Campbell: Pastoral Theologian and Bioethicist' (1996) 5(2) *Otago Bioethics Report* 1.
2 Alastair V. Campbell, Grant Gillett and D. Gareth Jones, *Medical Ethics* (4th edn, Oxford University Press 2005).
3 Alastair V. Campbell, *The Body in Bioethics* (Routledge 2009).
4 ibid 1.
5 *Royal Liverpool Children's Inquiry Report* (Stationery Office 2001).
6 Retained Organs Commission, *A Consultation Document on Unclaimed and Unidentifiable Organs and Tissues and a Possible Regulatory Framework* (Retained Organs Commission, National Health Service 2002).

of the commodification approach, and against this the centrality of the gift relationship and the significance of giving to unnamed strangers, with its basis in altruism: 'A society which fails to foster altruism and a real sense of communal responsibility and which fails to counter the natural human propensity for selfishness is doomed to moral failure and the collapse of humane social structures'.[7]

For Campbell, the embodiment of the person does not suddenly disappear at death, even though it will be let go in time. The body of the person who has now died once had relationships, interests, likes and dislikes, preferences, and obligations as a spouse, sibling, parent, and friend. If anatomists overlook this perspective, they fail to understand the human dimensions of their profession, and will treat dead bodies in a purely scientific manner on the premise that they can be totally objective about the human body. It is to act as though they are disinterested, disembodied observers of the human condition, who can do what they like to the cadavers at their disposal. The dangers of any such attitudes are poignantly highlighted by Campbell when he writes: 'To ignore the bodily aspects of ourselves, or to treat them in a merely instrumental way as a source of income or of social esteem, is ultimately threatening to the integrity of ourselves as individuals and as members of a human community.'[8]

Anatomists are one with the cadavers they study, a realisation that is central to any attempt at humanising their discipline. To quote Campbell again:

> Our bodies and the bodies of our fellow humans are always with us, an inescapable concomitant of being living, conscious beings. If we ignore this aspect of human life, we will end up with an abstract, theoretical and ultimately irrelevant bioethics.[9]

What applies to bioethics applies with equal force to anatomists, because any conduct by anatomists that ignores the welfare and interests of others directly imperils their welfare and interests no matter how significant it might be in elucidating bodily structure. It is my hope that these approaches to the dead human body will emerge in what follows, as I trace a series of issues that are central to the lives and functioning of anatomists.

An anatomical overview

An anatomist has the dubious distinction of reflecting on ethical developments against the background of a discipline with an unsavoury past. However, the centrality of dead human bodies in anatomical teaching and research raises ethical challenges of an intensely practical nature. The dimensions of these challenges span the well-known historical origins of the discipline with its plethora of questionable scandals that continued well into the nineteenth century. Nevertheless,

7 ibid 19.
8 Campbell, *The Body in Bioethics* (n 3) 103.
9 ibid 119.

the trajectory changed as the move from the use of unclaimed bodies to bequests gradually occurred from the 1960s onwards. Unfortunately, this took place largely for pragmatic reasons and with little ethical deliberation so that, when over the years the need for bodies for teaching outstripped supply, the old ways reasserted themselves. This was appallingly pronounced in the 1930s and 1940s during the Nazi regime when all semblance of ethical propriety disappeared in the quest for human bodies of 'high quality'. Scientific considerations reigned supreme and became the sole arbiter of anatomical practice. While the lessons learned from that grim episode have been taken on board, ethical challenges are encountered almost daily. The move to dependence upon bequests rather than unclaimed bodies has been a stuttering one, although the adoption by an international federation of anatomists of a set of recommendations for good anatomical practice, based on the use of donated bodies, is a harbinger of increasing ethical awareness.[10] This will be required as new sets of challenges emerge with the sale of bodies and body parts, the public display of dissected bodies, and the omnipresence of digitised images of human tissue.

Personal reminiscence

Only a few years ago, those in the discipline of anatomy would not have troubled themselves with ethical debate. What they did with, and to, dead human bodies was legal, and hence they had no need of any assistance from ethicists. Not only this, they regarded themselves as scientists living and working within a scientific paradigm, and hence objective and above the fray of philosophical and ethical speculation. They did not have to bother themselves with the uncertain values and value systems of those in the humanities, nor even of those working in clinical medicine. They simply got on with the job at hand, that of imparting the well-worn knowledge of anatomical minutiae to medical undergraduates and surgical postgraduates. The apparent assurance of these attitudes, prevalent in Western anatomy departments up to the 1980s and beyond, was bought at a price – that of ignoring the history of the discipline and the numerous vicissitudes through which it had come, many of which were deeply unethical with ongoing repercussions for the health of anatomy.

For someone like me who began to discover and face up to these problematic issues in the 1980s, the tension between the practice of anatomy and a growing interest in ethical issues stemming from anatomy was palpable. Not only this, it was looked upon with bemusement by other anatomists. At the very least, why waste one's time in this way when there was scientific research to be undertaken, albeit using animal rather than human tissues? At the worst, it was threatening the practice of anatomy, since it was beginning to question what one could, or should, do with the body parts and organs of adults, let alone human foetuses

---

10 See D. Gareth Jones, 'Searching for Good Practice Recommendations on Body Donation Across Diverse Cultures' (2016) 29 *Clinical Anatomy* 55.

and embryos, collected over the years under conditions considered unacceptable today. Secrecy was integral to the outlook of anatomists, since divulging to the public what the dissection of human bodies entailed may alienate them and force anatomists to justify what they did to the bodies at their disposal. There was no hint of unsavoury practices, but there was fear that anatomists would be taken out of their comfort zones and forced to face up to ethical questioning.

With hindsight, it is difficult to understand how this state of affairs could have come about, because anatomy's heritage is far from unsullied. Its dependence upon dead human bodies has been crucial, with the inevitable challenges of how to obtain these when our bodies are central to what we are as human beings.[11] We are our bodies, and hence there is no conceptual distance between the object of the studies of anatomists and our view of our own bodies. What anatomists study is nothing less than the study of themselves. And in doing so, it is they/ we who provide the raw material for those studies. Not unexpectedly, this raises ethical issues of immediate relevance to any who seek to discover more about the dead human body.

Dissonance in history

The travails over the last few centuries stand as ample testimony to this source of dissonance. The pressure to obtain bodies for dissection and study has led to unorthodox and, on occasion, illegal behaviour. The earliest modern developments stem from the early fourteenth century in Italy and Mondino de Luzzi (1276– 1326), who revived the practice of human dissection in Bologna against popular prejudice and superstitious respect for the dead. While there were differences between different European countries, there do not appear to have been signs of a generalised taboo against dismembering the human corpse.[12] For instance, the Christian cult of relics helped to normalise the practice of dismemberment.[13]

These fourteenth-century dissections were of executed criminals and were held in public. They were aimed at illustrating the much earlier texts of Galen (130–200), texts that had come to assume the status of infallible knowledge, even though not based on human dissections. Misleading as this was, they established dissection as an accepted part of the medical curriculum. While dependence upon dissection spread through major European cities, it added little new information to ideas already found in standard texts like Mondino's *Anatomy (Anathomia Corporis Humani)*.[14] Along with this lack of anatomical understanding, there was widespread belief that dissection of the human body was an act of desecration,

11 Philip Hefner, Ann Milliken Pederson and Susan Barreto, *Our Bodies Are Selves* (The Lutterworth Press 2015).
12 D. Gareth Jones and Maja I. Whitaker, *Speaking for the Dead: The Human Body in Biology and Medicine* (2nd edn, Ashgate 2009).
13 Katharine Park, 'The Life of the Corpse: Division and Dissection in Late Medieval Europe' (1995) 50 *Journal of the History of Medicine and Allied Sciences* 111.
14 Mondino de Luzzi, *Anathomia Corporis Humani* (1316, first printed 1478).

and this had a dampening effect on dissection until the fifteenth century.[15] Consequently, any dissection that was undertaken took place in secret.

In spite of these adverse circumstances, it was becoming obvious that any advances in human anatomy required dissection and an openness to scientific investigation of the interior of the body – the organs including the brain, the muscles, nerves, and vessels, and their interrelationships. Gradually the door was opened to such investigations by one university after another. At this point, Berengario da Carpi (*c*.1470–1530) and Leonardo da Vinci (1452–1519) entered the picture with their complementary contributions. Da Carpi carried out investigations critical both of Galen and Mondino. Leonardo da Vinci, the supreme artist, undertook anatomical dissections with that end in view, although at different periods in his life his emphasis shifted to and fro between anatomy and art.[16] Over many years, he dissected a large number of cadavers, and in the latter part of his life had ready access to corpses, often of executed criminals. Towards the end of the fifteenth century, there was an explosion in investigative anatomy. This was not regarded by the Church as an illicit activity, as long as it was done in a respectful way and the body parts buried together afterwards.[17] Unfortunately, Leonardo did not publish his seminal anatomical studies, with the sad result that his superb anatomical discoveries had little, if any, impact on the history of science despite the production of voluminous notebooks.

This revolution in anatomical understanding had to await the advent of Andreas Vesalius (1514–64), with his assiduous dissection of human bodies, frequently obtained from graveyards.[18] Vesalius was the epitome of the critical scientist, who stopped relying upon a reading of Galen and his traditional view of the body and based his knowledge of anatomy on direct study of the human body itself. This was a radical departure that relied entirely upon the availability of human cadavers and, in turn, upon accurate illustrations of bodily organs, their relationships to each other, and the interplay between structure and function.[19] In order to achieve these ends, he insisted upon actual dissections and first-hand experience of human dissection. The details of anatomical organisation emerged as critical to this venture with their dependence upon what is *actually* seen and not upon what one thinks *should* be seen. The end result was that observation gradually overtook the stultifying tradition embedded centuries before in the

15 Charles B. Rodning, '"O Death, Where is Thy Sting?"' Historical Perspectives on the Relationship of Human Postmortem Anatomical Dissection to Medical Education and Care' (1989) 2 *Clinical Anatomy* 277.
16 Alastair Sooke, 'Leonardo da Vinci: Anatomy of an Artist' *The Telegraph* (28 July 2013) <www.telegraph.co.uk/culture/art/leonardo-da-vinci/10202124/Leonardo-da-Vinci-Anatomy-of-an-artist.html> accessed 15 December 2017.
17 ibid.
18 Jones and Whitaker, *Speaking for the Dead* (n 12).
19 Andreas Vesalius, '*De Humani Corporis Fabrica*' (1543) <www.vesaliusfabrica.com/en/original-fabrica/the-art-of-the-fabrica/newly-digitized-1543-edition.html> accessed 15 December 2017.

texts of Galen.[20] However, human dissection and anatomy had a tenuous base in that they depended upon access to the bodies of condemned criminals.

While much changed between the sixteenth and early nineteenth centuries in Europe, the context within which anatomists operated remained remarkably consistent as the supply of bodies for dissection remained seriously deficient. In the eighteenth century, dissection was closely associated with punishment for murder, as it represented something over and above the execution itself, denying the wrongdoer a decent burial. Once again, this failed to provide a sufficient number of bodies, opening the way to grave robbing. Initially, this was carried out by surgeon-anatomists and their pupils, including well-known anatomists such as John Hunter (1728–93) and Astley Cooper (1768–1841). This became a lucrative and very extensive industry, employing an army of 'resurrectionists' in order to supply the needs of an increasing number of medical colleges and their students.[21] The majority of the resurrected corpses stolen from graveyards were predominantly those of the poor.[22]

Ethical reflections on historic incidents

Vesalius's insistence on studying the human body itself was a move into uncharted territory, dependent entirely upon a ready supply of dead human bodies, since the human body cannot be known from reflection alone. Ethical analysis is crucial, but not in isolation of the science that gives rise to the need for this analysis in the first place. Hence, the revolutionary nature of the research work undertaken by Vesalius provides the starting point for any analysis. The only avenue open to him for obtaining dead bodies was via grave robbing. This did not justify the same practice 200 years later in the nineteenth century, when the rationale was not research but the education of students in private medical schools within a climate of burgeoning public disquiet over the practice. In this later period, therefore, there was no scientific imperative to traverse new intellectual territory.

Vesalius should not be judged by today's standards with their emphasis upon informed consent, but neither should his manner of functioning be regarded as acceptable today. The elucidation of ethical standards concerning what can and cannot be done to dead human bodies has been fraught and has involved a medley of scandals and catastrophes (see the following section), and has been hard won. However, this does not mean that all historic practices can be justified. For instance, there is a profound difference between robbing graves in an effort

---

20 Jones and Whitaker, *Speaking for the Dead* (n 12).

21 E.H. Cornelius, 'John Hunter as an Expert Witness' (1978) 60 *Annals of the Royal College of Surgeons of England* 412; Wendy Moore, *The Knife Man: The Extraordinary Life and Times of John Hunter, Father of Modern Surgery* (Bantam Press 2005); Druin Burch, 'Astley Paston Cooper (1768–1841): Anatomist, Radical and Surgeon' (2010) 103 *Journal of the Royal Society of Medicine* 505.

22 Ruth Richardson, *Death, Dissection and the Destitute* (2nd edn, University of Chicago Press 2001).

to obtain dead bodies and committing murder in an effort to obtain dead bodies. Resurrectionists, no matter how one views them, were not murderers.

There is no going back to the time of Vesalius, either scientifically or ethically, and in both cases our task is to learn from the past and build upon it. There is no problem in doing this on the scientific front, because Vesalius provided anatomy with a solid foundation on which to build. The same cannot be said ethically, because this has reached its present stature only as a result of a series of disastrous episodes, scandals, and ethics commissions. Vesalius did not set the pace ethically, but he has to be viewed as a man of his time and cultural climate. The same comment can probably be made about Henry Gray of *Gray's Anatomy* fame.[23] Working in the 1850s, Gray, along with the illustrator, Henry Vandyke Carter, dissected bodies at St George's Hospital in London that would have come from the poor dying alone in workhouses, prisons, and hospitals.[24] They were unclaimed but, since misconduct was rife and few formal records were kept, it may well have been deception that led to some ending up as unclaimed. There are no references to their origin in *Gray's Anatomy*. This was (and still is) typical of anatomy texts, both in the mid-nineteenth century and much later, pointing as it does to a gap between the stunning illustrations of normal human anatomy and the sources of the bodies that provided the raw material for the illustrations.[25]

But where do I stand as an anatomist? This is my professional heritage from which there is no escape. In what ways can I, as an anatomist, make recompense for the unacceptable practices of the past, practices on which my discipline is based? Anatomists today must be made aware of these practices, and must be educated about how to act ethically. Even if there were no way around some of the historic practices, this should be acknowledged and assessed in terms of how one should act today on the basis of fundamental principles of informed consent, beneficence, non-maleficence, justice, and the dignity of all including the poor and disadvantaged.

Bridging the historic – contemporary divide

The Vesalius and Gray illustrations are, inevitably, of the past, but they have more immediate parallels in long-established anatomy departments. For instance, in my own Department of Anatomy at the University of Otago, the museum has material dating from 1879. Inevitably, there is little, if any, evidence of consent for the pre-1970s material, and this forced the department some years ago to consider what should be done with this material in light of today's radically different ethical environment. This is archival material, in the sense that it covers

---

23 Henry Gray, *Anatomy: Descriptive and Surgical* (John W. Parker and Son 1858).
24 Ruth Richardson, 'Historical Introduction' in Susan Standring (ed.), *Gray's Anatomy: The Anatomical Basis of Clinical Practice* (40th edn, Elsevier 2008).
25 D. Gareth Jones, 'Human Anatomy: A Review of the Science, Ethics and Culture of a Discipline in Transition' in Alina Maria Sisu (ed.), *Human Anatomy – Reviews and Medical Advances* (InTech Open Science 2017).

the long-term preservation of tissue or organs,[26] and is no longer needed to establish the cause of death; it is surplus to the requirements of medical diagnosis.[27] In the case of museum archives, the material will also be historic archival, having come from post-mortem examinations and surgical operations, and in anatomy museums from bodies left to the department (bequeathed or unclaimed) prior to the 1970s.[28] Generally, the material will be anonymous, meaning that it cannot be linked to any known individuals. Not only this, no information is available about the method of acquisition of the material nor its intended purpose; nor is it known whether consent was obtained.[29]

The ethical challenge is to determine what is to be done with this material, when there are no known next of kin or descendants to consult and possibly provide consent. Directives have been provided in response to the retention of pathology samples. For instance, in the UK, the Retained Organs Commission considered that decisions on retention and disposal needed to take account of the views of family members as well as the historic and educational value of the collections.[30] Material is to be treated with respect, and any use of the material today is to conform to contemporary ethical attitudes and values. Against this view is that of the National Bioethics Advisory Commission in the United States, with its conclusion that anonymous or anonymised specimens are not to be classed as research with human subjects, leading to the view that there is no place for informed consent; nor is ethics review required.[31]

With the historic archival material found in museums, there are no next of kin to consult, although it behoves the department to thoroughly check that this is the case and that there are no living relatives who can be traced. The questions that have to be answered are what will be in the best interests of the human community? What will show the greatest respect to those from whom this material was taken in the first place, in all likelihood without their consent?[32] The options that present themselves are: dispose of the tissue; use it in teaching; use it in research; or place it in continued storage.

Disposal may give the impression of showing respect for unknown people in the past, and yet this is based on the assumption that its use will fail to bring

26 Royal College of Pathologists, *Guidelines for the Retention of Tissue and Organs at Post-mortem Examination* (Royal College of Pathologists 2000).
27 'Research Based on Archived Information and Samples. Recommendations from the Royal College of Physicians Committee on Ethical Issues in Medicine' (1999) 33 *Journal of the Royal College of Physicians of London* 264.
28 Department of Health, *Report of a Census of Organs and Tissues Retained by Pathology Services in England* (The Stationery Office 2001).
29 D. Gareth Jones, 'Genetic Privacy and the Use of Archival Human Material in Genetic Studies – Current Perspectives' (2015) 5 *Medicolegal and Bioethics* 43.
30 Retained Organs Commission (n 6).
31 National Bioethics Advisory Commission, 'Research Involving Human Biological Materials: Ethical Issues and Policy Guidance' Vol 1: Report and Recommendations of the National Bioethics Advisory Commission (National Bioethics Advisory Commission 1999).
32 D. Gareth Jones, R. Gear and K.A. Galvin, 'Stored Human Tissue: An Ethical Perspective on the Fate of Anonymous, Archival Material' (2003) 29 *Journal of Medical Ethics* 343.

benefits to anyone in the present or future. In this vein, Ashcroft has made the point that disposal accentuates any effects on the burden of illness on current and future patients.[33] In other words, disposal is not an ethically neutral action.

The second option, that of using it for teaching, has the goal of producing immediate educational benefit, as usually encountered in the anatomy museum setting. The third option, research, may be more limited on account of the state of preservation of the material. However, if feasible, it brings with it the potential of leading to insights into clinical conditions that may benefit future patients. The fourth option is to retain the tissue in storage, although this may amount to no more than a means of avoiding a decision and hence of stockpiling the tissue. This is ethically unacceptable because the end result will be that no one benefits and that the retained tissue is wasted.[34]

The availability of archival material represents a compromise position that should not be used in such a way that it demeans the respect given to human beings and any tissue derived from them.[35] Routinely, it is preferable to strive for consent if at all possible, with its basis in altruism and a gift relationship.[36] Inevitably, this cannot occur when presented with anonymous archival material.[37] Despite this, an ideal is to seek to treat archival samples with the same level of care and respect one would show donated material.[38] This, in turn, requires an attitude that sees those with oversight of the material as custodians and not owners of it,[39] leading to a commitment to store this material safely and ensure that it is used in high-quality teaching and/or medically valuable research.[40]

There are sufficient constraints here to demonstrate that anonymous archival material can be approached ethically, even when there are elements of compromise on account of the manner in which it was obtained in the past when different ethical standards held sway. But there are limits. To investigate these, an illustration from the Nazi era will suffice. One of the living testaments to the Nazi regime to survive that period is an anatomical atlas created by Eduard Pernkopf, *Topographische Anatomie des Menschen*, published in 1937. The first American edition appeared in 1963.[41] Pernkopf was an ardent Nazi who became head of the Medical Faculty at the University of Vienna in 1938. He and the illustrators of the atlas had Nazi sympathies, as evidenced by the swastika and other Nazi symbols added to their

33 Richard Ashcroft, 'The Ethics of Reusing Archived Tissue for Research' (2000) 26 *Neuropathology and Applied Neurobiology* 408.

34 Jones, Gear and Galvin (n 32).

35 Medical Research Council, 'Human Tissue and Biological Samples for Use in Research' (Medical Research Council 2014).

36 Retained Organs Commission (n 6).

37 Ian Kennedy, *Learning from Bristol: The Report of the Public Inquiry into Children's Heart Surgery at the Bristol Royal Infirmary 1884–1995* (Cm 5207(I) 2001).

38 Jones, Gear and Galvin (n 32).

39 Kennedy (n 37).

40 Jones, 'Genetic Privacy and the Use of Archival Human Material in Genetic Studies' (n 29).

41 Eduard Pernkopf, *Atlas of Topographical and Applied Anatomy in Two Volumes: Volume 1: Head and Neck; Volume 2: Thorax, Abdomen and Extremities* (WB Saunders Company 1963).

signatures on some of the plates.[42] In the 1980s, the origins of the bodies used for the illustrations became public knowledge[43] – namely, that the University's Anatomy Department regularly received the cadavers of those executed by the Nazis.[44] There became general recognition that many of the subjects of the illustrations in the atlas were victims of the Nazi regime.[45]. An investigation by the University of Vienna in the 1990s revealed that Pernkopf was actively involved in the acquisition of bodies, to such an extent that there were difficulties in handling the rising number of bodies. Between 1937 and 1945, the Anatomical Institute received around 4,000 unclaimed bodies, about 7,000 bodies of foetuses and children, and at least 1,400 bodies of executed individuals.[46] About half the 791 illustrations in the Pernkopf atlas were created during the Nazi years.

There are two diametrically opposed views over the continued use of Pernkopf's atlas. Opposing positions have been put forward by Riggs[47] and Hildebrandt[48] and are summarised from the perspective of librarians by Atlas.[49] For some, the atlas should be banned on account of the evil implicit in its creation and because this evil may be further perpetrated by its continued use. Additionally, the atlas is easily replaced by other anatomical atlases or teaching material, even if they are less accurate and exquisite than that of Pernkopf. Those who argue for continued use of the atlas emphasise the beauty and extremely high quality of the illustrations that, in turn, reflect the beauty and wonder of the human body, as long as the source of the bodies and body parts is acknowledged. It has also been argued that continued use of the atlas is the most fitting tribute to those who died, and that rightly handled it can serve as a valuable tool for teaching ethics and history as much as anatomy.

Because the book is no longer being published, the pressing nature of the debate has disappeared. Nevertheless, the widespread debate elicited by the origins of Pernkopf remind anatomists that continued use of unethically derived human material, or even images as in this instance, taints anatomy as a discipline. The victims in this case were murdered, a sombre reminder of those murdered in the cause of anatomical education in the nineteenth century. To have failed to

42 Sabine Hildebrandt, *The Anatomy of Murder: Ethical Transgressions and Anatomical Science during the Third Reich* (Berghahn 2016).
43 Gerald Weissmann, *They All Laughed at Christopher Columbus: Tales of Medicine and the Art of Discovery* (Times Books 1987) 48.
44 Fred B. Charatan, 'Investigation of Nazi Anatomy Textbook to Start' (1997) 314 *British Medical Journal* 536.
45 Howard A. Israel and William E. Seidelman, 'Nazi Origins of an Anatomy Text: The Pernkopf Atlas' (1996) 276 *Journal of the American Medical Association* 1633.
46 See Hildebrandt, *The Anatomy of Murder* (n 42).
47 Garrett Riggs, 'What Should We Do about Eduard Pernkopf's Atlas?' (1998) 73 *Academic Medicine* 380.
48 Sabine Hildebrandt, 'How the Pernkopf Controversy Facilitated a Historical and Ethical Analysis of the Anatomical Sciences in Austria and Germany: A Recommendation for the Continued Use of the Pernkopf Atlas' (2006) 19 *Clinical Anatomy* 91.
49 Michel C. Atlas, 'Ethics and Access to Teaching Materials in the Medical Library: The Case of the Pernkopf Atlas' (2001) 89 *Bulletin of the Medical Library Association* 51.

learn from anatomy's dubious past is one of the tragic outcomes of the Pernkopf affair, with its failure to balance scientific objectivity with ethical behaviour. Spiro has commented: 'The brilliant depictions of the Pernkopf atlas are transfiguring; in each, I hear the scream of a person ... Like the head on the pike warning us where we must not go, they guard the slippery slope.'[50] If only anatomists during the Nazi era had clung to the centrality of informed consent, human dignity and equality, and justice. Instead, the medical ethics promulgated during the Nazi era were based on values that included 'the unequal worth of human beings, the moral imperative of preserving a pure Aryan people, the authoritarian role of the physician, the individual's obligation to stay healthy, and the priority of public health over individual-patient care'.[51] Clearly, many anatomists were operating by this set of values, allowing them to place their own interests and that of their 'science' above the welfare of those at odds with the state.

The halting trajectory from unclaimed bodies to bequests

The Pernkopf affair points to one much broader ethical issue implicit within the practice of anatomists, and this has been their widespread dependence upon the use of unclaimed bodies. These are the bodies of those with no one – family or friends – to look after their bodily remains at the time of death. Being unclaimed opens them up for use by anatomy departments for dissection and teaching, bypassing any informed consent for their use in this fashion. The pivotal legislation legitimising this practice was the 1832 Anatomy Act in the UK,[52] although this was not the first legislation involving unclaimed bodies. Richardson in her writings has argued strongly that the original decision in the 1820s and 1830s in the UK to use unclaimed rather than bequeathed bodies reflected negative social attitudes towards the poor and disadvantaged. The result was that poverty became the sole criterion for dissection, because it was principally the poor who found themselves unable to protect their relatives dying in hospitals. Perhaps surprisingly, even this did not bring exploitation of the poor to an end, as demonstrated by both English and Australian historians.[53]

The 1832 Act should have proved amenable to anatomists because it provided them with a relatively easy means of obtaining bodies within a short time of death. However, this was not the case because it was repeatedly manipulated or

---

50 H.M. Spiro, 'The Silence of Words – Some Thoughts on the Pernkopf Atlas' (1998) 110 *Wiener Klinische Wochenschrift* 183.
51 Florian Bruns and Tessa Chelouche, 'Lectures on Inhumanity: Teaching Medical Ethics in German Medical Schools Under Nazism' (2017) 166 *Annals of Internal Medicine* 591.
52 An Act for Regulating Schools of Anatomy 1832 (2 & 3 Gul IV c 75): Ruth Richardson, *Death, Dissection and the Destitute* (1st edn, Penguin 1988); Richardson, *Death, Dissection and the Destitute* (n 22); D. Gareth Jones and Maja I. Whitaker, 'Anatomy's Use of Unclaimed Bodies: Reasons Against Continued Dependence on an Ethically Dubious Practice' (2012) 25 *Clinical Anatomy* 246.
53 Richardson, *Death, Dissection and the Destitute* (n 22); Helen MacDonald, *Possessing the Dead: The Artful Science of Anatomy* (Melbourne University Press 2010).

ignored after 1832. For instance, in her book, *Possessing the Dead*, MacDonald shows that body snatching continued long after the Act had been passed, because the Act's means of obtaining unclaimed bodies from hospitals did not produce a sufficient number for the needs of some anatomy schools.[54] Bodies of the poor were surreptitiously and illegally diverted from the grave to the dissecting room. Even the anatomy inspectors were duped or complicit in these actions; senior anatomists expected them to be helpful to the anatomy cause by directing as many bodies as possible in their direction.

Anatomists, by and large, were driven by the pressing need to obtain bodies so that anatomical education could flourish. The argument was: no bodies, no dissecting, no medical training.[55] Unfortunately, this involved deception by anatomists and their employees, and a disregard for the feelings and concerns of families grieving the loss of a loved one. One would have expected at least a basic awareness of these concerns, even in the first part of the nineteenth century, but the drive for an adequate supply of bodies tended to override all other considerations, a drive that has emerged repeatedly in subsequent years. Anatomy, therefore, constantly straddles the interface between legitimate commitment to high-quality science and dubious ethical practices, an interface evident today as much as in the early nineteenth century.

Anatomists' dependence upon unclaimed bodies has opened the profession to a range of questionable unethical practices that continue to this day to blight many aspects of their practices and attitudes.[56] Throughout the latter part of the nineteenth century and much of the twentieth century, these unclaimed bodies have included those of the mentally ill[57] and African Americans,[58] as well as the appalling depths to which anatomists went during the Nazi era.[59] In all these instances, the pressures have been pragmatic ones – to use the bodies when needed and also, perhaps surprisingly, to desist from using them when the supply of bequests was sufficient to replace the supply of unclaimed ones. Until recent years, there has been little serious ethical reflection on how bodies are obtained, leading to the position that unclaimed bodies constitute a legitimate source of bodies for dissection, and indeed the routine source. From this it follows that dependence upon unclaimed bodies became normalised within the world of anatomy, leading to the assumption that there was no distinction between their legal and ethical legitimacy.[60]

---

54 MacDonald (n 53).

55 Jones and Whitaker, 'Anatomy's Use of Unclaimed Bodies' (n 52).

56 ibid.

57 D. Gareth Jones, 'The Anatomy Museum and Mental Illness: The Centrality of Informed Consent' in Catherine Coleborne and Dolly MacKinnon (eds), *Exhibiting Madness in Museums: Remembering Psychiatry through Collection and Display* (Routledge 2011).

58 Todd L. Savitt, *Medicine and Slavery: The Diseases and Health Care of Blacks in Antebellum Virginia* (University of Illinois Press 1978); Michael Sappol, *A Traffic of Dead Bodies: Anatomy and Embodied Social Identity in Nineteenth-Century America* (Princeton University Press 2002).

59 Hildebrandt, *The Anatomy of Murder* (n 42).

60 Jones and Whitaker, 'Anatomy's Use of Unclaimed Bodies' (n 52).

Wide-scale adoption of the use of unclaimed bodies was only possible by ignoring cultural inequities within societies, because anatomists paid little attention to those occupying less privileged strata than the ones they themselves occupied. This, coupled with their limited background in ethical thinking, has proved a major hindrance when faced with unusual and unexpected developments, such as the major public plastination exhibitions of dissected bodies and organs,[61] the dissections as seen on YouTube,[62] and the distribution of images of dissected bodies in various media.[63] Unthoughtful acceptance of the ready availability of bodies (especially, but not only, unclaimed ones) has removed any need for a base from which to analyse the interplay of ethical, cultural, and scientific factors.

A necessary change of paradigm

There can be little doubt that a major precipitating force for anatomists is to have at their disposal human material and tissue of the highest quality possible. This is a scientific imperative that cannot be dismissed as inconsequential. Hence, what is preferable from an anatomical standpoint is material from an individual who was well nourished prior to death and whose body is available within a short time of death. This is especially the case for research at a cellular level. And so, for anatomists to accept anything less than this is counter-intuitive within a scientific paradigm. To reject this scientific ideal will only be contemplated if anatomists are convinced on other grounds. My contention is that they will not be convinced on ethical grounds if they fail to engage with ethical reasoning that has not been integrated into their thinking as anatomists.

Reliance on bequests necessitates such ethical thinking, but it also has to take account of ingrained cultural and religious opposition of people to bequeath their bodies. This is where the use of human bodies and body parts differs significantly from the use of animals in research. While there is far from universal agreement on the latter, it is not usually problematic to obtain animals for research within well-established biomedical laboratories and systems. Animals are 'other' in a sense in which humans are not other – they are 'us', and cause us to confront death and one's own mortality.[64] One day I, too, will be a cadaver.

Integral to the donation paradigm is the claim that *altruism* is a fundamental ethical driver – the giving of one's body is preferable to being coerced into doing it. According to this, it is better to give than to receive, and the good of others

61 Gunther von Hagens (ed.), *Anatomy Art: Fascination Beneath the Surface. Catalogue on the Exhibition* (Institute for Plastination 2000).

62 Denis S. Barry *et al.*, 'Anatomy Education for the YouTube Generation' (2016) 9 *Anatomical Sciences Education* 90.

63 Jon Cornwall, David Callahan and Richman Wee, 'Ethical Issues Surrounding the Use of Images from Donated Cadavers in the Anatomical Sciences' (2016) 29 *Clinical Anatomy* 30.

64 Sandy C. Marks Jr, Sandra L. Bertman and June C. Penney, 'Human Anatomy: A Foundation for Education about Death and Dying in Medicine' (1997) 10 *Clinical Anatomy* 118; Christine Montross, *Body of Work: Meditations on Mortality from the Human Anatomy Lab* (Penguin 2007).

is better than self-interest.[65] The gift element is central to this value, with its premise that giving is preferable to taking.

It is the *absence of altruism* that characterises the use of unclaimed bodies. The 'unclaimedness' of these bodies stems from the weakness, vulnerability, and, frequently, dereliction of the people when alive, and it is this unclaimedness that mirrors their 'unwantedness'.[66] As a result, their interests have become subservient to the interests of others, leading to the distinct possibility of allowing for the exploitation of one individual by another, or one group by another. While the altruism may not always be an unsullied altruism, donation retains elements of goodness, and represents the autonomous choice of the donor unlike the use of unclaimed and unwanted bodies. An argument sometimes encountered in favour of the use of unclaimed bodies in some countries is that it bestows meaning upon an otherwise worthless life. The contention here is that a person considered value-less during life may actually acquire value at death through the use of his or her body for dissection. This is on the ground that an individual's limited value in the eyes of society *during* life is elevated by use of their remains *after* death, raising concerns about such a society and its ethical values.[67] In my estimation, this is an untenable view of human life and not one that should be encouraged by anatomists as a basis for serving their own interests.

This stance on the use of only bequests has implications for those societies and cultures where it is exceedingly difficult to obtain donated bodies because of cultural and religious opposition to body donation. There is no doubt that this is an ongoing challenge for many anatomy departments, and it is unlikely to be resolved in the short term. Far more studies are required to investigate the basis of these assertions, particularly about religious objections. As demonstrated by a number of scholars, there are some glaring exceptions within Buddhism and the debate on Confucianist opposition to body donation remains unresolved.[68] This is not to diminish what may be a clash of cultures, especially because acceptance of the legitimacy of donation in Western societies is relatively recent and was hard won. However, the situation should now have been reached whereby it is recognised that unclaimed bodies no longer represent the path of choice. Those in the community need to be shown how they can donate their bodies, how the bodies are treated, how the body is

65 William F. May, 'Religious Justifications for Donating Body Parts' (1985) 15(1) *Hastings Center Report* 38.

66 D. Gareth Jones, 'Use of Bequeathed and Unclaimed Bodies in the Dissecting Room' (1994) 7 *Clinical Anatomy* 102.

67 D. Gareth Jones, 'The Centrality of the Dead Human Body for Teaching and Research – Social, Cultural and Ethical Issues' (2011) 4 *South African Journal of Bioethics and Law* 18.

68 Steven C. Lin, Julia Hsu and Victoria Y. Fan, 'Silent Virtuous Taiwanese Teachers' (2009) 339 *British Medical Journal* 1438; Jong-Tae Park *et al.*, 'The Trend of Body Donation for Education Based on Korean Social and Religious Culture' (2011) 4 *Anatomical Sciences Education* 33; Sandeepani Kanchana Subasinghe and D. Gareth Jones, 'Human Body Donation Programs in Sri Lanka: Buddhist Perspectives' (2015) 8 *Anatomical Sciences Education* 484.

eventually disposed of, and ways in which close relatives can be assisted to come to terms with their own emotional, and perhaps religious, responses to a loved one's decision to bequeath their body.[69]

This is taking anatomists out of their comfort zone, but they need to realise that since the human body is central to their academic concerns, it is imperative that they pay attention to the value of individual free choice (on the part of an individual prior to death and the family at the time of death). They have to constantly weigh up the legitimacy of dissection and the use of human material against losses stemming from any downgrading of the value of human free choice.

An ethical code for anatomists

In 2014, the International Federation of Association of Anatomists produced 'Recommendations of Good Practice for the Donation and Study of Human Bodies and Tissues for Anatomical Examination'.[70] Among the 11 recommendations, the following constitute core elements:

- Informed consent from donors must be obtained in writing before any bequest can be accepted. Consent forms should take into account the following: donors must be entirely free in their decision to donate, this excludes donation by minors and prisoners condemned to death; although not essential, good practice is encouraged by having the next of kin also sign the form; whether the donor consents to their medical records being accessed.
- There should be no commercialisation in relation to bequests of human remains for anatomical education and research. This applies to the bequest process itself, where the decision to donate should be free from financial considerations, and also to the uses to which the remains are put following bequest. If bodies, body parts, or plastinated specimens are to be supplied to other institutions for educational or research purposes, this may not yield commercial gain. However, charging for real costs incurred, including the cost of maintaining a body donation program and preparation and transport costs, is considered appropriate. Payment for human material per se is not acceptable.
- There needs to be an urgent move towards the establishment of guidelines regulating the transport of human bodies, or body parts, within and between countries.
- Specimens must be treated with respect at all times. This includes, but is not limited to, storing and displaying human and non-human animal parts separately.

69 Jones, 'The Centrality of the Dead Human Body for Teaching and Research' (n 67).
70 See Jones, 'Searching for Good Practice Recommendations on Body Donation Across Diverse Cultures' (n 10).

- The normal practice is to retain donor anonymity. Any exceptions to this should be formally agreed to beforehand by the bequestee and, if appropriate, the family.
- Limits need to be placed on the extent to which images, or other artefacts produced from donations, are placed in the public domain, including in social media, both to respect the privacy of the donor (and their surviving relatives) and to prevent arousing morbid curiosity. No individual should be identifiable in images.
- A clear and rigorous legal framework should be established on a national and/or state level.
- There needs to be transparency between the institution and potential donors and their relatives at every stage, from the receipt of an initial enquiry to the final disposal of the remains.
- Special lectures/tutorials in ethics relating to the bequest of human remains should be made available to all students studying anatomy. This is to encourage the development of appropriate sensitivities in relation to the conduct and respect that is expected of those handling human remains used for purposes of anatomical education and research.
- Institutions should be encouraged to hold Services of Thanksgiving or Commemoration for those who have donated their bodies for medical education and research, to which can be invited relatives of the deceased, along with staff and students.

These recommendations are not to be considered the final word, because some of them have elicited further debate, including the way in which images are utilised (such as on YouTube[71]), the stipulation that anonymity should be maintained in the dissecting room,[72] and the movement of bodies between countries. However, they categorically stress the ethical values of informed consent, the importance of a non-commercial context, and the centrality of treating the families of donors with respect and of acknowledging the inestimable gift of the donations. These values, in turn, have helped anatomists stress the humanistic side of anatomical practice to complement its scientific side, within what an increasing number see as a gradual transformation of anatomy into a more humanistic discipline.[73] One manifestation of this is the increasing place given to commemorations of various sorts to give thanks for those who have donated their bodies for anatomical study.[74]

71 D. Gareth Jones, 'YouTube Anatomy Education: Source of Ethical Perplexity' (2016) 9 *Anatomical Sciences Education* 500.
72 D. Gareth Jones and Mike R. King, 'Maintaining the Anonymity of Cadavers in Medical Education: Historic Relic or Educational and Ethical Necessity?' (2017) 10 *Anatomical Sciences Education* 87.
73 Goran Štrkalj, *Humanistic Anatomy: A New Program for an Old Discipline* (Nova Biomedical 2016).
74 Goran Štrkalj and Nalini Pather, *Commemorations and Memorials: Exploring the Human Face of Anatomy* (World Scientific 2017).

Developments such as these provide an indication that anatomy as a profession is taking seriously its ethical and cultural responsibilities. There is a long way to go, but a start has been made. While most anatomists will not be aware of the contribution of Campbell, it is his ongoing involvement in medical ethics and in responding to organ retention scandals within clinical medicine and pathology that has proved a potent indirect influence on the maturation of anatomical ethics.

14 Ethics in research

An appraisal of Campbell's remarks

Ruth Macklin

Introduction

Professor Alastair V. Campbell has contributed to bioethics in so many ways that it is hard to single out any one contribution for well-deserved praise or cautious criticism. This essay focuses on research involving human beings. I comment on some points Campbell makes in his basic introduction to the topic, and I discuss recently revised international ethical guidelines as providing a helpful source for guidance on some of the more contentious issues in research ethics.

Campbell devotes Chapter 5 of his book, *Bioethics – the Basics*, to ethical issues in research.[1] Several points he makes in the chapter require further explication, lest they be misunderstood or taken at face value. The first example is his claim that 'consent may not be genuine, such as when researchers use natural disasters to conduct research under the guise of "treatment" or with food as an inducement to participate'.[2] A second example is a comment about one criterion for ethically acceptable research: 'that the risk to the subjects is minimal',[3] followed by the acknowledgement 'of course, defining what this means can be difficult!' These claims require further amplification, which I provide in this first section.

Informed consent and inducements to participate

Two cardinal ethical requirements are voluntary, informed consent from potential subjects of research, and an acceptable level of risks of the procedures to which participants are subjected in the study. More has been written about informed consent than about any other topic in bioethics. Still, uncertainties and disagreements remain, and on some issues reasonable people can disagree. One of the more controversial areas is conducting research during natural disasters. Campbell's comment raises two distinct issues about the legitimacy of consent

---

1 Alastair V. Campbell, Bioethics – The Basics (Routledge 2013).
2 ibid 117.
3 ibid 119.

in such situations. The first is that of conducting research under the guise of 'treatment' and the second is the use of inducements to participate.[4]

An overarching concern about conducting research during disasters is the vulnerability of the subject population. People caught in the wake of a disaster are rendered vulnerable by a variety of factors, including injuries, fear, grief, inadequate food and water, loss of housing, and disease outbreaks that sometimes accompany disasters. In addition, an entire population or segments of the population may have been vulnerable to some extent before the disaster struck: they may have food insecurity, lack of potable water, inadequate health care, or be at risk from endemic diseases. Therefore, many people are rendered doubly or even triply vulnerable in the wake of a disaster. The ethical question that arises is whether the vulnerability of victims of a disaster militates against conducting research during or soon after the event.

Arguments critical of research conducted in disasters focus on one or more of the following points: 1) victims in the midst of a disaster are rendered too vulnerable by the situation to permit their inclusion in research; 2) natural disasters or disease outbreaks in developing countries or poor areas in industrialized countries render the inhabitants even more vulnerable, since what they need is aid, not research; 3) people who are recruited by health workers during a disaster may confuse research with treatment and fall prey to the therapeutic misconception; 4) people caught in a disaster are too emotionally unstable to provide valid informed consent to be a research subject. To these arguments, Campbell adds a question about the problem of inducements: is the voluntariness with which consent is provided in such situations compromised when subjects are offered an inducement to participate, such as food?

Despite the truth of claims about the vulnerability of people caught in disasters, widespread agreement exists that with proper safeguards it is ethically acceptable to involve such vulnerable individuals in biomedical and behavioral research. Psychiatric research has determined that, despite the stress and other psychological and emotional factors affecting victims in a disaster, most such individuals remain capable of providing appropriate informed consent to participate in research.[5] Indeed, arguments supporting the ethical acceptability of research during disasters make the strong claim that such research is needed in order to inform future responses in these situations.[6]

---

4 The following four paragraphs are excerpted from my chapter, 'Studying Vulnerable Populations in the Context of Enhanced Vulnerability' in Dónal O'Mathúna *et al.* (eds), *Disaster Bioethics: Normative Issues When Nothing is Normal* (Springer 2014), 159–173.

5 Donald L. Rosenstein, 'Decision-making Capacity and Disaster Research' (2004) 17(5) *Journal of Traumatic Stress* 373.

6 Alan R. Fleischman and Emily B. Wood, 'Ethical Issues in Research Involving Victims of Terror' (2002) 79(3) *Journal of Urban Health* 315–321; Lauren Collogan *et al.*, 'Ethical Issues Pertaining to Research in the Aftermath of Disaster' (2004) 17(5) *Journal of Traumatic Stress* 363; Ruth Macklin, 'Global justice, human rights, and health' in Ronald M. Green (ed), *Global Bioethics* (New York: Oxford University Press, 2008) 141–160.

Coming now to Campbell's concerns about consent for research during disasters, we look first at his point that 'consent may not be genuine [...] when researchers use natural disasters to conduct research under the guise of "treatment"'.[7] It is not clear whether the situation Campbell describes is one in which researchers deliberately mislead potential subjects or, rather, one that constitutes the all-too-frequent situation known as the 'therapeutic misconception' on the part of research participants. The first possibility is clearly unethical and no more need be said about that. As for the second, Campbell appropriately acknowledges the likelihood of the therapeutic misconception even when subjects are properly informed: 'Often ... research participants wrongly believe it will be beneficial, even when they are told that there can be no guarantee of benefit.'[8] In some situations, there may be lack of clear evidence of what, in fact, took place during the consent process; or a population unfamiliar with biomedical research may simply misunderstand, regardless of what they have been told. Both of these factors were present in highly unethical research that took place during an outbreak of meningitis in Nigeria some years ago.[9]

The pharmaceutical giant, Pfizer, conducted a clinical trial in 1996 in Nigeria during a serious epidemic of meningitis in children. The company was testing trovafloxacin (under the trade name, Trovan), a drug that had not yet been approved by the Food and Drug Administration for use in the United States. Critics charged that it was unethical to use the circumstances of an epidemic to test a new drug. Numerous aspects of that clinical trial were cited as violations of widely accepted ethical rules. For example, the trial was in apparent violation of established industry guidelines for studies of meningitis, not only because it was carried out during an epidemic but also because the guidelines say that a follow-up spinal tap should be done a day or so after the drug is administered to see if it is working. Those follow-up tests were optional in the study in Nigeria. Despite these and other ethical shortcomings of that research, our focus here is on informed consent. Questions were raised about whether the research subjects – the children – or their parents were fully aware that they were part of a clinical trial. One laboratory technician was reported as saying that participants did not know that they were involved in research, they knew only that they were sick. The company claimed that local nurses had explained the research to the families, a procedure that could have been valid if it met the well-established requirements of informed consent. It is impossible to know what the nurses told the families, and whether they made it clear that the children were participants in research rather than patients receiving a 'new treatment' for the terrible disease they were suffering. In any case, the company produced no signed consent forms to document the consent process.[10]

---

7 Campbell (n 1) 117.

8 Campbell (n 1) 119.

9 The following paragraph describing the Nigerian research is excerpted from my book, *Double Standards in Medical Research in Developing Countries* (Cambridge University Press 2004).

10 Joe Stephens, 'The Body Hunters: Where Profits and Lives Hang in the Balance' (17 December 2000, *Washington Post*) <www.washingtonpost.com/wp-dyn/content/article/2007/07/02/AR2007070201255.html> retrieved 16 June 2017.

Campbell is certainly correct to state that in research 'there can be no guarantee of benefit'. But even the phrase used to make that point in the informed consent document or process is critical. For example, in my work serving on research ethics committees over many years, I would not accept the phrase in a consent document, 'there is no guarantee that you will benefit'. The wording implies that benefit is likely but cannot be guaranteed. A guarantee is a very strong warrant, whereas a phrase like 'you may not benefit from the research' is more straightforward. It is evident from many empirical studies of informed consent that regardless of what is written on consent forms or told to potential subjects in the consent discussion, at least some participants will mistake research for proven treatment. A phrase used by authors discussing the mistake research subjects in a disaster may make replaces the phrase 'therapeutic misconception' with one that is apt in a setting where aid workers both provide assistance and also conduct research: the 'philanthropic misconception'.[11]

Campbell makes a second point about whether consent to participate in research is 'genuine' in his statement quoted earlier: 'consent may not be genuine, such as when researchers use natural disasters to conduct research under the guise of "treatment" or with food as an inducement to participate'. The concern here is with 'food as an inducement to participate'. The implication seems to be that offering food as an inducement somehow destroys or weakens the voluntariness with which consent has been provided. A wide range of opinions exists on the ethics of inducements or incentives to participate in research. These opinions range from the belief that there is nothing unethical about offers of money or other benefits to participants in research to the view that there should be an absolute prohibition. At one end of this spectrum is the position of Ezekiel Emanuel, basically rejecting the idea that monetary payments constitute undue inducements,[12] and at the other end is the policy of a research ethics committee at GHESKIO Centers in Haiti, which contains an absolute prohibition against payment of any kind to research subjects (I learned this on a visit to Haiti when I met with members of the research ethics committee at the institution.) Many intermediary positions exist along this spectrum, with most cautioning against incentives that may be excessive; those are referred to as *undue* inducements.

Without further elaboration, it is unclear why Campbell contends that offering food in the context of a disaster imperils the 'genuineness' of consent. This may be another aspect of the 'philanthropic misconception'. Food shortages and food insecurity are common in disaster situations. Especially in hurricanes, earthquakes, and other natural disasters, the affected population may be cut off from food supplies. Aid organizations, such as the International Red Cross and *Médecins sans Frontières*, typically deliver food supplies as part of their rescue

11 Aasim Ahmad *et al.*, 'Evidence and Healthcare Needs During Disasters' in Donal O'Mathúna *et al.* (eds), *Disaster Bioethics: Normative Issues When Nothing is Normal* (Springer 2014) 95–106.

12 Ezekiel J. Emanuel, 'Ending Concerns about Undue Inducement' (2004) 32(1) *Journal of Law, Medicine and Ethics* 100–105.

operations. While it may be the case in some instances that food is offered as an incentive to participate in research, it is much more likely that providing food is a routine aspect of the mission of aid organizations. It is surely true that, when money is offered as an inducement to participate in research, individuals who decline to participate will not be given the money. But it is hard to imagine that an organization providing philanthropic aid and also conducting research would withhold food from individuals in need who decline to participate in research. This situation can most likely arise from a blurring of the lines between philanthropic assistance and conducting research, especially when one and the same organization is engaged in both activities. Moreover, in large-scale natural disasters, there are frequently numerous organizations that descend on the site – some local or national, others from different countries or international groups. It is not surprising that victims in a disaster would be confused regarding who is doing what in a stressful, chaotic situation. In the ongoing debates regarding what sorts of inducement may be 'undue', some commentators contend that the main worry lies with paying money to potential subjects, so they argue that small gifts or an offer of food would be preferable.

Acceptable level of risk in research

In Chapter 5 of *Bioethics – the Basics*, Campbell discusses the thorny problem of balancing risks to subjects against the potential benefits of research – to the participants themselves or to others in the future. He distinguishes between research involving competent and non-competent subjects. About the latter, he claims that 'the risk to the subjects [must be] minimal', while correctly acknowledging that 'defining what this means can be difficult!'[13] Despite that difficulty, the usual criteria for minimal risk research are considered to be the risks of everyday life, including routine medical examinations. Requiring that the risks of interventions in research involving non-competent subjects be minimal may be too restrictive. For example, experimental medications that have not been approved by a drug regulatory agency are considered more than minimal risk. The use of such experimental medications for research on, say, Alzheimer's patients would be precluded by Campbell's criterion. So, too, would the use of experimental medications on children, even if the drugs had been tested first in adults. Here we should recall the difference between requiring that risks be *minimal* as opposed to their being *minimized* in research. The 2016 revision of the Council for International Organizations of Medical Sciences (CIOMS)'s international ethical guidelines mentions in a number of them the requirement for minimizing risks to subjects. Campbell's limitation on the level of risk in research involving non-competent individuals would preclude studying a great many interventions

13 Campbell (n 1) 119. In response to an editor's query about whether Campbell had intended to say 'minimised' but mistakenly wrote 'minimal' in his book, we asked Campbell for clarification. He graciously acknowledged his error, replying that he should have written 'minimised' since to require that risks be minimal would badly affect worthwhile research.

that could be the only way of improving diagnosis or treatment for a great many individuals for whom no satisfactory interventions currently exist.

In fairness, however, I do acknowledge that Campbell's discussion of this topic occurs in a chapter of a book devoted to 'the basics' of bioethics. One cannot expect an exhaustive treatment of all the complex and detailed issues in bioethics in a book devoted to laying out the basics for readers not already familiar with the field.

A middle ground regarding acceptable risk levels for non-competent subjects can be found in the 2016 CIOMS international ethical guidelines. For this category of research subjects, CIOMS introduces the category 'a minor increase above minimal risk' when the research has no prospect of direct benefit to the subjects. For research in which there is a prospect of direct benefit, there are no restrictions on the risk level for non-competent subjects other than the requirement that risks be minimized. CIOMS does follow Campbell's presumption that the minimal risk level should be the norm for this population, but CIOMS is narrower than Campbell's restriction because the minimal risk criterion applies only to research that has no prospect of direct benefit. Use of the category 'minor increase above minimal risk' is intended to provide special protections for non-competent research subjects when there is no prospect of direct benefit, while still allowing for important research to be carried out that may benefit future patients. The only population of subjects to which this risk category applies in the U.S. Code of Federal Regulations governing research is children and adolescents. The CIOMS guidelines expand the target populations to include incapacitated adults and pregnant women. (Pregnant women should, of course, be presumed to be competent unless determined otherwise. As a member of the work group that revised the CIOMS guidelines, I objected to applying this intermediate category of risk to pregnant women but was overruled by some of my colleagues on the work group.)

The first thing to note is that if, as Campbell suggests, defining 'minimal risk' in research is difficult, how much more difficult it is to determine what constitutes a minor increase over minimal risk. There is no metric for determining that level of risk. There is not even a rough description such as exists for minimal risk – 'the risks of everyday life'. Here is what the CIOMS guidelines say:

> While there is no precise definition of a "minor increase" above minimal risk, the increment in risk must only be a fraction above the minimal risk threshold and considered acceptable by a reasonable person. It is imperative that judgements about a minor increase above minimal risk pay careful attention to context. Thus, research ethics committees need to determine the meaning of a minor increase above minimal risk in light of the particular aspects of the study they are reviewing.[14]

14 Council for International Organizations of Medical Sciences, *International Ethical Guidelines for Health-related Research Involving Humans* (Geneva 2016) 13.

One question is whether this risk level is a useful addition to the process of ethical review of proposed research. As a member of the work group that revised the CIOMS guidelines, I expressed skepticism regarding its ease of application. Another member of the work group and I coined the phrase 'pseudo-metric' to describe the vaguely worded phrase. Some years ago, I experienced an attempt to apply this criterion in a study involving children under review by the research ethics committee at my institution. The study had no prospect of direct benefit to the children and involved an invasive procedure. Committee members debated whether the risk level should be a minor increase over minimal risk or more than a minor increase above minimal risk. The group was moving toward consensus that the intervention was more than a minor increase above minimal risk when one committee member pointed out that, according to the U.S. Federal Regulations, deciding in favor of the latter would make the research 'unapprovable' by the committee. It would be necessary to contact the U.S. Department of Health and Human Services, the federal agency located in Washington, D.C., to seek approval of the research through a bureaucratic procedure. Reminded of this requirement, committee members quickly agreed that the proposed research carried only a minor increase over minimal risk.

Research and global justice

The issue of justice in research encompasses at least the following two broad questions: 1) Does the way in which research priorities are set meet the requirements of global justice in research? 2) What are the requirements of justice regarding the distribution of benefits and burdens in research conducted in low-resource settings? Campbell includes a discussion of the '10/90 gap':

> Less than 10 per cent of the billions of dollars spent on health research is devoted to the health problems which account for 90 per cent of the global disease burden; moreover, most of this disease burden is borne by poor nations least likely to benefit from most international research.[15]

Campbell correctly points out that a considerable portion of research funded and conducted by the pharmaceutical industry is carried out in low- or middle-income countries that are unlikely to benefit from the results of the research. He notes that 'these companies control the agenda for research determining which countries and institutions will gain any benefit'.[16] Industry also controls the pricing and distribution of successful products of research. The situation Campbell describes provides a partial answer to question 1): the way in which research priorities are set fails to meet the requirements for global justice in research. In concluding the chapter on research, Campbell suggests a number of different ways in which the current imbalance might be rectified. Some of these ways require new

15 Campbell (n 1) 131–2.
16 ibid 132.

forms of international agreements on trade, others might involve using market forces to shift the balance in a more favorable direction, and still others would require a change in attitudes towards the sharing of publicly funded scientific discoveries. It is heartening to observe that, in the few short years since the publication of Campbell's book, serious efforts are being made to bring about changes that could benefit low- and middle-income countries in obtaining the fruits of research.

Chapter 5 of Campbell's book is devoted to justice – in particular, social and distributive justice. The latter conception of justice is most relevant to the topic of justice in global research. Campbell's discussion of distributive justice in this chapter is confined to the healthcare system, not the research context, yet principles of justice are applicable as well to the distribution of benefits and burdens of research involving humans. This is what is needed to answer question 2) above: What are the requirements of justice regarding the distribution of benefits and burdens in research conducted in low-resource settings? Since distributive justice requires a fair distribution of benefits and burdens, it is necessary to look first at who are the beneficiaries and who are subjected to the burdens. In this analysis, the relevant recipients of burdens and benefits are groups, or populations, rather than individuals. The groups that stand to be burdened by research are the participants. They undergo whatever risks, discomforts, and inconveniences exist during the research. Although some members of these groups may also receive benefits of the research during their participation, as Campbell has noted, participation in research may not result in direct benefits to the subjects and often does not. But among those participants who do benefit from research during their participation, what if they still need the research product or intervention after their participation is concluded?

The groups that stand to benefit from research are those who have access to the successful products of research once the research is concluded. From a global perspective, those likely to benefit are populations in countries like those in Western Europe that provide universal, high-quality health care to their citizens, and upper middle-class and wealthy individuals in countries like the United States, which does not have government-sponsored health care for all its citizens but relies on private insurance mechanisms for the majority of citizens and government-sponsored programs only for the very poor, the elderly, and military veterans. Over the years, the hodge-podge healthcare system in the United States has typically left millions without any health insurance, public or private. But for low-resource countries with a large population of poor residents and a weak public health system, successful products of research may be available only to the relative few who can afford such products. A significant counter-example to this general picture is preventive and therapeutic medications for HIV/AIDS. Programs such as the Global Fund to Fight AIDS, Tuberculosis and Malaria, the U.S. multi-billion-dollar PEPFAR initiative, and other multilateral programs have made unprecedented gains in controlling the AIDS pandemic in some countries and providing significant relief in others. Yet aside from these unique efforts focused primarily on HIV/AIDS, from the standpoint of distributive justice, the situation is an inequitable global distribution of preventive and therapeutic products resulting from research. The question posed by this situation is: What are the obligations, if any, of researchers, sponsors of research, and host governments where research is carried out, once a study is concluded and has been demonstrated to yield successful products? Campbell's discussion of research ethics in his book does not take up this question directly, but his concerns about global justice point the way to some possible answers. The remainder of this chapter addresses the obligation to provide the successful products of research in low-resource settings where research is conducted but means are lacking for the government or the population affected to obtain such products.

International ethical guidance

A number of internationally recognized guidelines address the question of what is owed to research subjects when their participation has ended, and what, if anything, is owed to the community or country where research is conducted once it is concluded. Two key documents are: the *Declaration of Helsinki* (2013, *DoH*),[17] issued by the World Medical Association, and the CIOMS International Ethical Guidelines (2016).[18]

The *DoH* contains two paragraphs that address the distribution of successful products of research. Paragraph 20 says:

> Medical research with a vulnerable group is only justified if the research is responsive to the health needs or priorities of this group and the research cannot be carried out in a non-vulnerable group. In addition, this group should stand to benefit from the knowledge, practices or interventions that result from the research.

The ethical guidance in the *DoH* is limited to brief paragraphs such as this one. It offers no explication of terms such as 'vulnerable', nor does it provide an analysis of what it means to be 'responsive to the health needs or priorities of this group'. As a result, key terms in this paragraph are open to a variety of interpretations. For example, should all members of low-income groups – even those above the poverty line – be considered vulnerable? In countries where women are routinely subordinated to men – whether by law or by custom – should women be considered vulnerable? What about illiterate individuals in low-resource countries? They may be considered vulnerable because of their limited understanding of modern medical research, yet they may be most in need of the successful products of research carried out in their countries. The ethical principle that underlies this provision in the *DoH* relates specifically to vulnerability: 'Vulnerable individuals

---

17 World Medical Association, *WMA Declaration of Helsinki: Ethical Principles for Medical Research Involving Human Subjects* (France, Ferney-Voltaire 2013).
18 Council for International Organizations of Medical Sciences (n 14).

and groups stand in need of special protections.' However, the *DoH* does not address what those special protections should be.

The *DoH* has a second paragraph that pertains specifically to individuals who have served as subjects in research. Paragraph 34 says:

> In advance of a clinical trial, sponsors, researchers and host country governments should make provisions for post-trial access for all participants who still need an intervention identified as beneficial in the trial. This information must also be disclosed to participants during the informed consent process.

The ethical principle that underlies this paragraph is *justice as reciprocity*. That is, the group that was subjected to the burdens of research deserves to receive something in return: any benefits produced by the research. The post-trial benefits in this paragraph of the *DoH* accrue only to the research participants. Paragraph 20 (above) addresses a more controversial matter – that is, providing the successful products of research to the community or country where the research is carried out. But the *DoH* statement is narrower and weaker than a similar provision in CIOMS Guideline 2 (below). Paragraph 20 says only that the vulnerable group 'should stand to benefit from the knowledge, practices or interventions that result from the research'. This somewhat vague statement provides no practical guidance despite pointing in the direction of benefits to vulnerable populations.

The CIOMS's international ethical guidelines provide a great deal more detail than those in the *DoH*. The document contains lengthy commentaries following each guideline, providing explication of the meaning of key terms as well as a justification of the normative aspects of the guidelines themselves. Guideline 2 is entitled 'Research conducted in low-resource settings'. It reads as follows:

> Before instituting a plan to undertake research in a population or community in low-resource settings, the sponsor, researchers, and relevant public health authority must ensure that the research is responsive to the health needs or priorities of the communities or populations where the research will be conducted. As part of their obligation, sponsors, and researchers must also:
>
>   make every effort, in cooperation with government and other relevant stakeholders, to make available as soon as possible any intervention or product developed, and knowledge generated, for the population or community in which the research is carried out, and to assist in building local research capacity. In some cases, in order to ensure an overall fair distribution of the benefits and burdens of the research, additional benefits such as investments in the local health infrastructure should be provided to the population or community; and
>
>   consult with and engage communities in making plans for any intervention or product developed available, including the responsibilities of all relevant stakeholders.

Whereas the *DoH* refers to vulnerable groups in the paragraph that addresses post-trial access, this CIOMS guideline specifies research conducted in low-resource countries and communities.

In addition, whereas the *DoH* has a separate paragraph pertaining to post-trial benefits for research participants, Guideline 2 in CIOMS can be understood to apply not only to participants in research but also to the wider community.

Unlike the *DoH*, CIOMS provides an analysis of the concept of vulnerability and devotes a separate guideline to the topic. Guideline 15 is entitled 'Research involving vulnerable persons and groups':

> When vulnerable individuals and groups are considered for recruitment in research, researchers and research ethics committees must ensure that specific protections are in place to safeguard the rights and welfare of these individuals and groups in the conduct of the research.

An extensive commentary follows the guideline. The commentary first discusses the concept of vulnerability, citing a passage from the *DoH*: vulnerable groups and individuals 'may have an increased likelihood of being wronged or of incurring additional harm'. The commentary provides examples of what those specific protections might be, showing how such protections are geared to the characteristics that make individuals or groups vulnerable in the context of research.

Post-trial access to research results as a requirement of justice

Although worded somewhat differently, both the *DoH* and the CIOMS International Ethical Guidelines seek to provide a remedy for the great disparity that exists between rich and poor countries whose populations participate in research. But the proposals in their guidelines are controversial and have been subject to criticisms. One such criticism is embodied in the following comment:

> Distributive justice requires that each social member receives a just distribution of the benefits and burdens of society, i.e., what he or she deserves from being a member of the society. The question here is why do the members of the community who did not participate in the experiment deserve to receive the benefits of the experiment? They did not have to bear burdens as the test subjects do – or those the sponsoring agencies or pharmaceutical companies are required to shoulder – but receive an enormous benefit at no real cost to themselves...[19]

This analysis construes distributive justice to be a matter of what is owed to individuals, based on their contribution to an activity. However, a broader conception

19 D.R. Cooley, 'Distributive Justice and Clinical Trials in the Third World' (2001) 22 *Theoretical Medicine* 151–167.

of justice takes the unit of analysis to be the community or country, not the individuals residing there. Solomon Benatar criticizes the above-noted analysis as serving 'only to entrench further a neo-liberal economic mind-set deeply inimical to the progress required to rectify some of the widening disparities in wealth and health that characterize an increasingly unstable world'.[20] In this account, it is the 90/10 gap, as Campbell discussed, that constitutes the injustice. Benatar and many others address potential ways to reduce or eliminate the gap the obligation imposed by justice.

A different criticism argues that, if a guarantee to make products available were required before research could be initiated, it would prevent much important research from being conducted. A report by the Nuffield Council makes this point, arguing that if sponsors of research – including large pharmaceutical companies – were required to provide post-trial benefits in the form of successful products, many would simply cease to sponsor and conduct research in developing countries.[21] The reason is that they would be unable to afford the cost without curtailing other research. Both the conclusion and the reason may well be true. What is false, however, is the premise that it is the researchers or sponsors alone who would have to bear the burden of ensuring access to the fruits of research when trials have been concluded. My own view is that the host country – where the research is conducted – also has an obligation through its public health system to contribute to the effort.

Possibly the strongest and most sustained criticism of the post-trial access obligation appears in two publications that were the outcome of a conference whose participants were a group of bioethicists and researchers.[22] They argue not only that a scheme to ensure 'fair benefits' to developing countries need not include provision of the products of research but also that the requirement for post-trial access is flawed in other ways.[23] The authors advance several arguments, the first of which is that the requirement guarantees a benefit that may not be a fair benefit. They say, for example, 'research in which the subjects would be exposed to great risks or the sponsors stand to benefit enormously ... may be inadequate and unfair'.[24] This is surely an odd criticism, because research regulations and guidelines all require that risks be 'reasonable' in light of anticipated benefits. Very few clinical

---

20 Solomon Benatar, 'Global Disparities in Health and Human Rights: A Critical Commentary' (1998) 88 *American Journal of Public Health* 295–300.

21 Nuffield Council on Bioethics, *The Ethics of Research Related to Healthcare in Developing Countries* (London: Nuffield Council on Bioethics 2002) 123.

22 Participants in the 2001 Conference on Ethical Aspects of Research in Developing Countries, 'Moral Standards for Research in Developing Countries' (2004) 34(3) *Hastings Center Report* 17–27.

23 Portions of the following paragraphs are adapted from Macklin (n 5) 148–49, 151, 152. The article authored by the 'fair benefits' group criticized what was Guideline 10 in the 2002 revision of the CIOMS guidelines. The wording is slightly different in the 2016 revision, but the main points remain the same. I have slightly altered the wording of the criticisms by the 'fair benefits' authors to conform to Guideline 2 in the 2016 guideline without changing the meaning or the substance of their critique.

24 ibid 20.

trials involve 'great' risks to participants. Especially in research where there is no prospect of direct benefit to participants, it is hard to imagine a research ethics committee approving a study that exposes subjects to 'great risks'. As for the enormous benefits to sponsors, that is already the case in much industry-sponsored research. It is especially true of what Campbell refers to as 'me too' drug studies, in which a company conducts a clinical trial of its own copy-cat 'blockbuster' drug hoping to lure significant market share away from its competitor.

A second criticism by this group is that for very low- or no-risk research in which the benefits to sponsors are minimal, it could be unfair to sponsors to require them to make the product available. But tying the provision of successful products of research to the level of risk that participants undergo misses the entire point of the ethical requirement. Take vaccines, for example. Most vaccine studies pose low risk to subjects, especially in phase III trials where safety has been well established and the purpose is to demonstrate efficacy. Yet preventive vaccines are precisely the sort of products that ought to be made available to populations at risk for HIV/AIDS, malaria, and other dread diseases. The degree of benefits sponsors realize is just as irrelevant to this ethical requirement as is the level of risk the research participants undergo.

A more telling challenge is the authors' claim that requiring a prior agreement to supply a specific product resulting from successful research can turn out to be a ' " golden handcuff", constraining rather than benefiting the population'.[25] The population would be committed to using that specific product, even if a better one (more efficacious, fewer side effects) comes along at a later time. No one should be bound to use a product that is inferior to one that comes along at a later time. Furthermore, they argue, it would be unreasonable to require company A – which tested the original successful product – to purchase drugs from company B, which manufactures a better product at a later time. Of course the authors are right about this; however, it is an odd criticism that ignores the obvious way such contracts should be written. A properly executed contract would lay out appropriate conditions for such eventualities in an agreement negotiated by the various parties.

The 'fair benefit' critics contend that the requirement to make products available is paternalistic. It does not permit leaders of a country or representatives of the population decide what they would like by way of benefits, thus denying them their autonomous right to decide. It is true that there is an element of paternalism in this requirement. So, too, is there an element of paternalism in the more fundamental ethical requirement that research should be responsive to the health needs of the population where the research is carried out. Suppose the leaders of a strife-ridden country were to say to researchers or sponsors:

> Never mind the successful products of research. What we need are arms to combat our neighbors. Even a large segment of our healthy population will die in a conquest by our oppressive enemy. You may conduct your research

25 ibid 22.

here on the condition that you reimburse us with money for armaments when you realize a profit.

Would it be unacceptably paternalistic to refuse that request? More likely, however, the leaders would not mention what they would propose to do with the monetary profits they might ask for. The sad story of corruption and malfeasance by autocratic leaders in many countries suggests that it would be a bad idea to leave the decision about what should count as benefits entirely in the hands of leaders of countries where research is conducted. Beyond that, the criticism that ethics guidelines are 'paternalistic' is surely odd. By their very nature, guidelines are paternalistic in that they place constraints on researchers, sponsors, and subjects.

The 'fair benefits' authors have additional criticisms of the CIOMS requirement but space does not permit a longer discussion here. Suffice to say, the point of doing research in the first place is, as the CIOMS guideline says, to respond to the health needs and ultimately to improve the health of the population. Linking the type of benefit to the type of activity seems fitting, albeit somewhat narrow. Although the benefit does apply to a narrow range of research, that is precisely the intention: to avoid exploitation of populations in low-resource environments by ensuring that the community or country stands to gain something from research that yields successful products. The point of the requirement is to change the historical pattern of research conducted in developing countries, whereby the successful products that resulted became available only in industrialized countries where people could afford them.

In spite of the flaws in their criticisms of post-trial benefits as discussed in the CIOMS guideline, this group made several positive suggestions for a broad framework of fair benefits. These include providing collateral health services that are unnecessary for the research itself, both for the research participants and the population; public health measures for the country or community; long-term research collaboration; and sharing of financial rewards from research results, including intellectual property rights. The framework also includes two important procedural features: community involvement at all stages of the research process (a requirement CIOMS discusses in Guideline 7) and transparency, in the form of a central, publicly accessible repository of benefits agreements.

Final thoughts

This essay goes beyond what Campbell has written explicitly about research ethics in his book, *Bioethics – The Basics*. Nevertheless, it is my hope that both my gentle criticisms and my discussion regarding justice that goes beyond what he has addressed in that book are acceptable to him in the spirit of open intellectual dialogue. As a great admirer of so much of what Campbell has written and contributed to the field of bioethics, I look forward to our continuing academic friendship.

15 The republic of health

Motivating the republican turn in public health ethics

Richard Ashcroft

Preface: Alastair V. Campbell and his influence on my work

Like many people now established in the field of bioethics, I came to it by accident. My academic training was in history and philosophy of science, and it was only by good fortune that I found a postdoctoral fellowship in Liverpool working on ethics in clinical trials. I knew nothing about medical ethics – my PhD had been on ethics in the natural sciences. I assumed that medical ethics was all obvious and long since worked out – after all, doctors' work was inherently ethical and they had this Hippocratic Oath thing, didn't they? Ignorance is bliss. But it became clear that, in clinical research at least, there were all sorts of open ethical questions, and also questions where the ethical principles were well established but the implementation of those standards was not. Towards the end of my time in Liverpool, I saw an advertisement for a lectureship in Bristol on ethics in medicine. With the bravado of the ignorant, I applied, and was surprised and delighted to be called to interview. That was when I met Alastair. I had no idea who he was, but he was surrounded by people who thought he was Quite a Big Deal. Which, I was to discover, was entirely correct! He was, and is. After a fairly tough interview, I was amazed to be offered the job, and I did not hesitate to accept it.

I suppose I was a bit concerned that Alastair's background was in theology, rather than in philosophy, although I was hardly a 'pure' philosopher myself. I had had a religious upbringing and I had antibodies to that. I very quickly learned that Alastair's theology was broad, and literate, and humane. (And certainly broader, more literate, and more humane than I was). We quickly found that we had an enormous amount to talk about. He had to train me up in practically everything: I had hardly any teaching experience, knew next to nothing about medical ethics outside clinical trial ethics, had very limited exposure to medicine, nursing, or the organisation of health services – and rather limited social skills. Alastair trained me and mentored me in all aspects of the job, from how to give a lecture to how to plan a curriculum to how to establish a work-life balance. Although obviously a senior and well-respected professor, he thought it was important that he shared out the fun bits of the job (conference attendances and the like) and the tough administrative jobs that needed doing and we all have to learn somehow. He never pulled rank, although sometimes he did assert his authority. On a handful of occasions, I had the rough edge of his tongue – but this was so unusual, and when it happened so thoroughly deserved that it caused me real distress, and a desire to do better for him thenceforward. He has a real paternal manner without any of the paternalism we constantly challenged in our work together. This wasn't just division of labour – in some cases he was taking real risks in asking me to take something on, putting his own reputation on the line and the credibility of our centre. Let's just say that our relationship is still going strong all these years later, and I still rely on Alastair's mentorship when I find myself making hard choices or in a tight spot.

I have never, before or since, had a better boss. And I am proud to count Alastair among my dearest friends.

Intellectually and academically our minds ran along different lines, I think. Certainly back in the late 1990s, I had an enthusiasm for quite technical and mathematically inclined philosophical methods that were very different from the sorts of deliberative methods Alastair favoured. And Alastair's interests lay in the patient experience and in the hard problems of medical practice, whereas mine lay in the more 'political' issues of population health and rational decision making under uncertainty or risk. But nonetheless, if these two strategies in medical ethics do not talk to each other, medical ethics is much the poorer for it, and arguably runs into the sand as a result. One area where our interests coincided was in healthcare resource allocation, and we had fascinating conversations between ourselves, and with other academics and practitioners in Bristol, inside the university and in the health service organisations themselves. I learnt most of what I know about John Rawls's theory of justice from Alastair, both the internal mechanics of how it works and the external practice of how to apply it in practical cases.

This chapter is based on my inaugural lecture as Professor of Bioethics in the School of Law, Queen Mary University of London, delivered on 19 May 2010 under the title 'The republic of health – ethics and politics in twenty-first century health care'. It has benefited from significant editorial comments from John Coggon and Jürgen de Wispelaere. All errors that remain are mine. When I gave the lecture, I paid personal tribute to Alastair as my guide and mentor in medical ethics, and in so much else. Everything I have learnt in medical ethics started with him. This essay begins in discussions we had in Bristol in the late 1990s about resource allocation and the NHS, and the relationship between medical ethics and 'social medicine'. Although debates in health justice have developed in many directions since his first book on the topic in 1978, we are all in his debt. My gratitude to Alastair will never run out.[1]

Civic republicanism has been extensively discussed in the public health ethics context in a symposium in the journal *Public Health Ethics* edited by de Wispelaere and Coggon.[2] This essay was drafted well before that issue was planned but for various reasons is appearing well afterwards! The reader should take it as an

---

1 Alastair V. Campbell, *Medicine, Health And Justice* (Edinburgh, Churchill Livingstone 1978).
2 Jurgen de Wispelaere and John Coggon, 'Republican Special Symposium' (2016) 9(2) *Public Health Ethics* 123.

explication of how I get from medical ethics to civic republicanism. Other routes are no doubt possible. O'Shea works back from civic republicanism to medical ethics, completing the circuit.[3]

Introduction

In this essay, I will sketch an argument for the need to turn to the resources of civic republicanism to give foundations to public health ethics. I start by showing how there is an apparent natural link from mainstream contemporary medical ethics to political liberalism. I then show how this liberalism breaks down when we take account of some uncontroversial premises drawn from the behavioural sciences and public health practice. I then argue that civic republicanism offers some resources that may preserve what is of value in liberalism while addressing the difficulties I have identified. It is not my intention in this essay to present a fully worked-out theory of republicanism in public health; nor indeed is it to suggest that only republicanism can solve the problems that face liberalism. Indeed, I suspect that robust ethics and politics of public health would need a much more radical reconstruction. However, if we wish to preserve the central intuitions of contemporary medical ethics and public health ethics, civic republicanism is a promising candidate. As such, we can consider it what Imre Lakatos called a 'research programme': it doesn't present all the answers, but it presents a methodology for understanding and answering at least some of the questions in a coherent way.[4]

From healthcare ethics to public health ethics

Contemporary healthcare ethics is dominated by the ideal of the free, rational but vulnerable patient. The central role of healthcare ethics, as it has developed over the past half century, is to promote the autonomy of this patient. The autonomy of the patient is important for a number of reasons. First, patients are assumed to be vulnerable in two linked ways. They are vulnerable because they are sick and seeking help. And they are vulnerable because of the social power and authority of those from whom they seek help.[5] Contemporary healthcare ethics notes the former vulnerability, but has tended not to give it particular moral weight. This is in contrast to traditional medical ethics, which saw it as the fundamental fact about patients that gave normative justification for the second form of vulnerability. The weakness and need of the patient explain and justify the importance of the moral authority of the doctor. Traditional healthcare ethics focused on how best to use the healer's power in the interests of the patient.[6] The scope and

3 Tom O'Shea, 'Civic Republican Medical Ethics' (2017) 43 *Journal of Medical Ethics* 56.

4 Imre Lakatos, *The Methodology of Scientific Research Programmes: Philosophical Papers, Vol.1* (Cambridge University Press 1980).

5 Ian Kennedy, *The Unmasking of Medicine* (London, Allen and Unwin 1981).

6 Howard Brody, *The Healer's Power* (New Haven, Yale University Press 1992).

nature of those interests was in a certain sense transparent and obvious to the healer, and the patient's own account of those interests was of no special epistemic value. If anything, the patient's voice might be considered as expressing part of the set of symptoms displayed of the patient's illness. Traditional healthcare ethics recognised that under some circumstances this second form of vulnerability could lead to significant harm. But this could be limited or controlled by attention to the conduct of the professional. Protection of the individual by giving a say in decision making – possibly the final say – was not considered seriously, save in the context of elite, wealthy patients who could shop around between doctors. But here patient choice focused on choice of doctor, rather than on choice of treatment.[7] Contemporary healthcare ethics reinstates the patient's voice as authoritative, challenges the healer's power to define and control the situation, and therefore refocuses attention on the second form of vulnerability. The first form is taken to be overstated in the interests of the socially authoritative professionals. And the second form is taken to be crucial because only by challenging the authority of the professionals can this vulnerability be overcome.

The standard argument developed in contemporary healthcare ethics for the importance of patient autonomy has two elements. The first element is focused on the value of freedom. A patient's freedom is paramount and, to be protected, because in societies like ours the worst thing is to be treated as unfree, to be subjected to domination by another.

The second element is epistemic. The goals of treatment are not simply technical but normative. What treatment a patient needs depends on what is the goal of such treatment. But who is to define that goal? While the professional may well be obliged to point out that certain goals are unrealistic for reasons of feasibility, cost, or otherwise, the final determination of the goal or goals of treatment must rest with the patient. This is because only the patient can know and own her goals and values. Only she can have a clear grasp of the life she wishes to lead. And only she can make the choices that are necessary between competing or even conflicting values she may have.

Contemporary healthcare ethics makes these two elements of autonomy central and paramount. To protect the liberty of the patient, both from domination by professionals and from undue interference by the State or other social institutions, is crucial. And so is to protect the patient's privileged ability to live her *own* life as individual and specific, rather than as a simple instance of a generic type known to the professional or the social scientist. The difficulties of connecting the individual and the generic are great. It is well known to the clinician that there can be wide differences between the individual clinical case and the textbook account of the natural history of the disease instanced in this patient. But the 'personal factor', whereby not all individuals with the same illness and presented with the same options will want the same thing, adds an additional layer of complexity to the clinical encounter.

---

7 George B. Shaw, *The Doctor's Dilemma: A Tragedy* (London, The Bodley Head 1911).

Bootstrapping liberalism out of healthcare ethics

Contemporary healthcare ethics, therefore, has reconstructed the ethics of the doctor-patient encounter (possibly a better word than 'relationship', in a setting in which meetings may be brief and not necessarily repeated over time) with these joint emphases on personal liberty and personal normative authority at its heart. Now consider this encounter, from a different perspective. I have already begun to introduce the State into the story. Even where much of medicine proceeds on a purely private basis, the State plays a significant role in medical care. Modern states regulate entry to the professions; the conduct of professional-patient relationships; what treatments may be introduced to the marketplace; the achievement of certain public health goals (including certain types of screening and immunisations); and the achievement of a social-normative consensus on medical techniques that bear on fundamental moral values (abortion, euthanasia, assisted conception being obvious examples). It is in this context that a similar reconstruction of what is now called *bioethics* or *biomedical ethics* is taking place. The relationship between the individual and the State undergoes a similar shift to that I have described in the context of the doctor-patient encounter. Again, the fundamental concerns are with patient (now, citizen) liberty and with patients' (citizens') lives as their personal and non-exchangeable (so to speak) projects. The task of bioethics, in this model, is to make ethical analyses and normative prescriptions concerning public policy and law that govern the private and personal options and choices relating to healthcare issues of public concern. For instance, although no one can die my death in my place, many people can have an interest in the manner of my dying other than I. And the task of bioethics is in part to sort out whose interests are legitimate and whose are not, and how to weigh those legitimate interests with my own in order to craft a space of possibilities in which I can choose and act in a way most consistent with my own life goals.[8]

As Onora O'Neill has shown, this conflation of liberal political philosophy in the tradition of JS Mill with post-traditional person-centred healthcare ethics is far from obvious or inevitable.[9] And yet it hangs together in a pleasing way. The patient-citizen is a sovereign decision maker. There are strict moral limits to what may be done to her without her consent, and there are rather loose limits to what she may choose to do. Her moral ability to choose the shape of her own life, within the limits of what flesh may endure, is to be protected. We may not impose on that either because of our own interests, personal or sectional, or because we purport to know better than her what her interests are, or because we simply can. Nor can we impose on her choices *merely* to protect and promote our own, even when we believe that our choices are more rational, more public-spirited, or stand on firmer moral justification. And yet this is not a libertarian ethic: because

---

8 John H. Evans, *The History and Future of Bioethics: A Sociological View* (New York, Oxford University Press 2012).

9 Onora S O'Neill, *Autonomy and Trust in Bioethics* (Cambridge University Press 2002).

it is grounded in traditional healthcare ethics, even though it appears to be a radical reconstruction of that tradition, we do not necessarily leave the patient to bear the responsibility of her choices alone. Moreover, considerable room is left for coordination of choices, and for education and persuasion about the nature, contents and consequences of those choices. Indeed, there is arguably room for a degree of coercion, provided that the patient-citizen is consulted and compensated appropriately.[10]

This account is intentionally sketchy and minimalist. It is possible to fill it out in various ways. One attractive way to do so is as an application of Millian liberalism. Another is to stand back from the rather rapid translation of personal autonomy into the language of choice, and give an interpretation in terms of Kantian moral autonomy. Phenomenological, feminist, contractualist, and consequentialist variants of contemporary healthcare ethics exist and flourish in friendly rivalry. Nevertheless, these do not represent significant departures from the central paradigm, in which the assumption is that there is, at bottom, an ideally free and rational individual whose choices, were they made under ideally free and informed conditions, would truly represent what that person, all things considered, would want. And the task of healthcare ethics is largely seen, in this paradigm, as being to secure conditions for those choices as near to the ideal as possible, and to protect those near-ideal choices from interference, condescension, or the dominion of others, without prescribing the values guiding those choices.

Responding to liberal healthcare ethics

There are four obvious responses to this paradigm. The first is celebratory: it is a thoroughly good thing that the paradigm has emerged. It has made things much better for patients and empowered the citizenry at the same time. Defects and deficits may exist, but these mark the way for further extension and promotion of the paradigm. There may be some inherent and ineliminable instances where the paradigm fails, but even in those cases a suitably modified version of the authoritative patient choice model can be applied in a way consistent with its spirit. The second is condemnatory: the paradigm is bad. It is intellectually bankrupt. It has made things worse, and no doubt more expensive. It has betrayed the vulnerable and emptied out the professions of their distinctive moral characters. If we could go back, we should do so, but tragically that is not a road that lies open any more.[11] The third is reconstructive: the paradigm has important insights, but it is incoherent. There are some obvious flaws in its model of the patient-citizen and of the professional, and of its accounts of the various relationships and structures in play. But it is possible to take account of these defects and reconstruct the

10 Hugo Engelhardt, *The Foundations of Bioethics* (2nd edn, New York, Oxford University Press 1995).

11 For example, Raymond Tallis, *Hippocratic Oaths: Medicine and its Discontents* (London, Atlantic Books 2005).

paradigm in a way that preserves its crucial moral insights while avoiding its pitfalls. The fourth is reflexive: to evaluate the paradigm on the basis of its truth or falsity, or of its normative validity or illegitimacy, is a conceptual error. Rather, the paradigm is a model not of moral norms but of a social transformation. There is a dialectical relationship between the theory expressed by the paradigm and the practice it embodies. People have come to behave in the way the paradigm claims that they do, in response to being governed by its assumptions. Although there is an element of ideological mystification in the paradigm, it is a valid account of an emergent social reality.[12]

My own view is a hybrid of the reflexive and reconstructive responses to the paradigm of contemporary healthcare ethics. I can show you fairly easily why the first response is naïve and mistaken (see below). I am not sure I have an answer to the second response, beyond noting that its conservative pessimism is not one that is readily accompanied, as Gramsci teaches us it should be, by optimism of the will. And although I am a philosopher, and prone to pessimism of all kinds, as a practical philosopher I think optimism of the will matters. Healthcare ethics is nothing if not practical philosophy, both in the Kantian sense of being concerned with the nature of reasons and actions, and in the common-or-garden sense of being concerned with participation in public debates about 'what is to be done'.

I begin my argument by mentioning three major developments in healthcare ethics that challenge the contemporary paradigm. The first is the development of a challenge to the contemporary paradigm's privileging of the individual as source of moral authority, grounded in the analysis of the ethical challenges arising in the practice and policy of public health. The second is the development of a challenge to the paradigm's model of freedom as independence, arising from recent transformations in human rights theory and practice that have begun to insist on the necessary social and institutional conditions of individual freedom. The third is the development of a challenge to the contemporary paradigm's account of personal autonomy, grounded in empirically founded critiques of the model of rational agency assumed in this paradigm and which draw on the findings of the behavioural sciences. My argument will be that while none of these developments unsettle – indeed they arguable reinforce – the importance of *moral* autonomy and personal authenticity to healthcare, they do unsettle the *cognitive* and epistemic assumptions made by the paradigm, and the *political* assumptions of the paradigm. In the space available, I have only room to discuss one in detail: the psychological critique of autonomy.

The individual as source of moral authority

I will simply state this claim: public health practice, from outbreak control in epidemics, to vaccination policy, to the population paradox in preventive medicine, shows that, while individual behaviour is important, it is intervention at

---

12 For example, Nikolas Rose, *The Politics of Life Itself: Biomedicine, Power, and Subjectivity in the Twenty-First Century* (Princeton University Press 2006).

the population level that is necessary for the health of one and all. There are numerous contexts in which overriding or paternalistically shaping (nudging?) individual choice is necessary for public health protection and health promotion. Some would argue that these cases are instances of prudence taking priority over ethical norms. A better view would be that these interventions embody ethical norms, but these ethical norms are not those of individual-level morality and derive their authority from the collective, rather than the individual. The philosophical challenge is then to show the conditions under which the individual is protected from oppression, while securing the collective goods that underpin the ethical standing of the population level intervention.[13]

Freedom, independence and mutuality in human rights

Again, I can do no more here than state the claim. Notwithstanding distinguished recent work in the philosophical theory of human rights, which privileges those rights pertaining to the protection of individual autonomy, it is clear from the development of human rights doctrine and practice that securing those very 'autonomy rights' cannot be done in a vacuum.[14] Not only do they require a system of law and government to enshrine, promote and supervise their implementation and protection, they are indeed intimately connected to the so-called second-generation rights relating to economic and social equality, and indeed to third-generation rights relating to security, environmental protection and so on. Rather than seeing this, as some critics of the human rights system do, as 'mission creep' on the part of the human rights community, we should see these rights as interlinked. It is not that there are 'proper' rights, which are about individual freedom and 'pseudo'- or 'derived' rights (depending on one's level of enthusiasm for them), which are about collective welfare.[15] Human rights form a unity, and most liberalisms, by privileging individual rights, fail to reflect this unity.

The rational agent and the behavioural sciences

A standard criticism of some styles of intellectual thought is that they rely on an excessively narrow account of human rationality. Philosophers are often accused of this; so are economists. Both philosophers and economists are criticised for holding narrow and formalist accounts of what it is rational to do or believe; for applying them to human behaviour and finding the behaviour, rather than their theories, wanting; for missing or misunderstanding the political or ideological consequences of this systematic failure to understand human behaviour on its own terms (for instance, by marginalising or exploiting those who think differently); for ignoring

13 John Coggon, *What Makes Health Public? A Critical Evaluation of Moral, Legal and Political Claims In Public Health* (Cambridge University Press 2012).
14 For example, James Griffin, *On Human Rights* (Oxford University Press 2009).
15 Sandra Fredman, *Human Rights Transformed: Positive Rights and Positive Duties* (Oxford University Press 2008)

or misrepresenting empirical findings that cast doubt on their theories; and so on. Recently, thanks to Daniel Kahneman, Gerd Gigerenzer and others, research in cognitive psychology into practical failures of rationality, and limits to formal theories of rationality, have become part of the stock of public policy debate.[16] I want to consider another, different and perhaps more interesting criticism.

Famously in English law, a patient who is considered to have mental capacity must have their decision to consent (or – although this is more controversial – to refuse to consent) to a medical or surgical procedure respected, whether the decision is made for any reason or none at all. For example, in *Re T (Adult: Refusal of Treatment)*, Lord Donaldson, Master of the Rolls, said that the 'right of choice is not limited to decisions which others might regard as sensible. It exists notwithstanding that the reasons for making the choice are rational, irrational, unknown or even non-existent' ([1993] Fam 95, cited in Jackson, 2013, 217). It is thus no part of English law of consent to medical or surgical treatment that the patient be rational or consistent in his decision making, and it is no part of the duty of care owed by the professional to her patient that she ensure that his decision is rational. The offer must be consistent with the standard of care deemed responsible and the patient must be capable of making a decision, in terms of having the abilities to understand, retain and reflect upon the information necessary for a decision, and to make that decision. But beyond those tests of *ability* to do these things, there is no test that they actually *do* these things. So in this sense, English law is not particularly concerned with whether the patient makes a good choice; only that he is able to make a choice (the necessary skill is exercised in diagnosis and treatment planning and communication, and the necessary information for a decision is made available). And it therefore protects the *ownership* of the choice. We must be sure that it is *his* choice. Hence the importance in English law of ensuring that the decision is not coerced or unduly influenced by another.

So along this line of reasoning, we have nothing to concern us much about the imposition of an unrealistic norm of rationality as an evaluative yardstick for patient decision making. Now, it is true that for some patients, particularly children and the mentally disordered, a higher standard of rationality is applied. But for most patients it is not. Are we then to set aside the critique of philosophical (and economic) rationality as not a problem for theories of patient autonomy, or at least those seeking to involve the law? Perhaps. But there is another set of difficulties in our path. First of all, as philosophers of language have long argued, it is impossible to understand human behaviour as such without applying at least a minimal theory of rational agency to allow us to understand and explain human behaviour as human action (as opposed to mere automatism or reflex response). The action must make sense if we are to see it as an action; and in seeing something as an action we make sense of it by looking for reasons motivating it.[17]

---

16 Daniel Kahneman, *Thinking, Fast and Slow* (London, Allen Lane 2011); Gerd Gigenrenzer *et al.*, *Simple Heuristics That Make Us Smart* (New York, Oxford University Press 1999).

17 Onora S. O'Neill, *Towards Justice and Virtue: A Constructive Account of Practical Reasoning* (Cambridge University Press 1996) 66ff; Christine M Korsgaard, *Self-Constitution: Agency, Identity, and Integrity* (Oxford University Press 2009) 81ff.

Thus, to see a decision to undergo a medical or surgical procedure *as a decision*, it is not the case that we can sometimes say that the patient agreed for *no* reason. Some kind of reason must be imputable if we are to see the patient as an *agent* at all.

We may not need to rely on a formal theory of rationality, then, and it may not therefore be important to find ways of escaping criticisms of formal theories of rationality. But we do need to rely on some high-level assumptions about the relationship between agency and acting on reasons, on interpretation of behaviour and an account of the unity of the person, and so on. Here the behavioural sciences come into their own. They challenge every aspect of how we think we make decisions, and thereby challenge the normativity of the account of decision making central to the contemporary healthcare ethics paradigm.

To begin with, as any philosopher knows from direct personal experience, giving reasons is hard work. Explaining one's behaviour to oneself, for instance in writing, or to another, takes much thought and effort, especially if one's initial explanation is met with a question seeking further elaboration or challenging something said. And indeed, much of the time giving that explanation is not mere representational reporting of a decision-making process but something that shapes and changes that decision as it goes along. The act, and the self who acts, are shaped in the process of explanation. The traditional philosophical representation of practical reasoning, via the practical syllogism, is quite misleading as an account of the psychological process of making up one's mind, even within folk psychology. If this is plausible, then the standard model of the agent, who has preferences, and who makes up her mind in light of those preferences, and who in giving consent merely gives verbal representation to those preferences, and whose decisions must therefore be respected as representations of her settled and sovereign preferences, becomes quite implausible.

We can do better than this armchair philosophy of mind. We can draw on empirical psychological research. And from empirical psychology we know that there can be quite wide gaps between the reasons people may give for their decisions and the factors that actually motivate them, between how people reason about a decision before it is made and how they reason about it after it is made (especially if the actual consequence of the decision is not what they initially thought it would be). From the extensive literature on cognitive biases, we know that people are prone to all kinds of mistakes about relative probabilities, about how they will value things once they have them as opposed to how they think they will value them before they have them or how they will value them once they are lost, and so on.[18]

It is not simply a question of having an inadequate formal theory of rationality. One of the intriguing things about these cognitive errors and biases is that they are quite easy to explain to people, and people typically endorse the 'correct' theory once it is explained, and see how they are subject to various kinds of

18 Kahneman (n 16).

self-defeating reasoning strategies. They then go and carry on deciding as before, and make the same judgements that, on the theoretical model they have just endorsed, they would see as mistaken.

Think of smoking. Most smokers do not want to smoke. They may indeed want rather strongly not to smoke, and not to want to smoke. Nonetheless, they smoke. There are various explanations for this. The most obvious is that smoking is addictive. Smoking, considered as an addiction, would be considered not an autonomous behaviour at all. As such, banning it would present no moral problems, save one. That is that stopping a committed smoker from smoking imposes significant short-term discomfort and distress on that person, and we therefore have to reason out the trade-off between causing that short-term discomfort and distress and preventing the long-term illness and mortality caused by smoking. It is not necessarily the case, given this reasoning out of the trade-off, that we would ban smoking. But the autonomous wishes of the smoker are ruled out of court in this exercise, because they are not considered truly autonomous. For a non-autonomous person, acting in his best interests (as evaluated by us, who are autonomous) is what is normatively required. However, this seems too strong. Although the notion of weakness of will is not uncontroversial in philosophy, few would identify weakness of will as *eo ipso* a symptom of failed or defective autonomy.

Another possibility is that their wish to smoke is indeed autonomous, and that the failure of their desire not to smoke is because that desire is insufficiently strong, or that the benefits to the smoker of continuing to smoke dominate the benefits in the short or long term of not doing so. Here the agency of the smoker is not in question, and we are concerned with his autonomy. But we are troubled by his inability to hold long- and short-term interests together, and by the way long-term interests seem to have been discounted too much. The smoker is autonomous, but error prone.

How are we properly to respond to error proneness? Note, to make it more interesting still, that this is not so to speak random computational error. It is not the sort of error where in totting up a grocery bill we sometimes cannot get the sum to come out the same way twice. It is a more interesting kind of error, whereby we systematically and predictably make the same error over and over again. And our premise is that we do recognise it as an error. It is not that we have some kind of 'different arithmetic'. This is the kind of error that has attracted a lot of attention in recent years in the literature on 'behavioural economics'. One strand of that literature is to document and measure the types of systematic error to which we are prone. For my purposes, the more interesting strand of the literature is that which seeks to develop interventions that overcome this sort of error.

This type of error is habitual and ingrained. It is very difficult, if not impossible, to uproot it. It may even be, following Gigerenzer, that it would be harmful to do so, if in doing so we made everyday decision making more difficult, costly and subject to random computational error. The smart thing to do, therefore, is not to try to go against the grain, or, in Kant's lovely phrase, 'the crooked timber of humanity, out of which no straight thing was ever made'. Instead, we should use this cognitive habit for beneficial effect.

The worry is, first, that by using cognitive errors and biases to overcome behaviours caused or influenced by those same cognitive errors and biases, we undermine the ability of people to overcome those cognitive errors and biases themselves. Second, we are in an important sense treating people as *heteronomous*. That is to say, we treat them not as people capable of reasoning and choosing their own ends subject to the moral law, we treat them as empirical beings subject to natural laws, and in some sense *not* capable of choosing their own ends subject to the moral law.

The former objection I see as purely empirical. And I see the evidence as most unpromising for its proponents. The kinds of cognitive error in question are so pervasive, and so ingrained, and so situational in nature, that I see no prospect of training people out of them. For instance, even if we manage to train people not to discount 'irrationally' in the context of smoking, there is no reason to think that their decision making will become free of the same errors in other contexts. Indeed, psychologists tell us that the well-known phenomenon of risk compensation may well apply: I might think more carefully about cream buns, but shift my 'tomorrow is another day' attitude to another context. So it is far from clear that simply by making use of cognitive errors we undermine people's ability to overcome their errors. If we could free ourselves from these errors, that would be nice (although perhaps not always efficient). But this seems improbable.

The latter objection is much more interesting, and of course absolutely central to moral philosophy since Kant. However, as we've seen, we have real difficulties picking out the reasons people act on from those they merely say they act on; and tracking the relations between what reasons people have and what they actually do. This suggests two things in response to Kant's critique of heteronomy: first, we need, as O'Neill suggests, to focus on *public reason*, rather than psychological autonomy.[19] Second, we need to focus on the protection of individuals' values, not the decision making *as such*.

Forward to republicanism!

This brief essay has necessarily only sketched the argument without even a pretence to full rigour. What I hope I have done is motivate the thought that the apparent 'embedding' of contemporary healthcare ethics in political liberalism is not necessary, or helpful. A liberal healthcare ethics, by focusing on the primacy of individual choice and the avoidance of paternalism, cannot effectively address the relationship between personal choice and public health, or the unity of human rights, and moreover its model of individual decision making and practical reason is inconsistent with what we know of empirical psychology. I believe we are forced to go in a different direction to find a normative political philosophy that supports both healthcare ethics and public health ethics. My proposal

---

19 Onora S. O'Neill, *Constructions of Reason: Explorations of Kant's Practical Philosophy* (Cambridge University Press 1990).

is that civic republicanism presents us with certain valuable clues to what this philosophy should be like.

Civic republicanism shares with liberalism a concern with individual liberty, but unlike liberalism it is realistic about the fragility of individual choice, and unlike liberalism it is not committed to value neutrality in the public sphere. The civic republican sees individual choice as important, but vulnerable in itself to human weakness, and externally to the exercise of control by individuals over other individuals (principally in the form technically termed 'domination'). The civic republican does not think that choice can be totally free; but it can be freed, under certain conditions, from domination and arbitrary control. Securing this, however, requires not simply legislation but political practice – active citizenship – both in the form of active resistance to mechanisms of domination (for one's own sake, but also to protect others, and to preserve the liberty of the polity itself).[20] This political engagement requires commitment to a common good, the specification of which is a central element of the political argument of the community.[21] It seems to me that articulating the common good is central to the 'bioethical project' and thus (contra Evans)[22] healthcare ethics and public health ethics are both fully political and committed to a project of filling in the concept of the human good life – rather than leaving each individual to pursue his own goals (and fail in realising them).

---

20 Philip Pettit, 'Republican freedom: Three axioms, four theorems' in Cécile Laborde and
     John Maynor (eds), *Republicanism and Political Theory* (Oxford, Blackwell, 2008).
21 Iseult Honohan, Civic Republicanism (London, Routledge 2002).
22 Evans (n 8).

Index